JEREMIAH, LAMENTATIONS, AND BARUCH

THE IGNATIUS CATHOLIC STUDY BIBLE

REVISED STANDARD VERSION
SECOND CATHOLIC EDITION

JEREMIAH, LAMENTATIONS, AND BARUCH

With Introduction, Commentary, and Notes

by

Scott Hahn and Curtis Mitch

and

with Study Questions by

Dennis Walters

IGNATIUS PRESS   SAN FRANCISCO

Original Revised Standard Version, Catholic Edition
Nihil Obstat: Thomas Hanlon, S.T.L., L.S.S., Ph.L.
Imprimatur: + Peter W. Bartholome, D.D.
Bishop of St. Cloud, Minnesota
May 11, 1966

Introduction, commentaries, and notes:
Nihil Obstat: Ruth Ohm Sutherland, Ph.D., Censor Deputatus
Imprimatur: + The Most Reverend Salvatore Cordileone
Archbishop of San Francisco
April 27, 2023

Second Catholic Edition approved by the
National Council of the Churches of Christ in the USA

Cover art: *Jeremiah Lamenting the Destruction of Jerusalem*, 1630
Rembrandt van Rijn (1606–1669)
Rijksmuseum/Amsterdam/The Netherlands
Photo credit: Art Resource, NY

Cover design by Riz Boncan Marsella

Published by Ignatius Press in 2024

CONTENTS

INTRODUCTION TO
THE IGNATIUS STUDY BIBLE
by Scott Hahn, Ph.D.

You are approaching the "word of God". This is the title Christians most commonly give to the Bible, and the expression is rich in meaning. It is also the title given to the Second Person of the Blessed Trinity, God the Son. For Jesus Christ became flesh for our salvation, and "the name by which he is called is The Word of God" (Rev 19:13; cf. Jn 1:14).

The word of God is Scripture. The Word of God is Jesus. This close association between God's *written* word and his *eternal* Word is intentional and has been the custom of the Church since the first generation. "All Sacred Scripture is but one book, and this one book is Christ, 'because all divine Scripture speaks of Christ, and all divine Scripture is fulfilled in Christ'[1]" (CCC 134). This does not mean that the Scriptures are divine in the same way that Jesus is divine. They are, rather, divinely inspired and, as such, are unique in world literature, just as the Incarnation of the eternal Word is unique in human history.

Yet we can say that the inspired word resembles the incarnate Word in several important ways. Jesus Christ is the Word of God incarnate. In his humanity, he is like us in all things, except for sin. As a work of man, the Bible is like any other book, except without error. Both Christ and Scripture, says the Second Vatican Council, are given "for the sake of our salvation" (*Dei Verbum* 11), and both give us God's definitive revelation of himself. We cannot, therefore, conceive of one without the other: the Bible without Jesus, or Jesus without the Bible. Each is the interpretive key to the other. And because Christ is the subject of all the Scriptures, St. Jerome insists, "Ignorance of the Scriptures is ignorance of Christ"[2] (CCC 133).

When we approach the Bible, then, we approach Jesus, the Word of God; and in order to encounter Jesus, we must approach him in a prayerful study of the inspired word of God, the Sacred Scriptures.

Inspiration and Inerrancy The Catholic Church makes mighty claims for the Bible, and our acceptance of those claims is essential if we are to read the Scriptures and apply them to our lives as the Church intends. So it is not enough merely to nod at words like "inspired", "unique", or "inerrant". We

have to understand what the Church means by these terms, and we have to make that understanding our own. After all, what we believe about the Bible will inevitably influence the way we read the Bible. The way we read the Bible, in turn, will determine what we "get out" of its sacred pages.

These principles hold true no matter what we read: a news report, a search warrant, an advertisement, a paycheck, a doctor's prescription, an eviction notice. How (or whether) we read these things depends largely upon our preconceived notions about the reliability and authority of their sources—and the potential they have for affecting our lives. In some cases, to misunderstand a document's authority can lead to dire consequences. In others, it can keep us from enjoying rewards that are rightfully ours. In the case of the Bible, both the rewards and the consequences involved take on an ultimate value.

What does the Church mean, then, when she affirms the words of St. Paul: "All Scripture is inspired by God" (2 Tim 3:16)? Since the term "inspired" in this passage could be translated "God-breathed", it follows that God breathed forth his word in the Scriptures as you and I breathe forth air when we speak. This means that God is the primary author of the Bible. He certainly employed human authors in this task as well, but he did not merely assist them while they wrote or subsequently approve what they had written. God the Holy Spirit is the *principal* author of Scripture, while the human writers are *instrumental* authors. These human authors freely wrote everything, and only those things, that God wanted: the word of God in the very words of God. This miracle of dual authorship extends to the whole of Scripture, and to every one of its parts, so that whatever the human authors affirm, God likewise affirms through their words.

The principle of biblical inerrancy follows logically from this principle of divine authorship. After all, God cannot lie, and he cannot make mistakes. Since the Bible is divinely inspired, it must be without error in everything that its divine and human authors affirm to be true. This means that biblical inerrancy is a mystery even broader in scope than infallibility, which guarantees for us that the Church will always teach the truth concerning faith and morals. Of course the mantle of inerrancy likewise covers faith and morals, but it extends even farther to ensure that all the facts and events of salvation history are accurately presented for us in

---

[1] Hugh of St. Victor, *De arca Noe* 2, 8: PL 176, 642: cf. ibid. 2, 9: PL 176, 642–43.

[2] *DV* 25; cf. Phil 3:8 and St. Jerome, *Commentariorum in Isaiam libri xviii*, prol.: PL 24, 17b.

the Scriptures. Inerrancy is our guarantee that the words and deeds of God found in the Bible are unified and true, declaring with one voice the wonders of his saving love.

The guarantee of inerrancy does not mean, however, that the Bible is an all-purpose encyclopedia of information covering every field of study. The Bible is not, for example, a textbook in the empirical sciences, and it should not be treated as one. When biblical authors relate facts of the natural order, we can be sure they are speaking in a purely descriptive and "phenomenological" way, according to the way things appeared to their senses.

Biblical Authority Implicit in these doctrines is God's desire to make himself known to the world and to enter a loving relationship with every man, woman, and child he has created. God gave us the Scriptures not just to inform or motivate us; more than anything he wants to save us. This higher purpose underlies every page of the Bible, indeed every word of it.

In order to reveal himself, God used what theologians call "accommodation". Sometimes the Lord stoops down to communicate by "condescension"—that is, he speaks as humans speak, as if he had the same passions and weakness that we do (for example, God says he was "sorry" that he made man in Genesis 6:6). Other times he communicates by "elevation"—that is, by endowing human words with divine power (for example, through the Prophets). The numerous examples of divine accommodation in the Bible are an expression of God's wise and fatherly ways. For a sensitive father can speak with his children either by condescension, as in baby talk, or by elevation, by bringing a child's understanding up to a more mature level.

God's word is thus saving, fatherly, and personal. Because it speaks directly to us, we must never be indifferent to its content; after all, the word of God is at once the object, cause, and support of our faith. It is, in fact, a test of our faith, since we see in the Scriptures only what faith disposes us to see. If we believe what the Church believes, we will see in Scripture the saving, inerrant, and divinely authored revelation of the Father. If we believe otherwise, we see another book altogether.

This test applies not only to rank-and-file believers but also to the Church's theologians and hierarchy, and even the Magisterium. Vatican II has stressed in recent times that Scripture must be "the very soul of sacred theology" (*Dei Verbum* 24). As Joseph Cardinal Ratzinger, Pope Benedict XVI echoed this powerful teaching with his own, insisting that "the *normative theologians* are the authors of Holy Scripture" (emphasis added). He reminded us that Scripture and the Church's dogmatic teaching are tied tightly together, to the point of being inseparable: "Dogma is by definition nothing other than an interpretation of Scripture." The defined

dogmas of our faith, then, encapsulate the Church's infallible interpretation of Scripture, and theology is a further reflection upon that work.

The Senses of Scripture Because the Bible has both divine and human authors, we are required to master a different sort of reading than we are used to. First, we must read Scripture according to its *literal* sense, as we read any other human literature. At this initial stage, we strive to discover the meaning of the words and expressions used by the biblical writers as they were understood in their original setting and by their original recipients. This means, among other things, that we do not interpret everything we read "literalistically", as though Scripture never speaks in a figurative or symbolic way (it often does!). Rather, we read it according to the rules that govern its different literary forms of writing, depending on whether we are reading a narrative, a poem, a letter, a parable, or an apocalyptic vision. The Church calls us to read the divine books in this way to ensure that we understand what the human authors were laboring to explain to God's people.

The literal sense, however, is not the only sense of Scripture, since we interpret its sacred pages according to the *spiritual* senses as well. In this way, we search out what the Holy Spirit is trying to tell us, beyond even what the human authors have consciously asserted. Whereas the literal sense of Scripture describes a historical reality—a fact, precept, or event—the spiritual senses disclose deeper mysteries revealed through the historical realities. What the soul is to the body, the spiritual senses are to the literal. You can distinguish them; but if you try to separate them, death immediately follows. St. Paul was the first to insist upon this and warn of its consequences: "God ... has qualified us to be ministers of a new covenant, not in a written code but in the Spirit; for the written code kills, but the Spirit gives life" (2 Cor 3:5–6).

Catholic tradition recognizes three spiritual senses that stand upon the foundation of the literal sense of Scripture (see CCC 115). **(1)** The first is the *allegorical* sense, which unveils the spiritual and prophetic meaning of biblical history. Allegorical interpretations thus reveal how persons, events, and institutions of Scripture can point beyond themselves toward greater mysteries yet to come (OT) or display the fruits of mysteries already revealed (NT). Christians have often read the Old Testament in this way to discover how the mystery of Christ in the New Covenant was once hidden in the Old and how the full significance of the Old Covenant was finally made manifest in the New. Allegorical significance is likewise latent in the New Testament, especially in the life and deeds of Jesus recorded in the Gospels. Because Christ is the Head of the Church and the source of her spiritual life, what was accomplished in Christ the Head during his earthly life prefigures what he continually produces in his members through grace. The allegorical sense builds up the virtue of faith. **(2)** The second is the *tropological* or *moral* sense, which reveals how the actions of God's people in the Old Testament and the life of Jesus in the New Testament prompt us to form virtuous habits in our own lives. It therefore draws from Scripture warnings against sin and vice as well as inspirations to pursue holiness and purity. The moral sense is intended to build up the virtue of charity. **(3)** The third is the *anagogical* sense, which points upward to heavenly glory. It shows us how countless events in the Bible prefigure our final union with God in eternity and how things that are "seen" on earth are figures of things "unseen" in heaven. Because the anagogical sense leads us to contemplate our destiny, it is meant to build up the virtue of hope. Together with the literal sense, then, these spiritual senses draw out the fullness of what God wants to give us through his Word and as such comprise what ancient tradition has called the "full sense" of Sacred Scripture.

All of this means that the deeds and events of the Bible are charged with meaning beyond what is immediately apparent to the reader. In essence, that meaning is Jesus Christ and the salvation he died to give us. This is especially true of the books of the New Testament, which proclaim Jesus explicitly; but it is also true of the Old Testament, which speaks of Jesus in more hidden and symbolic ways. The human authors of the Old Testament told us as much as they were able, but they could not clearly discern the shape of all future events standing at such a distance. It is the Bible's divine Author, the Holy Spirit, who could and did foretell the saving work of Christ, from the first page of the Book of Genesis onward.

The New Testament did not, therefore, abolish the Old. Rather, the New fulfilled the Old, and in doing so, it lifted the veil that kept hidden the face of the Lord's bride. Once the veil is removed, we suddenly see the world of the Old Covenant charged with grandeur. Water, fire, clouds, gardens, trees, hills, doves, lambs—all of these things are memorable details in the history and poetry of Israel. But now, seen in the light of Jesus Christ, they are much more. For the Christian with eyes to see, water symbolizes the saving power of Baptism; fire, the Holy Spirit; the spotless lamb, Christ crucified; Jerusalem, the city of heavenly glory.

The spiritual reading of Scripture is nothing new. Indeed, the very first Christians read the Bible this way. St. Paul describes Adam as a "type" that prefigured Jesus Christ (Rom 5:14). A "type" is a real person, place, thing, or event in the Old Testament that foreshadows something greater in the New. From this term we get the word "typology", referring to the study of how the Old Testament prefigures Christ (CCC 128–30). Elsewhere St. Paul draws deeper meanings out of the story of Abraham's sons, declaring, "This is an allegory" (Gal

4:24). He is not suggesting that these events of the distant past never really happened; he is saying that the events both happened *and* signified something more glorious yet to come.

The New Testament later describes the Tabernacle of ancient Israel as "a copy and shadow of the heavenly sanctuary" (Heb 8:5) and the Mosaic Law as a "shadow of the good things to come" (Heb 10:1). St. Peter, in turn, notes that Noah and his family were "saved through water" in a way that "corresponds" to sacramental Baptism, which "now saves you" (1 Pet 3:20–21). It is interesting to note that the expression translated as "corresponds" in this verse is a Greek term that denotes the fulfillment or counterpart of an ancient "type".

We need not look to the apostles, however, to justify a spiritual reading of the Bible. After all, Jesus himself read the Old Testament this way. He referred to Jonah (Mt 12:39), Solomon (Mt 12:42), the Temple (Jn 2:19), and the brazen serpent (Jn 3:14) as "signs" that pointed forward to him. We see in Luke's Gospel, as Christ comforted the disciples on the road to Emmaus, that "beginning with Moses and all the prophets, he interpreted to them in all the Scriptures the things concerning himself" (Lk 24:27). It was precisely this extensive spiritual interpretation of the Old Testament that made such an impact on these once-discouraged travelers, causing their hearts to "burn" within them (Lk 24:32).

Criteria for Biblical Interpretation We, too, must learn to discern the "full sense" of Scripture as it includes both the literal and spiritual senses together. Still, this does not mean we should "read into" the Bible meanings that are not really there. Spiritual exegesis is not an unrestrained flight of the imagination. Rather, it is a sacred science that proceeds according to certain principles and stands accountable to sacred tradition, the Magisterium, and the wider community of biblical interpreters (both living and deceased).

In searching out the full sense of a text, we should always avoid the extreme tendency to "over-spiritualize" in a way that minimizes or denies the Bible's literal truth. St. Thomas Aquinas was well aware of this danger and asserted that "all other senses of Sacred Scripture are based on the literal" (*STh* I, 1, 10, *ad* 1, quoted in CCC 116). On the other hand, we should never confine the meaning of a text to the literal, intended sense of its human author, as if the divine Author did not intend the passage to be read in the light of Christ's coming.

Fortunately the Church has given us guidelines in our study of Scripture. The unique character and divine authorship of the Bible call us to read it "in the Spirit" (*Dei Verbum* 12). Vatican II outlines this teaching in a practical way by directing us to read the Scriptures according to three specific criteria:

1. We must "[b]e especially attentive 'to the content and unity of the whole Scripture'" (CCC 112).

2. We must "[r]ead the Scripture within 'the living Tradition of the whole Church'" (CCC 113).

3. We must "[b]e attentive to the analogy of faith" (CCC 114; cf. Rom 12:6).

These criteria protect us from many of the dangers that ensnare readers of the Bible, from the newest inquirer to the most prestigious scholar. Reading Scripture out of context is one such pitfall, and probably the one most difficult to avoid. A memorable cartoon from the 1950s shows a young man poring over the pages of the Bible. He says to his sister: "Don't bother me now; I'm trying to find a Scripture verse to back up one of my preconceived notions." No doubt a biblical text pried from its context can be twisted to say something very different from what its author actually intended.

The Church's criteria guide us here by defining what constitutes the authentic "context" of a given biblical passage. The first criterion directs us to the literary context of every verse, including not only the words and paragraphs that surround it, but also the entire corpus of the biblical author's writings and, indeed, the span of the entire Bible. The *complete* literary context of any Scripture verse includes every text from Genesis to Revelation—because the Bible is a unified book, not just a library of different books. When the Church canonized the Book of Revelation, for example, she recognized it to be incomprehensible apart from the wider context of the entire Bible.

The second criterion places the Bible firmly within the context of a community that treasures a "living tradition". That community is the People of God down through the ages. Christians lived out their faith for well over a millennium before the printing press was invented. For centuries, few believers owned copies of the Gospels, and few people could read anyway. Yet they absorbed the gospel—through the sermons of their bishops and clergy, through prayer and meditation, through Christian art, through liturgical celebrations, and through oral tradition. These were expressions of the one "living tradition", a culture of living faith that stretches from ancient Israel to the contemporary Church. For the early Christians, the gospel could not be understood apart from that tradition. So it is with us. Reverence for the Church's tradition is what protects us from any sort of chronological or cultural provincialism, such as scholarly fads that arise and carry away a generation of interpreters before being dismissed by the next generation.

The third criterion places scriptural texts within the framework of faith. If we believe that the Scriptures are divinely inspired, we must also believe them to be internally coherent and consistent with all the doctrines that Christians believe. Remember, the Church's dogmas (such as the Real Presence, the papacy, the Immaculate Conception) are not something *added* to Scripture; rather, they are the Church's infallible interpretation *of* Scripture.

Using This Study Guide This volume is designed to lead the reader through Scripture according to the Church's guidelines—faithful to the canon, to the tradition, and to the creeds. The Church's interpretive principles have thus shaped the component parts of this book, and they are designed to make the reader's study as effective and rewarding as possible.

Introductions: We have introduced the biblical book with an essay covering issues such as authorship, date of composition, purpose, and leading themes. This background information will assist readers to approach and understand the text on its own terms.

Annotations: The basic notes at the bottom of every page help the user to read the Scriptures with understanding. They by no means exhaust the meaning of the sacred text but provide background material to help the reader make sense of what he reads. Often these notes make explicit what the sacred writers assumed or held to be implicit. They also provide a great deal of historical, cultural, geographical, and theological information pertinent to the inspired narratives—information that can help the reader bridge the distance between the biblical world and his own.

Cross-References: Between the biblical text at the top of each page and the annotations at the bottom, numerous references are listed to point readers to other scriptural passages related to the one being studied. This follow-up is an essential part of any serious study. It is also an excellent way to discover how the content of Scripture "hangs together" in a providential unity. Along with biblical cross-references, the annotations refer to select paragraphs from the *Catechism of the Catholic Church*. These are not doctrinal "proof texts" but are designed to help the reader interpret the Bible in accordance with the mind of the Church. The *Catechism* references listed either handle the biblical text directly or treat a broader doctrinal theme that sheds significant light on that text.

Topical Essays, Word Studies, Charts: These features bring readers to a deeper understanding of select details. The *topical essays* take up major themes and explain them more thoroughly and theologically than the annotations, often relating them to the doctrines of the Church. Occasionally the annotations are supplemented by *word studies* that put readers in touch with the ancient languages of Scripture. These should help readers to understand better and appreciate the inspired terminology that runs throughout the sacred books. Also included are various *charts* that summarize biblical information "at a glance".

Icon Annotations: Three distinctive icons are interspersed throughout the annotations, each one corresponding to one of the Church's three criteria for biblical interpretation. Bullets indicate the passage or passages to which these icons apply.

Notes marked by the book icon relate to the "content and unity" of Scripture, showing how particular passages of the Old Testament illuminate the mysteries of the New. Much of the information in these notes explains the original context of the citations and indicates how and why this has a direct bearing on Christ or the Church. Through these notes, the reader can develop a sensitivity to the beauty and unity of God's saving plan as it stretches across both Testaments.

Notes marked by the dove icon examine particular passages in light of the Church's "living tradition". Because the Holy Spirit both guides the Magisterium and inspires the spiritual senses of Scripture, these annotations supply information along both of these lines. On the one hand, they refer to the Church's doctrinal teaching as presented by various popes, creeds, and ecumenical councils; on the other, they draw from (and paraphrase) the spiritual interpretations of various Fathers, Doctors, and saints.

Notes marked by the keys icon pertain to the "analogy of faith". Here we spell out how the mysteries of our faith "unlock" and explain one another. This type of comparison between Christian beliefs displays the coherence and unity of defined dogmas, which are the Church's infallible interpretations of Scripture.

Putting It All in Perspective Perhaps the most important context of all we have saved for last:

the interior life of the individual reader. What we get out of the Bible will largely depend on how we approach the Bible. Unless we are living a sustained and disciplined life of prayer, we will never have the reverence, the profound humility, or the grace we need to see the Scriptures for what they really are.

You are approaching the "word of God". But for thousands of years, since before he knit you in your mother's womb, the Word of God has been approaching you.

One Final Note. The volume you hold in your hands is only a small part of a much larger work still in production. Study helps similar to those printed in this booklet are being prepared for *all* the books of the Bible and will appear gradually as they are finished. Our ultimate goal is to publish a single, one-volume Study Bible that will include the entire text of Scripture, along with all the annotations, charts, cross-references, maps, and other features found in the following pages. Individual booklets will be published in the meantime, with the hope that God's people can begin to benefit from this labor before its full completion.

We have included a long list of Study Questions in the back to make this format as useful as possible, not only for individual study, but for group settings and discussions as well. The questions are designed to help readers both "understand" the Bible and "apply" it to their lives. We pray that God will make use of our efforts and yours to help renew the face of the earth!

INTRODUCTION TO JEREMIAH

Author The Book of Jeremiah is an anthology of prophetic sayings, sermons, and stories that were written down over the course of several decades and joined together into a single work. Jewish and Christian tradition have long identified the author of this collection as the prophet Jeremiah, a judgment based on the internal witness of the book, which presents itself as an account of the "words of Jeremiah" (1:1). Elsewhere it states that the Lord instructed Jeremiah to commit certain of his prophecies to writing (30:2; 36:2), which he did with the help of his secretary, Baruch (36:4, 32; 45:1). Other parts of the book attributed to Jeremiah include a letter sent to the Jewish exiles in Babylon (29:1–32) and a long oracle of judgment foretelling the fall of Babylon (51:60, referring to 50:1—51:58).

In addition to these portions of the book ascribed to Jeremiah, one also finds third-person accounts of Jeremiah's life and activities that are written from the perspective of someone who was knowledgeable about his ministry. Most likely this biographical information was supplied by Jeremiah's personal scribe and companion, Baruch. Moreover, since there are no unmistakable references in the book to persons or events that postdate the lives of Jeremiah and Baruch, it is plausible that the book is constructed mainly (or entirely) from the writings of these two individuals. Additions or updates made to the book after the time of Jeremiah and Baruch cannot be ruled out as a possibility but are not demanded by the evidence.

Nevertheless, several modern scholars have explained the origin and composition of the book differently. There has been a tendency to view the book's prose materials (its historical accounts and recorded sermons) as stemming, not from Jeremiah or his companion, Baruch, but from later authors and editors. Some attribute this prose material to Jeremiah's disciples, while others attribute it to scribes working in the exilic period who sought to promote the theology of Deuteronomy. Still others trace the bulk of the Book of Jeremiah to situations and struggles faced by the Jewish community in the postexilic period and thus see little or no connection between the prophet Jeremiah and the book that bears his name. Generally speaking, these modern hypotheses rest on limited evidence and depend heavily on imaginative reconstructions of the past, factors that make it difficult to verify such claims about how the book was written, compiled, and edited.

Date The Book of Jeremiah was not written down all at once. Jeremiah was first instructed to record his early prophecies in a scroll in 605 B.C. (36:2), but because that scroll was destroyed by King Jehoiakim of Judah, the prophet was forced to dictate a second copy to Baruch that included certain additions (36:4, 32). The contents of this rewritten and expanded scroll are debated, but many think its substance was incorporated into Jeremiah 1–25. Sometime after the deportation of captives from Judah in 597 B.C., Jeremiah sent a letter to the exiles in Babylon (29:1–23) with an oracle of doom against Babylon itself (50:1—51:58). The final chapter of the book is an account of Jerusalem's destruction in 586 B.C. (52:1–30) that includes a short postscript about the release of King Jehoiachin from prison, an event dated about 561 B.C. (52:31–39). From this information it is clear that some parts of the Book of Jeremiah were written in the late seventh century B.C., while other parts were written in the first half of the sixth century B.C. The final edition of the Book of Jeremiah can be reasonably dated around 550 B.C.

Title The book is named after Jeremiah, the son of Hilkiah, the prophet whose words and deeds are featured in its pages. His Hebrew name, *Yirmeyāhû*, sometimes shortened to *Yirmeyāh*, is of uncertain meaning. Possibilities include "the LORD exults" and "the LORD establishes". The title of the book appears in the Greek Septuagint as *Ieremias*, "Jeremiah", a heading expanded in the Latin Vulgate to *Ieremias Propheta*, "Jeremiah the Prophet". English titles for the book follow these ancient traditions.

Place in the Canon The canonicity of Jeremiah as a book of Sacred Scripture has never been seriously questioned in either Judaism or Christianity. In the Tanakh, or Jewish Bible, Jeremiah stands as the second of the Latter Prophets following the Book of Isaiah, although one rabbinic tradition places Jeremiah after 2 Kings (Babylonian Talmud, *Baba Bathra* 14b). In Christian Bibles, Jeremiah is the second of the Major Prophets following the Book of Isaiah. In Jewish, Catholic, and Protestant traditions, the Hebrew edition (MT) of Jeremiah is generally considered the canonical form of the book, whereas the shorter Greek edition (LXX) of Jeremiah is revered as authoritative in the Eastern Orthodox tradition. For the main differences between the Hebrew and Greek editions of Jeremiah, see *Literary Background*.

Structure Few books of the Bible are as complex in organization as Jeremiah. Its arrangement often seems haphazard and disjointed, which is due in part to the fact that neither its sayings nor its stories follow a chronological order. In some places, the book is arranged thematically; in others, the logic of its presentation is simply unclear. That said, it is possible to divide the book into four parts, two minor and two major. The two minor parts consist of a prologue that recounts the call of Jeremiah (chap. 1) and an epilogue that describes the conquest of Jerusalem and its aftermath (chap. 52). Between these endpoints one finds two major blocks of material that differ in some respects and yet mirror one another in other respects. Chapters 2–25 are predominately poetic (with some prose) and include only a few references to the historical context of Jeremiah's ministry. Chapters 26–51, by contrast, have a greater concentration of prose material (with some poetry) and make frequent reference to the historical setting of what is said or done by the prophet. Both halves of the book feature a sermon delivered by Jeremiah in the courts of the Temple (chaps. 7 and 26), and both halves conclude with oracles spoken against other nations (chaps. 25 and 46–51).

Literary Background The Book of Jeremiah exists in two distinct forms, one in Hebrew and one in Greek. These two editions differ in length as well as arrangement. **(1)** The traditional Hebrew edition preserved in the Masoretic text (MT) is the long form of the book. It is the one most commonly known and read today, since it is the basis for most English translations. **(2)** The Greek text preserved in the Septuagint (LXX) is shorter than the Masoretic text by nearly 15 percent and follows a different order. For instance, chapters 46–51 of the Hebrew edition stand near the midpoint of the Greek edition (after 25:13) rather than at its end (after 45:5). Besides these two major differences, there are several minor variations between the two editions as well.

The question of which edition represents the original text of Jeremiah remains unsettled to this day. Is the Greek edition an abridgment of the Hebrew edition? Or is the Hebrew edition an expansion of a shorter, more original text, which is preserved in the Greek edition? New light has been shed on this matter since the discovery of the Dead Sea Scrolls in the twentieth century. With the unearthing of the scrolls, scholars learned that two different Hebrew editions of the book circulated in antiquity. A few fragments of Jeremiah found among the scrolls exhibit close agreement with the long text of the MT (2Q Jer, 4Q Jer^a, 4Q Jer^c), while another Hebrew fragment agrees with the shorter text of the LXX (4Q Jer^b). The riddle of which version is more ancient is not thereby solved, but many scholars have concluded that the shorter Hebrew text (underlying the LXX) may be the original. If so, then the longer Hebrew text (MT) represents an early expansion of the text that supplies additional information for the benefit of later readers.

The Prophet and His Times Jeremiah is the most biographical of the Bible's prophetic books. More is known about the life, personality, and inner struggles of Jeremiah than of any other prophet in Scripture. He was born into a priestly family that lived in the town of Anathoth (1:1) and was called to prophetic ministry as a young man in 627 B.C. (1:6). Jeremiah's career as a prophet extended over the next forty years, which would prove to be the final decades of the Southern Kingdom of Judah and the Davidic monarchy (1:3). The Lord did not permit Jeremiah to marry (16:1–4), and he spent most of his life in the land of Judah, although his last years were spent in Egypt, where he was taken after the fall of Jerusalem in 586 B.C. (43:1–3). Nothing certain is known about the end of Jeremiah's life, although one ancient tradition relates that he was stoned to death by his own people (*Lives of the Prophets* 2, 1; Tertullian, *Scorpiace* 8).

Jeremiah is sometimes called "the weeping prophet", and for good reason. Apart from a small circle of friends and sympathizers, he was disliked by the majority of his contemporaries, including the royal and religious authorities of Judah. Jeremiah's vocation as God's messenger was thus fulfilled at great personal cost to himself. Among other things, he was plotted against (11:19–23), locked in stocks (20:1–6), put on trial (26:7–24), banned from the Temple (36:5), imprisoned (37:11–21), and cast into a cistern of sludge (38:1–13)—all for proclaiming the word of God faithfully. The turmoil that Jeremiah suffered as a result of these persecutions comes out in his "confessions" or personal dialogues with the Lord (11:18—12:6; 15:10–21; 17:14–18; 18:19–23; 20:7–13, 14–18).

Historically, Jeremiah lived during a transitional time in world politics. When he was called to be a prophet in 627 B.C., Assyria was the supreme ruler over the Near East, but this once-mighty empire had just entered a period of rapid decline from which it would not recover. Nineveh, its capital city, fell in 612 B.C., and after the fall of Haran in 610 B.C., the last remnants of the Assyrian government were swept away by the Babylonians, who emerged as the next imperial superpower on the world stage. Small states such as Judah lived at the mercy of these political and military giants, which also included at this time a newly resurgent Egypt. In the end, it was Judah's rebellion against Babylonian rule—contrary to the counsel of Jeremiah—that led to the overthrow of the Southern Kingdom of Judah. The final blow came in 586 B.C., when Babylonian invaders devastated the city of Jerusalem, destroyed the Lord's Temple, dismantled the Davidic monarchy, and deported thousands of Jewish captives into exile.

The Message of the Prophet The Book of Jeremiah is the longest of the Bible's prophetic books by word count. It is a sizeable collection of oracles and short narratives that touches upon a multitude of themes and concerns. This is not to say that Jeremiah forms a timeless treatise on theology or spirituality, since the book is firmly rooted in the final days of the kingdom of Judah. It no doubt communicates truths about God that are relevant for all times, but most of what is said and done in the book impinges directly on the events that led to Judah's conquest and exile in the sixth century B.C.

Jeremiah's prophetic vision ranges widely over Israel's past, present, and future. His opening sermon looks back on the Exodus when the Lord freed his people from bondage and led them through the wilderness to a new homeland. This was a honeymoon period, and the Lord, who wedded himself to Israel at Mt. Sinai, remembers with fondness the "devotion" of his young bride during these early years (2:2). But these days of marital joy, when Israel was "holy" to the Lord and the "first fruits" of his harvest (2:3), were shattered when the people crossed over into Canaan and lusted after idols (2:7–8). By their pursuit of these "lovers" (3:1), the promiscuous people committed "adultery" against their divine Husband (3:9) and polluted their land with "vile harlotry" (3:2). And none of this, the prophet insists, was the Lord's fault. He planted his people in Canaan as a "choice vine", but they made themselves a "wild vine" (2:21). The people of Israel committed the two evils of forsaking the Lord, the "fountain of living waters", and of turning their hearts to false gods, which are "broken cisterns that can hold no water" (2:13).

Because Israel's infidelities worsened over time, the Lord had no choice but to bring his people to judgment. By the time Jeremiah arrived on the scene, the Northern Kingdom of Israel had already been laid waste and the Southern Kingdom of Judah was teetering on the brink of destruction. Early in his ministry, Jeremiah supported King Josiah's reform, which attempted to purge the land of idolatry and restore proper observance of the Mosaic Law (2 Kings 23:1–25). But while the king's efforts were noble and sincere, his reform proved to be shallow and short-lived. Following the death of Josiah in 609 B.C., Judah quickly plunged back into the darkness of idolatry and immorality. Jeremiah had the unenviable task of sounding the alarm in this rapidly disintegrating society. His oracles of warning, most of them addressed to Jerusalem and Judah, aimed at stemming the tide of national apostasy before it was too late. Unless his call to repentance was heeded, the kingdom of Judah would condemn itself to a violent demise.

More than anything, Judah corrupted itself by false worship and faithless leadership. The Lord and his covenant were not merely neglected by the people—they were totally forsaken as the nation plunged itself into wanton iniquity. People made offerings to gods and goddesses (7:18); they set up idols and cult images in the Temple (7:30; 32:34);

and many sacrificed their children as offerings to pagan deities (7:31; 19:5). Jeremiah lays much of the blame for this rebellion at the feet of Judah's leaders. Its kings and princes were preoccupied with political affairs, such as forming alliances with powerful nations, and were enamored with luxurious living (22:13–17). Among religious leaders, the priests had no knowledge of God (2:8) and allowed themselves to be deceived by Judah's counterfeit prophets (20:6). False prophets were liars who led the people astray (14:14). Unlike Jeremiah, they had no admittance to the divine counsel (23:18). They claimed to speak the word of God, but they were never sent by him (23:14–32). Instead, they spoke empty words of comfort and made a living telling people what they wanted to hear. The false prophets countered Jeremiah's dire warnings of judgment with reassurance that Judah was safe from national threats (5:12). They proclaimed "Peace, peace" when there was "no peace" (6:14; 8:11) and popularized slogans that the Lord's Temple in Jerusalem was a guarantee against the danger of foreign conquest (7:4).

None of this passed unnoticed by the Lord (23:24; 32:19). Though he waited patiently for Judah's repentance over the years of Jeremiah's ministry, it never came. The nation only intensified its rebellion against the covenant, and so the Enforcer of the covenant had no choice but to put its curses of famine, sword, conquest, and exile into effect (15:2; 18:21; 21:7; 24:10; etc.). Judah had condemned itself to face the justice of the Lord, who alone wields the power to make and unmake nations and kingdoms (1:10). To the naked eye of history, the judgments that crushed Judah in the early sixth century were executed by the armies of Babylon; but according to the spiritual vision of the prophet, it was the Lord who summoned the Babylonians to bring suffering and woe upon his people for their defiant refusal to live by the covenant.

Besides threatening that God will make Jerusalem a "heap of ruins" (9:11), Jeremiah also bears a message of mercy (31:21). Looking beyond the horizons of imminent judgment, the prophet unveils the Lord's plan to give his people "a future and a hope" (29:11) as a sign of his "everlasting love" (31:3). Once the chastisements of defeat and exile are past, God will restore the fortunes of Israel and Judah (30:3) by bringing them back to Zion and blessing them once again (3:14; 31:12). He will rescue the remnant of his people from the nations to which they have been scattered (31:10). In fact, even the nations themselves—the Gentile peoples of the world—will forsake their idols and be gathered into the Lord's presence (3:17; 16:19). In response to these merciful acts of redemption, the covenant community will bring the God of Israel a continuous stream of thank offerings (33:11).

Jeremiah's vision of restoration clusters around the two hopes of a coming Messiah and the founding of a new covenant. The days when Israel and

15

Judah will be saved correspond to the days when God will raise up "one" of David's royal descendants to rule over the family of Abraham (33:26). This new King David (30:9) will be a righteous "Branch" who sits on David's throne and governs God's people with justice (23:5–6; 33:15–16). In addition, the Lord pledges to forge a new covenant with Israel and Judah that will surpass the broken covenant made at Mt. Sinai (31:31–32). Unlike the Law of Moses inscribed on stone tablets, the law of this new covenant will be written on the "hearts" of the people, enabling them to "know" God like never before (31:33–34). The Lord will thereby cleanse his people of their guilt (33:8), heal their stubborn unfaithfulness (3:22; 30:17), and give them a heart that fears him (32:40). And unlike the Mosaic covenant, which was destined to yield to a more perfect one, the new covenant will be "an everlasting covenant which will never be forgotten" (50:5).

Christian Perspective The Book of Jeremiah is quoted several times in the New Testament. Jesus cites the words of the prophet to accuse merchants and religious authorities of making the Jerusalem Temple a "den of robbers" (Jer 7:11; Mk 11:17). Paul quotes the book when he insists that whoever boasts should "boast in the Lord" (Jer 9:24; 1 Cor 1:31; 2 Cor 10:17). Matthew also draws select passages from Jeremiah to interpret events surrounding Jesus' infancy (Jer 31:15; Mt 2:18) and betrayal (Jer 32:6–9; Mt 27:9–10). More prominent in the New Testament are references to Jeremiah's prophecy of a "new covenant" (Jer 31:31–34). Jesus ratifies this new covenant in his blood at the Last Supper (Lk 22:20; 1 Cor 11:25); Paul views himself as a minister of this new covenant in mediating the life of the Spirit to the world (2 Cor 3:6); and the Book of Hebrews announces the arrival of the new covenant as the hearts of Christian believers are inscribed with God's Law and their sins are no longer remembered (Heb 8:8–12; 10:16–18). Beyond these explicit references to Jeremiah in the New Testament, Christian readings of the book frequently notice how the life of Jeremiah foreshadows the life of Jesus in several remarkable ways: both figures were prophets who delivered the word of the Lord but were rejected by the authorities of the day (Jer 1:5, 18–19; Mt 16:14; 20:18–19); both lived as unmarried, celibate men (Jer 16:1–2; Mt 19:12); both were rejected by their hometown (Jer 11:21; Mt 13:53–58; Lk 4:16–30); both foretold the fall of Jerusalem and the destruction of the Temple (Jer 19:15; 26:12; Mk 13:1–2; Lk 21:20); both were put on trial and accused of speaking falsehood (Jer 26:10–15; Mk 14:53–65); and both men, who suffered greatly at the hands of others, were likened to a sacrificial lamb led to the slaughter (Jer 11:19; Jn 1:29; Acts 8:32–35).

OUTLINE OF JEREMIAH

1. Prologue (chap. 1)
   A. The Call of Jeremiah (1:1–11)
   B. The Visions of Jeremiah (1:12–19)

2. First Collection of Oracles (chaps. 2–25)
   A. The Lord's Unfaithful Bride (2:1—4:4)
   B. Initial Announcements of Judgment (4:5—6:30)
   C. The Temple Sermon (7:1—9:26)
   D. Idols, Broken Covenant, Dialogue with the Lord (10:1—12:17)
   E. Prophetic Signs, Sayings, Dialogue with the Lord (13:1—17:27)
   F. Prophetic Signs, Sayings, Imprisonment (18:1—20:18)
   G. Denunciation of Corrupt Kings (21:1—23:8)
   H. Denunciation of False Prophets (23:9–40)
   I. Denunciation of Rebellious People (24:1—25:14)
   J. Denunciation of Judah and the Nations (25:15–38)

3. Second Collection of Oracles (chaps. 26–51)
   A. Initial Announcements of Judgment (26:1—28:17)
   B. Letter to Exiles in Babylon (29:1–32)
   C. Book of Consolation (30:1—33:26)
   D. Confrontations with the Kings of Judah (34:1—36:32)
   E. Jeremiah Imprisoned and Rescued (37:1—38:28)
   F. Jerusalem Besieged (39:1–18)
   G. Jeremiah in Mizpah and Egypt (40:1—45:5)
   H. Oracles against the Nations (46:1—51:64)

4. Epilogue (chap. 52)
   A. The Fall of Jerusalem (52:1–27)
   B. The Exiles of Judah (52:28–30)
   C. The Release of Jehoiachin (52:31–34)

THE BOOK OF

JEREMIAH

Introduction

1 The words of Jeremi′ah, the son of Hilki′ah, of the priests who were in An′athoth in the land of Benjamin, ²to whom the word of the LORD came in the days of Josi′ah the son of A′mon, king of Judah, in the thirteenth year of his reign. ³It came also in the days of Jehoi′akim the son of Josi′ah, king of Judah, and until the end of the eleventh year of Zedeki′ah, the son of Josiah, king of Judah, until the captivity of Jerusalem in the fifth month.

Jeremiah's Call and Commission

4 Now the word of the LORD came to me saying,

⁵"Before I formed you in the womb I knew you,
  and before you were born I consecrated you;
I appointed you a prophet to the nations."
⁶Then I said, "Ah, Lord GOD! Behold, I do not know how to speak, for I am only a youth."* ⁷But the LORD said to me,

"Do not say, 'I am only a youth';
  for to all to whom I send you you shall go,
  and whatever I command you you shall
    speak.
⁸Be not afraid of them,
  for I am with you to deliver you,

                                    says the LORD."

1:5: Is 49:1; Gal 1:15.   **1:8:** Is 43:5; Acts 18:9–10.

1:1–3 An introduction to Jeremiah the man. It identifies his father (Hilkiah), his family's occupation (priests), his hometown (Anathoth), and the length of his ministry (over 40 years, from 627 to 586 B.C.).

1:1 The words of Jeremiah: Functions as a title for the book. Jeremiah was involved in writing down his messages from the Lord (30:2; 36:2, 32; 51:60). His name, which may mean "the LORD exalts" or "the LORD establishes", was common in biblical times. **Hilkiah:** A high priest of this name ministered in Jerusalem during the reign of King Josiah (2 Kings 22:4). Evidence is lacking, however, to identify him as Jeremiah's father. **Anathoth:** A small town about three miles northeast of Jerusalem. It lay in Benjaminite territory and was one of 13 settlements in the land of Israel allotted as dwelling places for the Levitical priests and their families (Josh 21:18; 1 Kings 2:26).

1:2 the word of the LORD came: Biblical language for an instance of divine revelation. **Josiah:** King of Judah from 640 to 609 B.C. Jeremiah was called to be a prophet during Josiah's **thirteenth year**, i.e., in 627 B.C. See chart: *Kings of the Divided Monarchy* at 1 Kings 13.

1:3 Jehoiakim: The king of Judah from 609 to 598 B.C. He is Josiah's second son, who came to the throne after his younger brother, Jehoahaz, reigned for only three months in 609 B.C. Jehoiakim is one of Jeremiah's most determined

opponents. **Zedekiah:** The last king of Judah, who reigned from 597 to 586 B.C. He is the third son of Josiah to rule over the Southern Kingdom. Zedekiah is the successor to his nephew, Jehoiachin, who reigned for only three months in 598–97 B.C. **the captivity of Jerusalem:** The catastrophe of 586 B.C., when the Babylonians destroy Jerusalem and take survivors from Judah as exiles to Babylon (52:12–16; 2 Kings 25:8–12). This date for the end of Jeremiah's ministry is only an approximation, since he continues to proclaim the word of God among those who flee to Egypt in late 586 (44:1–30).

1:4 came to me: The following account is autobiographical, recounted by Jeremiah himself.

1:5 Before I formed you: God chose Jeremiah to be a prophet before his birth. The Hebrew verb *yāṣar* suggests the image of a potter forming a clay vessel with his hands, as in Gen 2:7. • Catholic tradition infers from this passage that unborn human life is willed by God and thus endowed with the right to life from the moment of conception (CCC 2270). • God is not ashamed to take flesh when he is its Creator. If he was unashamed of touching humanity when he fashioned it, he was not ashamed to make holy flesh the veil of his divinity. The body as formed from the beginning is undefiled unless one defiles it by fornication or adultery (St. Cyril of Jerusalem, *Catechesis* 12, 26). **I knew you:** The language of divine election, meaning "I chose you" (Amos 3:2; Rom 8:29). **consecrated:** Set apart by the Lord for a holy purpose (Sir 49:7). Similar descriptions are given of the Servant of the Lord in Isaiah (Is 49:1, 5) and of John the Baptist in the NT (Lk 1:15). **a prophet to the nations:** Jeremiah is sent mainly to the people of Judah, but he will also speak oracles of judgment against other nations (25:12–14; 46:1–51:58). • Paul alludes to this verse in Gal 1:15, where he relates that God set him apart before birth and called him to preach the gospel among the nations. He implies that a NT apostle, as a messenger entrusted with God's word, performs a ministry similar to that of an OT prophet.

1:6 I do not know how: An initial objection to God's call. Jeremiah's protest is typical of one who feels unworthy and unqualified for the divine task assigned to him. • The same reaction can be seen in figures such as Moses (Ex 3:11; 4:10), Gideon (Judg 6:15), and Isaiah (Is 6:5). The Lord responds to the resistance of those he calls to service by promising to be "with" them as a help and support (Ex 3:12; 4:12; Judg 6:16), just as he does for Jeremiah (1:8, 19) (CCC 2584). **a youth:** Jeremiah was probably a teenager when God called him.

Jeremiah, sometimes called a prophet of doom, lived at the most tragic period of Israel's history, during which Jerusalem was destroyed by Nebuchadrezzar and the people were carried off into captivity. He was of a priestly family, and he makes it clear in his book that he obeyed God's call to prophesy most reluctantly. It was his task, under the circumstances, to preach repentance and prophesy destruction if repentance was not forthcoming. But his words fell on deaf ears. In so far as the people heard at all, it was only to resent what he said and make him suffer for it. As the prophet was of a specially sensitive and affectionate nature, his sufferings were all the more acute.

He did not always prophesy doom. Thus in 31:31–34, he foretells the new covenant in terms that remind us of passages in the prophet Isaiah. His words may not have had much effect during his lifetime but after his death his influence was considerable, as was the case with other prophets also; cf. Mt 23:29–30. Not all the prophecies in the book are from Jeremiah himself but some have been inserted later. An important feature of the book is the quantity of biographical material, which tells us a great deal about the prophet.

*1:6: Typically, Jeremiah is reluctant to accept an office for which he feels himself ill suited, and which, he foresees, can bring nothing but suffering and disappointment.

⁹Then the LORD put forth his hand and touched my mouth; and the LORD said to me,

"Behold, I have put my words in your mouth.
¹⁰See, I have set you this day over nations and over kingdoms,

to pluck up and to break down,

to destroy and to overthrow,

to build and to plant."

11 And the word of the LORD came to me, saying, "Jeremi′ah, what do you see?" And I said, "I see a rod of almond."ᵃ ¹²Then the LORD said to me, "You have seen well, for I am watchingᵇ over my word to perform it."

13 The word of the LORD came to me a second time, saying, "What do you see?" And I said, "I see a boiling pot, facing away from the north." ¹⁴Then the LORD said to me, "Out of the north evil shall break forth upon all the inhabitants of the land. ¹⁵For, behold, I am calling all the tribes of the kingdoms of the north, says the LORD; and they shall come and every one shall set his throne at the entrance of the gates of Jerusalem, against all its walls round about,

and against all the cities of Judah. ¹⁶And I will utter my judgments against them, for all their wickedness in forsaking me; they have burned incense to other gods, and worshiped the works of their own hands. ¹⁷But you, gird up your loins; arise, and say to them everything that I command you. Do not be dismayed by them, lest I dismay you before them. ¹⁸And I, behold, I make you this day a fortified city, an iron pillar, and bronze walls, against the whole land, against the kings of Judah, its princes, its priests, and the people of the land. ¹⁹They will fight against you; but they shall not prevail against you, for I am with you, says the LORD, to deliver you."

Israel's Apostasy

2 The word of the LORD came to me, saying, ²"Go and proclaim in the hearing of Jerusalem, Thus says the LORD,

I remember the devotion of your youth,

your love as a bride,

how you followed me in the wilderness,

in a land not sown.

1:10: Rev 10:11.

1:9 touched my mouth: An encounter with God that equips Jeremiah to be his spokesman (CCC 707). Isaiah was similarly prepared for prophetic ministry when an angel cleansed his lips with a coal from the Temple altar (Is 6:6–7), as was Ezekiel, when the Lord gave him a scroll to eat (Ezek 3:1–3). **my words in your mouth:** The prophet is given words to speak that are not his own. It is a message invested with divine authority that God will communicate through him (2 Pet 1:21). • The passage uses language from Deut 18:18, where the Lord promises to raise up another prophet like Moses in the future. Jeremiah is thus a prophet in the likeness of Moses. However, the coming of a prophet of Moses' stature is fully realized only in Jesus Christ (Acts 7:37, 52).

1:10 pluck up ... plant: The main themes of Jeremiah's preaching, which includes divine judgment on sin as well as promises of mercy for repentance. The passage indicates that the word of God spoken through Jeremiah has the power to shape the course of history.

1:11–16 Two prophetic visions, one of an **almond** branch and another of a **boiling pot**. The first teaches that the fulfillment of God's *word* is certain; the second indicates that God's *wrath* will pour out over sinful Judah from the north. The almond tree is the first to put forth buds after winter and is said to "watch" for the coming of spring, a point made here by means of a wordplay (see textual notes a and b).

1:11 what do you see?: A question that directs attention to visions, as in Amos 7:8; 8:2; Zech 4:2; 5:2.

1:14 Out of the north: The scalding judgments of God will pour over Judah and Jerusalem when the Babylonians ravage the land. Babylon is geographically east of Judah rather than north, but armies coming from Mesopotamia did not risk crossing the Arabian Desert directly; instead, they followed the arc of the Fertile Crescent and invaded Israel from the north.

1:15 throne ... the gates: Fulfilled when the princes of Babylon sit in Jerusalem's middle gate (Jer 39:3).

1:16 all their wickedness: Spelled out in detail in chaps. 2–6. **works of their own hands:** Man-made idol images (Is 2:8; Acts 7:41).

1:17 gird up your loins: An idiom meaning "ready yourself for action." It involved tucking in or tying up one's robe in preparation for work or travel (Ex 12:11).

1:18 fortified city ... iron pillar ... bronze walls: Indestructible things. **kings:** Judah's last five kings reigned during Jeremiah's ministry (Josiah, Jehoahaz, Jehoiakim, Jehoiachin, Zedekiah). **princes:** Judah's royal authorities. **priests:** Judah's religious authorities.

1:19 They will fight against you: Jeremiah will face strong resistance and hostile persecution. Beyond needing courage, the prophet is made aware of the hardships that await him so that he will rely more completely on the Lord for protection and help (2 Cor 1:8–11). • Like Isaiah and Ezekiel, Jeremiah is tasked with delivering God's word to an obstinate people, many of whom will refuse it (cf. Is 6:9–13; Ezek 3:4–11; 12:2). Suffering for speaking the word of the Lord is characteristic of prophetic ministry in the OT and is likewise a hallmark of apostolic ministry in the NT (Acts 9:15–16; 1 Cor 4:9–13). • Saints and sinners are different. The former withstand great assaults of temptation, while even slight temptations overpower the latter. No victory is worthy of praise unless it is gained through struggle and conflict (St. John Cassian, *Conference* 3, 18).

2:1–37 Israel is charged with rebellion against the Lord and his covenant (2:9). The prophet speaks on behalf of God, the offended party, while the heavens are called upon to testify to the crimes of the people (2:12). They are guilty of forsaking the Lord **(1)** by worshiping foreign idols and **(2)** by seeking security in alliances with foreign nations.

2:2 devotion: The Hebrew *ḥesed* refers to love and loyalty within a covenant relationship. See word study: *Merciful Love* at Ex 34:7. **a bride:** The Mosaic covenant between God and Israel is viewed as a marital covenant between a husband and wife, as elsewhere in the prophets (Is 54:5; 62:5; Hos 1–3). Israel's sojourn in the wilderness corresponds to the honeymoon period, while its betrayal of the Lord in the form of worshiping other gods is denounced as harlotry (2:20) and adultery (3:9).

ᵃ Heb *shaqed.*
ᵇ Heb *shoqed.*

³Israel was holy to the LORD,
  the first fruits of his harvest.
All who ate of it became guilty;
  evil came upon them,
                    says the LORD."

4 Hear the word of the LORD, O house of Jacob, and all the families of the house of Israel. ⁵Thus says the LORD:
  "What wrong did your fathers find in me
    that they went far from me,
  and went after worthlessness, and became
    worthless?
⁶They did not say, 'Where is the LORD
    who brought us up from the land of Egypt,
  who led us in the wilderness,
    in a land of deserts and pits,
  in a land of drought and deep darkness,
    in a land that none passes through,
    where no man dwells?'
⁷And I brought you into a plentiful land
    to enjoy its fruits and its good things.
  But when you came in you defiled my land,
    and made my heritage an abomination.
⁸The priests did not say, 'Where is the LORD?'
    Those who handle the law did not know me;
  the rulers ᶜ transgressed against me;
    the prophets prophesied by Ba'al,
    and went after things that do not profit.

⁹"Therefore I still contend with you,
                    says the LORD,
  and with your children's children I will
    contend.
¹⁰For cross to the coasts of Cyprus and see,
    or send to Kedar and examine with care;
  see if there has been such a thing.
¹¹Has a nation changed its gods,
    even though they are no gods?
  But my people have changed their glory
    for that which does not profit.
¹²Be appalled, O heavens, at this,
    be shocked, be utterly desolate,
                    says the LORD,
¹³for my people have committed two evils:
    they have forsaken me,
  the fountain of living waters,
    and hewed out cisterns for themselves,
  broken cisterns,
    that can hold no water.

¹⁴"Is Israel a slave? Is he a homeborn servant?
    Why then has he become a prey?
¹⁵The lions have roared against him,
    they have roared loudly.
  They have made his land a waste;
    his cities are in ruins, without inhabitant.
¹⁶Moreover, the men of Memphis and Tah'panhes
    have broken the crown of your head.

2:3 holy: Set apart and dedicated to God for a sacred purpose. **the first fruits:** The first produce of the year's harvest, which is offered in thanksgiving to the Lord at his Temple (Ex 23:19; Lev 23:10). None but the priests and their families are allowed to eat the first fruits (Num 18:12–13). Theologically, Israel is the first fruits of the harvest of nations to enter a covenant relationship with the Lord. This is equivalent to saying that Israel is God's "first-born" among the family of nations (31:9; Ex 4:22). The same expression is applied to the earliest Christians in Jas 1:18. **became guilty:** Israel is under God's special protection as the family of Abraham (Gen 12:3; Num 24:9).
2:4 Jacob: Father of the twelve tribes of Israel (Gen 49:1–27).
2:5 worthlessness: Idols, which bring no profit (2:8, 11).
2:7 a plentiful land: Canaan, a land with abundant natural blessings (Ex 3:8; Deut 11:8–12). **my land:** Canaan, though occupied by Israel as a tenant, belongs to the Lord (Lev 25:23).
2:8 who handle the law: The Levitical priests, who are charged with teaching the Torah to the people (Lev 10:11; Deut 33:10). **the prophets:** False prophets (1 Kings 18:22). **Baal:** The storm and fertility god of Canaanite religion. He is depicted on ancient artifacts as a warrior wielding a lightning bolt. Baal is one of the Lord's chief rivals for Israel's religious devotion in Jeremiah's day. See word study: *Baal* at Hos 2:8.
2:9 contend: A covenant lawsuit is brought against the rebellious people.
2:10 Cyprus: An island northwest of Israel in the Mediterranean Sea. **Kedar:** A region of northern Arabia named after a tribal people who descended from Abraham's son Ishmael (Gen 25:13).
2:11 no gods: Echoes the Song of Moses, which declares that an idol is "no god" (Deut 32:21). **changed their glory:** Idolatry is a foolish exchange in which the glory of God

is traded away for worthless images that are lifeless and powerless to benefit their worshipers (Ps 106:20; Rom 1:25).
2:12 Be appalled, O heavens: Heaven and earth are witnesses to the covenant that God made with Israel in the time of Moses (Deut 30:19; 31:28).
2:13 cisterns: Stone reservoirs used for storing rainwater for the dry summer months. Here they represent the foreign gods and foreign nations that Israel has come to trust, forgetting that the Lord is the only true source of security and life for his people (CCC 2561). **living waters:** Fresh, drinkable water that gives life, as distinct from stagnant or polluted water. • Jesus uses this expression for the gift of the Holy Spirit that leads believers to eternal life (Jn 4:10–14; 7:37–39; CCC 694). • At first we did not exist, and then we came into being. But God, because he always exists, is always Father of the Son. The sacred writers have given us images of this, as when the Father says, "They have forsaken me, the fountain of living waters." Who can conceive of the fountain as empty of life and say that the Son came from nothing, when the Son himself says, "I am the life"? (St. Athanasias, *Defense of the Nicene Definition* 3, 12).
2:14 Is Israel a slave?: No, since Israel is the Lord's first-born son, and yet his people have given up the freedom of sonship to be a slave to other gods and governments.
2:15 lions: The Assyrians, who ravaged northern Israel in the eighth century B.C. and took the northern tribes as captives into exile (Is 5:29). These events stand as a warning to faithless Judah in the south.
2:16 Memphis ... Tahpanhes: Prominent cities in Egypt, the former along the Nile near modern Cairo and the latter in the northeast Delta near Lake Manzaleh. Diplomats from Judah presumably went to these locations to forge political alliances with Egypt in opposition to Babylon. Refugees from Judah settled in these cities after the fall of Jerusalem in 586 B.C. (43:7; 44:1).

ᶜ Heb *shepherds.*

¹⁷Have you not brought this upon yourself
 by forsaking the LORD your God,
 when he led you in the way?
¹⁸And now what do you gain by going to Egypt,
 to drink the waters of the Nile?
Or what do you gain by going to Assyria,
 to drink the waters of the Euphra′tes?
¹⁹Your wickedness will chasten you,
 and your apostasy will reprove you.
Know and see that it is evil and bitter
 for you to forsake the LORD your God;
 the fear of me is not in you,
     says the Lord GOD of hosts.

²⁰"For long ago you broke your yoke
 and burst your bonds;
 and you said, 'I will not serve.'
Yes, upon every high hill
 and under every green tree
 you bowed down as a harlot.
²¹Yet I planted you a choice vine,
 wholly of pure seed.
How then have you turned degenerate
 and become a wild vine?
²²Though you wash yourself with lye
 and use much soap,
 the stain of your guilt is still before me,
    says the Lord GOD.
²³How can you say, 'I am not defiled,
 I have not gone after the Ba′als'?
Look at your way in the valley;
 know what you have done—
a restive young camel interlacing her tracks,
²⁴ a wild donkey used to the wilderness,
 in her heat sniffing the wind!
 Who can restrain her lust?

None who seek her need weary themselves;
 in her month they will find her.
²⁵Keep your feet from going unshod
 and your throat from thirst.
But you said, 'It is hopeless,
 for I have loved strangers,
 and after them I will go.'

²⁶"As a thief is shamed when caught,
 so the house of Israel shall be shamed:
they, their kings, their princes,
 their priests, and their prophets,
²⁷who say to a tree, 'You are my father,'
 and to a stone, 'You gave me birth.'
For they have turned their back to me,
 and not their face.
But in the time of their trouble they say,
 'Arise and save us!'
²⁸But where are your gods
 that you made for yourself?
Let them arise, if they can save you,
 in your time of trouble;
for as many as your cities
 are your gods, O Judah.

²⁹"Why do you complain against me?
 You have all rebelled against me,
     says the LORD.
³⁰In vain have I struck down your children,
 they took no correction;
your own sword devoured your prophets
 like a ravening lion.
³¹And you, O generation, heed the word of the
 LORD.
Have I been a wilderness to Israel,
 or a land of thick darkness?

2:19 the fear of me: See note on Prov 1:7.

2:20 yoke: An image of the Lord's covenant with Israel (also in 5:5). After the Israelites were freed from the yoke of bondage in Egypt, they entered into the Lord's service and bound themselves to keep the laws of the Torah (Ex 24:3). Breaking the yoke is equivalent to breaking the covenant by refusing to serve the Lord as he commands. **high hill ... green tree:** Refers to pagan idol shrines with sacred groves unlawfully operating in the land of Judah. See note on 3:2. **harlot:** Idolatry is spiritual prostitution with other gods (3:1; Ex 34:15–16). The use of sexual metaphors for idolatry mirrors the fact that idol worship in the biblical world often involved acts of sexual impurity such as cultic prostitution (Ex 32:6; Num 25:1–2; Hos 4:13–14).

2:21 a choice vine: A traditional image of Israel (12:10; Ps 80:8–16; Is 5:1–7; Hos 10:1).

2:23 the Baals: Local idol images of the Canaanite god Baal. See note on 2:8. **the valley:** Probably the valley of the son of Hinnom, directly southwest of Jerusalem, where child sacrifice was practiced (7:31). **restive young camel:** A female camel in heat, which is easily excited and difficult to control.

2:24 sniffing the wind: A female donkey searches for a mate by the scent of urine.

2:25 hopeless: Because Judah is stubbornly determined to go after idols and will not be restrained. **loved strangers:** Like a prostitute who serviced her clients (2:20; Hos 2:5).

2:26 king ... princes ... priests ... prophets: Judah's royal and religious leaders, who lead the people astray and are most to blame for the national apostasy that prevails in Jeremiah's day (4:9).

2:27 a tree ... a stone: Pagan cult objects. The tree or wooden pole is associated with Asherah, the mother goddess of Canaanite religion, and the stone propped upright represents either Baal, the storm god, or El, the father of the gods in the Canaanite pantheon. Jeremiah, speaking with sarcasm, reverses the sexual roles of these objects in order to highlight the severity of Judah's spiritual confusion. **You are my father:** Implies a repudiation of the Lord, who is described in the Song of Moses as "your father, who created you" (Deut 32:6).

2:28 many ... are your gods: Points to rampant idolatry in Judah at this time (11:13; cf. 2 Kings 23:4–14). Ugaritic evidence indicates that the Canaanite pantheon had more than 50 deities.

2:30 took no correction: Repentance was refused despite divine discipline. The Lord's reproof is an expression of his fatherly love (Prov 3:11–12), since it is meant to turn his people from sin and bring them to a renewed commitment to his covenant (Deut 8:3–6; Heb 12:6). **prophets:** True prophets, who are often persecuted and killed (2 Chron 36:15–16; Mt 23:37; Acts 7:52).

Why then do my people say, 'We are free,
    we will come no more to you'?
³²Can a maiden forget her ornaments,
    or a bride her attire?
Yet my people have forgotten me
    days without number.

³³"How well you direct your course
    to seek lovers!
So that even to wicked women
    you have taught your ways.
³⁴Also on your skirts is found
    the lifeblood of guiltless poor;
    you did not find them breaking in.
    Yet in spite of all these things
³⁵you say, 'I am innocent;
    surely his anger has turned from me.'
Behold, I will bring you to judgment
    for saying, 'I have not sinned.'
³⁶How lightly you gad about,
    changing your way!
You shall be put to shame by Egypt
    as you were put to shame by Assyria.
³⁷From it too you will come away
    with your hands upon your head,

for the LORD has rejected those in whom you
    trust,
    and you will not prosper by them.

Unfaithful Israel

3 "If^d a man divorces his wife
    and she goes from him
and becomes another man's wife,
    will he return to her?
Would not that land be greatly polluted?
You have played the harlot with many lovers;
    and would you return to me?
               says the LORD.
²Lift up your eyes to the bare heights, and see!
    Where have you not been lain with?
By the waysides you have sat awaiting lovers
    like an Arab in the wilderness.
You have polluted the land
    with your vile harlotry.
³Therefore the showers have been withheld,
    and the spring rain has not come;
yet you have a harlot's brow,
    you refuse to be ashamed.
⁴Have you not just now called to me,
    'My father, you are the friend of my youth—

2:32 her attire: A sash worn in public that indicates a woman is married.

2:34 not ... breaking in: Bloodguilt is not imputed to a homeowner who strikes an intruder, causing his death (Ex 22:2). No such law protects Judah, who is guilty of grave injustices against the needy.

2:35 I am innocent: Proof of Judah's spiritual blindness (1 Jn 1:8).

2:36 Egypt: An ally of Judah that will quickly turn and become its taskmaster, e.g., Egypt unseated King Jehoahaz from the throne of Judah and replaced him with his brother, Jehoiakim, in 609 B.C. (2 Kings 23:34). It is ironic that God's people, delivered from servitude in Egypt, should seek its help for the welfare of the nation. **Assyria:** Seeking security in alliances with Assyria is also criticized by Hosea (Hos 7:11; 8:9; 12:1).

2:37 hands upon your head: A sign of humiliation (2 Sam 13:19).

3:1—4:4 An urgent call to repentance. The Lord appeals to his people as a grieving husband and father who earnestly desires reunion with his "faithless wife" (3:20) and "faithless sons" (3:22). See note on 2:2.

3:1 If a man divorces: The legal background is Deut 24:1-4, which forbids a husband to divorce and remarry the same woman if she enters a second marriage in the interim. Violation of this law brings guilt on the land of Israel (Deut 24:4; cf. 2:7). **played the harlot:** Judah has been promiscuous in serving gods other than the Lord. Jeremiah views this as spiritual prostitution with idols (3:2) as well as spiritual adultery against God, to whom they are joined by a marital covenant (3:8; CCC 2380).

3:2 the bare heights: Hilltops were popular places for pagan religious shrines, sometimes called "high places" in the Bible. Sexual impurity, possibly in the form of cult prostitution, is sometimes associated with these sites (3:23; Hos 4:13-14). **awaiting lovers:** Like a prostitute soliciting clients (Prov

7:10-12). **like an Arab:** Like a highway robber who waits to ambush travelers along lonely desert roads.

3:3 the spring rain: Arrives in March/April and helps to ensure that the spring harvest of barley and wheat is successful. Lack of rainfall is a sign that the Lord is displeased with his people (Deut 11:13-17). **a harlot's brow:** An attitude of willful defiance. Also, prostitutes may have advertised their occupation by wearing a jewel or decorative band on their foreheads (cf. Rev 17:4).

Word Study

Return (3:1)

Shûv (Heb.): A verb that appears over 1000 times in the OT, most often in Jeremiah. It expresses various meanings, including "turn", "turn around", and "turn back". The term can indicate changing direction (Deut 2:3), reverting to a prior condition (Gen 3:19), returning to a prior location (Gen 22:5), withdrawing from a hostile pursuit (1 Kings 22:33), or reneging on a vow (Judg 11:35). As a theological term, it speaks to Israel's relationship with the Lord, where it can signal rebellion (*turning away* from God and his commandments, Josh 23:12) as well as repentance (*turning back* to God through a conversion of heart, Ezek 14:6). Jeremiah makes several appeals for his people to "return" to the Lord in this way (Jer 3:12, 14; 22; 4:1; etc.). The danger is that Judah and Jerusalem will refuse the summons by not returning to God (Jer 3:7, 10). If they resist the prophet's call, judgment will be certain: God's anger will not "turn back" from his stubborn people (Jer 4:8).

---

^dGk Syr: Heb *Saying, If.*

23

[5]will he be angry for ever,
    will he be indignant to the end?'
Behold, you have spoken,
    but you have done all the evil that you could."

A Call to Repentance

6 The LORD said to me in the days of King Josi′ah: "Have you seen what she did, that faithless one, Israel, how she went up on every high hill and under every green tree, and there played the harlot? [7]And I thought, 'After she has done all this she will return to me'; but she did not return, and her false sister Judah saw it. [8]She saw that for all the adulteries of that faithless one, Israel, I had sent her away with a decree of divorce; yet her false sister Judah did not fear, but she too went and played the harlot. [9]Because harlotry was so light to her, she polluted the land, committing adultery with stone and tree. [10]Yet for all this her false sister Judah did not return to me with her whole heart, but in pretense, says the LORD."

11 And the LORD said to me, "Faithless Israel has shown herself less guilty than false Judah. [12]Go, and proclaim these words toward the north, and say,

'Return, faithless Israel,

                    says the LORD.

I will not look on you in anger,
    for I am merciful,

                    says the LORD;

I will not be angry for ever.
[13]Only acknowledge your guilt,
    that you rebelled against the LORD your
        God
and scattered your favors among strangers
    under every green tree,
    and that you have not obeyed my voice,

                    says the LORD.

[14]Return, O faithless children,

                    says the LORD;

    for I am your master;
I will take you, one from a city and two from a
    family,
    and I will bring you to Zion.

15 "'And I will give you shepherds after my own heart, who will feed you with knowledge and understanding. [16]And when you have multiplied and increased in the land, in those days, says the LORD, they shall no more say, "The ark of the covenant of the LORD." It shall not come to mind, or be remembered, or missed; it shall not be made again.* [17]At that time Jerusalem shall be called the throne of the LORD, and all nations shall gather to

---

3:5 spoken ... done: Points to the disparity between prayerful words and godless deeds.

3:6–11 The prophet compares the former rebellion of the Northern Kingdom of **Israel** with the current rebellion of the Southern Kingdom of **Judah**. Both kingdoms embrace a culture of sin and so place themselves under God's judgment. Nevertheless, Judah bears greater guilt because it is refusing to learn from the mistakes of its wicked sister, Israel, whose demise took place in 722 B.C., a full century before Jeremiah's time. For the metaphor of Israel (with its capital, Samaria) and Judah (with its capital, Jerusalem) as wayward sisters, see also Ezek 16:1–58 and 23:1–49.

3:6 Josiah: King of the Southern Kingdom of Judah from 640 to 609 B.C. **high hill ... green tree:** The northern Israelites had previously engaged in idolatry at various pagan shrines and sacred groves.

3:8 decree of divorce: A document that makes a divorce legally binding. A husband hands this certificate to his wife when he ends the marriage and sends her out of his home (Deut 24:1). Because the tribes of the Northern Kingdom of Israel had been sent into exile roughly a century earlier and had never returned to the land, it appears to Jeremiah's generation that a large part of the covenant people has been permanently "divorced" from the Lord. This is not so, however, since God pleads with the exiles of northern Israel to repent and return to him as an estranged wife goes back to her husband (3:12–14).

3:9 light to her: Judah underestimates the severity of her sins. **adultery:** See note on 2:2. **stone and tree:** See note on 2:27.

3:10 in pretense: The religious reform of King Josiah in 2 Kings 22–23 achieves limited success. It shows many outward signs of progress and renewal, but inside the people remain attached to their evil ways.

3:11 less guilty: Literally, "more righteous". This may be an allusion to Judah's confession that Tamar, whom he hired for sex as a roadside prostitute, is more righteous than he is (Gen 38:26).

3:12—4:2 Jeremiah urges the northern tribes of Israel, most of whom have remained in the Assyrian Exile since the eighth century B.C., to repent. If they do so, God will restore them (3:18).

3:12 I am merciful: The mercy of God is the sole basis for Israel's restoration (Ex 34:6) and for human salvation in general (Rom 9:15–16; 11:32) (CCC 210–11, 270).

3:14 master: The Hebrew involves a wordplay on the name Baal, a Canaanite deity worshiped by apostate Israelites in Jeremiah's day (2:23; 7:9; 11:13, etc.). See note on 2:8. **one from a city ... two from a family:** Only a remnant of northern Israel will be restored (50:17–20; Is 10:22). **Zion:** Another name for Jerusalem that features in prophetic visions of Israel's deliverance from sin and exile (Is 59:20–21; Joel 2:32). See note on 2 Sam 5:7.

3:15 shepherds: Wise and faithful leaders (23:4), unlike the corrupt authorities of Jeremiah's day who lead the people astray (23:1–2; Ezek 34:1–10). **after my own heart:** Echoes the description of David in 1 Sam 13:14.

3:16 ark of the covenant: A wooden chest overlaid with gold, carried with poles, and kept in the innermost chamber of the Temple. The ark was lidded with a slab of pure gold and topped with winged angelic creatures called cherubim, who formed a royal seat where the Lord sat invisibly "enthroned" (1 Sam 4:4; 2 Kings 19:15). • According to 2 Mac 2:5–6, Jeremiah hid the ark in an unmarked cave on Mt. Nebo before the Babylonians destroyed Solomon's Temple in 586 B.C., after which it was never found again. See note on Ex 25:10.

3:17 Jerusalem: The entire city will become the Lord's throne after the disappearance of the ark (3:16). **all nations shall gather:** A vision of the messianic future, when the nations will come streaming to Mt. Zion to worship the Lord and partake of the sumptuous feast he will prepare for

---

*3:16: The ark must have been destroyed at the same time as the temple in 586 B.C. In the Messianic times the presence of the Lord will not be restricted to the ark of the covenant; cf. Rev 21:22.

it, to the presence of the Lord in Jerusalem, and they shall no more stubbornly follow their own evil heart. ¹⁸In those days the house of Judah shall join the house of Israel, and together they shall come from the land of the north to the land that I gave your fathers for a heritage.

¹⁹" 'I thought
  how I would set you among my sons,
and give you a pleasant land,
  a heritage most beauteous of all nations.
And I thought you would call me, My Father,
  and would not turn from following me.
²⁰Surely, as a faithless wife leaves her husband,
  so have you been faithless to me, O house of
    Israel,
                        says the Lord.' "

²¹A voice on the bare heights is heard,
  the weeping and pleading of Israel's sons,
because they have perverted their way,
  they have forgotten the Lord their God.
²²"Return, O faithless sons,
  I will heal your faithlessness."
"Behold, we come to you;
  for you are the Lord our God.
²³Truly the hills are a delusion,
  the orgies on the mountains.
Truly in the Lord our God
  is the salvation of Israel.
24 "But from our youth the shameful thing has devoured all for which our fathers labored, their flocks and their herds, their sons and their daughters. ²⁵Let us lie down in our shame, and let our dishonor cover us; for we have sinned against the Lord our God, we and our fathers, from our youth even to this day; and we have not obeyed the voice of the Lord our God."

4 "If you return, O Israel,
                        says the Lord,
  to me you should return.
If you remove your abominations from my
    presence,
  and do not waver,
²and if you swear, 'As the Lord lives,'
  in truth, in justice, and in uprightness,
then nations shall bless themselves in him,
  and in him shall they glory."
3 For thus says the Lord to the men of Judah and to the inhabitants of Jerusalem:
"Break up your fallow ground,
  and sow not among thorns.
⁴Circumcise yourselves to the Lord,
  remove the foreskin of your hearts,
  O men of Judah and inhabitants of Jerusalem;
lest my wrath go forth like fire,
  and burn with none to quench it,
  because of the evil of your doings."

Judah Threatened with Invasion

5 Declare in Judah, and proclaim in Jerusalem, and say,
"Blow the trumpet through the land;
  cry aloud and say,
'Assemble, and let us go
  into the fortified cities!'
⁶Raise a standard toward Zion,
  flee for safety, stay not,
for I bring evil from the north,
  and great destruction.

---

them (Is 2:2-4; 25:6-9; Zech 2:10-11). • The NT views the gathering of all nations to Zion in spiritual rather than geographical terms. Coming to faith in Christ and joining the messianic community of the Church brings one to the heavenly Mt. Zion, the celestial Jerusalem above, where angels and saints worship the Lord in the New Covenant mediated by Jesus (Heb 12:22-24).

3:18 house of Judah ... Israel: A reunion of all the exiled tribes of Israel. The prophet foresees a restored community of the whole covenant people made up of captives taken away by the Babylonians in the sixth century B.C. (southern Judahites) as well as those taken into exile by the Assyrians in the eighth century B.C. (northern Israelites). The reunion of Israel and Judah is also envisioned in 50:17-20; Is 11:12; Ezek 37:15-23; Hos 1:11.

3:19 my sons: The people of Israel, who became God's children by covenant (Deut 14:1-2).

3:21 the bare heights: Repentance is called for at the site of rebellion. See note on 3:2.

3:22-25 A national confession of sin. The **we** who is speaking appears to be Jeremiah praying on behalf of penitent Israel. Similar confessions were made by Ezra (Ezra 9:6-15), Nehemiah (Neh 9:6-37), and Daniel (Dan 9:3-19).

3:23 orgies: The Hebrew refers to "noise" or "commotion".

3:24 the shameful thing: The Hebrew *habboshet* probably refers to Baal, the Canaanite storm god whose name is sometimes substituted with this word, e.g., Saul's son Eshbaal, "man of Baal" (1 Chron 9:39), also appears as Ish-bosheth, "man of shame" (2 Sam 2:8). See note on 2:8.

4:1 return: Another call for repentance, which includes acknowledging one's guilt (3:13) and seeking the Lord's mercy (3:12). See word study: *Return* at 3:1. **abominations:** Or "detestable things". The reference is to idols and the religious rites associated with them (Hos 9:10).

4:2 As the Lord lives: An oath formula. **shall bless themselves:** Or "shall be blessed". • Taking oaths in the name of the Lord implies not only Israel's conversion from sin, but a recommitment to its vocation as Abraham's offspring to mediate God's blessings to the world (Gen 22:18; 26:4). See note on Gen 12:3.

4:3 fallow ground: Hard and unreceptive to newly sown seed. It represents the hard hearts of the people (Ezek 36:26).

4:4 Circumcise ... your hearts: Echoing the words of Deut 10:16, the prophet urges the people to remove from their hearts all stubborn resistance to God's commandments. See note on 9:26.

4:5 Blow the trumpet: Like a watchman on a city wall who sounds the alarm when enemies approach (Ezek 33:2-3). It is a warning that people should seek protection inside a city's defenses. See word study: *Trumpet* at Judg 6:34.

4:6 a standard: A banner or visual sign to warn of imminent danger. **Zion:** Jerusalem. **evil from the north:** See note on 1:14.

⁷A lion has gone up from his thicket,
  a destroyer of nations has set out;
  he has gone forth from his place
to make your land a waste;
  your cities will be ruins
  without inhabitant.
⁸For this clothe yourself with sackcloth,
  lament and wail;
for the fierce anger of the LORD
  has not turned back from us."

9 "In that day, says the LORD, courage shall fail
both king and princes; the priests shall be appalled
and the prophets astounded." ¹⁰Then I said, "Ah,
Lord GOD, surely you have utterly deceived this
people and Jerusalem, saying, 'It shall be well with
you'; whereas the sword has reached their very
life."

11 At that time it will be said to this people and
to Jerusalem, "A hot wind from the bare heights in
the desert toward the daughter of my people, not to
winnow or cleanse, ¹²a wind too full for this comes
for me. Now it is I who speak in judgment upon
them."
¹³Behold, he comes up like clouds,
  his chariots like the whirlwind;
his horses are swifter than eagles—
  woe to us, for we are ruined!
¹⁴O Jerusalem, wash your heart from wickedness,
  that you may be saved.
How long shall your evil thoughts
  lodge within you?
¹⁵For a voice declares from Dan
  and proclaims evil from Mount E'phraim.

¹⁶Warn the nations that he is coming;
  announce to Jerusalem,
"Besiegers come from a distant land;
  they shout against the cities of Judah.
¹⁷Like keepers of a field they are against her round
    about,
  because she has rebelled against me,
                                    says the LORD.
¹⁸Your ways and your doings
  have brought this upon you.
This is your doom, and it is bitter;
  it has reached your very heart."

¹⁹My anguish, my anguish! I writhe in pain!
  Oh, the walls of my heart!
My heart is beating wildly;
  I cannot keep silent;
for I hear the sound of the trumpet,
  the alarm of war.
²⁰Disaster follows hard on disaster,
  the whole land is laid waste.
Suddenly my tents are destroyed,
  my curtains in a moment.
²¹How long must I see the standard,
  and hear the sound of the trumpet?
²²"For my people are foolish,
  they know me not;
they are stupid children,
  they have no understanding.
They are skilled in doing evil,
  but how to do good they know not."

²³I looked on the earth, and behold, it was waste
    and void;
  and to the heavens, and they had no light.

4:7 A lion: Nebuchadnezzar, king of Babylon, whose army is coming to destroy Jerusalem. **waste ... ruins without inhabitant:** Judah will suffer the same devastation that came to northern Israel when the lion of Assyria invaded, according to 2:15.

4:8 sackcloth: A coarse fabric spun from goat hair and worn in times of mourning (Gen 37:34).

4:9 king ... princes ... priests ... prophets: Judah's royal and religious leaders, who led the people astray and were most to blame for the national apostasy that prevails in Jeremiah's day (2:26). Their weakness as leaders will be clear when their courage fails in the midst of crisis.

4:10 GOD: Spelled with capital letters when it translates the Hebrew consonants YHWH, referring to "Yahweh", but supplied with the vowels of *'elōhîm*, meaning "God". **you ... deceived:** In a moment of distress and grief, the prophet audaciously accuses the Lord of misleading the people of Judah into a false sense of security. **It shall be well with you:** Or "you shall have peace." Many wrongly suppose that Jerusalem and the Temple would be immune to destruction since the Lord established Zion and promised to protect it (Ps 48:8; 87:5). He also made it clear, however, that rebellion against the covenant would bring conquering nations upon Israel (Deut 28:47–68).

4:11 hot wind: The coming distress is likened to a scorching and dusty wind, called a sirocco, that blows into the land from the Arabian desert (22:22). **daughter of my people:** A feminine depiction of Judah and Jerusalem. See word study:

The Daughter of Zion at Lam 1:6. **not to winnow:** The gales of judgment will be destructive, not like the normal breezes that assist farmers on threshing floors.

4:13 he comes: Nebuchadnezzar of Babylon, the destroyer of nations mentioned in 4:7. **woe:** A cry of anguish heard at funerals. See word study: *Woe* at Is 28:1.

4:14 wash your heart: A final appeal for repentance before the conquest of Jerusalem. Prophecies of destruction are initially conditional; their fulfillment depends on the response of the prophet's audience. See note on 4:4.

4:15 Dan: The northernmost tribe of Israel, bordering Syria. **Mount Ephraim:** The mountainous region of central Israel, north of Jerusalem.

4:19–21 Jeremiah, speaking in the first person ("I, me, my"), grieves aloud over the horrors he foresees for Judah and Jerusalem. It is the prophet's love for his people that makes their coming demise so painful.

4:22 stupid children: The children of Israel are God's children by covenant (Deut 14:1), but their rebellion against God exposes their foolishness (Is 1:2–3). This verse appears to be the Lord's answer to the prophet's question in 4:21.

4:23 the earth: Or "the land". **waste and void:** The same Hebrew expression used in Gen 1:2, translated "without form and void". This suggests the land of Judah will undergo a tragic experience of de-creation, reverting to the chaotic state of the world in the beginning before God formed it and filled it with life.

²⁴I looked on the mountains, and behold, they were
  quaking,
    and all the hills moved back and forth.
²⁵I looked, and behold, there was no man,
    and all the birds of the air had fled.
²⁶I looked, and behold, the fruitful land was a desert,
    and all its cities were laid in ruins
  before the Lord, before his fierce anger.
  27 For thus says the Lord, "The whole land shall
be a desolation; yet I will not make a full end.
²⁸For this the earth shall mourn,
    and the heavens above be black,
  for I have spoken, I have planned;
    I have not relented nor will I turn back."

²⁹At the noise of horseman and archer
    every city takes to flight;
  they enter thickets; they climb among rocks;
    all the cities are forsaken,
    and no man dwells in them.
³⁰And you, O desolate one,
  what do you mean that you dress in scarlet,
    that you deck yourself with ornaments of gold,
    that you enlarge your eyes with paint?
  In vain you beautify yourself.
    Your lovers despise you;
    they seek your life.
³¹For I heard a cry as of a woman with labor pains,
    anguish as of one bringing forth her first child,
  the cry of the daughter of Zion gasping for
    breath,
    stretching out her hands,
  "Woe is me! I am fainting before murderers."

The Godlessness of Jerusalem

5 Run back and forth through the streets of
    Jerusalem,
    look and take note!
  Search her squares to see
    if you can find a man,

one who does justice
    and seeks truth;
  that I may pardon her.
²Though they say, "As the Lord lives,"
    yet they swear falsely.
³O Lord, do not your eyes look for truth?
  You have struck them down,
    but they felt no anguish;
  you have consumed them,
    but they refused to take correction.
  They have made their faces harder than rock;
    they have refused to repent.

⁴Then I said, "These are only the poor,
    they have no sense;
  for they do not know the way of the Lord,
    the law of their God.
⁵I will go to the great,
    and will speak to them;
  for they know the way of the Lord,
    the law of their God."
  But they all alike had broken the yoke,
    they had burst the bonds.

⁶Therefore a lion from the forest shall slay them,
    a wolf from the desert shall destroy them.
  A leopard is watching against their cities,
    every one who goes out of them shall be torn
      in pieces;
  because their transgressions are many,
    their apostasies are great.

⁷"How can I pardon you?
    Your children have forsaken me,
    and have sworn by those who are no gods.
  When I fed them to the full,
    they committed adultery
    and trooped to the houses of harlots.
⁸They were well-fed lusty stallions,
    each neighing for his neighbor's wife.

4:27 I will not make a full end: Despite mass devastation, God will stop short of total annihilation. He will preserve a remnant of his people to ensure that the covenant community lives on (5:10, 18; Is 10:21–22; Amos 9:8) and enters a "new covenant" with him (31:31–34).

4:30 O desolate one: Judah, the Lord's bride (2:2), depicted as a prostitute who seduces lovers (3:1). She is unaware that her clients want her dead. **paint:** A mixture of soot and lead sulfide used as eye makeup.

4:31 labor pains: The intense agony of Judah's judgment (6:24). It will be like a woman in the throes of childbirth, only to learn that warriors are invading her city as her helpless newborn enters the world. **the daughter of Zion:** Jerusalem. See word study: *The Daughter of Zion* at Lam 1:6.

5:1–3 The Lord challenges Jeremiah to find a single righteous man in Jerusalem, since this would give him reason to pardon the city and restrain his judgment. Tragically, the capital has become so godless, so full of treachery, that none can be found, showing that its divine punishment is justly deserved. The passage is similar to Abraham's dialogue with the Lord in Gen 18:22–33.

5:2 they swear falsely: A violation of the second commandment of the Decalogue (Ex 20:7).

5:3 You have struck them: The Lord chastises his people in measured ways, inviting them to repent of their evildoing, but his discipline goes unheeded (2:30). Previously God had bemoaned a similar lack of response in northern Israel before its downfall (Amos 4:6–11). For the nature of divine correction, see note on Lev 26:14–39. **harder than rock:** Points to Judah's defiance.

5:4 they do not know: Because of a dereliction of duty on the part of Israel's priests, who are tasked with educating the people in the Torah (Lev 10:10–11).

5:5 the yoke: The Mosaic covenant. See note on 2:20.

5:6 lion ... wolf ... leopard: Predators representing the Babylonians.

5:7 those who are no gods: Idols (Deut 32:21). Serving gods other than the Lord is a violation of the first commandment of the Decalogue (Ex 20:3–6). **adultery:** A violation of the sixth commandment of the Decalogue (Ex 20:14).

5:8 lusty stallions: Hard to control when the instinct to mate overcomes them. Israel's lack of moral restraint in sexual matters is depicted. • The prophet likens godless men

⁹Shall I not punish them for these things?
> says the LORD;
> and shall I not avenge myself
> on a nation such as this?

¹⁰"Go up through her vine-rows and destroy,
> but make not a full end;
> strip away her branches,
> for they are not the LORD's.
¹¹For the house of Israel and the house of Judah
> have been utterly faithless to me,
> says the LORD.
¹²They have spoken falsely of the LORD,
> and have said, 'He will do nothing;
> no evil will come upon us,
> nor shall we see sword or famine.
¹³The prophets will become wind;
> the word is not in them.
> Thus shall it be done to them!'"

¹⁴Therefore thus says the LORD, the God of hosts:
> "Because they ᵉ have spoken this word,
> behold, I am making my words in your mouth a
> fire,
> and this people wood, and the fire shall devour
> them.
¹⁵Behold, I am bringing upon you
> a nation from afar, O house of Israel,
> says the LORD.
> It is an enduring nation,
> it is an ancient nation,
> a nation whose language you do not know,
> nor can you understand what they say.
¹⁶Their quiver is like an open tomb,
> they are all mighty men.

¹⁷They shall eat up your harvest and your food;
> they shall eat up your sons and your
> daughters;
> they shall eat up your flocks and your herds;
> they shall eat up your vines and your fig trees;
> your fortified cities in which you trust
> they shall destroy with the sword."

18 "But even in those days, says the LORD, I will not make a full end of you. ¹⁹And when your people say, 'Why has the LORD our God done all these things to us?' you shall say to them, 'As you have forsaken me and served foreign gods in your land, so you shall serve strangers in a land that is not yours.'"

²⁰Declare this in the house of Jacob,
> proclaim it in Judah:
²¹"Hear this, O foolish and senseless people,
> who have eyes, but see not,
> who have ears, but hear not.
²²Do you not fear me? says the LORD;
> Do you not tremble before me?
> I placed the sand as the bound for the sea,
> a perpetual barrier which it cannot pass;
> though the waves toss, they cannot prevail,
> though they roar, they cannot pass over it.
²³But this people has a stubborn and rebellious
> heart;
> they have turned aside and gone away.
²⁴They do not say in their hearts,
> 'Let us fear the LORD our God,
> who gives the rain in its season,
> the autumn rain and the spring rain,
> and keeps for us
> the weeks appointed for the harvest.'

5:21: Is 6:9–10; Mt 13:10–15; Mk 8:17–18.

---

to irrational animals. Because their conduct is irrational, they become like stallions lusting after females, each neighing for his neighbor's wife (St. Irenaeus, *Against Heresies* 5, 8, 3).

5:10 not a full end: See note on 4:27.

5:11 house of Israel … house of Judah: The Northern Kingdom of Israel and the Southern Kingdom of Judah, respectively.

5:12 He will do nothing: Propaganda made popular by false prophets, who tell the rulers and the people what they want to hear (2 Tim 4:3). Utterly deceived, they insist that Judah need not fear Jeremiah's grim prophecies that disaster is certain if repentance is refused. They proclaim "peace" (6:14) in the midst of violence (6:7) and wrongly believe that Jerusalem will escape destruction because the Lord's Temple is there (7:4).

5:13 The prophets: I.e., false prophets (5:31). **wind:** A wordplay on the Hebrew term *ruah*, which can also mean "Spirit". True prophets speak by God's Spirit; false prophets speak nothing but wind.

5:14 I am making my words … fire: The words of the prophet come from God (1:9) and are thus fully effective in

accomplishing God's purposes (Is 55:11). The Lord's sentence of destruction is enacted through the preaching of Jeremiah (1:10).

📖 **5:15 a nation from afar:** The Babylonians. **whose language you do not know:** Akkadian, an East Semitic language. Jeremiah is invoking the covenant curses of Deut 28:49–68, which foresees the Lord sending a nation from afar who speaks a foreign language to besiege, conquer, and exile rebellious Israel. An earlier fulfillment of this curse took place in the eighth century B.C., when the Lord sent the Assyrians against the Northern Kingdom of Israel (Is 28:11–13).

5:19 in a land that is not yours: The coming exile to Babylon is meant (52:28–30).

5:21 senseless: Or "heartless".

5:24 They do not say … fear the LORD: The most basic religious virtue is lacking in Judah. See note on Prov 1:7. **autumn rain:** The showers that water Israel in October/November after vineyards and orchards have been harvested. They help to prepare the ground for plowing and sowing and to refill cisterns after the dry summer months. **spring rain:** The showers that water Israel in March/April before the spring harvest of barley and wheat. **the weeks:** The seven weeks between the feasts of Passover and Pentecost, also known as the Feast of Weeks (Deut 16:9–11).

ᵉ Heb *you*.

²⁵Your iniquities have turned these away,
    and your sins have kept good from you.
²⁶For wicked men are found among my people;
    they lurk like fowlers lying in wait. **f**
  They set a trap;
    they catch men.
²⁷Like a basket full of birds,
    their houses are full of treachery;
  therefore they have become great and rich,
²⁸   they have grown fat and sleek.
  They know no bounds in deeds of wickedness;
    they judge not with justice
  the cause of the fatherless, to make it prosper,
    and they do not defend the rights of the
      needy.
²⁹Shall I not punish them for these things?
                                        says the LORD,

    and shall I not avenge myself
    on a nation such as this?"

³⁰An appalling and horrible thing
    has happened in the land:
³¹the prophets prophesy falsely,
    and the priests rule at their direction;
  my people love to have it so,
    but what will you do when the end comes?

A Warning to Judah

6 Flee for safety, O people of Benjamin,
    from the midst of Jerusalem!
  Blow the trumpet in Teko′a,
    and raise a signal on Beth″-hacche′rem;
  for evil looms out of the north,
    and great destruction.
²The comely and delicately bred I will destroy,
    the daughter of Zion.
³Shepherds with their flocks shall come against
      her;
    they shall pitch their tents around her,
    they shall pasture, each in his place.
⁴"Prepare war against her;
    up, and let us attack at noon!"

"Woe to us, for the day declines,
    for the shadows of evening lengthen!"
⁵"Up, and let us attack by night,
    and destroy her palaces!"

⁶For thus says the LORD of hosts:
  "Hew down her trees;
    cast up a siege mound against Jerusalem.
  This is the city which must be punished;
    there is nothing but oppression within her.
⁷As a well keeps its water fresh,
    so she keeps fresh her wickedness;
  violence and destruction are heard within her;
    sickness and wounds are ever before me.
⁸Be warned, O Jerusalem,
    lest I be alienated from you;
  lest I make you a desolation,
    an uninhabited land."

⁹Thus says the LORD of hosts:
  "Glean **g** thoroughly as a vine
    the remnant of Israel;
  like a grape-gatherer pass your hand again
    over its branches."
¹⁰To whom shall I speak and give warning,
    that they may hear?
  Behold, their ears are closed, **h**
    they cannot listen;
  behold, the word of the LORD is to them an object
      of scorn,
    they take no pleasure in it.
¹¹Therefore I am full of the wrath of the LORD;
    I am weary of holding it in.
  "Pour it out upon the children in the street,
    and upon the gatherings of young men, also;
  both husband and wife shall be taken,
    the old folk and the very aged.
¹²Their houses shall be turned over to others,
    their fields and wives together;
  for I will stretch out my hand
    against the inhabitants of the land,"
                                        says the LORD.

5:26–28 Social injustice flourishes in Judah alongside idolatry and sexual immorality (5:7–8). Jeremiah is not the first prophet of Israel to denounce the oppression and extortion of the poor by the rich and powerful (6:6; cf. Is 1:16–17; 3:14–15; Amos 2:6–8; 8:4–6).

5:31 prophets ... priests ... people: Corruption has reached all levels of Judean society, from religious leaders to the rank and file (6:28).

6:1 Benjamin: The tribal territory bordering northeast Judah. Jerusalem sits on the border of Benjaminite territory (Josh 18:16). **Tekoa:** Five miles south of Bethlehem in the highlands of Judah, near the edge of the Judean wilderness. It is the hometown of the prophet Amos (Amos 1:1). **Beth-haccherem:**

Translates "house of the vineyard". Its exact location is uncertain. Saint Jerome identifies it with a village called Bethacarma near Tekoa (*Commentary on Jeremiah* 6, 1). **out of the north:** See note on 1:14.

6:2 daughter of Zion: Jerusalem. See note on 4:31.

6:3 Shepherds ... flocks: Army commanders and their ranks of warriors.

6:4 Woe: See note on 4:13.

6:6 siege mound: Used as a ramp for bringing battering rams against city walls.

6:9 Glean thoroughly: The Babylonians are given permission to pick Judah clean, i.e., to make a total conquest of the land. In biblical law, farmers were instructed to leave a small portion of their crop, called the gleanings, in their fields and orchards so that the poor would have a source of food (Lev 19:9–10). No such restriction is placed on Judah.

6:12 stretch out my hand: The Lord is ready to strike a blow (Is 5:25; 9:12, 17, 21).

---

f Heb uncertain.
g Cn: Heb *they shall glean.*
h Heb *uncircumcised.*

¹³"For from the least to the greatest of them,
   every one is greedy for unjust gain;
and from prophet to priest,
   every one deals falsely.
¹⁴They have healed the wound of my people
      lightly,
   saying, 'Peace, peace,'
   when there is no peace.
¹⁵Were they ashamed when they committed
      abomination?
   No, they were not at all ashamed;
   they did not know how to blush.
Therefore they shall fall among those who
      fall;
   at the time that I punish them, they shall
      be overthrown,"

                              says the LORD.

¹⁶Thus says the LORD:
"Stand by the roads, and look,
   and ask for the ancient paths,
where the good way is; and walk in it,
   and find rest for your souls.
But they said, 'We will not walk in it.'
¹⁷I set watchmen over you, saying,
   'Give heed to the sound of the trumpet!'
But they said, 'We will not give heed.'
¹⁸Therefore hear, O nations,
   and know, O congregation, what will happen
      to them.
¹⁹Hear, O earth; behold, I am bringing evil upon
      this people,
   the fruit of their devices,
because they have not given heed to my words;
   and as for my law, they have rejected it.

²⁰To what purpose does frankincense come to me
      from Sheba,
   or sweet cane from a distant land?
Your burnt offerings are not acceptable,
   nor your sacrifices pleasing to me.
²¹Therefore thus says the LORD:
'Behold, I will lay before this people
   stumbling blocks against which they shall
      stumble;
fathers and sons together,
   neighbor and friend shall perish.'"

²²Thus says the LORD:
"Behold, a people is coming from the north
      country,
   a great nation is stirring from the farthest
      parts of the earth.
²³They lay hold on bow and spear,
   they are cruel and have no mercy,
   the sound of them is like the roaring sea;
they ride upon horses,
   set in array as a man for battle,
   against you, O daughter of Zion!"
²⁴We have heard the report of it,
   our hands fall helpless;
anguish has taken hold of us,
   pain as of a woman with labor pains.
²⁵Go not forth into the field,
   nor walk on the road;
for the enemy has a sword,
   terror is on every side.
²⁶O daughter of my people, put on sackcloth,
   and roll in ashes;
make mourning as for an only son,
   most bitter lamentation;

6:16: Mt 11:29. **6:25**: Jer 20:3, 10; 46:5; 49:29; Ps 31:13.

6:13 from prophet to priest: The failure of Judah's religious leadership is in view (8:10).

6:14 Peace, peace: The Hebrew *shalôm* implies prosperity and well-being as well as an absence of hostility. False prophets delude the masses into thinking that Judah and Jerusalem will be safe from threats of invasion and conquest, despite wickedness filling the land and city. The quotation appears to have been a popular slogan (see 8:11; Ezek 13:10).

6:16 the ancient paths: Marked out by the Torah, which shows God's people the way to blessing and life by giving commandments (Deut 30:15-20) and imparting lessons of faith and life through its accounts of Israel's early history (Deut 29:1-29). **rest for your souls:** Jesus borrows this language when he offers rest to those who exchange their heavy burdens for his light yoke (Mt 11:28-30). His teaching is implicitly contrasted with the laws of the Mosaic covenant, which Jeremiah depicts as a "yoke" (2:20; 5:5). See note on Acts 15:5.

6:17 watchmen: The Lord's prophets, like sentinels posted on city walls and towers, give warning to inhabitants if danger approaches (Is 21:6-8; Ezek 3:17; Hab 2:1). **trumpet:** A ram's horn. See word study: *Trumpet* at Judg 6:34.

6:19 evil: Means "disaster" or "calamity". See note on Amos 3:6.

6:20 frankincense: A key ingredient in the sacred blend of incense prescribed for Israel's sanctuary (Ex 30:34-38). **Sheba:** An ancient trading empire in the southern Arabian Peninsula (modern Yemen). It was an exporter of spices (1 Kings 10:1-2; Is 60:6). **sweet cane:** A key ingredient in sacred anointing oil (Ex 30:23-25). **burnt offerings:** See note on Lev 1:3-17. **not acceptable:** Not a condemnation of sacrifice per se, since the Torah called God's people to serve him in such ways (Lev 1-7). Israel's prophets insist, rather, that worship is displeasing to God when liturgy and life are out of alignment, i.e., when people go through the motions of religious ritual without devotion in their hearts and without a corresponding commitment to obey the Lord's covenant in daily life (Is 1:11-17; Mic 6:6-8). See note on Amos 5:21-24. • The Lord, before the coming of Christ, rejected the sacrifices of the people when they sinned against him and thought he would be appeased by sacrifices rather than repentance (*Apostolic Constitutions* 6, 4, 22).

6:22 a great nation: The Babylonians.

6:24 labor pains: The intense agony of Judah's judgment (4:31).

6:25 terror is on every side: Evokes a frightening image of Jerusalem under siege, a city surrounded by enemies from which none can escape to safety. This is one of Jeremiah's most memorable expressions (20:3, 10; 46:5; 49:29; cf. Lam 2:22).

6:26 sackcloth: A coarse fabric spun from goat hair and worn in times of mourning (Gen 37:34). **ashes:** Ancient expressions of mourning included sitting in ashes (Job 2:8; Is 58:5; Jon 3:6) and sprinkling ashes upon one's head (2 Sam 13:19;

for suddenly the destroyer
    will come upon us.
27"I have made you an assayer and tester among
    my people,
    that you may know and assay their ways.
28They are all stubbornly rebellious,
    going about with slanders;
    they are bronze and iron,
    all of them act corruptly.
29The bellows blow fiercely,
    the lead is consumed by the fire;
    in vain the refining goes on,
    for the wicked are not removed.
30Refuse silver they are called,
    for the Lord has rejected them."

Impending Punishment of Judah

7 The word that came to Jeremi'ah from the Lord: 2"Stand in the gate of the Lord's house, and proclaim there this word, and say, Hear the word of the Lord, all you men of Judah who enter these gates to worship the Lord. 3Thus says the Lord of hosts, the God of Israel, Amend your ways and your doings, and I will let you dwell in this place. 4Do not trust in these deceptive words: 'This is the temple of the Lord, the temple of the Lord, the temple of the Lord.'*

5 "For if you truly amend your ways and your doings, if you truly execute justice one with another, 6if you do not oppress the alien, the fatherless or the widow, or shed innocent blood in this place, and if you do not go after other gods to your own hurt, 7then I will let you dwell in this place, in the land that I gave of old to your fathers for ever.

8 "Behold, you trust in deceptive words to no avail. 9Will you steal, murder, commit adultery, swear falsely, burn incense to Ba'al, and go after other gods that you have not known, 10and then come and stand before me in this house, which is called by my name, and say, 'We are delivered!'— only to go on doing all these abominations? 11Has this house, which is called by my name, become a den of robbers in your eyes? Behold, I myself have seen it, says the Lord. 12Go now to my place that was in Shiloh, where I made my name dwell at first, and see what I did to it for the wickedness of my people Israel. 13And now, because you have done all these things, says the Lord, and when I spoke to you persistently you did not listen, and when I called you, you did not answer, 14therefore I will do to the

---

7:11: Mt 21:13; Mk 11:17; Lk 19:46.

Jud 4:11; 1 Mac 3:47). The image of rolling in ashes signifies the extreme grief that is coming to Judah (25:34; Ezek 27:30).

6:27 an assayer: Jeremiah is like one who examines the purity of a metal by a refining process.

6:30 Refuse silver: Ruined by impurities that cannot be separated out. The end product is worthless. **the Lord has rejected them:** I.e., the evildoers that make up Jeremiah's generation (7:29). The statement is not a complete repudiation of Israel as the Lord's covenant people (1 Sam 12:22; Ps 94:14).

7:1—8:3 Jeremiah's Temple sermon, delivered in 609 B.C. The prophet urges the sinful people of Judah to realign their lives with the covenant or they will be cast forth into exile (7:15) and the Temple will become a "desolation" (22:5). In particular, he debunks the popular belief that the presence of the Lord's Temple in Jerusalem guarantees the city's protection from conquest (7:4). Proof that this belief is naïve and unfounded is the former destruction of God's sanctuary at Shiloh (7:12). A summary account of Jeremiah's Temple sermon and the trial that followed appears in 26:1-19.

7:1 The word that came: Biblical language for an instance of divine revelation (11:1; 14:1).

7:2 the gate: One of the entrances into the Temple courts, where the prophet would be assured a large audience of worshipers.

7:3 this place: The land of Judah (7:7), which includes Jerusalem and its Temple (26:12).

7:4 the temple of the Lord: An empty slogan that Jeremiah calls a deception. Jerusalem's protection lies not in the presence of the Lord's house within its walls but in its adherence to the Lord's covenant. The belief that Zion is "inviolable" is probably based on passages of Scripture (e.g., Ps 46:4-5; 48:1-3; Is 31:5) that seem to be confirmed historically by the miracle of 701 B.C., when the Lord prevented the Assyrians from sacking Jerusalem (Is 37:33-35) despite conquering multiple towns in Judah (2 Kings 18:13; 19:32-36). The people, and the false prophets who deceive them, are forgetting that God spared Jerusalem on that occasion because Hezekiah heeded the instructions of the prophet Isaiah and sought the Lord's protection by fervent prayer (2 Kings 19:1-31). The only secure object of trust is the Lord himself (17:7; 39:18).

7:5 justice: The Hebrew *mishpat* means a fair and unprejudiced application of the Mosaic Law to the entire covenant community, regardless of a person's social situation.

7:6 alien ... fatherless ... widow: The most vulnerable members of ancient society, whose protection is a concern of the Torah (Ex 22:21-22; Deut 14:29; 24:19-21). The first category refers to non-Israelites sojourning in the land of Israel. **innocent blood:** e.g., King Jehoiakim's execution of the prophet Uriah (26:20-23).

7:9 steal ... other gods: Violations of five of the Ten Commandments (Ex 20:2-17; Deut 5:6-21).

7:10 called by my name: I.e., belongs to me (= the Lord).

7:11 den of robbers: The Temple is compared to a cave where bandits hide from justice, stash their loot, and find temporary rest between crimes. The Lord's house, by contrast, will not afford protection for his lawless people. • Jesus cites these words when he cleanses the Jerusalem Temple, accusing merchants of turning God's house of prayer into a place of profit (Mt 21:13; Mk 11:17; Lk 19:46).

7:12 Shiloh: A town in central Israel nearly 20 miles north of Jerusalem. The Tabernacle and the Ark of the Covenant are stationed at various times before the founding of the monarchy (Josh 18:1; Judg 18:31; 1 Sam 1-3). Jeremiah draws a lesson from the past: the Lord once dwelt in his sanctuary in Shiloh, yet because of the sins of his people, he abandoned its precincts and allowed it to be destroyed around 1050 B.C. (Ps 78:60). He even allowed the Philistines to capture the ark (1 Sam 4:11). Jerusalem can expect to fare no better, given the iniquity that resides in it (7:14). The Lord's holy sanctuary will afford no protection for an unholy people. **wickedness:** E.g., the sins of Eli's sons (1 Sam 2:12-17, 22-25).

---

*7:4: Trust in the temple's presence without true service of God and observance of his commands is vain, just as earlier a similar trust in the presence of the ark was fruitless without moral observance; 1 Sam 4:3.

house which is called by my name, and in which you trust, and to the place which I gave to you and to your fathers, as I did to Shiloh. ¹⁵And I will cast you out of my sight, as I cast out all your kinsmen, all the offspring of E′phraim.

The People's Disobedience

16 "As for you, do not pray for this people, or lift up cry or prayer for them, and do not intercede with me, for I do not hear you. ¹⁷Do you not see what they are doing in the cities of Judah and in the streets of Jerusalem? ¹⁸The children gather wood, the fathers kindle fire, and the women knead dough, to make cakes for the queen of heaven; and they pour out drink offerings to other gods, to provoke me to anger. ¹⁹Is it I whom they provoke? says the LORD. Is it not themselves, to their own confusion? ²⁰Therefore thus says the Lord GOD: Behold, my anger and my wrath will be poured out on this place, upon man and beast, upon the trees of the field and the fruit of the ground; it will burn and not be quenched."

21 Thus says the LORD of hosts, the God of Israel: "Add your burnt offerings to your sacrifices, and eat the flesh. ²²For in the day that I brought them out of the land of Egypt, I did not speak to your fathers or command them concerning burnt offerings and sacrifices. ²³But this command I gave them, 'Obey my voice, and I will be your God, and you shall be my people; and walk in all the way that I command you, that it may be well with you.' ²⁴But they did not obey or incline their ear, but walked in their own counsels and the stubbornness of their evil hearts, and went backward and not forward. ²⁵From the day that your fathers came out of the land of Egypt to this day, I have persistently sent all my servants the prophets to them, day after day; ²⁶yet they did not listen to me, or incline their ear, but stiffened their neck. They did worse than their fathers.

27 "So you shall speak all these words to them, but they will not listen to you. You shall call to them, but they will not answer you. ²⁸And you shall say to them, 'This is the nation that did not obey the voice of the LORD their God, and did not accept discipline; truth has perished; it is cut off from their lips.
²⁹Cut off your hair and cast it away;
    raise a lamentation on the bare heights,
for the LORD has rejected and forsaken
    the generation of his wrath.'

30 "For the sons of Judah have done evil in my sight, says the LORD; they have set their abominations in the house which is called by my name, to defile it. ³¹And they have built the high place *i* of To′pheth,

---

7:15 I will cast you out: Foretells the exile of Judah to Babylon (52:27–30). **Ephraim:** Another name for the Northern Kingdom of Israel, which includes Shiloh. Israel's northern tribes were taken into exile by the Assyrians in the eighth century B.C. (2 Kings 15:29; 17:6; 23:27).

7:16 do not pray: Intercessory prayer is disallowed in this dire situation, since the Lord is not willing to relent of his judgment on Judah, no matter who pleads its cause (11:14; 14:11). Not even the prayers of Moses or Samuel could save Jeremiah's generation from the consequences of its evildoing (15:1).

7:18 the queen of heaven: Ishtar, a Mesopotamian astral goddess of love and war who was associated with the planet Venus (1 Kings 11:5). She was served by incense offerings, wine libations, cakes baked over a fire, and had many devotees among women and families (44:15–19). Mesopotamian myths identify Ishtar as the wife of the fertility god Tammuz (cf. Ezek 8:14). She was known in Greek as Astarte.

7:21 burnt offerings: Animal holocausts given entirely to God. **eat the flesh:** Jeremiah speaks with sarcasm since none of the meat of a burnt offering was to be consumed by the worshiper. See note on Lev 1:3–17.

7:22 in the day: At the time of the Exodus. **I did not speak ... concerning ... sacrifices:** According to the Pentateuch, God's original covenant with Israel at Mt. Sinai did not include the ritual code of sacrifice found in Lev 1–7 or the prescribed sacrifices for feast days in Num 28–29. It initially consisted of the Ten Commandments spoken by God (Ex 20:1–17; Deut 5:6–22), along with a small body of laws, called the Covenant Code, in which sacrifice was purely discretionary (Ex 21–23). Laws mandating sacrifice were not given until *after* Israel broke the original Sinai covenant by worshiping the golden calf (Ex 32:1–6). Only when the Sinai covenant was renewed and expanded, beginning in Ex 34:10, did Israel receive detailed laws for regular sacrifice. For Jeremiah, a careful reading of this story shows that obedience to the Lord's voice was always the primary objective of the covenant in God's plan for Israel (1 Sam 15:22). • The prophet means that at first God gave his people the Decalogue, written by the finger of God on tablets of stone, but after their idolatry in the passage about the calf, he demanded sacrifices to be offered to him rather than to demons. As a concession, he granted them the blood of sacrifices and animal flesh (St. Jerome, *Commentary on Jeremiah 7*, 21–23). • Sacrifices were instituted to draw men away from sacrificing to idols. For this reason, precepts regarding sacrifice were not given until after the people worshiped the golden calf and fell into idolatry. They were established so that the people, inclined to make offerings, might sacrifice them to God and not to idols. Hence the passage that says God did not command burnt offerings and sacrifices in the day when he brought them out from Egypt (St. Thomas Aquinas, *Summa Theologiae* I-II, 102, 3).

7:23 your God ... my people: The Lord and Israel belong to one another by virtue of the covenant that bound them together as father and children (3:4; 31:9) as well as Bridegroom and bride (2:2). Scholars designate statements of mutual belonging as the "covenant formula" (30:22; Lev 26:12; Ezek 37:27; Hos 2:23).

7:26 stiffened their neck: An obstinate refusal to be guided by the yoke of the covenant (2:20).

7:29 Cut off your hair: An ancient mourning ritual (Is 15:2; Ezek 27:31; Mic 1:16).

7:30 abominations: Idols (4:1). Some were even placed in the Temple (Ezek 5:11; 8:6–18).

7:31 the high place: An unlawful shrine. See word study: *High Places* at 2 Kings 23:5. **Topheth:** Meaning unknown. Suggestions include "oven" or "fire pit" (cf. Is 30:33). It designates a specific cultic site where children were incinerated as sacrifices to pagan gods. **valley of the son of Hinnom:** Directly southwest of Jerusalem (modern Wadi er-Rababi). The Hinnom valley is an image of damnation in the NT. See word study: *Hell* at Mk 9:43. **burn their sons ... daughters:** Sacrificing children by fire to deities such as Molech, probably a

---

ⁱ Gk Tg: Heb *high places*.

which is in the valley of the son of Hin'nom, to burn their sons and their daughters in the fire; which I did not command, nor did it come into my mind. ³²Therefore, behold, the days are coming, says the LORD, when it will no more be called To'pheth, or the valley of the son of Hinnom, but the valley of Slaughter: for they will bury in Topheth, because there is no room elsewhere. ³³And the dead bodies of this people will be food for the birds of the air, and for the beasts of the earth; and none will frighten them away. ³⁴And I will make to cease from the cities of Judah and from the streets of Jerusalem the voice of mirth and the voice of gladness, the voice of the bridegroom and the voice of the bride; for the land shall become a waste.

A Lament for Judah

8 "At that time, says the LORD, the bones of the kings of Judah, the bones of its princes, the bones of the priests, the bones of the prophets, and the bones of the inhabitants of Jerusalem shall be brought out of their tombs; ²and they shall be spread before the sun and the moon and all the host of heaven, which they have loved and served, which they have gone after, and which they have sought and worshiped; and they shall not be gathered or buried; they shall be as dung on the surface of the ground. ³Death shall be preferred to life by all the remnant that remains of this evil family in all the places where I have driven them, says the LORD of hosts.

⁴"You shall say to them, Thus says the LORD:
When men fall, do they not rise again?
  If one turns away, does he not return?
⁵Why then has this people turned away
  in perpetual backsliding?
They hold fast to deceit,
  they refuse to return.
⁶I have given heed and listened,
  but they have not spoken rightly;
no man repents of his wickedness,
  saying, 'What have I done?'
Every one turns to his own course,
  like a horse plunging headlong into battle.
⁷Even the stork in the heavens
  knows her times;
and the turtledove, swallow, and crane ʲ
  keep the time of their coming;
but my people know not
  the ordinance of the LORD. *

⁸"How can you say, 'We are wise,
  and the law of the LORD is with us'?
But, behold, the false pen of the scribes
  has made it into a lie.
⁹The wise men shall be put to shame,
  they shall be dismayed and taken;
behold, they have rejected the word of the
    LORD,
  and what wisdom is in them?
¹⁰Therefore I will give their wives to others
  and their fields to conquerors,

7:34: Rev 18:23.

---

god of the underworld (32:35), is an abomination condemned by the Torah (Lev 18:21; 20:2-5; Deut 18:10). King Josiah launched religious reforms to halt this murderous crime in Judah (2 Kings 23:10), but apparently the practice of child sacrifice made a comeback after his death in 609 B.C. (19:4-5; 32:35; Ezek 16:20-21). Archaeological finds at Carthage and Tyre confirm that the cremation of children was a religious practice in biblical times.

7:32 the valley of Slaughter: The ravine will be filled with the unburied corpses of the slain when Jerusalem is conquered in 586 B.C. (19:6).

7:33 food for the birds ... beasts: Human corpses eaten by scavengers are one of the curses of the Mosaic covenant triggered by Israel's disobedience (Deut 28:26).

7:34 voice of the bridegroom: The joyous sounds of wedding celebrations will cease when disaster strikes (16:9; 25:10). They will not be heard again until the Lord restores his people after judgment (33:10-11). Jeremiah himself is forbidden to marry in view of Judah's imminent demise (16:1-4).

8:1 bones ... brought out: Exhuming and exposing the remains of idolaters is a symbolic act of insult and judgment (2 Kings 23:16; cf. Bar 2:24-25). Jerusalem's royal tombs hold the bones of David and his successors (1 Kings 2:10; 11:43; Neh 3:16). **kings ... princes ... priests ... prophets ... inhabitants:** Religious corruption spreads through the whole of Judean society from top to bottom.

8:2 the host of heaven: The sun, moon, stars, and planets visible in the day and night sky. Worship of the heavenly bodies is strictly forbidden in Israel (Deut 4:19), although disregard for the prohibition is well documented in the Bible (2 Kings 17:16; 23:5; Ezek 8:16; Amos 5:26; Zeph 1:5).

8:3 Death shall be preferred: A curse of the Mosaic covenant triggered by the disobedience of Israel (Deut 28:64-68). **the remnant:** The survivors of the conquest of Jerusalem who will be taken into exile in Babylon. For them, life will be worse than death.

8:4-17 The Lord marvels at Judah's stubborn defiance. Instead of repentance, the people are living in a constant state of rebellion.

8:5 hold fast to deceit: They delude themselves with reassuring slogans of peace and protection while standing on the brink of disaster (6:14; 7:4; 8:11).

8:6 turns to his own: Implies a turning away from God. See word study: *Return* at 3:1.

8:7 stork ... crane: Even the birds of the air know when to begin their seasonal migrations, thanks to the instinct given them by God. The people of Judah, by contrast, are less perceptive than non-rational animals when it comes to taking action and changing the direction of their lives as the Lord commands (cf. Is 1:3).

8:8 We are wise: Foolish self-deception. Wisdom is found, not merely in possessing the Torah, but in obeying its commandments (Deut 4:5-6). **the scribes:** A professional class of scholars, writers, and copyists (1 Chron 2:55; 2 Chron 34:13).

8:10 from prophet to priest: The failure of Judah's religious leadership is meant (6:13).

ʲ The meaning of the Hebrew word is uncertain.
*8:7: cf. Is 1:3.

Jeremiah 8, 9

because from the least to the greatest
  every one is greedy for unjust gain;
from prophet to priest
  every one deals falsely.
[11]They have healed the wound of my people
    lightly,
  saying, 'Peace, peace,'
    when there is no peace.
[12]Were they ashamed when they committed
    abomination?
  No, they were not at all ashamed;
    they did not know how to blush.
  Therefore they shall fall among the fallen;
    when I punish them, they shall be
      overthrown,

                              says the LORD.
[13]When I would gather them, says the LORD,
    there are no grapes on the vine,
  nor figs on the fig tree;
    even the leaves are withered,
      and what I gave them has passed away from
        them."[k]

[14]Why do we sit still?
  Gather together, let us go into the fortified cities
    and perish there;
  for the LORD our God has doomed us to perish,
    and has given us poisoned water to drink,
    because we have sinned against the LORD.
[15]We looked for peace, but no good came,
  for a time of healing, but behold, terror.

[16]"The snorting of their horses is heard from Dan;
    at the sound of the neighing of their stallions
      the whole land quakes.
  They come and devour the land and all that fills
    it,
    the city and those who dwell in it.

[17]For behold, I am sending among you serpents,
    adders which cannot be charmed,
      and they shall bite you,"

                              says the LORD.

[18]My grief is beyond healing,[1]
  my heart is sick within me.
[19]Listen, the cry of the daughter of my people
    from the length and breadth of the land:
  "Is the LORD not in Zion?
    Is her King not in her?"
  "Why have they provoked me to anger with their
      graven images,
    and with their foreign idols?"
[20]"The harvest is past, the summer is ended,
    and we are not saved."
[21]For the wound of the daughter of my people my
      heart is wounded,
  I mourn, and dismay has taken hold on me.

[22]Is there no balm in Gilead?
  Is there no physician there?
Why then has the health of the daughter of my
      people
  not been restored?
9 [m]O that my head were waters,
    and my eyes a fountain of tears,
  that I might weep day and night
    for the slain of the daughter of my people!
[2][n]O that I had in the desert
    a wayfarers' lodging place,
  that I might leave my people
    and go away from them!
For they are all adulterers,
    a company of treacherous men.
[3]They bend their tongue like a bow;
    falsehood and not truth has grown strong[o] in
      the land;

8:13 no grapes: Judah has produced no good fruit for the Lord's harvest. **vine . . . fig tree:** Images of the covenant people of Israel (2:21; Ps 80:8; Is 5:7; Hos 9:10; Lk 13:6–9).

8:14 Why do we sit still?: The words of sinful Judahites when they suddenly realize that catastrophe has come. **poisoned water:** Makes death certain in the midst of a siege.

8:15 We looked for peace . . . terror: This saying also appears in 14:19.

8:16 their horses: The cavalry of Nebuchadnezzar, commander of the Babylonian army. **Dan:** One of the northernmost cities of the land of Israel. For Babylon's invasion of Judah from the north, see note on 1:14.

8:17 serpents: The Babylonian hordes are compared to poisonous snakes. For a literal example of divine judgment by serpents, see Num 21:6. **cannot be charmed:** Judah will not be able to avert the judgment that is coming. Snake charming by incantations and other techniques was widely practiced in the ancient Near East (Ps 58:4–5; Eccles 10:11).

8:18—9:1 Jeremiah agonizes over Judah's fatal wounds and certain doom, quoting the words of the people (8:19b, 20) as well as the Lord (8:19c).

8:19 the daughter of my people: Jerusalem. See word study: *The Daughter of Zion* at Lam 1:6. **King:** The Lord, who is enthroned in his Temple on Zion (Ps 48:1–2; 84:1–4). **provoked me to anger:** Just as the Israelites did when they served idols in the wilderness after leaving Egypt (Deut 32:16, 21).

8:22 Gilead: The highlands east of the Jordan River. The region exports balsam, extracted from trees and plants, that is used for medicinal purposes (46:11; Gen 37:25).

9:1 that I might weep: Explains why Jeremiah is remembered as a "weeping prophet" (13:17; 14:17).

9:2 that I might leave: Jeremiah wishes aloud that he could flee the apostate city of Jerusalem. At least then he would not have to witness the calamity that is coming.

9:3 tongue: Can be used as a weapon to inflict wounds on other people, much like a warrior's bow and arrows (9:8). For the destructive potential of the tongue, see Prov 16:27; Sir 28:17–26; Jas 3:1–12. **from evil to evil:** A profusion of slander, deception, and lies in Judah points to a rapidly disintegrating society and shows that God's judgment is entirely deserved. No one can be trusted in a community that lacks a

---

[k]Heb uncertain.
[1]Cn Compare Gk: Heb uncertain.
[m]Ch 8:23 in Heb.
[n]Ch 9:1 in Heb.
[o]Gk: Heb *and not for truth they have grown strong.*

34

for they proceed from evil to evil,
and they do not know me, says the LORD.

4Let every one beware of his neighbor,
and put no trust in any brother;
for every brother is a supplanter,
and every neighbor goes about as a slanderer.
5Every one deceives his neighbor,
and no one speaks the truth;
they have taught their tongue to speak lies;
they commit iniquity and are too weary to repent.[p]
6Heaping oppression upon oppression, and deceit upon deceit,
they refuse to know me, says the LORD.

7Therefore thus says the LORD of hosts:
"Behold, I will refine them and test them,
for what else can I do, because of my people?
8Their tongue is a deadly arrow;
it speaks deceitfully;
with his mouth each speaks peaceably to his neighbor,
but in his heart he plans an ambush for him.
9Shall I not punish them for these things? says the LORD;
and shall I not avenge myself
on a nation such as this?

10"Take up[q] weeping and wailing for the mountains,
and a lamentation for the pastures of the wilderness,
because they are laid waste so that no one passes through,
and the lowing of cattle is not heard;
both the birds of the air and the beasts
have fled and are gone.
11I will make Jerusalem a heap of ruins,
a lair of jackals;
and I will make the cities of Judah a desolation,
without inhabitant."

12 Who is the man so wise that he can understand this? To whom has the mouth of the LORD spoken, that he may declare it? Why is the land ruined and laid waste like a wilderness, so that no one passes through?
13And the LORD says: "Because they have forsaken my law which I set before them, and have not obeyed my voice, or walked in accord with it,
14but have stubbornly followed their own hearts and have gone after the Ba′als, as their fathers taught them.
15Therefore thus says the LORD of hosts, the God of Israel: Behold, I will feed this people with wormwood, and give them poisonous water to drink.
16I will scatter them among the nations whom neither they nor their fathers have known; and I will send the sword after them, until I have consumed them."

17Thus says the LORD of hosts:
"Consider, and call for the mourning women to come;
send for the skilful women to come;
18let them make haste and raise a wailing over us,
that our eyes may run down with tears,
and our eyelids gush with water.
19For a sound of wailing is heard from Zion:
'How we are ruined!
We are utterly shamed,
because we have left the land,
because they have cast down our dwellings.'"

20Hear, O women, the word of the LORD,
and let your ear receive the word of his mouth;
teach to your daughters a lament,
and each to her neighbor a dirge.
21For death has come up into our windows,
it has entered our palaces,
cutting off the children from the streets
and the young men from the squares.
22Speak, "Thus says the LORD:
'The dead bodies of men shall fall
like dung upon the open field,

---

basic commitment to honesty and justice (9:4–6) (CCC 2464–70, 2475–87).

9:4 a supplanter: A pun on the name Jacob, popularly taken to mean "one who supplants" (Gen 27:36). The name is linked with Jacob's shrewd actions, especially his acquisition of Esau's birthright (Gen 25:27–34) and first-born blessing (Gen 27:1–40).

9:11 a heap of ruins: A picture of Jerusalem after the Babylonian destruction of the city of 586 B.C. This will confirm the warning God gave to Solomon centuries earlier, that if Israel abandons the covenant and serves other gods, the people will be driven off their land and the Temple will be left "a heap of ruins" (1 Kings 9:8). **jackals:** Known to haunt the ruins of settlements long deserted (49:33; Lam 5:18; Is 34:13).

9:14 the Baals: Baal is the storm and fertility god of Canaanite religion. Use of the plural may point to multiple images and shrines of Baal in Judah or may be a way of indicating the proliferation of "idols" in general.

9:15 wormwood: A shrub that grows in arid regions and has leaves that are extremely bitter (23:15; Prov 5:4; Lam 3:15; Rev 8:11).

9:16 I will scatter them: Exile from the Promised Land is the climactic curse of the Mosaic covenant that is triggered by Israel's disobedience (Deut 28:64–68).

9:17 the mourning women: Women and girls play a leading role in mourning rituals in the biblical world. Sometimes they are hired as professional lamenters to wail, beat their breasts, and chant dirges for the deceased (Mk 5:38–39). Jerusalem is urged to summon these women, i.e., to make preparations for its coming funeral.

9:21 death: Pictured as a murderous intruder who climbs in windows, sparing neither the rich and ruling class nor the young of the next generation.

[p] Cn Compare Gk: Heb *your dwelling*.
[q] Gk Syr: Heb *I will take up*.

like sheaves after the reaper,
  and none shall gather them.'"

23 Thus says the Lord: "Let not the wise man glory in his wisdom, let not the mighty man glory in his might, let not the rich man glory in his riches; ²⁴but let him who glories glory in this, that he understands and knows me, that I am the Lord who practice steadfast love, justice, and righteousness in the earth; for in these things I delight, says the Lord."*

25 "Behold, the days are coming, says the Lord, when I will punish all those who are circumcised but yet uncircumcised—²⁶Egypt, Judah, E'dom, the sons of Ammon, Moab, and all who dwell in the desert that cut the corners of their hair; for all these nations are uncircumcised, and all the house of Israel is uncircumcised in heart."

Idolatry Has Brought Ruin on Israel

10 Hear the word which the Lord speaks to you, O house of Israel. ²Thus says the Lord:
"Learn not the way of the nations,
  nor be dismayed at the signs of the heavens
  because the nations are dismayed at them,
³for the customs of the peoples are false.
A tree from the forest is cut down,
  and worked with an axe by the hands of a craftsman.

⁴Men deck it with silver and gold;
  they fasten it with hammer and nails
  so that it cannot move.
⁵Their idolsʳ are like scarecrows in a cucumber field,
  and they cannot speak;
they have to be carried,
  for they cannot walk.
Be not afraid of them,
  for they cannot do evil,
  neither is it in them to do good."

⁶There is none like you, O Lord;
  you are great, and your name is great in might.
⁷Who would not fear you, O King of the nations?
  For this is your due;
for among all the wise ones of the nations
  and in all their kingdoms
  there is none like you.
⁸They are both stupid and foolish;
  the instruction of idols is but wood!
⁹Beaten silver is brought from Tar'shish,
  and gold from U'phaz.
They are the work of the craftsman and of the hands of the goldsmith;
  their clothing is violet and purple;
  they are all the work of skilled men.

9:24: 1 Cor 1:31; 2 Cor 10:17. **9:26:** Acts 7:51.

9:24 but let him who glories: Judah cannot be saved by any human ingenuity or resource. Only a wholehearted return to the Lord can help now. The Greek LXX reads: "But let the one who boasts boast in this, to understand and know that I am the Lord." • Paul paraphrases this passage in 1 Cor 1:31 to insist that believers should boast in the Lord and not in themselves, for the knowledge, might, and wealth of the world cannot compare to the wisdom, strength, and riches of God.

9:25 circumcised: Circumcision of the male foreskin was widely practiced in the Near East, often as a custom for boys nearing the age for marriage. In OT times, the Philistines are one of the few peoples that stand out from their neighbors for being uncircumcised (1 Sam 18:25–27). Male circumcision in Israel takes place on the eighth day after birth; it is a rite of initiation into the Lord's covenant with Abraham (Gen 17:10–14) and the first step toward full participation in Israel's life of worship (Lev 12:3). See note on Gen 17:11.

9:26 dwell in the desert: Arabs, who in biblical times circumcise boys at age 13 (Josephus, *Antiquities* 1, 214). **cut the corners of their hair:** Shaving hair from the temples is a religious rite among Arabian tribes (Herodotus, *Histories* 3, 8). **uncircumcised in heart:** Judah, because of its failure to observe the covenant, has become no different from neighboring peoples outside the covenant (cf. Rom 2:25). The unstated premise is that circumcision is an exterior sign of an interior commitment. Cutting away the foreskin of the flesh symbolizes the need for God's people to cut away the stubbornness of the heart that resists obedience to the Lord's commandments (Deut 10:16). But while efforts at circumcising the heart are needed (4:4), it will become clear to Jeremiah that the heart

is "desperately corrupt" (17:9), so much so that the Lord himself must act to "heal" the faithlessness of his people (3:22). • Moses foresaw that the Lord, by an interior act of grace, would someday circumcise the hearts of his people, giving them a new strength for obedience (Deut 30:6; Bar 2:31). According to Paul, this promised circumcision of the heart takes place in Baptism (Col 2:11–12), when believers in Christ have their hearts filled with the Spirit, empowering them to fulfill God's Law (Rom 2:29; 5:5; 8:4). See word study: *Heart* at Deut 30:6.

10:1–5 The Lord declares that idols and astrological signs pose no threat to his people because they are "false" (10:3). Images of gods and goddesses are products of human craftsmanship that are no more real than "scarecrows" propped up in a field (10:5). They can neither speak nor hear, much less help or harm others. For similar passages that polemicize against idols, see Ps 115:4–8; Is 40:18–20; 44:9–20; 46:5–7.

10:2 the nations: The pagan peoples and civilizations that surround Israel. **signs of the heavens:** Astral phenomena such as comets, eclipses, constellations, and planetary sightings that are believed to impact peoples' lives for good or ill.

10:4 hammer and nails: Used to secure an idol in place and keep it from falling over (Is 41:7).

10:5 scarecrows: An image reused in Bar 6:70.

10:6 none like you, O Lord: The God of Israel is incomparable, meaning he has no peer among the myriad deities professed by other nations. He alone is "the true God" (10:10). **your name:** Yhwh, probably pronounced "Yahweh" and translated "Lord" in the RSV2CE. This name, which was revealed to Moses at the burning bush (Ex 3:14), bears the mystery of the divine presence within it (CCC 206–9) and must be treated with the utmost reverence (CCC 2807).

10:9 Tarshish: Probably the mining colony of Tartessos in southern Spain (Ezek 27:12). **Uphaz:** Location unknown (Dan 10:5).

ʳHeb *They.*
*9:23–24: The basis of true religion.

¹⁰But the LORD is the true God;
    he is the living God and the everlasting
        King.
  At his wrath the earth quakes,
    and the nations cannot endure his indignation.

11 Thus shall you say to them: "The gods who did not make the heavens and the earth shall perish from the earth and from under the heavens."ˢ

¹²It is he who made the earth by his power,
    who established the world by his wisdom,
    and by his understanding stretched out the
        heavens.
¹³When he utters his voice there is a tumult of
        waters in the heavens,
    and he makes the mist rise from the ends of
        the earth.
  He makes lightning for the rain,
    and he brings forth the wind from his
        storehouses.
¹⁴Every man is stupid and without knowledge;
    every goldsmith is put to shame by his
        idols;
  for his images are false,
    and there is no breath in them.
¹⁵They are worthless, a work of delusion;
    at the time of their punishment they shall
        perish.
¹⁶Not like these is he who is the portion of Jacob,
    for he is the one who formed all things,
  and Israel is the tribe of his inheritance;
    the LORD of hosts is his name.

¹⁷Gather up your bundle from the ground,
    O you who dwell under siege!
¹⁸For thus says the LORD:
  "Behold, I am slinging out the inhabitants of the
        land
    at this time,

and I will bring distress on them,
    that they may feel it."

¹⁹Woe is me because of my hurt!
    My wound is grievous.
  But I said, "Truly this is an affliction,
    and I must bear it."
²⁰My tent is destroyed,
    and all my cords are broken;
  my children have gone from me,
    and they are not;
  there is no one to spread my tent again,
    and to set up my curtains.
²¹For the shepherds are stupid,
    and do not inquire of the LORD;
  therefore they have not prospered,
    and all their flock is scattered.

²²Listen, a rumor! Behold, it comes!—
    a great commotion out of the north
        country
  to make the cities of Judah a desolation,
    a lair of jackals.

²³I know, O LORD, that the way of man is not in
        himself,
    that it is not in man who walks to direct his
        steps.
²⁴Correct me, O LORD, but in just measure;
    not in your anger, lest you bring me to
        nothing.

²⁵Pour out your wrath upon the nations that know
        you not,
    and upon the peoples that call not on your
        name;
  for they have devoured Jacob;
    they have devoured him and consumed
        him,
    and have laid waste his habitation.

10:25: 1 Thess 4:5; Rev 16:1.

10:11 Thus ... the heavens: The entire verse is written in Aramaic.

10:12–16 Jeremiah contrasts the almighty Creator, who alone is worthy of worship as Lord, with useless idols that are destined for destruction. These words also appear in 51:15–19.

10:12 by his power ... wisdom: Creation bears witness to the supreme power and intelligence of its divine Maker (Ps 19:1; Wis 13:5; Rom 1:20). For wisdom personified as God's master craftsman, see Prov 8:22–31; Wis 7:22—8:1.

10:13 lightning ... rain: A glimpse of God's power is seen in a thunderstorm (Ps 135:7). The statement implies that the Lord—not Baal, the storm god of Canaanite religion—is the one who brings the rainfall needed for Israel to prosper (14:22; Deut 11:13–17). See note on 2:8.

10:17 Gather up your bundle: I.e., collect your things, since the long journey into exile is about to begin. Deportations from Judah to Babylon take place in 605 (Dan 1:1–4), 597 (2 Kings 24:10–16), and 586 B.C. (2 Kings 25:8–11).

10:19–21 Jerusalem speaks as a mother robbed of her children whose family tent has been torn down.

10:21 shepherds: The corrupt authorities of Jeremiah's day who lead the people astray (23:1–2; Ezek 34:1–10). See note on 4:9.

10:22 out of the north: See note on 1:14.

10:23–25 A final prayer that beseeches the Lord to temper his justice with mercy. The petitioner, either Jeremiah or the personified city of Jerusalem, asks for a measure of restraint, lest Judah be annihilated completely. God is asked to divert some of his wrath to godless nations who have brought suffering upon Israel.

10:25 Jacob: The people of Israel.

ˢ This verse is in Aramaic.

Israel and Judah Have Broken the Covenant

11 The word that came to Jeremi'ah from the LORD: ²"Hear the words of this covenant, and speak to the men of Judah and the inhabitants of Jerusalem. ³You shall say to them, Thus says the LORD, the God of Israel: Cursed be the man who does not heed the words of this covenant ⁴which I commanded your fathers when I brought them out of the land of Egypt, from the iron furnace, saying, Listen to my voice, and do all that I command you. So shall you be my people, and I will be your God, ⁵that I may perform the oath which I swore to your fathers, to give them a land flowing with milk and honey, as at this day." Then I answered, "So be it, LORD."

6 And the LORD said to me, "Proclaim all these words in the cities of Judah, and in the streets of Jerusalem: Hear the words of this covenant and do them. ⁷For I solemnly warned your fathers when I brought them up out of the land of Egypt, warning them persistently, even to this day, saying, Obey my voice. ⁸Yet they did not obey or incline their ear, but every one walked in the stubbornness of his evil heart. Therefore I brought upon them all the words of this covenant, which I commanded them to do, but they did not."

9 Again the LORD said to me, "There is revolt among the men of Judah and the inhabitants of Jerusalem. ¹⁰They have turned back to the iniquities of their forefathers, who refused to hear my words; they have gone after other gods to serve them; the house of Israel and the house of Judah have broken my covenant which I made with their fathers. ¹¹Therefore, thus says the LORD, Behold, I am bringing evil upon them which they cannot escape; though they cry to me, I will not listen to them. ¹²Then the cities of Judah and the inhabitants of Jerusalem will go and cry to the gods to whom they burn incense, but they cannot save them in the time of their trouble. ¹³For your gods have become as many as your cities, O Judah; and as many as the streets of Jerusalem are the altars you have set up to shame, altars to burn incense to Ba'al.

14 "Therefore do not pray for this people, or lift up a cry or prayer on their behalf, for I will not listen when they call to me in the time of their trouble. ¹⁵What right has my beloved in my house, when she has done vile deeds? Can vows[t] and sacrificial flesh avert your doom? Can you then exult? ¹⁶The LORD once called you, 'A green olive tree, fair with excellent fruit'; but with the roar of a great tempest he will set fire to it, and its branches will be consumed. ¹⁷The LORD of hosts, who planted you, has pronounced evil against you, because of the evil which the house of Israel and the house of Judah have done, provoking me to anger by burning incense to Ba'al."

11:1–17 Jeremiah's sermon against Judah and Jerusalem, often dated to 622 B.C., the year the "book of the law" was found in the Temple (2 Kings 22:8). This discovery, which was a partial or complete copy of Deuteronomy, gave new energy to King Josiah's religious reforms (2 Kings 22–23). The prophet warns fellow Judahites that revolt against God's covenant, especially by worshiping "other gods" (11:10), will provoke the Lord's anger (11:17) and bring certain doom (11:15).

11:2 this covenant: The Mosaic covenant that binds God and Israel together as a father to his children (Deut 8:5; 14:1; 32:6). The terms of this covenant were revealed partly at Sinai (the laws of Exodus and Leviticus), partly in the wilderness (the laws of Numbers), and partly on the plains of Moab just before entering Canaan (the laws of Deuteronomy).

11:3 Cursed: Similar to formulas in the Mosaic covenant itself (e.g., Deut 27:15–26). The curses of the covenant are the dreadful penalties that threaten those who fail to uphold its terms. The Lord is not only a partner in this covenant with Israel but is the Enforcer who puts the curses into effect when his people break its commandments (Deut 28:15–68).

11:4 iron furnace: Used for smelting metals at extremely high temperatures. The image signifies the intensity of Israel's suffering in Egypt (Ex 1:8–14) before God delivered the people from slavery and made them his own special possession (Deut 4:20). **my people ... your God:** Known as the covenant formula, which expresses a mutual belonging between the Lord and Israel (30:22; Gen 17:7–8; Lev 26:12; Ezek 37:27).

11:5 the oath which I swore: The divine pledge to give the land of Canaan to the descendants of Abraham (Gen 15:18–21; 26:3). **So be it:** The Hebrew is *'āmēn*, a liturgical acclamation used to express consent to an oath (Num 5:19–22) and ratify the terms of a covenant (Deut 27:15–26) (CCC 1061–65).

11:8 the words of this covenant: The curses of the covenant that brought disaster upon the unfaithful of previous generations. Tragically, Jeremiah's generation is failing to learn the lessons of the past (11:10).

11:10 house of Israel: The northern tribes of Israel, whom the Assyrians have already exiled from the land in the eighth century B.C. **house of Judah:** The southern tribes of Judah. Having committed the same sins as northern Israel, they are destined to meet the same fate.

11:12 the time of their trouble: The day when God's judgment falls.

11:13 your gods ... many: The most basic violation of the Mosaic covenant, which demands allegiance to the Lord alone (Ex 20:2–3; Deut 5:6–7). **shame:** A derogatory name for Baal, the storm and fertility god of Canaanite religion. See note on 3:24. **burn incense:** Sacrifice offered to any god except the Lord invites destruction (Ex 22:20).

11:14 do not pray: Prophets typically intercede for others (Gen 20:7), but Jeremiah is forbidden to pray that Judah will escape the punishment that its rebellion deserves (7:16). The Lord will answer neither the prophet's pleas nor the cries of the people when disaster strikes. The futility of intercession is an ominous sign that Judah's fate is sealed.

11:15 my beloved: Judah is the Lord's unfaithful wife (2:2). **avert your doom?:** Sacrifices offered in the Temple will not atone for Judah's national apostasy. The sinfulness of the people makes their worship unacceptable to the Lord in any case (6:20).

11:16 olive tree: An image of all Israel as the people planted and cultivated by God but whose branches are about to be set ablaze (11:17). • Paul employs the same image of Israel as an olive tree in Rom 11:17–24. He, too, describes the tree losing some of its branches, but he adds that Gentile believers in Jesus are made sharers in Israel's spiritual blessings by being grafted onto its trunk (Rom 15:27).

11:17 incense to Baal: See note on 11:13.

---

¹⁸The LORD made it known to me and I knew;
  then you showed me their evil deeds.
¹⁹But I was like a gentle lamb
  led to the slaughter.
I did not know it was against me
  they devised schemes, saying,
"Let us destroy the tree with its fruit,
  let us cut him off from the land of the living,
  that his name be remembered no more."
²⁰But, O LORD of hosts, who judge righteously,
  who test the heart and the mind,
let me see your vengeance upon them,
  for to you have I committed my cause.

21 Therefore thus says the LORD concerning the men of An'athoth, who seek your life, and say, "Do not prophesy in the name of the LORD, or you will die by our hand"—²²therefore thus says the LORD of hosts: "Behold, I will punish them; the young men shall die by the sword; their sons and their daughters shall die by famine; ²³and none of them shall be left. For I will bring evil upon the men of An'athoth, the year of their punishment."

Jeremiah Complains to God

12 Righteous are you, O LORD, when I complain
  to you;
  yet I would plead my case before you.
Why does the way of the wicked prosper?
  Why do all who are treacherous thrive?
²You plant them, and they take root;
  they grow and bring forth fruit;
you are near in their mouth
  and far from their heart.
³But you, O LORD, know me;
  you see me, and test my mind toward you.

Pull them out like sheep for the slaughter,
  and set them apart for the day of slaughter.
⁴How long will the land mourn,
  and the grass of every field wither?
For the wickedness of those who dwell in it
  the beasts and the birds are swept away,
  because men said, "He will not see our latter
    end."

⁵"If you have raced with men on foot, and they
    have wearied you,
  how will you compete with horses?
And if in a safe land you fall down,
  how will you do in the jungle of the Jordan?
⁶For even your brothers and the house of your
    father,
  even they have dealt treacherously with you;
  they are in full cry after you;
believe them not,
  though they speak fair words to you."

⁷"I have forsaken my house,
  I have abandoned my heritage;
I have given the beloved of my soul
  into the hands of her enemies.
⁸My heritage has become to me
  like a lion in the forest,
she has lifted up her voice against me;
  therefore I hate her.
⁹Is my heritage to me like a speckled bird of
    prey?
  Are the birds of prey against her round
    about?
Go, assemble all the wild beasts;
  bring them to devour.

11:18—12:6 The first of Jeremiah's "confessions" to the Lord (followed by 15:10–21; 17:14–18; 18:19–23). Here God reveals to Jeremiah that a plot against his life is brewing in his hometown of Anathoth (1:1). Once informed of the treachery, the prophet commits his cause to God (11:20), who in turn decrees death for these would-be murderers and their families (11:22–23).

11:19 lamb led to the slaughter: Jeremiah is both innocent and unaware that others are conspiring to kill him. • The imagery resembles Isaiah's Song of the Suffering Servant, which describes the future Messiah as a man rejected, abused, and slain by his own people despite being as blameless and unknowing as a lamb led to the slaughter (Is 52:13—53:12, in particular 53:7). Jeremiah is thus a messiah-like figure who provokes hostility for speaking the word of God faithfully (11:21). • From these words it can be seen that Christ would be crucified and slain. As also Isaiah prophesied, he is the innocent lamb led to the slaughter (St. Justin Martyr, *Dialogue with Trypho* 72).

11:21 Anathoth: Jeremiah's hometown, about three miles northeast of Jerusalem (1:1).

11:23 none ... shall be left: I.e., not even a remnant will survive when the Babylonians overrun Anathoth. This will be another act of divine judgment on the priestly family of Eli (1 Sam 2:27–36), which had been banished to the town of Anathoth by Solomon (1 Kings 2:26–27).

12:1 Righteous: Faithful to the covenant and fair in administering its blessings and curses. See word study: *Righteous* at

Neh 9:8. **Why ... the wicked prosper?:** The prophet is puzzled and irked to see evildoers flourishing instead of facing justice (cf. Ps 73:3–12). The situation is temporary, says the Lord, because beasts are coming to devour them (12:9).

12:2 near in their mouth: Hypocrites who speak of the Lord with pious words but fail to honor him in their hearts (Is 29:13; Ezek 33:31).

12:3 sheep for the slaughter: Proposed as a fitting punishment for those plotting the murder of Jeremiah (11:19). **day of slaughter:** A dreadful day of reckoning (Jas 5:5).

12:4 How long ...?: The cry of one who waits impatiently for God's justice (Ps 35:17; Rev 6:10).

12:5 If.... And if ...: Two proverbial sayings warning Jeremiah that even greater trials of suffering lie ahead for him. **the jungle:** The lush growth around the Jordan was once home to lions (49:19).

12:6 even your brothers: Some of Jeremiah's kinsmen were among the co-conspirators planning to take his life (11:21).

12:7 I have forsaken my house: The Lord has abandoned Judah and Jerusalem, handing them over to judgment. • Jesus alludes to this verse when he laments over Jerusalem, the city that rejected his call to repentance (Mt 23:38; Lk 13:35). In both cases, the abandonment of God's dwelling is a prelude to foreign destruction—by the Babylonians in 586 B.C. and by the Romans in A.D. 70. **the beloved of my soul:** The covenant people, described as the Lord's bride (2:1–2).

12:9 wild beasts: The warriors of Babylon.

¹⁰Many shepherds have destroyed my vineyard,
  they have trampled down my portion,
they have made my pleasant portion
  a desolate wilderness.
¹¹They have made it a desolation;
  desolate, it mourns to me.
The whole land is made desolate,
  but no man lays it to heart.
¹²Upon all the bare heights in the desert
  destroyers have come;
for the sword of the LORD devours
  from one end of the land to the other;
  no flesh has peace.
¹³They have sown wheat and have reaped thorns,
  they have tired themselves out but profit
    nothing.
They shall be ashamed of their ᵘ harvests
  because of the fierce anger of the LORD."

The Lord's Answer

14 Thus says the LORD concerning all my evil neighbors who touch the heritage which I have given my people Israel to inherit: "Behold, I will pluck them up from their land, and I will pluck up the house of Judah from among them. ¹⁵And after I have plucked them up, I will again have compassion on them, and I will bring them again each to his heritage and each to his land. ¹⁶And it shall come to pass, if they will diligently learn the ways of my people, to swear by my name, 'As the LORD lives,' even as they taught my people to swear by Ba'al, then they shall be built up in the midst of my people. ¹⁷But if any nation will not listen, then I will utterly pluck it up and destroy it, says the LORD."

The Linen Waistcloth

13 *Thus said the LORD to me, "Go and buy a linen waistcloth, and put it on your loins, and do not dip it in water." ²So I bought a waistcloth according to the word of the LORD, and put it on my loins. ³And the word of the LORD came to me a second time, ⁴"Take the waistcloth which you have bought, which is upon your loins, and arise, go to the Euphra'tes, and hide it there in a cleft of the rock." ⁵So I went, and hid it by the Euphra'tes, as the LORD commanded me. ⁶And after many days the LORD said to me, "Arise, go to the Euphra'tes, and take from there the waistcloth which I commanded you to hide there." ⁷Then I went to the Euphra'tes, and dug, and I took the waistcloth from the place where I had hidden it. And behold, the waistcloth was spoiled; it was good for nothing.

8 Then the word of the LORD came to me: ⁹"Thus says the LORD: Even so will I spoil the pride of Judah and the great pride of Jerusalem. ¹⁰This evil people, who refuse to hear my words, who stubbornly follow their own heart and have gone after other gods to serve them and worship them, shall be like this waistcloth, which is good for nothing. ¹¹For as the waistcloth clings to the loins of a man, so I made the whole house of Israel and the whole house of Judah cling to me, says the LORD, that they might be for me a people, a name, a praise, and a glory, but they would not listen.

The Jars Filled with Wine

12 "You shall speak to them this word: 'Thus says the LORD, the God of Israel, "Every jar shall be filled with wine."' And they will say to you, 'Do we

---

12:10 shepherds: Either the corrupt leaders of Judah, who have led the people astray (23:1–2), or the foreign army officers who will direct the invasion of the land (6:3). **my vineyard:** A traditional image of Israel (2:21; Is 5:1–7; Hos 10:1). **they have trampled:** The Babylonian conquest of Judah is so certain that Jeremiah speaks as if it has already happened.

12:12 sword of the LORD: An image of God's judgment on his adversaries (Deut 32:42; Ezek 21:1–17). **no flesh has peace:** Peace is withdrawn in times of judgment (16:5; 30:5).

12:14–17 Both a warning and an invitation to Israel's neighbors in the region. The small nations of Moab, Ammon, and Syria will be exiled by the Babylonians along with Judah (12:14). Nevertheless, the Lord will show them compassion, restore them to their ancestral lands, and invite them to serve him instead of the idols that formerly ensnared both them and Judah. If so, they will prosper (12:16). The language of the passage ("pluck up, build, destroy") has links with Jeremiah's prophetic commission in 1:10.

13:1–11 Jeremiah buys a new waistcloth, buries it under a rock on the banks of the Euphrates River, and then retrieves it once the elements have ruined it. God commanded these actions to signify how Israel, bound to him by covenant and called to cling to him in obedience, is about to have its "pride" spoiled by its conquest and exile to Babylon on the Euphrates (13:9). By serving gods other than the Lord, the "evil people" of Judah and Jerusalem have made themselves worthless

(13:10). For other symbolic actions performed by Jeremiah, see 16:1–4; 19:1–13; 32:1–44; 43:8–13.

13:1 waistcloth: A loincloth wrapped loosely around the waist and thighs and tied. **not ... in water:** The garment is not to be washed after the prophet wears it.

13:4 the Euphrates: One of the two great rivers of Mesopotamia. The long trip of several hundred miles from Judah to the Euphrates anticipates the long road to exile in Babylon (cf. 51:63–64). Some think the location (Heb., *perāt*) meant is Wadi Fara, the site of ancient Parah of Benjamin, approximately three miles northeast of Jeremiah's hometown of Anathoth (Josh 18:23).

13:11 cling: The Hebrew verb *dabaq* means "cleave" or "hold fast to" and signals Israel's obligation to give exclusive allegiance to the Lord and his covenant (Deut 10:20; 11:22; 13:4). It is comparable to the way a husband and wife cleave to one another in marriage (Gen 2:24). • The loincloth is the patriarchs and prophets who form the garment of Christ. Do you not realize that the saints are like God's vestment? For his people are as close to him as clothing on the body (St. Jerome, *Homilies on the Psalms* 26).

13:12–14 Another symbolic action. Jeremiah, standing before a collection of empty wine jugs, declares that God is about to intoxicate his people as a prelude to their demise (cf. 25:15–29; Is 29:9–10). The large number of vessels to be filled with wine signifies all the many people of Judah, from authorities to average families. Perhaps the prophet is at a banquet or possibly in a potter's workshop, as in 18:1–4.

13:12 jar: The Greek LXX has "wineskin". **Do we not indeed know ...?:** The onlookers respond as if insulted by such an obvious question.

ᵘHeb *your*.
*13:1–11: Note here and elsewhere the use of symbolic action throughout Jeremiah's ministry.

not indeed know that every jar will be filled with wine?' ¹³Then you shall say to them, 'Thus says the LORD: Behold, I will fill with drunkenness all the inhabitants of this land: the kings who sit on David's throne, the priests, the prophets, and all the inhabitants of Jerusalem. ¹⁴And I will dash them one against another, fathers and sons together, says the LORD. I will not pity or spare or have compassion, that I should not destroy them.'"

¹⁵Hear and give ear; be not proud,
for the LORD has spoken.
¹⁶Give glory to the LORD your God
before he brings darkness,
before your feet stumble
on the twilight mountains,
and while you look for light
he turns it into gloom
and makes it deep darkness.
¹⁷But if you will not listen,
my soul will weep in secret for your pride;
my eyes will weep bitterly and run down with tears,
because the LORD's flock has been taken captive.

¹⁸Say to the king and the queen mother:
"Take a lowly seat,
for your beautiful crown
has come down from your head."ᵛ
¹⁹The cities of the Neg'eb are shut up,
with none to open them;
all Judah is taken into exile,
wholly taken into exile.

²⁰"Lift up your eyes and see
those who come from the north.

Where is the flock that was given you,
your beautiful flock?
²¹What will you say when they set as head over you
those whom you yourself have taught
to be friends to you?
Will not pangs take hold of you,
like those of a woman with labor pains?
²²And if you say in your heart,
'Why have these things come upon me?'
it is for the greatness of your iniquity
that your skirts are lifted up,
and you suffer violence.
²³Can the Ethiopian change his skin
or the leopard his spots?
Then also you can do good
who are accustomed to do evil.
²⁴I will scatter youʷ like chaff
driven by the wind from the desert.
²⁵This is your lot,
the portion I have measured out to you, says the LORD,
because you have forgotten me
and trusted in lies.
²⁶I myself will lift up your skirts over your face,
and your shame will be seen.
²⁷I have seen your abominations,
your adulteries and neighings, your lewd harlotries,
on the hills in the field.
Woe to you, O Jerusalem!
How long will it be
before you are made clean?"

The Great Drought

14 The word of the LORD which came to Jeremi'ah concerning the drought:

13:14 I will dash them: An image of jars smashing against one another in the midst of chaos. Based on the preceding verse, the prophecy pictures drunken people staggering and falling into one another (6:21).

13:16 Give glory to the LORD: Instead of glorying in human wisdom, might, and riches (9:23–24). **gloom ... deep darkness:** Recalls the ominous "day of the Lord" as described by the prophet Amos in the eighth century B.C. (Amos 5:18–20) and the prophet Zephaniah in the seventh century B.C. (Zeph 1:14–16).

13:17 my eyes will weep: Jeremiah's reputation for being Israel's "weeping prophet" is confirmed (9:1; 14:17).

13:18 the king: Jehoiachin, grandson of Josiah, who reigned over the Southern Kingdom of Judah for three months before his exile to Babylon in 597 B.C. (2 Kings 24:10–15). **the queen mother:** Nehushta, mother of Jehoiachin and a prominent royal figure in Judah's government (2 Kings 24:8). See essay: *The Queen Mother* at 1 Kings 2. **crown:** Both the king and queen wore a royal headpiece, probably made of fine gold and studded with jewels (Ps 21:3; Zech 9:16).

13:19 the Negeb: The southernmost territory of Judah. **shut up:** Under siege. **all Judah is taken into exile:** The event

is so certain that Jeremiah describes it as an already accomplished fact.

13:20 from the north: See note on 1:14. **you:** The Hebrew is feminine singular, presumably referring back to the "queen mother" (13:18).

13:21 friends: The Babylonians were once on friendly terms with Judah (2 Kings 20:12–15). **a woman with labor pains:** Points to the sudden and intense agony of Judah's judgment (4:31; 6:24).

13:23 Ethiopian: A Cushite from the land south of Egypt. The question is rhetorical: Judah is so bent on evil that its people are no more able to change their ways than an African can change the color of his skin or an animal can change the pattern of its hide.

13:24 I will scatter: The language of exile to foreign lands (Lev 26:33; Deut 28:64). **like chaff:** Like the useless husks that are separated from grain on threshing floors and blown away by the wind (Ps 1:4; Mt 3:12).

13:26 your shame will be seen: The coming humiliation of Judah, who has whored after other gods (13:27), is compared to the public exposure of an adulteress (Ezek 16:35–39; Nahum 3:5).

13:27 Woe: A cry of anguish heard at funerals. See word study: *Woe* at Is 28:1.

14:1–6 The whole land of Judah, people and animals, groans under the weight of a drought. Lack of rainfall

---

ᵛGk Syr Vg: Heb obscure.
ʷHeb *them*.

²"Judah mourns
    and her gates languish;
her people lament on the ground,
    and the cry of Jerusalem goes up.
³Her nobles send their servants for water;
    they come to the cisterns,
they find no water,
    they return with their vessels empty;
they are ashamed and confounded
    and cover their heads.
⁴Because of the ground which is dismayed,
    since there is no rain on the land,
the farmers are ashamed,
    they cover their heads.
⁵Even the deer in the field forsakes her newborn
        fawn
    because there is no grass.
⁶The wild donkeys stand on the bare heights,
    they pant for air like jackals;
their eyes fail
    because there is no herbage.

⁷"Though our iniquities testify against us,
    act, O LORD, for your name's sake;
for our backslidings are many,
    we have sinned against you.
⁸O you hope of Israel,
    its savior in time of trouble,
why should you be like a stranger in the land,
    like a wayfarer who turns aside to linger for a
        night?
⁹Why should you be like a man confused,
    like a mighty man who cannot save?

Yet you, O LORD, are in the midst of us,
    and we are called by your name;
    leave us not."

¹⁰Thus says the LORD concerning this people:
"They have loved to wander thus,
    they have not restrained their feet;
therefore the LORD does not accept them,
    now he will remember their iniquity
    and punish their sins."

11 The LORD said to me: "Do not pray for the welfare of this people. ¹²Though they fast, I will not hear their cry, and though they offer burnt offering and cereal offering, I will not accept them; but I will consume them by the sword, by famine, and by pestilence."

Denunciation of Lying Prophets; and a Prayer for Mercy

13 Then I said: "Ah, Lord GOD, behold, the prophets say to them, 'You shall not see the sword, nor shall you have famine, but I will give you assured peace in this place.'" ¹⁴And the LORD said to me: "The prophets are prophesying lies in my name; I did not send them, nor did I command them or speak to them. They are prophesying to you a lying vision, worthless divination, and the deceit of their own minds. ¹⁵Therefore thus says the LORD concerning the prophets who prophesy in my name although I did not send them, and who say, 'Sword and famine shall not come on this land': By sword and famine those prophets shall be

---

14:12: Rev 6:8.

(14:4) has left water supplies depleted (14:3) and the landscape denuded of growth (14:5–6). These extreme conditions seem to have come after the Babylonian deportation of 597 B.C. (2 Kings 24:10–17). • The implied background is the curse of Deut 28:23–24, where the Lord threatens to withhold rain from the Promised Land if his people abandon the covenant (cf. 3:2–3).

14:3 cisterns: Stone reservoirs used for storing rainwater for the dry summer months.

14:7–10 Jeremiah intercedes for Judah, confessing the sinfulness of his people and calling upon the Lord to halt his chastisement. Use of the first-person plural ("we, us, our") shows that he is speaking as a representative of his people. Judah's wickedness is not excused or denied; rather, the Lord's historic role as Israel's "savior" is affirmed as a basis for hope (14:8, 22). The prophet desires, if nothing else, that God will show mercy in order to preserve his reputation ("for your name's sake", 14:7).

14:8 stranger ... wayfarer: Persons from other countries who stay in the land of Israel for a time without making it their permanent home.

14:9 in the midst of us: The Lord's presence in the Temple is not a guarantee that Judah will never suffer harm, as the false slogan of 7:4 implies, but it means that a mighty Deliverer is near at hand should he choose to act in answer to prayer. **called by your name:** Israel has been chosen to be God's special possession (Deut 7:6).

14:10 does not accept: A refusal of Jeremiah's prayer in 14:7–9. Judah's iniquity has reached an appalling level that demands punitive justice. **remember:** Means the Lord will

take action against sin at a time of his choosing (Hos 8:13; 9:9). Conversely, forgiveness is indicated when God does "not remember" sins (31:34).

14:11 Do not pray: The third time Jeremiah is forbidden to pray for Judah (7:16; 11:14). The futility of intercession, as well as of the people's fasting and sacrifice (11:12), is an ominous sign that the nation's fate is sealed. Now the prophet can only lament what is coming (14:17–18).

14:12 fast: See note on Joel 1:14. **burnt offering:** Even Judah's sacrifices in the Temple have become unacceptable to the Lord. See note on 6:20. **cereal offering:** See note on Lev 2:1–16. **sword ... famine ... pestilence:** Curses of the covenant that bring suffering and death to violators of the covenant (Lev 26:25–26; Ezek 7:15).

14:13–16 Jeremiah, unwilling to give up on intercessory prayer, responds to 14:10–12 with a second attempt to win the Lord's favor. His plea is that Judah is not fully culpable because the people have been led astray by false prophets. The divine reply: the people remain guilty of great "wickedness", and so their judgment will not be averted (14:16).

14:13 the prophets: False prophets who receive neither message nor mandate from the Lord. They gave false assurances that Judah would always have peace (6:14; 8:11), thanks to the presence of God's Temple in Jerusalem (7:3). In reality, they are shameless liars (14:14).

14:15 By sword and famine: An instance of poetic justice in which those who deny the dangers of sword and famine are doomed to perish by them.

consumed. ¹⁶And the people to whom they prophesy shall be cast out in the streets of Jerusalem, victims of famine and sword, with none to bury them—them, their wives, their sons, and their daughters. For I will pour out their wickedness upon them.

¹⁷"You shall say to them this word:
'Let my eyes run down with tears night and
    day,
    and let them not cease,
for the virgin daughter of my people is struck
    down with a great wound,
    with a very grievous blow.
¹⁸If I go out into the field,
    behold, those slain by the sword!
And if I enter the city,
    behold, the diseases of famine!
For both prophet and priest ply their trade
    through the land,
    and have no knowledge.'"

¹⁹Have you utterly rejected Judah?
    Does your soul loathe Zion?
Why have you struck us down
    so that there is no healing for us?
We looked for peace, but no good came;
    for a time of healing, but behold, terror.
²⁰We acknowledge our wickedness, O LORD,
    and the iniquity of our fathers,
    for we have sinned against you.
²¹Do not spurn us, for your name's sake;
    do not dishonor your glorious throne;
    remember and do not break your covenant
        with us.

²²Are there any among the false gods of the nations
    that can bring rain?
Or can the heavens give showers?
Are you not he, O LORD our God?
    We set our hope on you,
    for you do all these things.

Anguish and Terror Foretold

15 Then the LORD said to me, "Though Moses and Samuel stood before me, yet my heart would not turn toward this people. Send them out of my sight, and let them go! ²And when they ask you, 'Where shall we go?' you shall say to them, 'Thus says the LORD:
"Those who are for pestilence, to pestilence,
    and those who are for the sword, to the sword;
those who are for famine, to famine,
    and those who are for captivity, to captivity."'
³"I will appoint over them four kinds of destroyers, says the LORD: the sword to slay, the dogs to tear, and the birds of the air and the beasts of the earth to devour and destroy. ⁴And I will make them a horror to all the kingdoms of the earth because of what Manas′seh the son of Hezeki′ah, king of Judah, did in Jerusalem.

⁵"Who will have pity on you, O Jerusalem,
    or who will bemoan you?
Who will turn aside
    to ask about your welfare?
⁶You have rejected me, says the LORD,
    you keep going backward;
so I have stretched out my hand against you and
        destroyed you;—
    I am weary of relenting.

15:2: Rev 13:10.

14:16 none to bury them: A great indignity. See note on Tob 1:17.

14:17 tears night and day: Jeremiah's reputation for being Israel's "weeping prophet" is confirmed (9:1; 13:17). **virgin daughter of my people:** A poetic name for Jerusalem. See word study: *The Daughter of Zion* at Lam 1:6.

14:18 no knowledge: Judah's spiritual leaders, tasked with religious instruction, fail to impart true knowledge of God to the people. The same problem plagued northern Israel in Hosea's day (Hos 4:1–6).

14:19–22 Jeremiah, still unwilling to abandon Judah to conquest and exile, prays again for clemency. This time he confesses the sins of multiple generations (14:20), begs the Lord to uphold his covenant with Israel (14:21), and acknowledges the inability of idols to bring rain (14:22).

14:19 Zion: Jerusalem. **We looked for peace ... terror:** This saying also appears in 8:15.

14:21 your glorious throne: Either the Jerusalem Temple (17:12) or the Ark of the Covenant specifically, where the Lord sits enthroned on the wings of the cherubim (2 Sam 6:2; Is 37:16).

14:22 Are there: The first two rhetorical questions expect a negative answer. **false gods ... bring rain?:** It takes a searing drought (14:1) for Judah to acknowledge that the God of Israel controls the rainfall—not Baal, the Canaanite storm god whose idol the people have worshiped (11:13). See note on 10:13.

15:1–4 The Lord declines Jeremiah's second appeal for leniency in 14:19–22. Judah has reached such an advanced stage of moral and spiritual depravity that not even Israel's most celebrated intercessors, the prophets **Moses** and **Samuel**, could hope to elicit God's compassion and turn back his judgment (Ps 99:6–8). For the effectiveness of these intercessors in the past, see Ex 32:11–14; Num 14:13–24; 1 Sam 7:1–14; 12:7–25.

15:2 pestilence ... sword ... famine: Curses of the covenant that bring suffering and death to violators of the covenant (Lev 26:25–26). **captivity:** The climactic curse of the Mosaic covenant is Israel's dispersion to foreign lands (Lev 26:33; Deut 28:64–68). Of those who escape the curse of death, many will be torn from the land to live as exiles in Babylon (52:28–30). Captivity is feared as a fate worse than death (8:3).

15:4 Manasseh: The most wicked of the Davidic kings of Judah (696–642 B.C.). His policies over several decades allowed countless abominations to flourish in the land (2 Kings 21:1–15), setting Judah on a path toward ruin from which it never recovered, despite King Josiah's efforts at reform (2 Kings 23:24–27).

15:5–9 A divine address to Jerusalem, a mother once blessed but about to be bereaved of her children.

15:6 I am weary of relenting: God is tired of waiting for Jerusalem to repent. His patience is now spent, and he is unwilling to postpone the city's punishment any longer.

⁷I have winnowed them with a winnowing fork
    in the gates of the land;
I have bereaved them, I have destroyed my
    people;
    they did not turn from their ways.
⁸I have made their widows more in number
    than the sand of the seas;
I have brought against the mothers of young
    men
    a destroyer at noonday;
I have made anguish and terror
    fall upon them suddenly.
⁹She who bore seven has languished;
    she has swooned away;
her sun went down while it was yet day;
    she has been shamed and disgraced.
And the rest of them I will give to the sword
    before their enemies,

                says the LORD."

Jeremiah Pleads Again and Is Reassured

10 Woe is me, my mother, that you bore me, a man of strife and contention to the whole land! I have not lent, nor have I borrowed, yet all of them curse me. ¹¹So let it be, O LORD,ˣ if I have not entreatedʸ you for their good, if I have not pleaded with you on behalf of the enemy in the time of trouble and in the time of distress! ¹²Can one break iron, iron from the north, and bronze?

¹³"Your wealth and your treasures I will give as spoil, without price, for all your sins, throughout all your territory. ¹⁴I will make you serve your enemies in a land which you do not know, for in my anger a fire is kindled which shall burn for ever."

¹⁵O LORD, you know;
    remember me and visit me,
    and take vengeance for me on my persecutors.
In your forbearance take me not away;
    know that for your sake I bear reproach.
¹⁶Your words were found, and I ate them,
    and your words became to me a joy
    and the delight of my heart;
for I am called by your name,
    O LORD, God of hosts.
¹⁷I did not sit in the company of merrymakers,
    nor did I rejoice;
I sat alone, because your hand was upon me,
    for you had filled me with indignation.
¹⁸Why is my pain unceasing,
    my wound incurable,
    refusing to be healed?
Will you be to me like a deceitful brook,
    like waters that fail?
¹⁹Therefore thus says the LORD:
"If you return, I will restore you,
    and you shall stand before me.

15:7 a winnowing fork: A shovel-like instrument used by farmers to separate edible grains from their useless husks, called chaff, after threshing (Is 30:24). For winnowing as an image of divine judgment, see 51:2; Ps 1:4-5; Is 21:9-10.

15:8 more ... than the sand: An ominous play on God's pledge to make Abraham's descendants as many as the sands on the seashore (Gen 22:17; 32:12).

15:9 She who bore seven: A woman abundantly blessed (1 Sam 2:5; Job 42:13). **her sun went down:** Her happiness prematurely gave way to darkness and grief.

15:10-21 The second of Jeremiah's "confessions" to the Lord (cf. 11:18–12:6; 17:14-18; 18:19-23). The prayer begins with lament and complaint about his trials (15:10-11), continues with a plea for vindication (15:15), and ends with divine words of reassurance (15:20-21).

15:10 Woe: A cry of anguish heard at funerals. See word study: *Woe* at Is 28:1. **my mother:** Either the prophet's natural mother, whose name is unknown (20:14), or possibly the mother city of Jerusalem (15:5). **all of them curse me:** Jeremiah wrestles with discouragement as he faces opposition, isolation, and rejection of his message.

15:11 So let it be: Follows the Greek LXX, which reads the Hebrew as the liturgical acclamation ʾāmēn (as in 11:5). The Hebrew reads ʾāmar YHWH, "the LORD said". This suggests the passage is a conditional self-curse: [May I be cursed] **if I have not entreated you**, etc. See word study: *If* at Job 31:5.

15:12 iron: Jeremiah, whom the Lord promised to make an "iron pillar" against Judah's assaults (1:18), or perhaps the "iron yoke" of Babylon (28:14), which invades from the north. See note on 1:14.

15:13-14 The Lord's response to Jeremiah, which also addresses the nation. It closely resembles the oracle spoken in 17:3-4. Judah's wealth is about to be plundered, and those who survive sword, famine, and pestilence will be enslaved to an enemy nation, just as the Mosaic Law foretold (Deut 28:68).

15:15 take vengeance: It is the Lord's responsibility to avenge himself and his servants against evildoers (Deut 32:35). **my persecutors:** E.g., the men of Anathoth (11:21), the priest Pashur (20:1-2), and the mob enraged by his Temple sermon (26:7-19). **for your sake ... reproach:** The prophet suffers for being God's spokesman (Ps 69:7).

15:16 Your words ... I ate them: Jeremiah remembers his prophetic calling, when God put divine "words" into his "mouth" (1:9). This suggests the idea of eating and ingesting the message he was to deliver (Ezek 2:8–3:3; Rev 10:8-11). Some relate this passage to the finding of "the book of the law" in the Temple in 622 B.C. (2 Kings 22:8). **delight of my heart:** The word of the Lord is sweetness to those who accept it (Ps 119:103).

15:18 pain unceasing: Due to relentless persecution. **like waters that fail?:** Jeremiah questions whether the Lord can still be trusted to defend him as promised at the time of his call (1:18-19). The prophet pictures a seasonal stream or wadi that dries up in the hot summer months.

15:19-21 Jeremiah is recommissioned as the Lord's prophet.

15:19 If you return: Implies that Jeremiah, at the end of his rope, has decided to abandon his difficult mission. See word study: *Repent* at 3:1. **I will restore you:** The Lord will renew Jeremiah's call if he accepts again his prophetic task to speak God's word, as in 1:9. **stand before me:** As a servant who stands ready before a king (1 Kings 10:8). **what is worthless:** The prophet's insinuation in 15:18 that God's help has evaporated.

ˣGk Old Latin: Heb *the LORD said.*
ʸCn: Heb obscure.

If you utter what is precious, and not what is
worthless,
you shall be as my mouth.
They shall turn to you,
but you shall not turn to them.
²⁰And I will make you to this people
a fortified wall of bronze;
they will fight against you,
but they shall not prevail over you,
for I am with you
to save you and deliver you, says the LORD.
²¹I will deliver you out of the hand of the wicked,
and redeem you from the grasp of the ruthless."

Jeremiah's Celibacy and Message

16 The word of the LORD came to me: ²"You
shall not take a wife, nor shall you have sons
or daughters in this place. ³For thus says the LORD
concerning the sons and daughters who are born
in this place, and concerning the mothers who bore
them and the fathers who begot them in this land:
⁴They shall die of deadly diseases. They shall not
be lamented, nor shall they be buried; they shall be
as dung on the surface of the ground. They shall
perish by the sword and by famine, and their dead
bodies shall be food for the birds of the air and for
the beasts of the earth.

5 "For thus says the LORD: Do not enter the house
of mourning, or go to lament, or bemoan them; for I
have taken away my peace from this people, says the
LORD, my steadfast love and mercy. ⁶Both great and
small shall die in this land; they shall not be buried,
and no one shall lament for them or cut himself or
make himself bald for them. ⁷No one shall break
bread for the mourner, to comfort him for the dead;

nor shall any one give him the cup of consolation
to drink for his father or his mother. ⁸You shall not
go into the house of feasting to sit with them, to
eat and drink. ⁹For thus says the LORD of hosts, the
God of Israel: Behold, I will make to cease from this
place, before your eyes and in your days, the voice
of mirth and the voice of gladness, the voice of the
bridegroom and the voice of the bride.

10 "And when you tell this people all these words,
and they say to you, 'Why has the LORD pronounced
all this great evil against us? What is our iniquity?
What is the sin that we have committed against
the LORD our God?' ¹¹then you shall say to them:
'Because your fathers have forsaken me, says the
LORD, and have gone after other gods and have
served and worshiped them, and have forsaken
me and have not kept my law, ¹²and because you
have done worse than your fathers, for behold, every
one of you follows his stubborn evil will, refusing
to listen to me; ¹³therefore I will hurl you out of this
land into a land which neither you nor your fathers
have known, and there you shall serve other gods
day and night, for I will show you no favor.'

God Will Restore Israel

14 "Therefore, behold, the days are coming,
says the LORD, when it shall no longer be said, 'As
the LORD lives who brought up the sons of Israel
out of the land of Egypt,' ¹⁵but 'As the LORD lives
who brought up the sons of Israel out of the north
country and out of all the countries where he had
driven them.' For I will bring them back to their own
land which I gave to their fathers.

16 "Behold, I am sending for many fishers, says
the LORD, and they shall catch them; and afterwards

16:9: Jer 7:34; 25:10; Rev 18:23.

15:20 wall of bronze: A restatement of the promise in
1:18. **they will fight:** See note on 1:19.

16:1–9 Jeremiah is forbidden to take a wife (16:2), start
a family (16:2), mourn the dead (16:5), or join in any feasting (16:8). These are prophetic actions, i.e., they are signs of
judgment for the people, whose wives and children will be lost
in the coming judgment, and signs of *mercy* for the prophet,
who will be spared the extreme grief that others will face when
they watch their families perish. No funerals, burials, festal
banquets, or weddings will be possible in the dreadful days
ahead (16:4, 6, 9).

16:2 in this place: In the land of Judah.

16:4 diseases ... sword ... famine: See note on 14:12.

16:5 house of mourning: A place where people gather
to comfort a bereaved family with a funerary meal (16:7).
peace: Withdrawn from Judah, despite the claims of the false
prophets (6:14; 8:11; 14:13). **steadfast love and mercy:** The
withdrawal of these divine gifts is a frightful sign that Judah
has lost God's favor and now faces destruction.

16:6 cut himself ... make himself bald: None will survive
or remain in the land to grieve over the dead. Gashing or
lacerating the skin and shaving one's hair are pagan mourning
rituals that are forbidden in Israel (Lev 19:28; Deut 14:1). The
practice of cutting one's hair as an expression of grief is known
in Israel, however (Is 22:12; Amos 8:10).

16:7 bread ... cup: Food and drink given to comfort a bereaved family in their time of mourning (Ezek 24:17; Hos 9:4).

16:9 voice of the bridegroom: The joyous sounds of
wedding celebrations will cease when disaster strikes (7:34;
25:10). They will not be heard again until the Lord restores his
people after judgment (33:10–11).

16:13 I will hurl you: Expulsion from the land of Israel.
neither you nor your fathers: Echoes the covenant
curses of Deut 28:36 and 28:64, which foresee exile as a place
where Israelite captives will serve other gods.

16:15 As the LORD lives: A new formula for swearing
oaths that will replace the old formula in 16:14. For
other things Judah will no longer say in the future, see 3:16;
7:32; 31:29. **brought up ... Israel:** The prophet foresees a
new and greater exodus of the Israelites from Babylon and the
lands of exile that will surpass the original Exodus from Egypt.
After the coming judgment, he expects a new deliverance and
a new outpouring of mercy, as elaborated in Jer 31–33. See
essay: *The New Exodus in Isaiah* in Is 43. **the north country:**
Babylon and Assyria (50:17–20). See note on 1:14.

16:16 fishers ... hunters: A picture of enemy soldiers
rounding up the inhabitants of Judah for the march into
exile (Eccles 9:12; Amos 4:2). • Jesus uses a fishing metaphor
to speak of the missionary role of the apostles, whose task will
be to gather men and women into God's kingdom (Mt 4:19;
Mk 1:17; Lk 5:10).

I will send for many hunters, and they shall hunt them from every mountain and every hill, and out of the clefts of the rocks. [17]For my eyes are upon all their ways; they are not hidden from me, nor is their iniquity concealed from my eyes. [18]And[z] I will doubly recompense their iniquity and their sin, because they have polluted my land with the carcasses of their detestable idols, and have filled my inheritance with their abominations."

[19]O Lord, my strength and my stronghold,
   my refuge in the day of trouble,
to you shall the nations come
   from the ends of the earth and say:
"Our fathers have inherited nothing but lies,
   worthless things in which there is no profit.
[20]Can man make for himself gods?
   Such are no gods!"

21 "Therefore, behold, I will make them know, this once I will make them know my power and my might, and they shall know that my name is the Lord."

Judah's Sin and Shame

17 "The sin of Judah is written with a pen of iron; with a point of diamond it is engraved on the tablet of their heart, and on the horns of their altars, [2]while their children remember their altars and their Ashe'rim, beside every green tree, and on the high hills, [3]on the mountains in the open country. Your wealth and all your treasures I will give for spoil as the price of your sin[a] throughout all your territory. [4]You shall loosen your hand[b] from your heritage which I gave to you, and I will make you serve your enemies in a land which you do not know, for in my anger a fire is kindled which shall burn for ever."

[5]Thus says the Lord:
"Cursed is the man who trusts in man
   and makes flesh his arm,
   whose heart turns away from the Lord.
[6]He is like a shrub in the desert,
   and shall not see any good come.
He shall dwell in the parched places of the
     wilderness,
   in an uninhabited salt land.

[7]"Blessed is the man who trusts in the Lord,
   whose trust is the Lord.
[8]He is like a tree planted by water,
   that sends out its roots by the stream,
and does not fear when heat comes,
   for its leaves remain green,
and is not anxious in the year of drought,
   for it does not cease to bear fruit."

[9]The heart is deceitful above all things,
   and desperately corrupt;
   who can understand it?

17:7–8: Ps 1:1–3.

16:18 doubly recompense: A way of saying that Judah will pay for its sins in full (Is 40:2).

16:19–21 The prayer of Jeremiah (16:19a–b), the confession of the nations (16:19c–20), and the Lord's response (16:21). The prophet foresees Gentiles coming to faith in the God of Israel as they acknowledge that the whole tradition of idolatry is bankrupt—a corrupted form of religion that deals in lies and brings no benefit. For Jeremiah's critique of idols, see note on 10:1–5.

16:19 my stronghold: A fortress of protection (Ps 9:9; 18:2; 37:39). **the nations come:** Conversion of the world beyond Israel is also envisioned in 3:17 and 12:16. For the expectation of a future incoming of the nations, see also Is 2:2–4; Mic 4:1–3; Zech 2:11; 8:20–23.

16:20 no gods: Echoes the Song of Moses, which declares that an idol is "no god" (Deut 32:21).

16:21 my name is the Lord: Yhwh, probably pronounced "Yahweh", the name of God revealed to Moses at the burning bush. See note on Ex 3:15.

17:1 pen of iron: A stylus tipped with diamond or another hard stone, used for inscribing on rock (Job 19:24). The image implies that Judah's heart has become stone (Ezek 36:26). **horns of their altars:** Altars discovered from ancient Canaan typically have four projections at the top four corners. They are marked by Judah's sin because they are used to make offerings to idols (2 Kings 21:5).

17:2 Asherim: Trees or wooden poles that serve as cultic symbols of the Canaanite mother goddess Asherah (Deut 16:21). **the high hills:** Idol shrines with sacred groves were often found on mountain tops and hills. See word study: *High Places* at 2 Kings 23:5.

17:3 I will give for spoil: Wealth obtained by injustice (17:11) will be lost to plundering warriors (15:13).

17:4 your heritage: The Promised Land. **your enemies:** The Babylonians.

17:5–8 A contrast between the wicked of Judah, who are like a desert shrub clinging to life (17:6), and the righteous, who are like a thriving fruit tree drawing life from a stream (17:8). The difference between them is the object of their trust, whether it is placed in human resources (17:5) or in God, the fountain of living water (17:13; Ps 40:5; CCC 215). The passage encourages the remnant of devout Jews to rely upon the Lord on the eve of judgment (= the coming **heat** of 17:8). For the blessings and curses of the covenant, see Deut 28:1–68, and for the righteous as flourishing trees, see Ps 1:3 and 92:12–15.

17:5 his arm: I.e., his strength.

17:9 The heart is deceitful: Inclinations to sin are lodged deep in our being, affecting our thoughts, decisions, and actions in devious ways. It is a spiritual pathology that fights against our obligation to love the Lord with our whole "heart" (Deut 6:5). Although we still possess free will (Sir 15:11–20), Jeremiah recognizes that our hearts are desperately in need of grace so that God can heal our "faithlessness" (3:22) by writing his laws on our "hearts" (31:33). Even the prophet needs this healing (17:14). See note on 9:26. • Jesus likewise teaches that the evil thoughts, words, and actions that defile us come from the heart (Mk 7:21–23). **corrupt:** Or "sick". **who can understand it?:** Sinful man is a mystery to himself. Only the Lord can search out the depths of his heart (17:10; 1 Sam 16:7; Acts 1:24).

---

[z]Gk: Heb *And first.*
[a]Cn: Heb *your high places for sin.*
[b]Cn: Heb *and in you.*

¹⁰"I the LORD search the mind
    and test the heart,
  to give to every man according to his ways,
    according to the fruit of his doings."

¹¹Like the partridge that gathers a brood which she
    did not hatch,
  so is he who gets riches but not by right;
  in the midst of his days they will leave him,
    and at his end he will be a fool.

¹²A glorious throne set on high from the beginning
    is the place of our sanctuary.
¹³O LORD, the hope of Israel,
    all who forsake you shall be put to shame;
  those who turn away from you ᶜ shall be written
    in the earth,
    for they have forsaken the LORD, the fountain
    of living water.

¹⁴Heal me, O LORD, and I shall be healed;
    save me, and I shall be saved;
    for you are my praise.
¹⁵Behold, they say to me,
    "Where is the word of the LORD?
    Let it come!"
¹⁶I have not pressed you to send evil,
    nor have I desired the day of disaster,
    you know;
  that which came out of my lips
    was before your face.
¹⁷Be not a terror to me;
    you are my refuge in the day of evil.

¹⁸Let those be put to shame who persecute me,
    but let me not be put to shame;
  let them be dismayed,
    but let me not be dismayed;
  bring upon them the day of evil;
    destroy them with double destruction!

19 Thus said the LORD to me: "Go and stand in the Benjamin ᵈ Gate, by which the kings of Judah enter and by which they go out, and in all the gates of Jerusalem, ²⁰and say: 'Hear the word of the LORD, you kings of Judah, and all Judah, and all the inhabitants of Jerusalem, who enter by these gates. ²¹Thus says the LORD: Take heed for the sake of your lives, and do not bear a burden on the sabbath day or bring it in by the gates of Jerusalem. ²²And do not carry a burden out of your houses on the sabbath or do any work, but keep the sabbath day holy, as I commanded your fathers. ²³Yet they did not listen or incline their ear, but stiffened their neck, that they might not hear and receive instruction.

24 "'But if you listen to me, says the LORD, and bring in no burden by the gates of this city on the sabbath day, but keep the sabbath day holy and do no work on it, ²⁵then there shall enter by the gates of this city kings ᵉ who sit on the throne of David, riding in chariots and on horses, they and their princes, the men of Judah and the inhabitants of Jerusalem; and this city shall be inhabited for ever. ²⁶And people shall come from the cities of Judah and the places round about Jerusalem, from the land of Benjamin, from the Shephe'lah, from the hill country, and from the Neg'eb, bringing burnt offerings and sacrifices,

---

17:10: Ps 62:12; Rev 2:23; 22:12.

17:10 according to his ways: Judgment according to works is a classic teaching of Scripture (32:19; Ps 62:12; Prov 24:12; Mt 16:27; Rom 2:5–8; 1 Pet 1:17).

17:12 A glorious throne: The glory of the Lord is enthroned in the Temple (Ps 26:8) on the Ark of the Covenant (2 Sam 6:2), which is an image of his eternal throne in heaven (Ps 11:4). See note on 3:16.

17:13 hope: Or "pool". **living water:** See note on 2:13.

17:14–18 The third of Jeremiah's "confessions" to the Lord (cf. 11:18–12:6; 15:10–21; 18:19–23). Here he struggles with two opposing desires: the prophet does not want to see disaster come upon Judah (17:16), yet he wants his enemies to get what they deserve (17:18).

17:15 Where is the word of the LORD?: The scoffing words of Jeremiah's opponents. He is beginning to look foolish because his prophecies of judgment have not yet come true (cf. 2 Pet 3:3–4). What scoffers fail to realize is that the "delay" of God's punishment is a mercy, a final opportunity for repentance (13:16; Rom 2:4; 2 Pet 3:9).

17:16 the day of disaster: Equivalent to "the day of the LORD" (Amos 5:18–20).

17:18 Let those be put to shame: A prayer of imprecation. See essay: *Imprecatory Psalms* at Ps 109.

17:19 the Benjamin Gate: The Hebrew is "gate of the sons of the people". Its location is uncertain, but it apparently allowed access into the Temple from the royal palaces on Zion. **all the gates:** The various city gates in the wall surrounding Jerusalem.

17:21 the sabbath day: The seventh day of the Jewish week and a sacred day of rest. Being one of the Ten Commandments, it is one of the fundamental obligations of the covenant (Ex 20:8–11; Lev 23:3) and a perpetual "sign" that the Lord made heaven and earth (Ex 31:13–17). Breaking the Sabbath by doing unnecessary work is a serious offense (Num 15:32–36). Here and elsewhere the Sabbath is broken by merchants greedy for gain (Neh 13:15–22; Amos 8:4–6) (CCC 2168–73).

17:25 the throne of David: A conditional promise that renewed obedience to the covenant will prolong the Davidic dynasty in Jerusalem. Tragically, this possibility will go unrealized. Judah's stubborn rebellion will bring ruin on the nation and the collapse of the monarchy until the coming of Jesus as the messianic heir to David's throne (Mt 1:1; Lk 1:32–33; Acts 2:29–36).

17:26 land of Benjamin: Borders the land of Judah on the northeast. **the Shephelah:** The low hills of western Judah. **the Negeb:** The arid region in the deep south of Judah. **burnt offerings:** See note on Lev 1:3–17. **cereal offerings:** See note on Lev 2:1–16. **frankincense:** A key ingredient in the sacred blend of incense prescribed for Israel's sanctuary (Ex 30:34–38). **thank offerings:** See note on Ps 50:14.

ᶜ Heb *me*.
ᵈ Cn: Heb *sons of people*.
ᵉ Cn: Heb *kings and princes*.

cereal offerings and frankincense, and bringing thank offerings to the house of the LORD. ²⁷But if you do not listen to me, to keep the sabbath day holy, and not to bear a burden and enter by the gates of Jerusalem on the sabbath day, then I will kindle a fire in its gates, and it shall devour the palaces of Jerusalem and shall not be quenched.'"

The Potter and the Clay

18 The word that came to Jeremi'ah from the LORD: ²"Arise, and go down to the potter's house, and there I will let you hear my words." ³So I went down to the potter's house, and there he was working at his wheel. ⁴And the vessel he was making of clay was spoiled in the potter's hand, and he reworked it into another vessel, as it seemed good to the potter to do.

5 Then the word of the LORD came to me: ⁶"O house of Israel, can I not do with you as this potter has done? says the LORD. Behold, like the clay in the potter's hand, so are you in my hand, O house of Israel. ⁷If at any time I declare concerning a nation or a kingdom, that I will pluck up and break down and destroy it, ⁸and if that nation, concerning which I have spoken, turns from its evil, I will repent of the evil that I intended to do to it. ⁹And if at any time I declare concerning a nation or a kingdom that I will build and plant it, ¹⁰and if it does evil in my sight, not listening to my voice, then I will repent of the good which I had intended to do to it. ¹¹Now, therefore, say to the men of Judah and the inhabitants of Jerusalem:

'Thus says the LORD, Behold, I am shaping evil against you and devising a plan against you. Return, every one from his evil way, and amend your ways and your doings.'

Israel's Stubborn Idolatry

12 "But they say, 'That is in vain! We will follow our own plans, and every one will act according to the stubbornness of his evil heart.'

¹³"Therefore thus says the LORD:
   Ask among the nations,
      who has heard the like of this?
   The virgin Israel
      has done a very horrible thing.
¹⁴Does the snow of Lebanon leave
      the crags of Sir'ion? **f**
   Do the mountain **g** waters run dry, **h**
      the cold flowing streams?
¹⁵But my people have forgotten me,
      they burn incense to false gods;
   they have stumbled **i** in their ways,
      in the ancient roads,
   and have gone into bypaths,
      not the highway,
¹⁶making their land a horror,
      a thing to be hissed at for ever.
   Every one who passes by it is horrified
      and shakes his head.
¹⁷Like the east wind I will scatter them
      before the enemy.

18:6: Rom 9:21.

📖 **18:1-12** The lesson of the potter at his wheel. Jeremiah learns that the Lord, the divine potter, wants to shape Israel, his clay, into a useful vessel, yet the vessel has become ruined by its determination to do evil. Still, God has the power to reshape the fortunes of Judah, and of all nations, if they repent and yield to his will. • The potter and clay as an image of the Lord's authority to form his people goes back to Isaiah (Is 29:16; 45:9; 64:8) and is later reused by the apostle Paul (Rom 9:21). It stems from the biblical picture of the first man, Adam, who was formed from the dust or clay of the ground (Gen 2:7).

18:3 his wheel: The Hebrew reads "the two stones". Potters fashioned cups, pots, and other earthenware on the surface of the top stone while rotating the bottom stone with his feet (Sir 38:29).

18:4 spoiled: It failed to hold its intended shape. The image of the potter balling up the clay and starting again with the same lump suggests that God is giving Judah a second chance to become a worthy vessel.

18:7 pluck ... break ... destroy: God's Lordship over history and the world means that he can remove even the mightiest of nations from the earth (1:10; 31:28).

18:8 if: The prophecy is conditional, meaning the outcome depends on how the people respond to the prophet's message (26:3, 13, 19; Jon 3:10). **turns:** The language of repentance. See word study: *Return* at 3:1. **I will repent:** God deals mercifully with those who repent of sin and deals severely with

those who refuse to cease their wicked ways (18:10-11). The notion of God "repenting" is not intended literally, but is a figurative expression based on the analogy of human behavior. It is a way of saying that his decree of judgment can still be delayed or repealed if his people recommit themselves to him. See note on Gen 6:6. **the evil that I intended:** Not moral evil, which is incompatible with God's goodness, but the "disaster" or "calamity" he sends to those who refuse to repent of moral evil. See note on Amos 3:6.

18:10 repent of the good: The blessings that God wants to give his people will be withheld because of their defiant rebellion.

18:12 evil heart: See note on 17:9.

18:13 The virgin Israel: The title, which also appears in 31:4, 21, is ironic, seeing that God's people are guilty of spiritual prostitution (3:2-5).

18:14-15 snow of Lebanon: Covers the mountain peaks north of Israel. **Sirion:** Another name for Mt. Hermon, the largest in the anti-Lebanon range. It is normal for Hermon's summit to be capped with snow throughout the year; this is contrasted with how strange and abnormal it is for a people (= Judah) to forsake their god (= the Lord) to serve foreign deities (18:15; cf. 2:11). **the ancient roads:** The ways of the covenant leading to blessing and life (Deut 30:15-20).

18:16 hissed ... shakes his head: Gestures of derision and disgust by passersby (Zeph 2:15). Jerusalem will experience this after its destruction (Lam 2:15).

📖 **18:17 east wind:** Sometimes represents God's judgment (Is 27:8; Jon 4:8). **I will scatter them:** Exile from the Promised Land is the climactic curse of the Mosaic covenant that is triggered by Israel's disobedience (Deut 28:64-68).

---

f Cn: Heb *the field.*
g Cn: Heb *foreign.*
h Cn: Heb *Are...plucked up?*
i Gk Syr Vg: Heb *they made them stumble.*

I will show them my back, not my face,
    in the day of their calamity."

Plots against Jeremiah

18 Then they said, "Come, let us make plots against Jeremi′ah, for the law shall not perish from the priest, nor counsel from the wise, nor the word from the prophet. Come, let us strike him with the tongue, and let us not heed any of his words."

¹⁹Give heed to me, O LORD,
    and listen to my plea.ʲ
²⁰Is evil a recompense for good?
    Yet they have dug a pit for my life.
Remember how I stood before you
    to speak good for them,
    to turn away your wrath from them.
²¹Therefore deliver up their children to famine;
    give them over to the power of the sword,
let their wives become childless and widowed.
    May their men meet death by pestilence,
    their youths be slain by the sword in battle.
²²May a cry be heard from their houses,
    when you bring the marauder suddenly upon
      them!
For they have dug a pit to take me,
    and laid snares for my feet.
²³Yet, you, O LORD, know
    all their plotting to slay me.

Forgive not their iniquity,
    nor blot out their sin from your sight.
Let them be overthrown before you;
    deal with them in the time of your anger.

The Broken Earthen Flask

19 Thus said the LORD, "Go, buy a potter's earthen flask, and take some of the elders of the people and some of the senior priests, ²and go out to the valley of the son of Hinnom at the entry of the Potsherd Gate, and proclaim there the words that I tell you. ³You shall say, 'Hear the word of the LORD, O kings of Judah and inhabitants of Jerusalem. Thus says the LORD of hosts, the God of Israel, Behold, I am bringing such evil upon this place that the ears of every one who hears of it will tingle. ⁴Because the people have forsaken me, and have profaned this place by burning incense in it to other gods whom neither they nor their fathers nor the kings of Judah have known; and because they have filled this place with the blood of innocents, ⁵and have built the high places of Ba′al to burn their sons in the fire as burnt offerings to Baal, which I did not command or decree, nor did it come into my mind; ⁶therefore, behold, days are coming, says the LORD, when this place shall no more be called To′pheth, or the valley of the son of Hinnom, but the valley of Slaughter. ⁷And in this place I will make void the plans of Judah and Jerusalem, and will cause their

---

18:18 the priest ... the wise ... the prophet: The religious leaders of Judah, whom Jeremiah rebukes for leading the people astray (2:8; 8:8–10). Priests are supposed to teach the Torah (Lev 10:11); sages are supposed to teach the wisdom of fearing the Lord (Prov 1:7); and prophets are supposed to speak for the Lord and not for false gods such as Baal (23:13). **strike him with the tongue:** Suggests a campaign of slander, although 18:23 suggests that murder is part of the plot as well.

18:19–23 The fourth of Jeremiah's "confessions" to the Lord (cf. 11:18—12:6; 15:10–21; 17:14–18). Having learned that opponents are plotting against him (18:18), he protests his innocence (18:20) and prays for divine judgment to fall on the conspirators and their families (18:21–23).

18:20 dug a pit: A hunter's trap (18:22; Ps 119:85). **I stood before you:** As a servant who stands ready before a king (1 Kings 10:8). **to speak good:** By interceding for the welfare of Judah (e.g., 14:7–9, 20–22).

18:21 deliver up: Imprecations that call down God's judgments on the prophet's would-be assassins. For moral issues raised by these types of prayers, see essay: *The Imprecatory Psalms* at Ps 109. **their children:** See note on Ps 137:9. **famine ... sword ... pestilence:** Curses of the Mosaic covenant (Lev 26:25–26).

18:23 Forgive not their iniquity: A prayer, not for the damnation of one's enemies, but for evildoers to bear the temporal consequences of their sins. Jeremiah, who had prayed that fellow Judahites would be spared divine wrath (18:20), now prays that the men plotting his murder will bear God's wrath that is coming to the nation (cf. Neh 4:4–5).

19:1–13 Jeremiah buys a clay vessel, gathers leaders from Jerusalem as witnesses, stands at the southern gate of the city, and smashes the vessel beyond repair. God commanded these

prophetic actions to drive home the message that Judah and Jerusalem are doomed to utter destruction (19:10). Judah, in other words, is no longer the malleable clay it was in 18:4; the people have since become hardened in their disobedience, and their fate is now sealed (19:15).

19:1 earthen flask: A ceramic bottle or jug (18:3–4).

19:2 valley of the son of Hinnom: Directly southwest of Jerusalem, identified with modern Wadi er-Rababi. The Hinnom valley is an image of damnation in the NT. See word study: *Hell* at Mk 9:43. **the Potsherd Gate:** In the southern wall of Jerusalem, perhaps later known as the Dung Gate (Neh 2:13). It is probably the exit where broken pottery and other refuse is carried out of the city to be discarded in the valley below.

19:3 evil: The Hebrew *rāʿāh* here means "disaster" or "calamity". See note Amos 3:6.

19:5 high places: Unlawful worship sites, commonly associated with idolatry. See word study: *High Places* at 2 Kings 23:5. **sons ... as burnt offerings:** For this abomination, see note on 7:31. **Baal:** The storm and fertility god of Canaanite religion. Only here is it mentioned that Baal worship involved the murder of children (unless Baal, meaning "lord", was a title for Molech, 32:35).

19:6 Topheth: A cult site where children were incinerated as offerings to pagan deities. The meaning of the name is unknown; suggestions include "oven" or "fire pit" (cf. Is 30:33). **the valley of Slaughter:** The ravine will be filled with the unburied corpses of the slain when Jerusalem is conquered in 586 B.C. (7:32).

19:7–9 The calamities in store for Judah and Jerusalem are curses of the Mosaic covenant triggered by disobedience. These include death by the sword (19:7; Lev 26:25), scavengers eating human corpses (19:7; Deut 28:26), becoming a horror in the eyes of others (19:8; Deut 28:37), being besieged by enemies (19:9; Deut 28:52), and resorting to cannibalism when food supplies run out (19:9; Lev 26:29; Deut 28:53).

ʲ Gk Compare Syr Tg: Heb *my adversaries.*

people to fall by the sword before their enemies, and by the hand of those who seek their life. I will give their dead bodies for food to the birds of the air and to the beasts of the earth. ⁸And I will make this city a horror, a thing to be hissed at; every one who passes by it will be horrified and will hiss because of all its disasters. ⁹And I will make them eat the flesh of their sons and their daughters, and every one shall eat the flesh of his neighbor in the siege and in the distress, with which their enemies and those who seek their life afflict them.'

10 "Then you shall break the flask in the sight of the men who go with you, ¹¹and shall say to them, 'Thus says the LORD of hosts: So will I break this people and this city, as one breaks a potter's vessel, so that it can never be mended. Men shall bury in To′pheth because there will be no place else to bury. ¹²Thus will I do to this place, says the LORD, and to its inhabitants, making this city like To′pheth. ¹³The houses of Jerusalem and the houses of the kings of Judah—all the houses upon whose roofs incense has been burned to all the host of heaven, and drink offerings have been poured out to other gods—shall be defiled like the place of To′pheth.'"

14 Then Jeremi′ah came from To′pheth, where the LORD had sent him to prophesy, and he stood in the court of the LORD's house, and said to all the people: ¹⁵"Thus says the LORD of hosts, the God of Israel, Behold, I am bringing upon this city and upon all its towns all the evil that I have pronounced against it, because they have stiffened their neck, refusing to hear my words."

Jeremiah Is Persecuted by Pashhur and Complains to God

20 Now Pashhur the priest, the son of Im′mer, who was chief officer in the house of the LORD, heard Jeremi′ah prophesying these things. ²Then Pashhur beat Jeremi′ah the prophet, and put him in the stocks that were in the upper Benjamin Gate of the house of the LORD. ³On the next day, when Pashhur released Jeremi′ah from the stocks, Jeremiah said to him, "The LORD does not call your name Pashhur, but Terror on every side. ⁴For thus says the LORD: Behold, I will make you a terror to yourself and to all your friends. They shall fall by the sword of their enemies while you look on. And I will give all Judah into the hand of the king of Babylon; he shall carry them captive to Babylon, and shall slay them with the sword. ⁵Moreover, I will give all the wealth of the city, all its gains, all its prized belongings, and all the treasures of the kings of Judah into the hand of their enemies, who shall plunder them, and seize them, and carry them to Babylon. ⁶And you, Pashhur, and all who dwell in your house, shall go into captivity; to Babylon you shall go; and there you shall die, and there you shall be buried, you and all your friends, to whom you have prophesied falsely."

⁷O LORD, you have deceived me,
and I was deceived;

19:13: Acts 7:42.   **20:3, 10:** Jer 6:25; 46:5; 49:29; Ps 31:13.

19:7 make void: The Hebrew verb *bāqaq* may be a pun on *baqbuq*, translated "flask" in 19:1.

19:8 hissed at: See note on 18:16.

19:11 never be mended: In contrast to an earlier time in Jeremiah's ministry, when Judah was still like wet clay that could be reshaped into a worthy vessel (18:1–11).

19:13 the host of heaven: The sun, moon, stars, and planets visible in the day and night sky. Worship of the heavenly bodies is strictly forbidden in Israel (Deut 4:19), although disregard for the prohibition is well documented in the Bible (2 Kings 17:16; 23:5; Ezek 8:16; Amos 5:26; Zeph 1:5). **drink offerings:** Libations made to idols.

19:14 in the court: Jeremiah, having delivered his message to a few in 19:10–13, now stands in the Temple to announce Judah's demise before the general public.

19:15 I am bringing ... evil: The Lord's judicial verdict is now rendered: Judah and Jerusalem, found guilty of grievous crimes and unwilling to repent, are headed for destruction.

20:1–6 The response to Jeremiah's message spoken in the Temple in 19:15. The prophet is seized, beaten, and locked in stocks overnight. His persecutor, Pashhur, a priest and head of the Temple security force, learns that he and his family will die as exiles in Babylon for this hostile attempt to silence the Lord's prophet (20:6). The incident likely occurred before 605 B.C., when Jeremiah was banned from the Temple (36:5). The prophet Amos was similarly opposed and censured by a priest at a sanctuary in Bethel (Amos 7:10–17).

20:1 Pashhur: A common name in preexilic Judah (21:1). **Immer:** A priestly family since the time of King David (1 Chron 24:14). **chief officer:** In charge of the sanctuary police. He is a priest of senior rank authorized to put troublemakers in "stocks and collar" (29:26).

20:2 upper Benjamin Gate: Possibly the "upper gate" built on the north side of the Temple by King Jotham (2 Kings 15:35).

20:3 Terror on every side: Evokes a frightening image of Jerusalem under siege, a city surrounded by enemies from which none can escape to safety. This is one of Jeremiah's most memorable expressions (6:25; 20:10; 46:5; 49:29; cf. Lam 2:22).

20:4 Babylon: The Neo-Babylonian empire, ruled by Nebuchadnezzar from 605 to 562 B.C. This is the first time Judah's conqueror is identified by name in the book.

20:5 all the wealth: Judah's riches are destined to become spoils of war (15:13; 17:3). For the fulfillment of this prophecy, see 27:16; 28:3, 6; 52:17–23.

20:6 into captivity: Pashhur may have been among the "chief men" of Judah that Nebuchadnezzar exiles to Babylon in 597 B.C. (2 Kings 24:15). **prophesied falsely:** Suggests that Pashhur peddles a vain message of "peace" in the face of imminent war (6:14; 8:11).

20:7–13 The fifth of Jeremiah's "confessions" to the Lord (11:18–12:6; 15:10–21; 17:14–18; 18:19–23; 20:14–18). It is marked by greater emotional intensity than previous confessions. Jeremiah is coming to realize the personal cost of his preaching, which is not only rejected by most but is now provoking violent actions from authorities (20:2). His prayer, which begins in great distress, ends with a surge of renewed confidence in the Lord as his Deliverer (20:12–13) (CCC 2584).

you are stronger than I,
  and you have prevailed.
I have become a laughingstock all the day;
  every one mocks me.
⁸For whenever I speak, I cry out,
  I shout, "Violence and destruction!"
For the word of the LORD has become for me
  a reproach and derision all day long.
⁹If I say, "I will not mention him,
  or speak any more in his name,"
there is in my heart as it were a burning fire
  shut up in my bones,
and I am weary with holding it in,
  and I cannot.
¹⁰For I hear many whispering.
  Terror is on every side!
"Denounce him! Let us denounce him!"
  say all my familiar friends,
  watching for my fall.
"Perhaps he will be deceived,
  then we can overcome him,
  and take our revenge on him."
¹¹But the LORD is with me as a dread warrior;
  therefore my persecutors will stumble,
  they will not overcome me.
They will be greatly shamed,
  for they will not succeed.
Their eternal dishonor
  will never be forgotten.
¹²O LORD of hosts, who test the righteous,
  who see the heart and the mind,

let me see your vengeance upon them,
  for to you have I committed my cause.

¹³Sing to the LORD;
  praise the LORD!
For he has delivered the life of the needy
  from the hand of evildoers.

¹⁴Cursed be the day
  on which I was born!
The day when my mother bore me,
  let it not be blessed!
¹⁵Cursed be the man
  who brought the news to my father,
  "A son is born to you,"
  making him very glad.
¹⁶Let that man be like the cities
  which the LORD overthrew without pity;
let him hear a cry in the morning
  and an alarm at noon,
¹⁷because he did not kill me in the womb;
  so my mother would have been my
    grave,
  and her womb for ever great.
¹⁸Why did I come forth from the womb
  to see toil and sorrow,
  and spend my days in shame?

The Fall of Jerusalem

21 This is the word which came to Jeremi'ah from the LORD, when King Zedeki'ah sent to

---

20:14–18: Job 3:3–13.

20:7 LORD, you have deceived me: A daring accusation spoken in bitter anguish. Jeremiah feels misled by God's promise that enemies "shall not prevail" over him (1:19). He is discovering this was a promise to protect his life, not a promise to protect him from hostility and abuse. **stronger than I:** Implies an accusation that God muscled Jeremiah into accepting his call in 1:4–19.

20:9 I will not ... speak: Jeremiah attempts to keep silent, lest he bring even more "reproach" upon himself (20:8), but his attempt is unsuccessful because his prophetic message is like a **burning fire** that cannot be contained. His dilemma is that speaking and silence both seem unbearable. **in my bones:** At times, prophets have an irresistible urge from within to speak the words that God has entrusted to them (Num 22:38; Amos 3:8). The image suggests his message concerns fiery wrath and destruction (6:11; Lam 1:13).

20:10 Terror is on every side: A quotation from Ps 31:13. Jeremiah used this expression in 20:3 to pronounce God's judgment on another, but now he is besieged by enemies (cf. 6:25; 46:5; 49:29).

20:11 the LORD is with me: As promised at the time of Jeremiah's call (1:8, 19) and later reaffirmed (15:20).

20:12 test the righteous: The Lord allows Jeremiah to suffer adversity in order to strengthen his faith and to ensure that his motives for serving God are purified of selfish interests (Sir 2:1–6; Jas 1:2–3; 1 Pet 1:6–7). See note on Job 1:9. **let me see your vengeance:** Vengeance against enemies is entrusted to the Lord (Deut 32:35). For prayers that wish ill on persecutors, see essay: *Imprecatory Psalms* at Ps 109.

20:13 he has delivered: Jeremiah's release from the stocks in 20:3 may be meant (cf. Ps 35:10; 109:31).

20:14–18 The sixth of Jeremiah's "confessions" to the Lord. Like Job in the midst of his agony, he curses the day of his birth as a day that made possible his present misery (Job 3:1–26). Cursing one's birthday is not the same as cursing one's parents, which was a capital offense in ancient Israel (Ex 21:17; Lev 20:9).

20:15 my father: Hilkiah (1:1).

20:16 the cities: Sodom and Gomorrah, overthrown by fire and brimstone (Gen 19:24–25). **an alarm:** An audible signal of war, such as a trumpet blast (Judg 7:19–23).

21:1–10 The king of Judah seeks assurance from Jeremiah that God will save Jerusalem from conquest (21:2), only to learn that its fall is certain (21:10), for God himself will fight against it (21:5–6). The only options left for the city: resist the enemy and die or surrender to the enemy and live (21:8–9).

21:1 Zedekiah: The last of the Davidic line of kings to rule in Jerusalem. He is installed on the throne in 597 B.C. after his predecessor, Jehoiachin, is exiled to Babylon (2 Kings 24:10–17). But after Zedekiah rebels against Babylonian rule in 588 B.C., Jerusalem is besieged by the Babylonian army (52:3–5), which will end in 586 B.C. with the city and Temple destroyed (52:12–14). **Pashhur:** Not the priest mentioned in 20:1, but another adversary who seeks Jeremiah's death (38:1–6). **Zephaniah:** A leading priest in Jerusalem (29:29) who is executed by the Babylonians at Riblah (52:24–27).

him Pashhur the son of Malchi'ah and Zephani'ah the priest, the son of Ma·asei'ah, saying, ²"Inquire of the LORD for us, for Nebuchadrez'zar king of Babylon is making war against us; perhaps the LORD will deal with us according to all his wonderful deeds, and will make him withdraw from us."

3 Then Jeremi'ah said to them: ⁴"Thus you shall say to Zedeki'ah, 'Thus says the LORD, the God of Israel: Behold, I will turn back the weapons of war which are in your hands and with which you are fighting against the king of Babylon and against the Chalde'ans who are besieging you outside the walls; and I will bring them together into the midst of this city. ⁵I myself will fight against you with outstretched hand and strong arm, in anger, and in fury, and in great wrath. ⁶And I will strike the inhabitants of this city, both man and beast; they shall die of a great pestilence. ⁷Afterward, says the LORD, I will give Zedeki'ah king of Judah, and his servants, and the people in this city who survive the pestilence, sword, and famine, into the hand of Nebuchadrez'zar king of Babylon and into the hand of their enemies, into the hand of those who seek their lives. He shall strike them with the edge of the sword; he shall not pity them, or spare them, or have compassion.'

8 "And to this people you shall say: 'Thus says the LORD: Behold, I set before you the way of life and the way of death. ⁹He who stays in this city shall die by the sword, by famine, and by pestilence; but he who goes out and surrenders to the Chalde'ans who are besieging you shall live and shall have his life as a prize of war. ¹⁰For I have set my face against this city for evil and not for good, says the LORD: it shall be given into the hand of the king of Babylon, and he shall burn it with fire.'

Message to the King of Judah

11 "And to the house of the king of Judah say, 'Hear the word of the LORD, ¹²O house of David! Thus says the LORD:

"'Execute justice in the morning,
    and deliver from the hand of the oppressor
    him who has been robbed,
lest my wrath go forth like fire,
    and burn with none to quench it,
    because of your evil doings.'"

¹³"Behold, I am against you, O inhabitant of the valley,
O rock of the plain,

                                    says the LORD;
you who say, 'Who shall come down against us,
    or who shall enter our habitations?'
¹⁴I will punish you according to the fruit of your doings,

                                    says the LORD;
    I will kindle a fire in her forest,
    and it shall devour all that is round about her."

Exhortation to Repentance

22 Thus says the LORD: "Go down to the house of the king of Judah, and speak there this word, ²and say, 'Hear the word of the LORD, O King of Judah, who sit on the throne of David, you, and your servants, and your people who enter these gates. ³Thus says the LORD: Do justice and righteousness, and deliver from the hand of the oppressor him who has been robbed. And do no wrong or violence to the alien, the fatherless, and the widow, nor shed innocent blood in this place. ⁴For if you will indeed obey this word, then there shall enter the gates of this house kings who sit

---

21:2 Nebuchadrezzar: An alternate spelling for Nebuchadnezzar, the founder and ruler of the Neo-Babylonian empire from 605 to 562 B.C. **all his wonderful deeds:** Zedekiah presumes upon the Lord's election of Zion, as though the city were unconquerable because the Temple resides there. Also, the Lord miraculously defended the city against an Assyrian assault in 701 B.C. See note on 7:4.

21:4 the Chaldeans: Another name for the Babylonians, its leading tribe in southern Mesopotamia being the Kaldu tribe.

21:5 I myself will fight: The fall of Jerusalem is assured by divine decree (21:10). **outstretched hand ... strong arm:** Expressions familiar from the Exodus story, only now the dreadful power of God is turned against Israel rather than against Egypt on Israel's behalf (Deut 4:34; 5:15). **anger ... fury ... great wrath:** Moses used this language when he foresaw the Lord punishing Israel with exile from the land (Deut 29:28).

21:7 pestilence, sword, and famine: Curses of the Mosaic covenant that bring death to violators of the covenant (Lev 26:25–26).

21:8 I set before you ... life ... death: A parody of the "two ways" of the covenant described by Moses, who assured Israel that obedience would lead to blessings and disobedience to curses (Deut 11:26–28; 30:15–20). In Jeremiah's day, the curse of national conquest is certain, and

the only way to save one's life is to surrender to the enemy as a captive destined for exile.

21:10 set my face against: An idiom for determined opposition. **burn it with fire:** Fulfilled in 52:13.

21:12 O house of David: An address to the Davidic royal family in Jerusalem. **Execute justice:** The administration of justice, especially for the poor and powerless, is one of the chief duties of the king (22:3; 1 Kings 3:28; Ps 72:1–4). **my wrath:** The chastisements that David is warned about when God makes a covenant of kingship with him (2 Sam 7:14–15).

21:13 O inhabitant ... O rock: An address to the city and surrounding villages of Jerusalem. The people, like their king, are deceived into thinking that Zion is invincible to attack (21:2).

21:14 her forest: An allusion to the royal palace built by Solomon, called "The House of the Forest of Lebanon" because of its towering cedar beams (1 Kings 7:20).

22:1–9 Jeremiah speaks in the Judean royal palace on the social responsibilities of kingship.

22:3 Do justice and righteousness: See notes on 21:12 and 2 Sam 8:15. **alien ... fatherless ... widow:** See note on 7:6.

22:4 if ... then: The continuation of the Davidic monarchy is conditional, i.e., it depends on the conduct of the Davidic kings (22:2).

on the throne of David, riding in chariots and on horses, they, and their servants, and their people. [5]But if you will not heed these words, I swear by myself, says the LORD, that this house shall become a desolation. [6]For thus says the LORD concerning the house of the king of Judah:

"'You are as Gilead to me,
    as the summit of Lebanon,
yet surely I will make you a desert,
    an uninhabited city.[k]
[7]I will prepare destroyers against you,
    each with his weapons;
and they shall cut down your choicest cedars,
    and cast them into the fire.

8 "'And many nations will pass by this city, and every man will say to his neighbor, "Why has the LORD dealt thus with this great city?" [9]And they will answer, "Because they forsook the covenant of the LORD their God, and worshiped other gods and served them."'"

[10]Weep not for him who is dead,
    nor bemoan him;
but weep bitterly for him who goes away,
    for he shall return no more
    to see his native land.

Message to the Sons of Josiah

11 For thus says the LORD concerning Shallum the son of Josi'ah, king of Judah, who reigned instead of Josiah his father, and who went away from this place: "He shall return here no more, [12]but in the place where they have carried him captive, there shall he die, and he shall never see this land again."

[13]"Woe to him who builds his house by
        unrighteousness,
    and his upper rooms by injustice;
who makes his neighbor serve him for nothing,
    and does not give him his wages;
[14]who says, 'I will build myself a great house
        with spacious upper rooms,'
    and cuts out windows for it,
        paneling it with cedar,
        and painting it with vermilion.
[15]Do you think you are a king
        because you compete in cedar?
Did not your father eat and drink
        and do justice and righteousness?
    Then it was well with him.
[16]He judged the cause of the poor and needy;
    then it was well.
Is not this to know me?
    says the LORD.
[17]But you have eyes and heart
        only for your dishonest gain,
    for shedding innocent blood,
        and for practicing oppression and violence."
[18]Therefore thus says the LORD concerning
        Jehoi'akim the son of Josi'ah, king of Judah:
"They shall not lament for him, saying,
    'Ah my brother!' or 'Ah sister!'
They shall not lament for him, saying,
    'Ah lord!' or 'Ah his majesty!'
[19]With the burial of a donkey he shall be buried,
        dragged and cast forth beyond the gates of
        Jerusalem."

[20]"Go up to Lebanon, and cry out,
        and lift up your voice in Bashan;

22:5: Mt 23:38; Lk 13:35.

22:5 this house: The royal house of David, which the Lord himself established by his covenant with David (2 Sam 7:12-16). See essay: *The Davidic Covenant* at 2 Sam 7.

22:6 Gilead ... Lebanon: Forested regions east and north of the land of Israel. The felling and burning of their trees in 22:7 signify the destruction of the king's palaces in Jerusalem, which in turn points to the fiery end of the Davidic monarchy in Judah. The Southern Kingdom of Judah, which endured for more than three centuries, will become like a deforested wasteland.

22:10-30 Oracles concerning three of the last four kings of Judah: Shallum/Jehoahaz (22:10-12), Jehoiakim (22:13-23), and Coniah/Jehoiachin (22:24-30).

22:10 him who is dead: Josiah, the fifteenth king of Judah, who was mortally wounded on the field of battle in 609 B.C. (2 Kings 23:29-30). **him who goes away:** Shallum, renamed Jehoahaz, the sixteenth king of Judah. He was taken captive by Pharaoh Neco after a short reign of three months in 609 B.C. (2 Kings 23:31-34). Shallum is the fourth son of Josiah (1 Chron 3:15).

22:12 there shall he die: In the land of Egypt (2 Kings 23:34).

22:13 Woe to him: Jehoiakim, the seventeenth king of Judah, who reigns from 609 to 598 B.C. He cares little about the appalling injustice in his realm; instead, he is preoccupied with building a luxurious palace for himself out of imported cedar (22:14-15). His corrupt regime is guilty of defrauding laborers, murdering innocents, and violent oppression (22:17; 2 Kings 24:4). Jehoiakim is the second son of Josiah (1 Chron 3:15). **serve him for nothing:** Suggests he conscripts forced laborers for his building projects, as Solomon did (1 Kings 5:13; 11:28). **wages:** Unlawful to withhold (Deut 24:14-15; Jas 5:4). • According to Catholic tradition, defrauding wage earners of payment is one of the sins that cries out to heaven (CCC 1867, 2213).

22:15 your father: Josiah, one of Judah's most righteous kings (2 Kings 22:1-2; 23:24-25).

22:18 Ah...!: The Hebrew exclamation is *hôy*, often translated "woe". It is a cry of anguish heard at funerals in biblical times. See word study: *Woe* at Is 28:1.

22:19 a donkey: Not actually buried but taken outside city walls to decay in the wild. The imagery is poetic, signifying the dishonorable end that Jehoiakim deserves in contrast to the elaborate state funeral expected for a king. Historically, he is buried with his ancestors (2 Kings 24:6).

22:20 Lebanon ... Bashan ... Abarim: Mountainous regions north of Israel, east of the Sea of Galilee and east of the Jordan River, respectively.

---

[k]Cn: Heb *cities*.

cry from Ab′arim,
    for all your lovers are destroyed.
[21]I spoke to you in your prosperity,
    but you said, 'I will not listen.'
This has been your way from your youth,
    that you have not obeyed my voice.
[22]The wind shall shepherd all your shepherds,
    and your lovers shall go into captivity;
then you will be ashamed and confounded
    because of all your wickedness.
[23]O inhabitant of Lebanon,
    nested among the cedars,
how you will groan[1] when pangs come upon you,
    pain as of a woman with labor pains!"

Message concerning Coniah
the Son of Jehoiakim

24 "As I live, says the LORD, though Coni′ah the son of Jehoi′akim, king of Judah, were the signet ring on my right hand, yet I would tear you off [25]and give you into the hand of those who seek your life, into the hand of those of whom you are afraid, even into the hand of Nebuchadrez′zar king of Babylon and into the hand of the Chalde′ans. [26]I will hurl you and the mother who bore you into another country, where you were not born, and there you shall die. [27]But to the land to which they will long to return, there they shall not return."
[28]Is this man Coni′ah a despised, broken pot,
    a vessel no one cares for?

Why are he and his children hurled and cast
    into a land which they do not know?
[29]O land, land, land,
    hear the word of the LORD!
[30]Thus says the LORD:
"Write this man down as childless,
    a man who shall not succeed in his days;
for none of his offspring shall succeed
    in sitting on the throne of David,
    and ruling again in Judah."

A Remnant to Be Restored after Exile

23 "Woe to the shepherds who destroy and scatter the sheep of my pasture!" says the LORD. [2]Therefore thus says the LORD, the God of Israel, concerning the shepherds who care for my people: "You have scattered my flock, and have driven them away, and you have not attended to them. Behold, I will attend to you for your evil doings, says the LORD. [3]Then I will gather the remnant of my flock out of all the countries where I have driven them, and I will bring them back to their fold, and they shall be fruitful and multiply. [4]I will set shepherds over them who will care for them, and they shall fear no more, nor be dismayed, neither shall any be missing, says the LORD.

The Righteous Branch

5 "Behold, the days are coming, says the LORD, when I will raise up for David a righteous Branch, and he shall reign as king and deal wisely, and shall

---

23:5: Jer 33:15; Is 4:2; Zech 3:8; 6:12.

22:24 As I live: An oath formula. **Coniah:** A shortened form of Jeconiah (24:1), also known as King Jehoiachin, who reigns over Judah for three months in 598–597 B.C. He is taken as a captive to Babylon in 597 B.C. (2 Kings 24:15) and eventually released from prison around 560 B.C. (52:31–34). **signet ring:** One of a king's most prized possessions. It was engraved with royal insignia and was used to seal official documents.

22:25 Nebuchadrezzar: An alternate spelling for Nebuchadnezzar, ruler of the Neo-Babylonian empire from 605 to 562 B.C.

22:26 the mother who bore you: Nehushta, the royal queen mother, who is exiled to Babylon with her son in 597 B.C. (2 Kings 24:8, 15).

📖 **22:30 childless:** Dynastically, not literally. Jeconiah/Jehoiachin already has several sons (= the "children" of 22:28), but the prophecy declares that none of them will reign as a king in Jerusalem, since the Davidic monarchy is about to collapse and disappear from the stage of history. • Not until the coming of Jesus will another heir from David's royal line (Mt 1:1–16) assume David's throne (Lk 1:32–33). Peter sees its fulfillment in Jesus' enthronement at the Father's right hand in heaven (Acts 2:29–36). **his offspring:** Jeconiah/Jehoiachin and his sons are mentioned outside the Bible on clay tablets from ancient Babylon. In harmony with 52:34 and 2 Kings 25:30, they speak of the exiled king and his family receiving food rations from the Babylonian government.

23:1–40 Jeremiah denounces Judah's kings (23:1–8) and false prophets (23:9–40) for failing the Lord's people (23:2)

and deceiving them into thinking that all is well (23:17). Judgment is near at hand, but the prophet envisions a more distant future when the Lord will raise up faithful shepherds to care for his flock (23:4) along with a truly godly king, the Davidic Messiah (23:5–6).

23:1 Woe: A cry of anguish heard at funerals. See word study: *Woe* at Is 28:1. **the shepherds:** The wicked kings of Israel and Judah, whose godless reigns have left the flock of God's people (Ps 95:7) scattered and exiled (Ezek 34:1–10). These will be replaced by worthy shepherds in the future (23:4).

23:2 driven them away: Israel's northern tribes have long since gone into Assyrian exile (2 Kings 15:29; 17:6), and the Babylonian Exile of the southern tribes already began in 605 (Dan 1:1–7) and 597 B.C. (2 Kings 24:10–16). Thousands more will go to Babylon in 586 B.C. (52:28–30; 2 Kings 25:11).

23:3 I will gather the remnant: Those who repent and return to the Lord in exile will be restored, as foreseen in the Law of Moses (Deut 30:1–5).

📖🕊 **23:5 the days are coming:** The days of restoration that will follow Judah's imminent judgment. **I will raise up for David:** A messianic prophecy. The future Messiah will be a wise and upright king from David's line who will rule over the reunited family of Israel and Judah (23:6) at an unspecified time after the disappearance of the Davidic monarchy in 586 B.C. For similar prophecies of a Davidic Messiah, see 30:9; 33:15; Is 9:6–7; 11:1–10; Ezek 34:23; Hos 3:5. • Only one remedy could help the fallen human race, namely, that one of the sons of Adam should be born innocent of the original transgression and achieve victory for the rest by his example and merits. Yet there could be no offspring from our sinful race without seed. Only the Lord could do this, and

---

[1]Gk Vg Syr: Heb *be pitied.*

execute justice and righteousness in the land. [6]In his days Judah will be saved, and Israel will dwell securely. And this is the name by which he will be called: 'The LORD is our righteousness.'

7 "Therefore, behold, the days are coming, says the LORD, when men shall no longer say, 'As the LORD lives who brought up the sons of Israel out of the land of Egypt,' [8]but 'As the LORD lives who brought up and led the descendants of the house of Israel out of the north country and out of all the countries where he[m] had driven them.' Then they shall dwell in their own land."

False Prophets Denounced

9 Concerning the prophets:
My heart is broken within me,
   all my bones shake;
I am like a drunken man,
   like a man overcome by wine,
because of the LORD
   and because of his holy words.

[10]For the land is full of adulterers;
   because of the curse the land mourns,
   and the pastures of the wilderness are dried up.
Their course is evil,
   and their might is not right.
[11]"Both prophet and priest are ungodly;
   even in my house I have found their
    wickedness,
               says the LORD.
[12]Therefore their way shall be to them
   like slippery paths in the darkness,
   into which they shall be driven and fall;
   for I will bring evil upon them
   in the year of their punishment,
               says the LORD.
[13]In the prophets of Samar'ia
   I saw an unsavory thing:
   they prophesied by Ba'al
   and led my people Israel astray.
[14]But in the prophets of Jerusalem
   I have seen a horrible thing:

---

so he made David's Lord a son of David, and from the fruit of the promised Branch sprang one without fault, one Person in whom two natures come together. By one and the same conception and birth sprang our Lord Jesus Christ, in whom was present true divinity and true humanity (St. Leo the Great, *Sermons* 28, 3). **justice and righteousness:** Required by the kings of Israel and Judah as earthly representatives of God and his rule. See note 2 Sam 8:15.

23:6 The LORD is our righteousness: A play on the name of Judah's last king, Zedekiah, which means "The LORD is my righteousness."

23:8 As the LORD lives: A new formula for swearing oaths that will replace the old formula (23:7). For other things that Judah will no longer say in the future, see 3:16; 7:32; 31:29. **brought up ... Israel:** The prophet foresees a new and greater exodus of the Israelites from Babylon and the lands of exile that will surpass their original Exodus from Egypt. After the coming judgment, he expects a new deliverance and a new outpouring of mercy, more fully elaborated in Jer 31–33. See essay: *The New Exodus in Isaiah* in Is 43.

the north country: Babylon and Assyria (50:17–20). See note on 1:14.

23:9–40 Jeremiah exposes the false prophets of his day. They present themselves as divine messengers, but the Lord did not send them, speak his word to them, or admit them to his secret counsel (23:18, 21). They allege having prophetic dreams, but their visions come from their own minds (23:16). Worst of all, they embolden people to continue in evil (23:14) by prophesying nothing but peace and security (23:17).

23:9 My heart is broken: The distraught cries of Jeremiah, who sees his country headed for ruin (23:12).

23:10 adulterers: Marital infidelity was a serious problem (23:14; 29:23). Alternatively, the prophet could be speaking about idolaters, whose worship of pagan gods is a betrayal of Israel's marital covenant with the Lord (2:2). **the curse:** Perhaps the drought mentioned in 14:1.

23:11 prophet and priest: Judah's corrupt religious leaders, who are often linked together in the book (2:8; 4:9; 6:13; 8:10). **even in my house:** For abominations in the Temple, see 2 Kings 23:7; Ezek 8:5–18.

23:13 the prophets of Samaria: The northern prophets of Baal, the storm and fertility god of Canaanite religion (1 Kings 18:20–40).

[m] Gk: Heb *I*.

Word Study

Branch (23:5)

Ṣemaḥ (Heb.): a noun indicating various types of vegetative growth, from the stem and branches of a plant or tree (Is 61:11) to the tendrils of a vine (Ezek 17:8) to the herbage that covers landscapes in the wild (Gen 19:25). It is this "growth" of the earth that God blesses with rain (Ps 65:10). Less frequently but more significantly, the image of a branch represents a sign of hope. In one passage, the Lord's "branch" is the holy remnant of his people who dwell in a purified Jerusalem (Is 4:2). In several others, it serves as a title for a royal descendant of David. Initially this "branch" refers to Zerubbabel, who is a key figure in the rebuilding of the Jerusalem Temple after the Babylonian Exile (Zech 3:8; 6:12). Ultimately, however, it is a title for the Davidic Messiah, an ideal king who will shepherd God's people with perfect justice and righteousness (Jer 23:5; 33:15). This image of the Messiah as a sprouting "branch" is likely indebted to Is 11:1, where the stump of David's royal house shows signs of life—a "branch" (Heb., *nēṣer*) that rises up as a king anointed with God's Spirit (Is 11:2) and sought by the nations (Is 11:10). There is a difference in the terms used by Jeremiah and Isaiah, but both prophets paint the same picture of the same royal person.

they commit adultery and walk in lies;
  they strengthen the hands of evildoers,
  so that no one turns from his wickedness;
all of them have become like Sodom to me,
  and its inhabitants like Gomor′rah."
[15]Therefore thus says the LORD of hosts concerning the prophets:
  "Behold, I will feed them with wormwood,
  and give them poisoned water to drink;
for from the prophets of Jerusalem
  ungodliness has gone forth into all the land."

16 Thus says the LORD of hosts: "Do not listen to the words of the prophets who prophesy to you, filling you with vain hopes; they speak visions of their own minds, not from the mouth of the LORD. [17]They say continually to those who despise the word of the LORD, 'It shall be well with you'; and to every one who stubbornly follows his own heart, they say, 'No evil shall come upon you.'"

[18]For who among them has stood in the council of
    the LORD
    to perceive and to hear his word,
    or who has given heed to his word and
    listened?
[19]Behold, the storm of the LORD!
    Wrath has gone forth,
  a whirling tempest;
    it will burst upon the head of the wicked.
[20]The anger of the LORD will not turn back
    until he has executed and accomplished
    the intents of his mind.
  In the latter days you will understand it clearly.

[21]"I did not send the prophets,
    yet they ran;
  I did not speak to them,
    yet they prophesied.
[22]But if they had stood in my council,
    then they would have proclaimed my words to
    my people,

and they would have turned them from their evil
    way,
  and from the evil of their doings.

23 "Am I a God at hand, says the LORD, and not a God afar off? [24]Can a man hide himself in secret places so that I cannot see him? says the LORD. Do I not fill heaven and earth? says the LORD. [25]I have heard what the prophets have said who prophesy lies in my name, saying, 'I have dreamed, I have dreamed!' [26]How long shall there be lies[n] in the heart of the prophets who prophesy lies, and who prophesy the deceit of their own heart, [27]who think to make my people forget my name by their dreams which they tell one another, even as their fathers forgot my name for Ba′al? [28]Let the prophet who has a dream tell the dream, but let him who has my word speak my word faithfully. What has straw in common with wheat? says the LORD. [29]Is not my word like fire, says the LORD, and like a hammer which breaks the rock in pieces? [30]Therefore, behold, I am against the prophets, says the LORD, who steal my words from one another. [31]Behold, I am against the prophets, says the LORD, who use their tongues and say, 'Says the LORD.' [32]Behold, I am against those who prophesy lying dreams, says the LORD, and who tell them and lead my people astray by their lies and their recklessness, when I did not send them or charge them; so they do not profit this people at all, says the LORD.

33 "When one of this people, or a prophet, or a priest asks you, 'What is the burden of the LORD?' you shall say to them, 'You are the burden,[o] and I will cast you off, says the LORD.' [34]And as for the prophet, priest, or one of the people who says, 'The burden of the LORD,' I will punish that man and his household. [35]Thus shall you say, every one to his neighbor and every one to his brother, 'What has the LORD answered?' or 'What has the LORD spoken?' [36]But 'the burden of the LORD' you shall mention no more, for the burden is every man's own word, and you pervert the words of the living

---

23:15 wormwood: A shrub that grows in arid regions and has leaves that are extremely bitter (9:15; Prov 5:4; Lam 3:15; Rev 8:11).

23:17 It shall be well with you: The false assurance that Judah can expect "peace" when death and disaster approach (6:14; 8:11).

23:18 the council of the LORD: The heavenly court, with God presiding on his throne over an assembly of angels (1 Kings 22:19–23). True prophets like Jeremiah are given privileged access to the deliberations and decisions of this council, enabling them to proclaim the Lord's plan for his people and for the course of salvation history. False prophets never have admission to these secret proceedings, and so their claims to speak for God or his plans for the future are fraudulent.

23:20 the latter days: See word study: *The Latter Days* at Is 2:2.

23:24 Do I not fill heaven and earth?: A rhetorical question implying that God is omnipresent (1 Kings 8:27). Because he transcends the limits of space, there is no place in his creation that is beyond the reach of his power or sight (CCC 300).

23:25 I have dreamed: Sometimes dreams are channels of divine revelation in Scripture, but claims to have received a communication from God must be measured by the standard of the covenant (Deut 13:1–5) to make sure they are not "lying dreams" (23:32). See word study: *Dream* at Gen 37:5.

23:28 straw ... wheat: A contrast between false prophecy and true prophecy, only the latter of which gives nourishment to God's people.

23:33 burden: The Hebrew *massāʾ* can mean both "burden" (Ex 23:5) and "oracle" (Is 14:28). It is the subject of a wordplay: Judah accepts the words of the false prophets when they claim to deliver an oracle from God (23:26); but because they "pervert the words of the living God" (23:36), they have become a burden to the Lord that he is ready to cast off (23:33).

---

[n] Cn Compare Syr: Heb obscure.
[o] Gk Vg: Heb *What burden*.

God, the LORD of hosts, our God. ³⁷Thus you shall say to the prophet, 'What has the LORD answered you?' or 'What has the LORD spoken?' ³⁸But if you say, 'The burden of the LORD,' thus says the LORD, 'Because you have said these words, "The burden of the LORD," when I sent to you, saying, "You shall not say, 'The burden of the LORD,'" ³⁹therefore, behold, I will surely lift you up and cast you away from my presence, you and the city which I gave to you and your fathers. ⁴⁰And I will bring upon you everlasting reproach and perpetual shame, which shall not be forgotten.'"

Two Baskets: Good and Bad Figs

24 After Nebuchadrez'zar king of Babylon had taken into exile from Jerusalem Jeconi'ah the son of Jehoi'akim, king of Judah, together with the princes of Judah, the craftsmen, and the smiths, and had brought them to Babylon, the LORD showed me this vision: Behold, two baskets of figs placed before the temple of the LORD. ²One basket had very good figs, like first-ripe figs, but the other basket had very bad figs, so bad that they could not be eaten. ³And the LORD said to me, "What do you see, Jeremi'ah?" I said, "Figs, the good figs very good, and the bad figs very bad, so bad that they cannot be eaten."

4 Then the word of the LORD came to me: ⁵"Thus says the LORD, the God of Israel: Like these good figs, so I will regard as good the exiles from Judah, whom I have sent away from this place to the land of the Chalde'ans. ⁶I will set my eyes upon them for good, and I will bring them back to this land. I will build them up, and not tear them down; I will plant them, and not uproot them. ⁷I will give them a heart to know that I am the LORD; and they shall be my people and I will be their God, for they shall return to me with their whole heart.

8 "But thus says the LORD: Like the bad figs which are so bad they cannot be eaten, so will I treat Zedeki'ah the king of Judah, his princes, the remnant of Jerusalem who remain in this land, and those who dwell in the land of Egypt. ⁹I will make them a horror**ᵖ** to all the kingdoms of the earth, to be a reproach, a byword, a taunt, and a curse in all the places where I shall drive them. ¹⁰And I will send sword, famine, and pestilence upon them, until they shall be utterly destroyed from the land which I gave to them and their fathers."

The Babylonian Captivity Foretold

25 The word that came to Jeremi'ah concerning all the people of Judah, in the fourth year of Jehoi'akim the son of Josi'ah, king of Judah (that was the first year of Nebuchadrez'zar king of Babylon), ²which Jeremi'ah the prophet spoke to all the people of Judah and all the inhabitants of Jerusalem: ³"For twenty-three years, from the thirteenth year of Josi'ah the son of A'mon, king of Judah, to this day, the word of the LORD has come to me, and I have spoken persistently to you, but you have not listened. ⁴You have neither listened nor inclined your ears to hear, although the LORD persistently sent to you all his servants the prophets, ⁵saying, 'Turn now, every one of you, from his evil way and wrong doings, and dwell upon the land which the LORD has given to you and your fathers from of old and for ever; ⁶do not go after other gods to serve

---

24:1–10 A vision of good and bad figs. The **good figs** are the captives from Judah taken to Babylon in 597 B.C.; they are blessed and will eventually return to the land to start a new life (24:4–7). The **bad figs** are the people left behind in Judah after the first deportations; they seem to have been spared God's wrath, but in fact they are headed for destruction (23:8–10; 29:16–17). The vision corrects a misunderstanding among the bad figs, who wrongly think they are favored by God because they escaped captivity in 597 (cf. Ezek 11:14–16). A key theological premise is that exile and its sufferings purge the sins of the good figs (Is 40:1–2) (CCC 710).

24:1 Nebuchadrezzar: An alternate spelling of Nebuchadnezzar, ruler of the Neo-Babylonian empire from 605 to 562 B.C. **Jeconiah:** King Jehoiachin, who is exiled to Babylon in 597 B.C. (2 Kings 24:10–15). His name appears as Coniah in 22:24. **vision:** A prophetic message that God conveys through images (as in Amos 7:1—9:15). **figs:** First become ripe in early summer.

24:5 Chaldeans: Babylonians.

📖 **24:7 I will give them a heart:** One of the great hopes of biblical prophecy: the Lord will heal his people in the depths of their being and will give them a new strength to obey him. Moses describes this as a circumcision of the heart (Deut 30:6), whereas Jeremiah and Ezekiel describe it as God giving his people a new heart inscribed with his Law (Jer 31:33; Ezek 11:19–20; 36:26). See note on Bar 2:31. **my people ... their God:** The covenant between the Lord and

Israel (Lev 26:12) will be reaffirmed with the remnant that returns from exile (Ezek 37:27).

24:8 Zedekiah: The last king of Judah, who reigns from 597 to 586 B.C.

24:10 sword, famine, and pestilence: Curses of the Mosaic covenant that bring suffering and death to violators of the covenant (Lev 26:25–26).

25:1–14 Jeremiah prophesies that Judah, overrun with idolatry, is about to become a wasteland. The same devastation awaits neighboring nations in the region, who will likewise fall before the oncoming armies of Babylon (25:9). The good news is that after 70 years of Babylonian rule, the Lord will punish this conquering nation for its iniquities (25:12–14).

25:1 the fourth year: 605 B.C. **Jehoiakim:** King of Judah from 609 to 598 B.C. **Nebuchadrezzar:** An alternate spelling of Nebuchadnezzar, ruler of the Neo-Babylonian empire from 605 to 562 B.C. His forces defeated the Egyptians at Carchemish in 605, making Babylonia the imperial superpower of the Near East for the next several decades.

25:3 For twenty-three years: Since 627 B.C., the time of Jeremiah's initial call to ministry (1:2).

25:4 sent ... prophets: Jeremiah is not the only genuine prophet who speaks God's word to the Southern Kingdom of Judah in the years before its demise. Another is Uriah, son of Shemaiah (26:20).

25:5 Turn now, every one: Summarizes the prophet's repeated call for repentance. See word study: *Return* at 3:1.

25:6 the work of your hands: Idol images, which are products of human craftsmanship (10:3–5).

ᵖ Compare Gk: Heb *horror for evil.*

and worship them, or provoke me to anger with the work of your hands. Then I will do you no harm.' [7]Yet you have not listened to me, says the LORD, that you might provoke me to anger with the work of your hands to your own harm.

8 "Therefore thus says the LORD of hosts: Because you have not obeyed my words, [9]behold, I will send for all the tribes of the north, says the LORD, and for Nebuchadrez'zar the king of Babylon, my servant, and I will bring them against this land and its inhabitants, and against all these nations round about; I will utterly destroy them, and make them a horror, a hissing, and an everlasting reproach.ᑫ [10]Moreover, I will banish from them the voice of mirth and the voice of gladness, the voice of the bridegroom and the voice of the bride, the grinding of the millstones and the light of the lamp. [11]This whole land shall become a ruin and a waste, and these nations shall serve the king of Babylon seventy years. [12]Then after seventy years are completed, I will punish the king of Babylon and that nation, the land of the Chalde'ans, for their iniquity, says the LORD, making the land an everlasting waste. [13]I will bring upon that land all the words which I have uttered against it, everything written in this book, which Jeremi'ah prophesied against all the nations. [14]For many nations and great kings shall make slaves even of them; and I will recompense them according to their deeds and the work of their hands."

The Cup of the Lord's Wrath

15 Thus the LORD, the God of Israel, said to me: "Take from my hand this cup of the wine of wrath, and make all the nations to whom I send you drink it. [16]They shall drink and stagger and be crazed because of the sword which I am sending among them."

17 So I took the cup from the LORD's hand, and made all the nations to whom the Lord sent me drink it: [18]Jerusalem and the cities of Judah, its kings and princes, to make them a desolation and a waste, a hissing and a curse, as at this day; [19]Pharaoh king of Egypt, his servants, his princes, all his people, [20]and all the foreign folk among them; all the kings of the land of Uz and all the kings of the land of the Philis'tines (Ash'kelon, Gaza, Ek'ron, and the remnant of Ash'dod); [21]E'dom, Moab, and the sons of Ammon; [22]all the kings of Tyre, all the kings of Sidon, and the kings of the islands across the sea; [23]De'dan, Te'ma, Buz, and all who cut the corners of their hair; [24]all the kings of Arabia and all the kings of the mixed tribes that dwell in the desert; [25]all the kings of Zimri, all the kings of E'lam, and all the kings of Med'ia; [26]all the kings of the north, far and near, one after another, and all the kingdoms of the

---

25:10: Jer 7:34; 16:9; Rev 18:23.   **25:15:** Jer 51:7; Rev 14:8, 10; 16:19; 17:4; 18:3.

25:9 the north: See note on 1:14. **my servant:** Means, not that the Babylonian king is a devout worshiper of the Lord, but that God will use him as an instrument of his wrath against Judah and other nations. The Lord, who steers the course of world history, can direct even the mightiest nations and rulers to fulfill his purposes (27:6; Is 10:5-11). God will similarly raise up Cyrus II of Persia as his anointed servant to release Judah's exiles from Babylon and to help finance the rebuilding of the Jerusalem Temple (Ezra 1:1-4; Is 44:28—45:1). **a hissing:** See note on 18:16.

25:10 voice of the bridegroom: The joyous sounds of wedding celebrations will cease when disaster strikes (7:34; 16:9). They will not be heard again until the Lord restores his people after judgment (33:10-11). **grinding of the millstones:** Represents the ordinary activities of life.

25:11 seventy years: A round number for the period of Judah's subjugation to Babylon, after which the Lord will judge Babylon and the return of Judah's exiles will begin (25:12; 29:10). This period begins in 605 B.C., when Judah becomes a vassal state of Babylon, and extends to 539 B.C., when Babylon falls to the Persians, and even to 538 B.C., when Cyrus II of Persia releases the Jewish exiles from Babylon—a period approximating seven decades. Seventy years also represents a full lifespan, and so part of the message is that only the children of Judah's exiles will reap the blessings of the prophecy, not their parents (Ps 90:10; Is 23:15). For other references to Jeremiah's prophecy, see 2 Chron 36:22-23; Ezra 1:1-4; Dan 9:2.

25:13 in this book: Meaning obscure, since Jeremiah has not prophesied against other nations prior to this point. However, in the Greek LXX, which may preserve a more ancient form of the book, Jeremiah's oracles against the nations (= chaps.

46-51) appear immediately following this verse. See introduction: *Literary Background*.

25:14 many nations: Such as the Persians and the Medes. **great kings:** Such as Cyrus II of Persia.

25:15-29 A vision that confirms Jeremiah's appointment as "a prophet to the nations" (1:5, 10).

25:15 cup of the wine of wrath: An image of judgment, in which evildoers are made to drink wine that causes them to stumble in a drunken stupor toward destruction (Ps 75:8; Is 51:17; Ezek 23:31-34; Obad 16; Rev 18:6). Nations set to imbibe God's wrath include Judah, its closest neighbors, peoples east of Mesopotamia, and finally Babylon (25:18-26). Oracles against these nations appear in chaps. 46-51. See note on Is 51:17.

25:16 the sword: Another image of the Lord's judgment (Deut 32:41; Ezek 21:9-10).

25:20 the land of Uz: Associated with Edom, southeast of Judah (Gen 36:28; Lam 4:21). It was home to the biblical figure of Job (Job 1:1). **Ashkelon ... Ashdod:** Philistine coastal cites west of Judah.

25:21 Edom: South of the Dead Sea. **Moab ... Ammon:** East of the Jordan River.

25:22 Tyre ... Sidon: Phoenician port cities northwest of the land of Israel.

25:23 Dedan, Tema, Buz: Peoples in northern Arabia. **cut the corners of their hair:** Shaving hair from the temples was a religious rite among ancient Arabian tribes (Herodotus, *Histories* 3, 8).

25:25 Zimri: Location unknown. **Elam ... Media:** Ancient lands within the borders of modern Iran.

25:26 Babylon: The Hebrew is *shēshakh*, a cipher for Babylon created by reversing the order of the Hebrew alphabet, with the last letter of the alphabet corresponding to the first letter, the second-to-last letter to the second letter, etc.

ᑫGk Compare Syr: Heb *desolations*.

world which are on the face of the earth. And after them the king of Babylon[r] shall drink.

27 "Then you shall say to them, 'Thus says the LORD of hosts, the God of Israel: Drink, be drunk and vomit, fall and rise no more, because of the sword which I am sending among you.'

28 "And if they refuse to accept the cup from your hand to drink, then you shall say to them, 'Thus says the LORD of hosts: You must drink! [29]For behold, I begin to work evil at the city which is called by my name, and shall you go unpunished? You shall not go unpunished, for I am summoning a sword against all the inhabitants of the earth, says the LORD of hosts.'

30 "You, therefore, shall prophesy against them all these words, and say to them:

'The LORD will roar from on high,
    and from his holy habitation utter his voice;
he will roar mightily against his fold,
    and shout, like those who tread grapes,
    against all the inhabitants of the earth.
[31]The clamor will resound to the ends of the earth,
    for the LORD has an indictment against the
        nations;
he is entering into judgment with all flesh,
    and the wicked he will put to the sword,
                    says the LORD.'

[32]"Thus says the LORD of hosts:
Behold, evil is going forth
    from nation to nation,
and a great tempest is stirring
    from the farthest parts of the earth!

33 "And those slain by the LORD on that day shall extend from one end of the earth to the other. They shall not be lamented, or gathered, or buried; they shall be dung on the surface of the ground.
[34]"Wail, you shepherds, and cry,
    and roll in ashes, you lords of the flock,

for the days of your slaughter and dispersion
        have come,
    and you shall fall like choice rams.[s]
[35]No refuge will remain for the shepherds,
    nor escape for the lords of the flock.
[36]Listen, the cry of the shepherds,
    and the wail of the lords of the flock!
For the LORD is despoiling their pasture,
[37]and the peaceful folds are devastated,
    because of the fierce anger of the LORD.
[38]Like a lion he has left his den,
    for their land has become a waste
because of the sword of the oppressor,
    and because of his fierce anger."

Jeremiah Threatened with Death

26 In the beginning of the reign of Jehoi'akim the son of Josi'ah, king of Judah, this word came from the LORD, [2]"Thus says the LORD: Stand in the court of the LORD's house, and speak to all the cities of Judah which come to worship in the house of the LORD all the words that I command you to speak to them; do not hold back a word. [3]It may be they will listen, and every one turn from his evil way, that I may repent of the evil which I intend to do to them because of their evil doings. [4]You shall say to them, 'Thus says the LORD: If you will not listen to me, to walk in my law which I have set before you, [5]and to heed the words of my servants the prophets whom I send to you urgently, though you have not heeded, [6]then I will make this house like Shiloh, and I will make this city a curse for all the nations of the earth.'"

7 The priests and the prophets and all the people heard Jeremi'ah speaking these words in the house of the LORD. [8]And when Jeremi'ah had finished speaking all that the LORD had commanded him to speak to all the people, then the priests and the prophets and all the people laid hold of him, saying,

---

25:30 will roar: The Lord is pictured as a fearsome lion (25:38; 50:44), as elsewhere in the prophets (Hos 5:14; Amos 1:2; Joel 3:16). **his holy habitation:** His "holy temple" in heaven (Ps 11:4). **those who tread grapes:** It was customary at the vintage harvest to press out the juice with songs and shouts (Is 16:10). Here it is an image of God stomping down the nations in judgment (Is 63:1–3; Joel 3:13).

25:33 that day: See note on Is 2:12 and word study: *The Day of the LORD* at Joel 1:15. **shall not be lamented ... or buried:** Because none will survive to weep for the slain or bury their dead (14:16; 16:6).

25:34 you shepherds: Kings and rulers of nations are addressed. **roll in ashes:** A mourning ritual. See note on 6:26.

26:1–24 Jeremiah's Temple sermon, delivered in 609 B.C. A fuller account of this sermon appears in 7:1–8:3, but here attention is focused on the reaction that follows his preaching. In this instance, the religious leaders of Judah clamor for the prophet's death (26:8), while the royal leaders of Judah intervene to prevent his death (26:16, 24). His alleged blasphemy:

Jeremiah uttered God's threat to destroy the city and Temple of Jerusalem (26:9, 11) if the people failed to repent (26:4–6). Other prophets such as Micah and Uriah issue the same warning (26:18, 20).

26:1 Jehoiakim: King of Judah from 609 to 598 B.C.

26:2 the LORD's house: The Temple in Jerusalem. **do not hold back:** I.e., out of fear of the opposition that God's message will provoke (1:17–19).

26:3 I may repent: See note on 18:8. **the evil which I intend:** Not moral evil, which is incompatible with God's goodness, but the "disaster" or "calamity" he sends to those who refuse to repent of moral evil. See note on Amos 3:6.

26:6 Shiloh: A former location of God's sanctuary (Josh 18:1). See note on 7:12.

26:7 priests ... prophets: The corrupt priests and false prophets of Judah (2:8; 4:9; 6:13; 8:10; 23:11).

26:8 You shall die!: Jeremiah's words are perceived as blasphemy against the divine name (Lev 24:10–23), which is linked with "the place" where the Lord dwells and where his people offer sacrifice (Deut 12:10–11; 1 Kings 5:5). That Judah's leaders think the Temple guarantees Jerusalem's safety, see note on 7:4.

---

[r] Heb *Sheshach*, a cipher for Babylon.
[s] Gk: Heb *a choice vessel*.

"You shall die! ⁹Why have you prophesied in the name of the Lᴏʀᴅ, saying, 'This house shall be like Shiloh, and this city shall be desolate, without inhabitant'?" And all the people gathered about Jeremi′ah in the house of the Lᴏʀᴅ.

10 When the princes of Judah heard these things, they came up from the king's house to the house of the Lᴏʀᴅ and took their seat in the entry of the New Gate of the house of the Lᴏʀᴅ. ¹¹Then the priests and the prophets said to the princes and to all the people, "This man deserves the sentence of death, because he has prophesied against this city, as you have heard with your own ears."

12 Then Jeremi′ah spoke to all the princes and all the people, saying, "The Lᴏʀᴅ sent me to prophesy against this house and this city all the words you have heard. ¹³Now therefore amend your ways and your doings, and obey the voice of the Lᴏʀᴅ your God, and the Lᴏʀᴅ will repent of the evil which he has pronounced against you. ¹⁴But as for me, behold, I am in your hands. Do with me as seems good and right to you. ¹⁵Only know for certain that if you put me to death, you will bring innocent blood upon yourselves and upon this city and its inhabitants, for in truth the Lᴏʀᴅ sent me to you to speak all these words in your ears."

16 Then the princes and all the people said to the priests and the prophets, "This man does not deserve the sentence of death, for he has spoken to us in the name of the Lᴏʀᴅ our God." ¹⁷And certain of the elders of the land arose and spoke to all the assembled people, saying, ¹⁸"Micah of Mo′resheth prophesied in the days of Hezeki′ah king of Judah, and said to all the people of Judah: 'Thus says the Lᴏʀᴅ of hosts,

Zion shall be plowed as a field;
     Jerusalem shall become a heap of ruins,
          and the mountain of the house a wooded height.'

¹⁹Did Hezeki′ah king of Judah and all Judah put him to death? Did he not fear the Lᴏʀᴅ and entreat the favor of the Lᴏʀᴅ, and did not the Lᴏʀᴅ repent of the evil which he had pronounced against them? But we are about to bring great evil upon ourselves."

20 There was another man who prophesied in the name of the Lᴏʀᴅ, Uri′ah the son of Shemai′ah from Kir′iath-je′arim. He prophesied against this city and against this land in words like those of Jeremi′ah. ²¹And when King Jehoi′akim, with all his warriors and all the princes, heard his words, the king sought to put him to death; but when Uri′ah heard of it, he was afraid and fled and escaped to Egypt. ²²Then King Jehoi′akim sent to Egypt certain men, Elna′than the son of Achbor and others with him, ²³and they fetched Uri′ah from Egypt and brought him to King Jehoi′akim, who slew him with the sword and cast his dead body into the burial place of the common people.

²⁴But the hand of Ahi′kam the son of Sha′phan was with Jeremi′ah so that he was not given over to the people to be put to death.

The Sign of the Thongs and Yoke-bars

27 In the beginning of the reign of Zedeki′ahᵘ the son of Josi′ah, king of Judah, this word came to Jeremi′ah from the Lᴏʀᴅ. ²Thus the Lᴏʀᴅ said to me: "Make yourself thongs and yoke-bars, and put them on your neck. ³Send wordᵛ to the king of E′dom, the king of Moab, the king of the sons of Ammon, the king of Tyre, and the king of Si′don by

---

26:10 princes: Royal officials who serve as judges in Jerusalem (cf. Ps 122:3–5). **New Gate:** Location uncertain.

26:16 in the name of the Lᴏʀᴅ: The first criterion of a true prophet, which is met in Jeremiah as well as his contemporary, Uriah (26:20). False prophets of the day sometimes spoke in the name of the Lord (27:15) but also in the name of Baal (2:8; 23:13).

26:18 Micah of Moresheth: Prophesied in the Southern Kingdom of Judah in the late eighth century. He is one of the Minor Prophets whose oracles are preserved in the Bible (Mic 1:1). The court elders argue that sparing Jeremiah's life and heeding his call to repentance would be wise, just as sparing Micah's life and heeding his message proved to be wise in the past (26:19). **Hezekiah:** King of Judah from 729 to 686 ʙ.ᴄ. **Zion ... a wooded height:** A citation from Mic 3:12 that foretells the conquest of Jerusalem.

26:20 Uriah the son of Shemaiah: An otherwise unknown prophet who was recently martyred for speaking God's word to Judah (26:23). **Kiriath-jearim:** A town of Judah less than ten miles northwest of Jerusalem.

26:22 Elnathan: Identified in 36:12 as one of the princes of Judah.

26:23 slew him: Makes Jehoiakim guilty of shedding "innocent blood" (7:6; 22:3).

26:24 Ahikam the son of Shaphan: Served as a royal official under King Josiah, who died in 609 ʙ.ᴄ. (2 Kings 22:12). His son, Gedaliah, is made governor of Judah after the conquest of Jerusalem in 586 ʙ.ᴄ. (40:5) and is given custody of Jeremiah (39:14).

27:1–22 Jeremiah delivers the Lord's message that Judah and its neighbors must submit to the yoke of Babylonian rule (27:7, 12) or face Babylonian reprisal (27:8, 13). Because God gave Nebuchadnezzar the authority to rule these small states for a time, any attempt at rebellion against Babylon amounts to a rebellion against God's will (see 28:16). The episode also draws a sharp contrast between true and false prophets (27:14–18).

27:1 Zedekiah: The last king of Judah, who reigns from 597 to 586 ʙ.ᴄ. He is the third son of Josiah to rule over the Southern Kingdom. The episode in this chapter takes place in 594 ʙ.ᴄ., his fourth regnal year, according to 28:1.

27:2 thongs and yoke-bars: Wooden bars and a collar that were fastened to the neck and shoulders of an ox with leather straps. Jeremiah carries such a yoke, which represents subjugation to a powerful nation, as a symbolic act that dramatizes his message in a visual way. For similar prophetic acts, see 13:1–11 and 19:1–15.

27:3 Edom: South of the Dead Sea. **Moab ... Ammon:** East of the Jordan River. **Tyre ... Sidon:** Phoenician port cities northwest of the land of Israel. **envoys:** Foreign delegates present in Jerusalem and discussing a plan to declare their

---

ᵘ Another reading is *Jehoiakim.*
ᵛ Cn: Heb *send them.*

the hand of the envoys who have come to Jerusalem to Zedeki'ah king of Judah. [4]Give them this charge for their masters: 'Thus says the LORD of hosts, the God of Israel: This is what you shall say to your masters: [5]"It is I who by my great power and my outstretched arm have made the earth, with the men and animals that are on the earth, and I give it to whomever it seems right to me. [6]Now I have given all these lands into the hand of Nebuchadnez'zar, the king of Babylon, my servant, and I have given him also the beasts of the field to serve him. [7]All the nations shall serve him and his son and his grandson, until the time of his own land comes; then many nations and great kings shall make him their slave.

[8] "'"But if any nation or kingdom will not serve this Nebuchadnez'zar king of Babylon, and put its neck under the yoke of the king of Babylon, I will punish that nation with the sword, with famine, and with pestilence, says the LORD, until I have consumed it by his hand. [9]So do not listen to your prophets, your diviners, your dreamers,[w] your soothsayers, or your sorcerers, who are saying to you, 'You shall not serve the king of Babylon.' [10]For it is a lie which they are prophesying to you, with the result that you will be removed far from your land, and I will drive you out, and you will perish. [11]But any nation which will bring its neck under the yoke of the king of Babylon and serve him, I will leave on its own land, to till it and dwell there, says the LORD."'"

[12] To Zedeki'ah king of Judah I spoke in like manner: "Bring your necks under the yoke of the king of Babylon, and serve him and his people, and live. [13]Why will you and your people die by the sword, by famine, and by pestilence, as the LORD has spoken concerning any nation which will not serve the king of Babylon? [14]Do not listen to the words of the prophets who are saying to you, 'You shall not serve the king of Babylon,' for it is a lie which they are prophesying to you. [15]I have not sent them, says the LORD, but they are prophesying falsely in my name, with the result that I will drive you out and you will perish, you and the prophets who are prophesying to you."

[16] Then I spoke to the priests and to all this people, saying, "Thus says the LORD: Do not listen to the words of your prophets who are prophesying to you, saying, 'Behold, the vessels of the LORD's house will now shortly be brought back from Babylon,' for it is a lie which they are prophesying to you. [17]Do not listen to them; serve the king of Babylon and live. Why should this city become a desolation? [18]If they are prophets, and if the word of the LORD is with them, then let them intercede with the LORD of hosts, that the vessels which are left in the house of the LORD, in the house of the king of Judah, and in Jerusalem may not go to Babylon. [19]For thus says the LORD of hosts concerning the pillars, the sea, the stands, and the rest of the vessels which are left in this city, [20]which Nebuchadnez'zar king of Babylon did not take away, when he took into exile from Jerusalem to Babylon Jeconi'ah the son of Jehoi'akim, king of Judah, and all the nobles of Judah and Jerusalem—[21]thus says the LORD of hosts, the God of Israel, concerning the vessels which are left in the house of the LORD, in the house of the king of Judah, and in Jerusalem: [22]They shall be carried to Babylon and remain

---

independence from Babylon, whom they serve as vassals. Perhaps word has reached them of the revolt that broke out in Nebuchanezzar's army in 594 B.C.

27:5 to whomever it seems right to me: The Lord, as Creator, asserts his total sovereignty over all the earth, which includes his control over the historical destiny of nations and kingdoms (1:10; CCC 269).

27:6 Nebuchadnezzar: Ruler of the Neo-Babylonian empire from 605 to 562 B.C. **my servant:** See note on 25:9. **also the beasts:** Emphasizes the extent of the king of Babylon's authority. The prophet Daniel says the same thing of Nebuchadnezzar in Dan 2:37-38.

27:7 until the time: Until the fall of Babylon in 539 B.C. **many nations:** Such as the Persians and the Medes. **great kings:** Such as Cyrus II of Persia.

27:9 prophets: Advisors to foreign kings who claim to speak on behalf of their nation's gods and goddesses. **diviners ... sorcerers:** Practitioners of superstitious arts who counsel foreign kings. These professions, which specialize in techniques for ascertaining the future, are strictly forbidden in Israel (Deut 18:9-12) (CCC 2116).

27:10-11 The choice between serving and opposing Babylon is a choice between expulsion from one's land (for rebellion) and continued possession of one's land (for submission). Judah is faced with the same options (27:12-15).

27:13 sword ... famine ... pestilence: Curses of the covenant that bring suffering and death to violators of the covenant (Lev 26:25-26; Ezek 7:15).

27:14 the prophets: The false prophets of Judah, who are leading the nation astray with deceptive words and promises.

27:16 the vessels: The sacred articles of the Temple, some of which were taken to Babylon in 605 B.C. (Dan 1:1-2) and some in 597 B.C. (2 Kings 24:10-13). False prophets claim that these spoils will return to Jerusalem soon. Just the opposite is true: Babylonian soldiers will confiscate the remaining vessels when the Temple is destroyed in 586 B.C. (2 Kings 25:13-17), and none will return to the Temple until after the Babylonian Exile, ca. 537 B.C. (Ezra 1:5-11).

27:18 let them intercede: Successful intercession is a test of a true prophet (Gen 20:7). Failure in this regard exposes a self-professed prophet as a deceiver.

27:19 the pillars: The two bronze columns, Jachin and Boaz, that stand at the entrance to the Temple building (1 Kings 7:15-22). **the sea:** The giant bronze laver that stands in the Temple courtyard (1 Kings 7:23-26). **the stands:** Supported water basins where sacrificial offerings are washed (1 Kings 7:27-37).

27:20 Jeconiah: King Jehoiachin, who is exiled to Babylon with the royal family in 597 B.C. (2 Kings 24:10-15).

27:22 carried to Babylon: Fulfilled in 52:17-23. **I will bring them back:** Fulfilled when God inspires Cyrus II of Persia to end the Babylonian Exile in 538 B.C. and to send the Temple vessels back to Jerusalem (Ezra 1:7-11).

---

[w]Gk Syr Vg: Heb *dreams.*

there until the day when I give attention to them, says the LORD. Then I will bring them back and restore them to this place."

Hananiah's False Prophecy

28 In that same year, at the beginning of the reign of Zedeki′ah king of Judah, in the fifth month of the fourth year, Hanani′ah the son of Azzur, the prophet from Gib′eon, spoke to me in the house of the LORD, in the presence of the priests and all the people, saying, ²"Thus says the LORD of hosts, the God of Israel: I have broken the yoke of the king of Babylon. ³Within two years I will bring back to this place all the vessels of the LORD's house, which Nebuchadnez′zar king of Babylon took away from this place and carried to Babylon. ⁴I will also bring back to this place Jeconi′ah the son of Jehoi′akim, king of Judah, and all the exiles from Judah who went to Babylon, says the LORD, for I will break the yoke of the king of Babylon."

5 Then the prophet Jeremi′ah spoke to Hanani′ah the prophet in the presence of the priests and all the people who were standing in the house of the LORD; ⁶and the prophet Jeremi′ah said, "Amen! May the LORD do so; may the LORD make the words which you have prophesied come true, and bring back to this place from Babylon the vessels of the house of the LORD, and all the exiles. ⁷Yet hear now this word which I speak in your hearing and in the hearing of all the people. ⁸The prophets who preceded you and me from ancient times prophesied war, famine, and pestilence against many countries and great kingdoms. ⁹As for the prophet who prophesies peace, when the word of that prophet comes to pass,

then it will be known that the LORD has truly sent the prophet."

10 Then the prophet Hanani′ah took the yoke-bars from the neck of Jeremi′ah the prophet, and broke them. ¹¹And Hanani′ah spoke in the presence of all the people, saying, "Thus says the LORD: Even so will I break the yoke of Nebuchadnez′zar king of Babylon from the neck of all the nations within two years." But Jeremi′ah the prophet went his way.

12 Sometime after the prophet Hanani′ah had broken the yoke-bars from off the neck of Jeremi′ah the prophet, the word of the LORD came to Jeremi′ah: ¹³"Go, tell Hanani′ah, 'Thus says the LORD: You have broken wooden bars, but I[x] will make in their place bars of iron. ¹⁴For thus says the LORD of hosts, the God of Israel: I have put upon the neck of all these nations an iron yoke of servitude to Nebuchadnez′zar king of Babylon, and they shall serve him, for I have given to him even the beasts of the field.'" ¹⁵And Jeremi′ah the prophet said to the prophet Hanani′ah, "Listen, Hananiah, the LORD has not sent you, and you have made this people trust in a lie. ¹⁶Therefore thus says the LORD: 'Behold, I will remove you from the face of the earth. This very year you shall die, because you have uttered rebellion against the LORD.'"

17 In that same year, in the seventh month, the prophet Hanani′ah died.

Jeremiah's Letters to the Exiles in Babylon

29 These are the words of the letter which Jere-mi′ah the prophet sent from Jerusalem to the elders[y] of the exiles, and to the priests, the prophets, and all the people, whom Nebuchadnez′zar had taken into exile from Jerusalem to Babylon.

28:1 that same year: 594 B.C. **Zedekiah:** See note on 27:1. **Hananiah:** A false prophet who claims to speak for the Lord (28:2) but was never sent by the Lord (28:15). He is deceiving people with the promise that, within two years, Judah will be free from Babylonian rule, its exiles will return home, and the Temple vessels confiscated by Nebuchadnezzar's army in 597 B.C. will be returned safely (28:3–4). All of this, according to Jeremiah, is a "lie" (28:15). **Gibeon:** About six miles northwest of Jerusalem.

28:3 Within two years: By 592 B.C. **the vessels:** See note on 27:16.

28:4 Jeconiah: King Jehoiachin, who is exiled to Babylon with the royal family (2 Kings 24:10–15). **all the exiles:** The captives from Judah who are taken to Babylon in 605 B.C. (Dan 1:1–4) and 597 B.C. (2 Kings 24:10–16).

28:6 Amen!: A Hebrew acclamation meaning "so be it" (CCC 1062–65). Jeremiah is speaking sarcastically to poke fun at a prophecy he knows to be untrue (28:15).

28:8 prophets ... from ancient times: e.g., Isaiah and Amos, who spoke oracles against foreign nations in the eighth century B.C. (Is 13–23; Amos 1–2).

📖 **28:9 peace:** The keynote theme of the false prophets in Jeremiah's day (6:14; 8:11; Ezek 13:10). See note on 6:14. **comes to pass:** One of the tests of a true prophet set forth in Deuteronomy: if an alleged prophet predicts the future, and what he foretells does not come to pass, then he

has spoken falsely a word that does not come from the Lord (Deut 18:20–22). Applied to the two prophets who square off in this episode, Hananiah's prediction that Judah's exiles will return home within two years will be exposed as false, while Jeremiah's prophecy that Hananiah will die within one year will be verified (28:16–17).

28:10 broke them: An attempt to subvert Jeremiah's prophetic action in 27:2 and prevent its fulfillment. The gesture is foolish and makes the outcome more bleak: instead of a wooden yoke, the Babylonians will become an "iron yoke of servitude" forced upon the neck of Judah and its neighbors (28:14).

28:14 even the beasts: See note on 27:6.

28:16 This very year: 594 B.C. **rebellion:** By encouraging Judah to refuse submission to Babylonian rule. See note on 27:1–22.

29:1–32 Jeremiah's letter to the Jewish exiles in Babylon. He gives reassurance that the Lord has neither forgotten nor forsaken them, although their restoration will not take place immediately. For the time being, they should prepare for an extended stay in Babylon (29:5–6), pray for the welfare of Babylon (29:7), and reject the lies of false prophets (29:8–9). But after the "seventy years" of subjection to Babylon are complete, God will bring his people back to their homeland (29:10). He thus has "plans" to bless the exiled community with a brighter "future" (29:11). The community still living in Judah can only expect disaster for their stubborn persistence in sin (29:16–19).

29:1 the elders: The community leaders of Judah in Babylon (Ezek 8:1). **exile from Jerusalem:** Refers to the deportation of 597 B.C. (2 Kings 24:10–16).

---

[x] Gk: Heb *you.*
[y] Gk: Heb *the rest of the elders.*

²This was after King Jeconi'ah, and the queen mother, the eunuchs, the princes of Judah and Jerusalem, the craftsmen, and the smiths had departed from Jerusalem. ³The letter was sent by the hand of Ela'sah the son of Sha'phan and Gemari'ah the son of Hilki'ah, whom Zedeki'ah king of Judah sent to Babylon to Nebuchadnez'zar king of Babylon. It said: ⁴"Thus says the LORD of hosts, the God of Israel, to all the exiles whom I have sent into exile from Jerusalem to Babylon: ⁵Build houses and live in them; plant gardens and eat their produce. ⁶Take wives and have sons and daughters; take wives for your sons, and give your daughters in marriage, that they may bear sons and daughters; multiply there, and do not decrease. ⁷But seek the welfare of the city where I have sent you into exile, and pray to the LORD on its behalf, for in its welfare you will find your welfare. ⁸For thus says the LORD of hosts, the God of Israel: Do not let your prophets and your diviners who are among you deceive you, and do not listen to the dreams which they dream,ᶻ ⁹for it is a lie which they are prophesying to you in my name; I did not send them, says the LORD.

10 "For thus says the LORD: When seventy years are completed for Babylon, I will visit you, and I will fulfil to you my promise and bring you back to this place. ¹¹For I know the plans I have for you, says the LORD, plans for welfare and not for evil, to give you a future and a hope. ¹²Then you will call upon me and come and pray to me, and I will hear you. ¹³You will seek me and find me; when you seek me with all your heart, ¹⁴I will be found by you, says the LORD, and I will restore your fortunes and gather you from all the nations and all the places where I have driven you, says the LORD, and I will bring you back to the place from which I sent you into exile.

15 "Because you have said, 'The LORD has raised up prophets for us in Babylon,'—¹⁶Thus says the LORD concerning the king who sits on the throne of David, and concerning all the people who dwell in this city, your kinsmen who did not go out with you into exile: ¹⁷Thus says the LORD of hosts, Behold, I am sending on them sword, famine, and pestilence, and I will make them like vile figs which are so bad they cannot be eaten. ¹⁸I will pursue them with sword, famine, and pestilence, and will make them a horror to all the kingdoms of the earth, to be a curse, a terror, a hissing, and a reproach among all the nations where I have driven them, ¹⁹because they did not heed my words, says the LORD, which I persistently sent to you by my servants the prophets, but you would not listen, says the LORD.'—²⁰Hear the word of the LORD, all you exiles whom I sent away from Jerusalem to Babylon: ²¹Thus says the LORD of hosts, the God of Israel, concerning A'hab the son of Kolai'ah and Zedeki'ah the son of Ma-asei'ah, who are prophesying a lie to you in my name: Behold, I will deliver them into the hand of Nebuchadrez'zar king of Babylon, and he shall slay them before your eyes. ²²Because of them this curse shall be used by all the exiles from Judah in Babylon: "The LORD make you like Zedeki'ah and A'hab, whom the king of Babylon roasted in the fire," ²³because they have committed folly in Israel, they have committed adultery with their neighbors' wives, and they have spoken in my name lying words which I did not command them. I am the one who knows, and I am witness, says the LORD.'"

24 To Shemai'ah of Nehel'am you shall say: ²⁵"Thus says the LORD of hosts, the God of Israel: You have sent letters in your name to all the people who are in Jerusalem, and to Zephani'ah the son of

---

29:2 Jeconiah: Jehoiachin, who is king of Judah for three months in 598–597 B.C. **the queen mother:** Nehushta (2 Kings 24:8). **eunuchs … princes:** Royal officials of the Judahite government.

29:3 Elasah: Possibly a brother of Ahikam, a defender of Jeremiah (26:24). **Gemariah:** Possibly a son of the high priest Hilkiah (2 Kings 22:4). **Zedekiah:** See note on 27:1. **sent to Babylon:** The nature of the king's errand is unknown, but Jeremiah's letter is conveniently sent to Babylon with the delegates.

29:7 pray to the LORD: Because the security and prosperity of Judah's exiles depend on the security and prosperity of Babylon. On praying for nations and civil authorities, see Ezra 6:10; 1 Mac 7:33; 1 Tim 2:1–2 (CCC 1900).

29:8 your prophets: False prophets. **diviners:** Those who claim to access the secrets of the future. These deceivers create false hopes of a quick return from exile. Jeremiah counters this by stressing that Judah should prepare for a long exile by building homes, making marriages, and raising families (29:5–6). See note on 27:9.

29:10 seventy years: The length of Babylon's dominion over Judah. See note on 25:11.

29:13 seek: I.e., pursue a deeper relationship with God. It is a condition for Israel's restoration according to Deut 4:29. See word study: *Sought* at 2 Chron 1:5.

29:16 the king: Zedekiah, the last king of Judah (29:3). **kinsmen who did not go:** Those who are left behind in Judah after the deportation in 597 B.C.

29:17 sword, famine, and pestilence: Curses of the covenant that bring suffering and death to violators of the covenant (Lev 26:25–26; Ezek 7:15). **vile figs:** See note on 24:1–10.

29:18 a hissing: See note on 18:16.

29:21 Ahab … Zedekiah: False prophets, otherwise unknown, who are peddling false hopes among the exiles in Babylon. The Lord pronounces judgment on them for lying to the people in his name and committing adultery with other men's wives (29:23).

29:22 roasted in the fire: A horrific death that is wished upon others as a curse. Most likely Ahab and Zedekiah's message that Judah's exile is about to end implies that Babylon is about to fall, and this provokes Babylonian authorities to punish them as instigators of insurrection.

29:23 the one who knows: The God of Israel, from whom nothing is hidden. See note on 23:24.

29:24 Shemaiah: One of the exiles who writes to the Jerusalem priests, complaining that Jeremiah has not been arrested as a "madman" (29:26) for predicting a long exile (29:27–28).

29:25 Zephaniah: A priest with oversight of the Temple (21:1; 37:3). He should not be confused with the biblical prophet Zephaniah, son of Cushi (Zeph 1:1).

ᶻ Cn: Heb *your dreams which you cause to dream.*

Ma-asei′ah the priest, and to all the priests, saying, ²⁶"The LORD has made you priest instead of Jehoi′ada the priest, to have charge in the house of the LORD over every madman who prophesies, to put him in the stocks and collar. ²⁷Now why have you not rebuked Jeremi′ah of An′athoth who is prophesying to you? ²⁸For he has sent to us in Babylon, saying, "Your exile will be long; build houses and live in them, and plant gardens and eat their produce."'"

29 Zephani′ah the priest read this letter in the hearing of Jeremi′ah the prophet. ³⁰Then the word of the LORD came to Jeremi′ah: ³¹"Send to all the exiles, saying, 'Thus says the LORD concerning Shemai′ah of Nehel′am: Because Shemaiah has prophesied to you when I did not send him, and has made you trust in a lie, ³²therefore thus says the LORD: Behold, I will punish Shemai′ah of Nehel′am and his descendants; he shall not have any one living among this people to see^a the good that I will do to my people, says the LORD, for he has talked rebellion against the LORD.'"

Hope for the Restoration of Israel

30 The word that came to Jeremi′ah from the LORD: ²"Thus says the LORD, the God of Israel: Write in a book all the words that I have spoken to you. ³For behold, days are coming, says the LORD, when I will restore the fortunes of my people, Israel and Judah, says the LORD, and I will bring them back to the land which I gave to their fathers, and they shall take possession of it."

4 These are the words which the LORD spoke concerning Israel and Judah:

⁵"Thus says the LORD:
 We have heard a cry of panic,
  of terror, and no peace.
⁶Ask now, and see,
  can a man bear a child?
 Why then do I see every man
  with his hands on his loins like a woman in labor?
 Why has every face turned pale?
⁷Alas! that day is so great
  there is none like it;
 it is a time of distress for Jacob;
  yet he shall be saved out of it.

8 "And it shall come to pass in that day, says the LORD of hosts, that I will break the yoke from off their^b neck, and I will burst their^b bonds, and strangers shall no more make servants of them.^c* ⁹But they shall serve the LORD their God and David their king, whom I will raise up for them.

¹⁰"Then fear not, O Jacob my servant, says the LORD,
  nor be dismayed, O Israel;
 for behold, I will save you from afar,
  and your offspring from the land of their captivity.
 Jacob shall return and have quiet and ease,
  and none shall make him afraid.
¹¹For I am with you to save you,
                    says the LORD;
 I will make a full end of all the nations
  among whom I scattered you,
  but of you I will not make a full end.
 I will chasten you in just measure,
  and I will by no means leave you unpunished.

29:26 in the stocks: Jeremiah receives this treatment in 20:1-2.

29:30-32 A personalized message on the divine punishment of Shemaiah, whose family will never return to Judah.

30:1—33:26 Chapters 30-33 form a collection of oracles called "The Book of Consolation". They look beyond the chastisements of conquest and exile to a future restoration, sounding a note of optimism amidst the prevailing pessimism of surrounding chapters. The Lord pledges **(1)** to rescue and reunite the exiles of Israel and Judah who have been dispersed among foreign nations (30:3, 10), **(2)** to return the exiles to the Promised Land (30:3), **(3)** to raise up a Davidic Messiah whom they will serve (30:9), and **(4)** to ratify a new covenant that surpasses the Mosaic covenant of old (31:31-34).

30:2 Write in a book: For similar statements indicating that Jeremiah is directly involved in writing his oracles, sometimes with the help of the scribe Baruch, see 29:1; 36:1-4, 32; 51:60.

30:3 Israel and Judah: Jeremiah's vision expands beyond the Babylonian Exile of Judah (the Southern Kingdom) in the sixth century B.C. and includes the Assyrian Exile of Israel (the Northern Kingdom), which has continued since the eighth century B.C. The Lord's promise of restoration is thus intended for all twelve tribes, called "all the families of Israel" (31:1). For this theme elsewhere in Jeremiah, see 3:6-14; 31:18-20; 50:17-20.

30:5-7 The paralyzing fear that seizes men when God's judgment falls.

30:7 that day: A day of panic and distress for sinners, known to the prophets as "the day of the LORD" (Amos 5:18-20). See note on Is 2:12 and word study: *The Day of the LORD* at Joel 1:15. **Jacob:** A name for the whole people of Israel, which is descended from the twelve sons of the patriarch Jacob.

30:8 the yoke: A symbol of foreign domination (27:12). **strangers:** Nations such as Egypt, Assyria, and Babylon.

30:9 David their king: The Davidic Messiah, a royal figure who will come at an unspecified time after the collapse of the Davidic monarchy in 586 B.C. See note on 23:5.

30:10-11 Verses that reappear in 46:27-28.

30:10 Jacob my servant: Israel, a nation set apart to serve the one true God (46:27-28; Is 41:8; 44:1).

30:11 I scattered you: Expulsion from the Promised Land and dispersion among the nations is a divine curse that was made necessary by the brazen disobedience of Israel and Judah (Lev 26:33; Deut 28:64). **not ... a full end:** A limit to God's judgment means that a remnant is preserved (4:27; 5:10, 18; 31:7).

---

^aGk: Heb *and he shall not see.*
^bGk Old Latin: Heb *your.*
^cHeb *make a servant of him.*
*30:8: The new covenant and the restoration.

¹²"For thus says the LORD:
Your hurt is incurable,
and your wound is grievous.
¹³There is none to uphold your cause,
no medicine for your wound,
no healing for you.
¹⁴All your lovers have forgotten you;
they care nothing for you;
for I have dealt you the blow of an enemy,
the punishment of a merciless foe,
because your guilt is great,
because your sins are flagrant.
¹⁵Why do you cry out over your hurt?
Your pain is incurable.
Because your guilt is great,
because your sins are flagrant,
I have done these things to you.
¹⁶Therefore all who devour you shall be devoured,
and all your foes, every one of them, shall go
into captivity;
those who despoil you shall become a spoil,
and all who prey on you I will make a prey.
¹⁷For I will restore health to you,
and your wounds I will heal,
says the LORD,
because they have called you an outcast:
'It is Zion, for whom no one cares!'

¹⁸"Thus says the LORD:
Behold, I will restore the fortunes of the tents of
Jacob,
and have compassion on his dwellings;
the city shall be rebuilt upon its mound,
and the palace shall stand where it used
to be.

¹⁹Out of them shall come songs of thanksgiving,
and the voices of those who make merry.
I will multiply them, and they shall not be
few;
I will make them honored, and they shall
not be small.
²⁰Their children shall be as they were of old,
and their congregation shall be established
before me;
and I will punish all who oppress them.
²¹Their prince shall be one of themselves,
their ruler shall come forth from their
midst;
I will make him draw near, and he shall approach
me,
for who would dare of himself to approach
me?
says the LORD.
²²And you shall be my people,
and I will be your God."
²³Behold the storm of the LORD!
Wrath has gone forth,
a whirling tempest;
it will burst upon the head of the wicked.
²⁴The fierce anger of the LORD will not turn back
until he has executed and accomplished
the intents of his mind.
In the latter days you will understand this.

31 "At that time, says the LORD, I will be the God of all the families of Israel, and they shall be my people."
²Thus says the LORD:
"The people who survived the sword
found grace in the wilderness;
when Israel sought for rest,

30:12–17 An oracle addressed to Zion, personified as a woman, who is wounded, guilty, and eventually healed by the Lord. The conquest of Jerusalem and its rebuilding after the Babylonian Exile is the story being summarized.

30:14 your lovers: Former political allies (27:3) who abandon Zion at the time of the Babylonian conquest of Judah (Lam 1:2). **blow of an enemy:** For a similar image of God warring against Jerusalem, see Lam 2:4–5.

30:16 all who devour ... devoured: Recalls the divine promise to Abraham and his descendants: "him who curses you I will curse" (Gen 12:3; cf. Deut 30:7). In this instance, God will overthrow Babylon for its role in overthrowing Judah.

30:19 songs of thanksgiving: Translates the Hebrew *tôdāh*, which here indicates a vocal expression of gratitude rising to God from the restored community. Thanksgiving for salvation was also ritualized as a sacrificial liturgy; see note on Ps 50:14.

30:21 he shall approach me: The leader of the restored Israel has priestly access to the Lord's presence.

30:22 my people ... your God: Reaffirms the covenant between the Lord and Israel, who are bound together as a father to his children (31:9) as well as a bridegroom to his bride (2:2–3). Scholars designate such statements of mutual belonging as the "covenant formula" (Lev 26:12; Ezek 37:27; Hos 2:23). It is found four times in Jeremiah's "Book of Consolation" (also 31:1, 33; 32:38).

30:24 the latter days: The days of messianic fulfillment. See word study: *The Latter Days* at Is 2:2.

31:1–40 The homecoming of the exiles of Ephraim (= the northern tribes of Israel) and Judah (= the southern tribes of Israel). The Lord chastises his people for a time by scattering them among the nations (31:10), but only because, in his "everlasting love" (31:3), he wishes to correct their misbehavior and draw them back to himself as a "father" seeks the return of a "first-born" (31:9; Deut 8:5). Ultimately God wants to show "mercy" to his wayward child (31:20).

31:1 God ... my people: Reaffirms the covenant bond between the Lord and Israel. See note on 30:22.

31:2 The people who survived: Exiles of the northern tribes of Israel living in the lands of the Assyrian dispersion (2 Kings 15:29; 17:6; Tob 1:1–3). **grace in the wilderness:** The journey home from exile recalls Israel's original journey through the wilderness after escaping Egypt. The homecoming of the exiles is thus presented as a new exodus that brings God's people to the Promised Land once again. See essay: *The New Exodus in Isaiah* at Is 43.

3 the LORD appeared to him[d] from afar.
I have loved you with an everlasting love;
    therefore I have continued my faithfulness to
    you.
4 Again I will build you, and you shall be built,
    O virgin Israel!
Again you shall adorn yourself with timbrels,
    and shall go forth in the dance of the
      merrymakers.
5 Again you shall plant vineyards
    upon the mountains of Samar′ia;
the planters shall plant,
    and shall enjoy the fruit.
6 For there shall be a day when watchmen will call
    in the hill country of E′phraim:
'Arise, and let us go up to Zion,
    to the LORD our God.'"

7 For thus says the LORD:
"Sing aloud with gladness for Jacob,
    and raise shouts for the chief of the nations;
proclaim, give praise, and say,
    'The LORD has saved his people,
    the remnant of Israel.'
8 Behold, I will bring them from the north country,
    and gather them from the farthest parts of the
      earth,
among them the blind and the lame,
    the woman with child and her who has labor
      pains, together;
    a great company, they shall return here.
9 With weeping they shall come,
    and with consolations[e] I will lead them back,
I will make them walk by brooks of water,

in a straight path in which they shall not
    stumble;
for I am a father to Israel,
    and E′phraim is my first-born.

10 "Hear the word of the LORD, O nations,
    and declare it in the islands afar off;
say, 'He who scattered Israel will gather him,
    and will keep him as a shepherd keeps his
      flock.'
11 For the LORD has ransomed Jacob,
    and has redeemed him from hands too strong
      for him.
12 They shall come and sing aloud on the height of
    Zion,
    and they shall be radiant over the goodness of
      the LORD,
over the grain, the wine, and the oil,
    and over the young of the flock and the herd;
their life shall be like a watered garden,
    and they shall languish no more.
13 Then shall the maidens rejoice in the dance,
    and the young men and the old shall be merry.
I will turn their mourning into joy,
    I will comfort them, and give them gladness
      for sorrow.
14 I will feast the soul of the priests with abundance,
    and my people shall be satisfied with my
      goodness,
                says the LORD."

15 Thus says the LORD:
"A voice is heard in Ra′mah,
    lamentation and bitter weeping.

31:15: Mt 2:18.

31:3 everlasting love: The undying affection that a father has for his children (31:9). At times this love can be expressed as discipline (Prov 3:11–12); but it ensures the covenant people that God will neither forget nor forsake them (Deut 4:31; 1 Sam 12:22). Divine love has been the foundation of Israel's election from the beginning (Deut 7:6–8) (CCC 220; 1611). **faithfulness:** The Hebrew *ḥesed* refers to the unfailing loyalty that governs a covenant relationship. See word study: *Merciful Love* at Ex 34:7.

31:4 O virgin Israel: The title, which also appears in 18:13, is ironic, seeing that God's people are guilty of spiritual prostitution (3:2–5).

31:5 Samaria: The central hill country of Israel. It was the heart of the Northern Kingdom of Israel until the Assyrian conquest of 722 B.C. Growing crops in these highlands symbolizes God's intention to bless the northern tribes once again.

31:6 Ephraim: The tribal territory of Ephraim in central Israel. Ephraim is the dominant tribe of the Northern Kingdom of Israel and the tribe of its first king, Jeroboam I (1 Kings 12:25). **let us go up to Zion:** A sign of repentance. Israel's northern tribes, since the founding of the Northern Kingdom, has severed all ties with Jerusalem, rejecting even the Lord's Temple and establishing its own illegitimate sanctuaries

(1 Kings 12:25–33). The return to Zion points to a spiritual renewal and realignment with the covenant.

31:7 Jacob: Father of the whole family of Israel, chosen to be the Lord's "first-born" among the family of nations (31:9). **chief of the nations:** Or "head of the nations". The same expression is used of King David (2 Sam 22:44; Ps 18:43). **remnant of Israel:** The survivors of Israel who return to the Lord in faith and obedience (Is 10:20–22).

31:8 gather ... from the farthest parts: Confirms the promise of restoration from exile stated in Deut 30:1–5.

31:9 I am a father: For the divine Fatherhood of God, see notes on Wis 14:3 and Is 63:16. **my first-born:** Israel was chosen to be the first nation among the family of nations to enter a covenant of kinship with the Lord (Ex 19:5–6; Deut 14:1). See note on Ex 4:22.

31:10 a shepherd: A common scriptural image for God (Gen 49:24; Ps 23:1; Is 40:11; Ezek 34:15).

31:11 redeemed: I.e., reclaimed by the Lord, who acts as a kinsman coming to Israel's aid. See word study: *Redeem* at Lev 25:25. **hands too strong:** The mighty nations that hold exiled Israelites captive.

31:15 A voice is heard in Ramah: Bitter cries of lamentation echo in Ramah, a town of Benjamin five miles north of Jerusalem. According to one tradition, this town was the burial site of Rachel, the favored wife of Jacob (1 Sam 10:2). In Jeremiah's time, Ramah is a staging point where Babylonian soldiers gather the captives of Judah for the long

---

[d] Gk: Heb *me*.
[e] Gk Compare Vg Tg: Heb *supplications*.

Rachel is weeping for her children;
    she refuses to be comforted for her children,
    because they are not.'"*

¹⁶Thus says the LORD:
    "Keep your voice from weeping,
    and your eyes from tears;
    for your work shall be rewarded, says the LORD,
    and they shall come back from the land of the
        enemy.
¹⁷There is hope for your future,
                                        says the LORD,
    and your children shall come back to their own
        country.
¹⁸I have heard E′phraim bemoaning,
    'You have chastened me, and I was chastened,
    like an untrained calf;
    bring me back that I may be restored,
    for you are the LORD my God.
¹⁹For after I had turned away I repented;
    and after I was instructed, I struck my
        thigh;
    I was ashamed, and I was confounded,
    because I bore the disgrace of my youth.'
²⁰Is E′phraim my dear son?
    Is he my darling child?
For as often as I speak against him,
    I do remember him still.
Therefore my heart yearns for him;
    I will surely have mercy on him,
                                        says the LORD.

²¹"Set up waymarks for yourself,
    make yourself guideposts;
    consider well the highway,
    the road by which you went.

Return, O virgin Israel,
    return to these your cities.
²²How long will you waver,
    O faithless daughter?
For the LORD has created a new thing on the
        earth:
    a woman protects a man."

23 Thus says the LORD of hosts, the God of Israel: "Once more they shall use these words in the land of Judah and in its cities, when I restore their fortunes:
    'The LORD bless you, O habitation of righteousness,
    O holy hill!'
²⁴And Judah and all its cities shall dwell there together, and the farmers and those who wander ᶠ with their flocks. ²⁵For I will satisfy the weary soul, and every languishing soul I will replenish."

26 Thereupon I awoke and looked, and my sleep was pleasant to me.

Individual Responsibility for Conduct

27 "Behold, the days are coming, says the LORD, when I will sow the house of Israel and the house of Judah with the seed of man and the seed of beast. ²⁸And it shall come to pass that as I have watched over them to pluck up and break down, to overthrow, destroy, and bring evil, so I will watch over them to build and to plant, says the LORD. ²⁹In those days they shall no longer say:
    'The fathers have eaten sour grapes,
    and the children's teeth are set on edge.'
³⁰But every one shall die for his own sin; each man who eats sour grapes, his teeth shall be set on edge.

A New Covenant Promised

31 †"Behold, the days are coming, says the LORD, when I will make a new covenant with the house of

---

31:31: Lk 22:20; 1 Cor 11:25. **31:31–34:** Jer 32:38–40; Heb 8:8–12; 10:16–17.

---

journey into exile (40:1). Rachel is said to mourn the loss of these Israelite children from the land, but the Lord assures her they will "come back" in the future (31:17). Another tradition locates Rachel's tomb in Bethlehem (Gen 35:19). • According to Mt 2:18, this passage also finds fulfillment when Herod the Great, threatened by reports of a newborn king of the Jews, slaughters the innocent children of Bethlehem. In this instance, Rachel's children (= baby Israelites) are taken from the land of Israel when they are taken from this life.

31:20 my dear son: See note on 31:9.

31:22 a woman protects a man: Indicates something strange and unexpected.

31:23 O holy hill: Mt. Zion in Jerusalem (Ps 2:6).

31:27 Behold, the days are coming: Words that introduce prophecies in 31:31 and 31:38 also.

31:28 pluck ... break ... destroy ... build ... plant: The various actions of judgment and restoration that God promises to accomplish through Jeremiah's ministry (1:10).

31:29 sour grapes ... set on edge: A proverb about the intergenerational effects of sin. Apparently it was misused to deflect responsibility for God's judgment, as if previous generations were solely to blame for calamities suffered in the present (Lam 5:7). The Lord is not so unjust; he holds individuals responsible for their own actions (Ezek 18:2–3). Besides that, Jeremiah's generation is guilty of "worse" sins than their ancestors (16:12).

31:31–34 Jeremiah prophesies a "new covenant" (31:31) that will be unlike the Mosaic covenant (31:32). Its distinctive features: **(1)** it entails a great act of deliverance, in which the Lord will rescue both the northern ("the house of Israel") and southern tribes of Israel ("the house of Judah") after long years of exile (31:31); **(2)** unlike the Sinai Torah, with the Decalogue inscribed on tablets of stone, the Law of the new covenant will be written on the hearts of the people, instructing them and assisting their obedience from the inside (31:33); **(3)** the whole covenant community will come to a new knowledge of God (31:34); and **(4)** the Lord will accomplish a definitive forgiveness of sins (31:34). Related prophecies of a future covenant include 32:40; Is 54:10; 59:21; 61:8; Ezek 34:25; Hos 2:18. • Jesus ratifies Jeremiah's new covenant at the Last Supper, when he offers his Body and Blood as a sacrifice for the forgiveness of sins (Lk 22:19–20; 1 Cor 11:23–25). Paul sees himself as a minister of this new covenant because the Spirit, who indwells and gives life to believers, writes on the tablets of human hearts instead of tablets of stone (2 Cor 3:1-6). According to the Book of

---

ᶠ Cn Compare Syr Vg Tg: Heb *and they shall wander.*
*31:15: Quoted by Matthew and applied to the Holy Innocents (Mt 2:18).
†31:31–34: The new covenant; cf. Mt 26:28.

Israel and the house of Judah, ³²not like the covenant which I made with their fathers when I took them by the hand to bring them out of the land of Egypt, my covenant which they broke, and I showed myself their Master, says the LORD. ³³But this is the covenant which I will make with the house of Israel after those days, says the LORD: I will put my law within them, and I will write it upon their hearts; and I will be their God, and they shall be my people. ³⁴And no longer shall each man teach his neighbor and each his brother, saying, 'Know the LORD,' for they shall all know me, from the least of them to the greatest, says the LORD; for I will forgive their iniquity, and I will remember their sin no more."

³⁵Thus says the LORD,
who gives the sun for light by day
and the fixed order of the moon and the stars
for light by night,
who stirs up the sea so that its waves roar—
the LORD of hosts is his name:
³⁶"If this fixed order departs
from before me, says the LORD,
then shall the descendants of Israel cease
from being a nation before me for ever."

³⁷Thus says the LORD:
"If the heavens above can be measured,
and the foundations of the earth below can be
explored,

then I will cast off all the descendants of Israel
for all that they have done,
says the LORD."

The City Will Be Rebuilt

38 "Behold, the days are coming, says the LORD, when the city shall be rebuilt for the LORD from the tower of Hanan'el to the Corner Gate. ³⁹And the measuring line shall go out farther, straight to the hill Ga'reb, and shall then turn to Goah. ⁴⁰The whole valley of the dead bodies and the ashes, and all the fields as far as the brook Kid'ron, to the corner of the Horse Gate toward the east, shall be sacred to the LORD. It shall not be uprooted or overthrown any more for ever."

Jeremiah Buys a Field at Anathoth

32 The word that came to Jeremi'ah from the LORD in the tenth year of Zedeki'ah king of Judah, which was the eighteenth year of Nebuchadrez'zar. ²At that time the army of the king of Babylon was besieging Jerusalem, and Jeremi'ah the prophet was shut up in the court of the guard which was in the palace of the king of Judah. ³For Zedeki'ah king of Judah had imprisoned him, saying, "Why do you prophesy and say, 'Thus says the LORD: Behold, I am giving this city into the hand of the king of Babylon, and he shall take it; ⁴Zedeki'ah king of Judah shall not escape out of the hand of the Chalde'ans, but shall surely be given into the hand of the king of Babylon, and shall speak with him

---

Hebrews, the sacrifice of Jesus ratifies the new covenant and effects the forgiveness of sins, making obsolete the animal sacrifices of the Mosaic covenant that provided a constant reminder of sins (Heb 10:11–18) (CCC 580; 715; 1965). • I have read of a final law and of a covenant greater than all others. The law given at Horeb is old and belongs to a single people only, but the law to which I refer is for all peoples. Now a newer law abrogates an older one, and a later covenant nullifies a previous one. We have been given an eternal and final law, namely, Christ, and a trustworthy covenant that will not be succeeded by any other law, commandment, or ordinance (St. Justin Martyr, *Dialogue with Trypho* 11). • What is this law that God writes on the hearts of men but the presence of the Holy Spirit, by whom the love that fulfills the law is poured into our hearts? Apart from its sacramental rites, which foreshadow things to come, the promises of the Old Covenant are earthly and temporal. What is promised in the new covenant is good for the heart, mind, and spirit, indicating that men would not fear the alarm of the external law but love the righteousness of the law dwelling within them (St. Augustine, *On the Spirit and the Letter* 36).

31:32 their Master: Or "their Husband". For the Mosaic covenant as a marital covenant, see note on 2:2.

31:33 their God ... my people: The covenant formula. See note on 30:22.

31:34 know me: Refers to a close relationship with the Lord based in part on obedience to his laws (e.g., the righteous King Josiah comes to "know" God in 22:16). • Teachers of the word of God come and go in succession, but Sacred Scripture stands for all time and will not pass away until the Lord's appearance at the end of time. Then we will no longer need the Scriptures or people to interpret it because the promise will be fulfilled that everyone shall know the Lord, from the least of them to the greatest (St. Bede, *On the Tabernacle* 1, 7). **remember their sin no more:** Remembering sin is a reference to punishing it (14:10).

31:36 this fixed order: The stability of creation mirrors the Lord's enduring commitment to Israel. See note on 31:3.

31:37 measured ... explored: Two impossible things, reinforcing the message that God will not forsake his people (1 Sam 12:22; Ps 94:14; Rom 11:1).

31:38 the city: Jerusalem, destroyed in 586 B.C., but rebuilt in stages after the Babylonian Exile. **the tower of Hananel:** North of the Temple site (Neh 12:39). **the Corner Gate:** In the northwest wall of Jerusalem (Zech 14:10).

31:39 Gareb ... Goah: Seem to mark the western boundaries of Jerusalem. Exact locations are unknown.

31:40 valley of the dead ... ashes: The ravine southwest of Jerusalem, called the "valley of the son of Hinnom" in 7:31 and 19:2. **brook Kidron:** The ravine east of Jerusalem, separating the city from the Mt. of Olives (Jn 18:1). **the Horse Gate:** In the eastern wall of the city (Neh 3:28).

32:1–15 Jeremiah purchases a plot of land from his cousin, Hanamel, as a prophetic sign that the people of Judah, soon to be forced into exile, will eventually return from Babylon, reoccupy their homeland, and resume economic activities such as buying and selling property. For other symbolic actions performed by Jeremiah, see 13:1–11; 16:1–4; 19:1–13; 27:1–15.

32:1 tenth year: 587 B.C. **Zedekiah:** The last king of Judah, from 597 to 586 B.C. **Nebuchadrezzar:** An alternate spelling for Nebuchadnezzar, ruler of the Neo-Babylonian empire from 605 to 562 B.C.

32:2 besieging: The siege began the preceding year in 588 B.C. (2 Kings 25:1–2). Details of the siege appear in chaps. 37–38. **court of the guard:** The royal palace-yard in Jerusalem that allows detainees limited interaction with others. Jeremiah is kept here for announcing the impending fall of the city (33:1).

32:4 Chaldeans: Babylonians. **face to face:** Fulfilled when Zedekiah is captured during an attempt to flee the city. He is brought before Nebuchadnezzar, who slays his sons and gouges out his eyes (2 Kings 25:4–7).

face to face and see him eye to eye; ⁵and he shall take Zedeki'ah to Babylon, and there he shall remain until I visit him, says the Lord; though you fight against the Chalde'ans, you shall not succeed'?"

6 Jeremi'ah said, "The word of the Lord came to me: ⁷Behold, Han'amel the son of Shallum your uncle will come to you and say, 'Buy my field which is at An'athoth, for the right of redemption by purchase is yours.' ⁸Then Han'amel my cousin came to me in the court of the guard, in accordance with the word of the Lord, and said to me, 'Buy my field which is at An'athoth in the land of Benjamin, for the right of possession and redemption is yours; buy it for yourself.' Then I knew that this was the word of the Lord.

9 "And I bought the field at An'athoth from Han'amel my cousin, and weighed out the money to him, seventeen shekels of silver. ¹⁰I signed the deed, sealed it, got witnesses, and weighed the money on scales. ¹¹Then I took the sealed deed of purchase, containing the terms and conditions, and the open copy; ¹²and I gave the deed of purchase to Baruch the son of Neri'ah son of Mah'seiah, in the presence of Han'amel my cousin, in the presence of the witnesses who signed the deed of purchase, and in the presence of all the Jews who were sitting in the court of the guard. ¹³I charged Baruch in their presence, saying, ¹⁴'Thus says the Lord of hosts, the God of Israel: Take these deeds, both this sealed deed of purchase and this open deed, and put them in an earthen-ware vessel, that they may last for a long time. ¹⁵For thus says the Lord of hosts, the God of Israel: Houses and fields and vineyards shall again be bought in this land.'

God's Assurance of the People's Return

16 "After I had given the deed of purchase to Baruch the son of Neri'ah, I prayed to the Lord, saying: ¹⁷'Ah Lord God! It is you who have made the heavens and the earth by your great power and by your outstretched arm! Nothing is too hard for you, ¹⁸who show mercy to thousands, but repay the guilt of fathers to their children after them, O great and mighty God whose name is the Lord of hosts, ¹⁹great in counsel and mighty in deed; whose eyes are open to all the ways of men, rewarding every man according to his ways and according to the fruit of his doings; ²⁰who have shown signs and wonders in the land of Egypt, and to this day in Israel and among all mankind, and have made you a name, as at this day. ²¹You brought your people Israel out of the land of Egypt with signs and wonders, with a strong hand and outstretched arm, and with great terror; ²²and you gave them this land, which you swore to their fathers to give them, a land flowing with milk and honey; ²³and they entered and took possession of it. But they did not obey your voice or walk in your law; they did nothing of all you commanded them to do. Therefore you have made all this evil come upon them. ²⁴Behold, the siege mounds have come up to the city to take it, and because of sword and famine and pestilence the city is given into the hands of the Chalde'ans who are fighting against it. What you spoke has come to pass, and behold, you see it. ²⁵Yet you, O Lord God, have said to me, "Buy the field for money and get witnesses"—though the city is given into the hands of the Chalde'ans.' "

32:5 until I visit him: Zedekiah's peaceful death in Babylon appears to be meant (34:5).

32:7 Shallum: Jeremiah's uncle, but otherwise unknown. **Anathoth:** Jeremiah's hometown, about three miles northeast of Jerusalem in Benjaminite territory (1:1; 32:8). **right of redemption:** Efforts were made in ancient Israel to keep family lands within family lines, lest ancestral property become alienated from its heirs. In times of financial hardship, when land had to be sold, it was offered first to a near kinsman. If he could afford the purchase, as in this episode, he would act as a "kinsman redeemer". Land purchased by someone outside the kinship group reverted to the original family owners at the Jubilee year (Lev 25:25–28).

32:8 my cousin: Literally, "the son of my uncle".

32:9 seventeen shekels: About seven ounces of silver. • Matthew sees Jeremiah's purchase of the field foreshadowing a key event in the Gospel story: the purchase of a field with the 30 pieces of silver returned by Judas Iscariot after he regrets betraying Jesus (Mt 27:3–10).

32:10 sealed it: The deed of sale was rolled up and fastened shut with clay or wax that was stamped with a ring or a small cylinder. Duplicate copies of the deed were stored for safekeeping in a lidded pottery jar so that ownership of the property could be verified at a later time (32:14). **witnesses:** Render the business transaction legally valid.

32:11 open copy: Kept unsealed for ease of reference.

32:12 Baruch: Jeremiah's personal scribe. See note on 36:4.

32:14 earthen-ware vessel: Many of the Dead Sea Scrolls, as well as documents from the Jewish colony at Elephantine, Egypt, were also stored in this way.

32:16–25 Jeremiah's prayer summarizes Israel's history from the Exodus to the Babylonian Exile. It praises the Lord for his power, justice, and marvelous deeds. For similar prayers that review the course of salvation history, see Ezra 9:6–15; Neh 9:6–37; Dan 9:4–19.

32:17 Nothing is too hard: An assertion of God's omnipotence, meaning that nothing that is logically possible is beyond his power (Lk 1:37). The Lord can thus accomplish anything he wills (Ps 135:6), but he will not deny himself by acting contrary to his nature (2 Tim 2:13; Heb 6:18) (CCC 268–71).

32:18 mercy to thousands: One of the Lord's divine attributes revealed to Moses on Mt. Sinai (Ex 34:6–7).

32:19 according to his ways: Judgment according to works is a classic teaching of Scripture (17:10; Ps 62:12; Prov 24:12; Mt 16:27; Rom 2:5–8; 1 Pet 1:17).

32:24 siege mounds: Ramps made of stone, packed earth, and wooden planks. They enabled siege towers and battering rams to get close to a city's defensive walls. **sword and famine and pestilence:** Curses of the Mosaic covenant that bring suffering and death to violators of the covenant (Lev 26:25–26).

32:25 though the city is given: The prophet has second thoughts about buying land on the eve of the Babylonian conquest. He seeks reassurance from the Lord that life in Judah and its capital will return to normal following the calamity of 586 B.C. Divine reassurance follows in 32:26–44.

26 The word of the LORD came to Jeremi′ah: ²⁷"Behold, I am the LORD, the God of all flesh; is anything too hard for me? ²⁸Therefore, thus says the LORD: Behold, I am giving this city into the hands of the Chalde′ans and into the hand of Nebuchad-rez′zar king of Babylon, and he shall take it. ²⁹The Chalde′ans who are fighting against this city shall come and set this city on fire, and burn it, with the houses on whose roofs incense has been offered to Ba′al and drink offerings have been poured out to other gods, to provoke me to anger. ³⁰For the sons of Israel and the sons of Judah have done nothing but evil in my sight from their youth; the sons of Israel have done nothing but provoke me to anger by the work of their hands, says the LORD. ³¹This city has aroused my anger and wrath, from the day it was built to this day, so that I will remove it from my sight ³²because of all the evil of the sons of Israel and the sons of Judah which they did to provoke me to anger—their kings and their princes, their priests and their prophets, the men of Judah and the inhabitants of Jerusalem. ³³They have turned to me their back and not their face; and though I have taught them persistently they have not listened to receive instruction. ³⁴They set up their abominations in the house which is called by my name, to defile it. ³⁵They built the high places of Ba′al in the valley of the son of Hinnom, to offer up their sons and daughters to Mo′lech, though I did not command them, nor did it enter into my mind, that they should do this abomination, to cause Judah to sin.

36 "Now therefore thus says the LORD, the God of Israel, concerning this city of which you say, 'It is given into the hand of the king of Babylon by sword, by famine, and by pestilence': ³⁷Behold, I will gather them from all the countries to which I drove them in my anger and my wrath and in great indignation; I will bring them back to this place, and I will make them dwell in safety. ³⁸And they shall be my people, and I will be their God. ³⁹I will give them one heart and one way, that they may fear me for ever, for their own good and the good of their children after them. ⁴⁰I will make with them an everlasting covenant, that I will not turn away from doing good to them; and I will put the fear of me in their hearts, that they may not turn from me. ⁴¹I will rejoice in doing them good, and I will plant them in this land in faithfulness, with all my heart and all my soul.

42 "For thus says the LORD: Just as I have brought all this great evil upon this people, so I will bring upon them all the good that I promise them. ⁴³Fields shall be bought in this land of which you are saying, It is a desolation, without man or beast; it is given into the hands of the Chalde′ans. ⁴⁴Fields shall be bought for money, and deeds shall be signed and sealed and witnessed, in the land of Benjamin, in the places about Jerusalem, and in the cities of Judah, in the cities of the hill country, in the cities of the Sheph′elah, and in the cities of the Neg′eb; for I will restore their fortunes, says the LORD."

Healing after Punishment

33 The word of the LORD came to Jeremi′ah a second time, while he was still shut up in the court of the guard: ²"Thus says the LORD who made the earth, ᵍ the LORD who formed it to establish it—the LORD is his name: ³Call to me and I will

---

32:38–40: Jer 31:31–34.

32:27 all flesh: All living things. **anything too hard for me?:** Expects a negative answer (Gen 18:14). Resuming normal life in the land may look impossible from Jeremiah's vantage point, but all things are possible for God (Mt 19:26).

32:29 this city on fire: Fulfilled in 52:13. **Baal:** The storm and fertility god of Canaanite religion. See note on 11:10.

32:30 Israel ... Judah: The Northern and Southern Kingdoms, respectively.

32:34 abominations: The religious aberrations that defiled the Temple. In the late monarchical period, the Lord's sanctuary was defiled with graven images, idolatrous vessels, the worship of foreign gods, and living quarters for cult prostitutes (2 Kings 23:4, 6–7; Ezek 8:7–18).

32:35 valley of the son of Hinnom: Directly southwest of Jerusalem. **Molech:** Probably a god of the underworld who is served by child sacrifice (Lev 20:1–5; 2 Kings 23:10). See note on 7:31.

32:37 I will gather: Those who repent and return to the Lord in exile will be restored, as foreseen in the Law of Moses (Deut 30:1–5).

32:38 my people ... their God: The covenant formula. See note on 30:22.

32:40 an everlasting covenant: A reference to the "new covenant" promised in 31:31. The gift of a new heart that fears the Lord is one of its primary blessings (Bar 2:35; Ezek 16:60; 36:26). See note on 31:31–34.

32:41 I will rejoice: The Lord will not merely permit his people to return home and rebuild their lives in the land; he will take delight in prospering them once again.

32:42 evil: The Hebrew *rā 'āh* here means, not moral evil, but "calamity" or "disaster".

32:44 Shephelah: The low hills of western Judah. **Negeb:** The arid region in the deep south of Judah.

33:1–26 The final chapter of the "Book of Consolation" (chaps. 30–33) affirms the Lord's faithfulness to his commitments. These are grouped into three categories: **(1)** God promises to heal (33:6), restore (33:7), and cleanse the exiles of Israel and Judah (33:8); **(2)** God promises to reestablish the joys of community life in Judah and Jerusalem (33:10–13); and **(3)** God promises to honor his covenant of kingship with David and his sons as well as his covenant of priesthood with Aaron and his sons (33:14–26).

33:1 still shut up: Jeremiah had been imprisoned by Zedekiah (32:2–3).

33:2 the LORD: YHWH, probably pronounced "Yahweh", the name of God revealed to Moses at the burning bush. See note on Ex 3:15.

33:3 answer you ... tell you: The personal pronoun ("you") is singular in both cases, indicating that God is addressing Jeremiah individually. **hidden things:** Future things that are unknown until the Lord reveals them to his prophets (Deut 29:29).

ᵍGk: Heb *it.*

answer you, and will tell you great and hidden things which you have not known. [4]For thus says the LORD, the God of Israel, concerning the houses of this city and the houses of the kings of Judah which were torn down to make a defense against the siege mounds and before the sword:[h] [5]The Chalde'ans are coming in to fight[i] and to fill them with the dead bodies of men whom I shall strike in my anger and my wrath, for I have hidden my face from this city because of all their wickedness. [6]Behold, I will bring to it health and healing, and I will heal them and reveal to them abundance[j] of prosperity and security. [7]I will restore the fortunes of Judah and the fortunes of Israel, and rebuild them as they were at first. [8]I will cleanse them from all the guilt of their sin against me, and I will forgive all the guilt of their sin and rebellion against me. [9]And this city[k] shall be to me a name of joy, a praise and a glory before all the nations of the earth who shall hear of all the good that I do for them; they shall fear and tremble because of all the good and all the prosperity I provide for it.

10 "Thus says the LORD: In this place of which you say, 'It is a waste without man or beast,' in the cities of Judah and the streets of Jerusalem that are desolate, without man or inhabitant or beast, there shall be heard again [11]the voice of mirth and the voice of gladness, the voice of the bridegroom and the voice of the bride, the voices of those who sing, as they bring thank offerings to the house of the LORD:

'Give thanks to the LORD of hosts,
　for the LORD is good,
　for his mercy endures for ever!'

For I will restore the fortunes of the land as at first, says the LORD.

12 "Thus says the LORD of hosts: In this place which is waste, without man or beast, and in all of its cities, there shall again be habitations of shepherds resting their flocks. [13]In the cities of the hill country, in the cities of the Shephe'lah, and in the cities of the Neg'eb, in the land of Benjamin, the places about Jerusalem, and in the cities of Judah, flocks shall again pass under the hands of the one who counts them, says the LORD.

14 "Behold, the days are coming, says the LORD, when I will fulfil the promise I made to the house of Israel and the house of Judah. [15]In those days and at that time I will cause a righteous Branch to spring forth for David;* and he shall execute justice and righteousness in the land. [16]In those days Judah will be saved and Jerusalem will dwell securely. And this is the name by which it will be called: 'The LORD is our righteousness.'

17 "For thus says the LORD: David shall never lack a man to sit on the throne of the house of Israel, [18]and the Levitical priests shall never lack a man in my presence to offer burnt offerings, to burn cereal offerings, and to make sacrifices for ever."

19 The word of the LORD came to Jeremi'ah: [20]"Thus says the LORD: If you can break my covenant with the day and my covenant with the

---

33:15: Jer 23:5; Is 4:2; Zech 3:8; 6:12.

33:4 torn down: Building materials from dismantled homes are repurposed in order to strengthen Jerusalem's defenses. **siege mounds:** See note on 32:24.

33:5 Chaldeans: Babylonians. **I shall strike:** Underscores the theological truth that Babylon's army will administer the Lord's justice against the wicked city.

33:7 Judah ... Israel: Envisions a reunion of all twelve tribes of Israel. See note on 30:3.

33:10 desolate: Judah's population was greatly reduced after several thousand captives were taken to Babylon (52:28–30).

33:11 voice of the bridegroom: The joyous sounds of wedding celebrations will be heard again after the Lord reestablishes the covenant community in Judah. These voices have fallen silent during the decades of the Exile (7:34; 25:10). **thank offerings:** Peace offerings sacrificed in the Temple in gratitude for divine deliverance. Thanksgiving for the Lord's restoration of his people is here in view. According to later rabbinic tradition, all sacrifices will cease in the age to come except one: the *tôdāh*, or "sacrifice of thanksgiving" (*Leviticus Rabbah* 9, 7). See notes on Lev 7:12 and Ps 50:14. **Give thanks ... his mercy endures for ever:** Words found in several biblical psalms (Ps 100:5; 106:1; 107:1; 118:1; 136:1). This song of praise recalls David's song of thanksgiving when the ark was brought in musical procession to its first dwelling tent

in Jerusalem (1 Chron 16:34), as well as in the laying of the foundation for the rebuilding of the Temple after the Babylonian Exile (Ezra 3:11).

33:14–26 These verses, translated from the Hebrew text (MT), do not appear in the Greek translation of the book (LXX). For other differences between these two versions of Jeremiah, see introduction: *Literary Background*.

33:15 a righteous Branch: The Davidic Messiah, whom God will raise up after the collapse of the Davidic monarchy. See word study: *Branch* at 23:5. **justice and righteousness:** Required of the kings of Israel and Judah as earthly representatives of God and his rule. See note on 2 Sam 8:15.

33:16 it: The pronoun is feminine, referring back to Jerusalem. **the LORD is our righteousness:** The name of the coming king in 23:6. It is here a name for the restored city, also called "the throne of the LORD" (3:17).

33:17–18 God pledges to uphold his covenant of kingship with **David** and his covenant of priesthood with Israel's **Levitical priests**. In the Davidic covenant, the Lord swore to establish David's "throne" and "kingdom" and "line" forever (2 Sam 7:13, 16; Ps 89:29). In the Levitical covenant, he called Aaron and his descendants and admitted them to a "perpetual priesthood throughout their generations" (Ex 40:15; Sir 45:7; Neh 13:29). These pledges are renewed in view of the disappearance of the Davidic monarchy and the destruction of the Jerusalem Temple in 586 B.C.

33:20 my covenant with the day ... the night: The Lord's covenant with creation, which established the alternating cycles of day and night (Gen 1:3–5, 14–19) and which was reaffirmed as part of his covenant with Noah (Gen 8:22). If

---

[h] Heb obscure.

[i] Cn: Heb *They are coming in to fight against the Chaldeans.*

[j] Heb uncertain.

[k] Heb *and it.*

*33:15: cf. Is 11:1: "a shoot from the stump of Jesse."

night, so that day and night will not come at their appointed time, [21]then also my covenant with David my servant may be broken, so that he shall not have a son to reign on his throne, and my covenant with the Levitical priests my ministers. [22]As the host of heaven cannot be numbered and the sands of the sea cannot be measured, so I will multiply the descendants of David my servant, and the Levitical priests who minister to me."

23 The word of the LORD came to Jeremi'ah: [24]"Have you not observed what these people are saying, 'The LORD has rejected the two families which he chose'? Thus they have despised my people so that they are no longer a nation in their sight. [25]Thus says the LORD: If I have not established my covenant with day and night and the ordinances of heaven and earth, [26]then I will reject the descendants of Jacob and David my servant and will not choose one of his descendants to rule over the seed of Abraham, Isaac, and Jacob. For I will restore their fortunes, and will have mercy upon them."

Death in Captivity Predicted for Zedekiah

34 The word which came to Jeremi'ah from the LORD, when Nebuchadrez'zar king of Babylon and all his army and all the kingdoms of the earth under his dominion and all the peoples were fighting against Jerusalem and all of its cities: [2]"Thus says the LORD, the God of Israel: Go and speak to Zedeki'ah king of Judah and say to him, 'Thus says the LORD: Behold, I am giving this city into the hand of the king of Babylon, and he shall burn it with fire. [3]You shall not escape from his hand, but shall surely be captured and delivered into his hand; you shall see the king of Babylon eye to eye and speak with him face to face; and you shall go to Babylon.' [4]Yet hear the word of the LORD, O Zedeki'ah king of Judah! Thus says the LORD concerning you: 'You shall not die by the sword. [5]You shall die in peace. And as spices were burned for your fathers, the former kings who were before you, so men shall burn spices for you and lament for you, saying, "Alas, lord!"' For I have spoken the word, says the LORD."

6 Then Jeremi'ah the prophet spoke all these words to Zedeki'ah king of Judah, in Jerusalem, [7]when the army of the king of Babylon was fighting against Jerusalem and against all the cities of Judah that were left, La'chish and Aze'kah; for these were the only fortified cities of Judah that remained.

Treatment of Hebrew Slaves

8 The word which came to Jeremi'ah from the LORD, after King Zedeki'ah had made a covenant with all the people in Jerusalem to make a proclamation of liberty to them, [9]that every one should set free his Hebrew slaves, male and female, so that no one should enslave a Jew, his brother. [10]And they obeyed, all the princes and all the people who had entered into the covenant that every one would set free his slave, male or female, so that they would not be enslaved again; they obeyed and set them free. [11]But afterward they turned around and took back the male and female slaves they had set free, and brought them into subjection as slaves. [12]The word of the LORD came to Jeremi'ah from the LORD: [13]"Thus says the LORD, the God of Israel: I made a covenant with your fathers when I brought them out

---

people cannot break this covenant by preventing the continuous coming of day and night—a thing utterly impossible—then God's covenants with David and the Levitical priests will likewise remain unbroken (33:21). See note on Gen 1:1—2:4.

📖 33:22 the host ... the sands: The pledge of unmeasurable fruitfulness linked to the Abrahamic covenant in Gen 22:17 is here applied to the Davidic and Levitical covenants.

33:24 the two families: The northern tribes of Israel and the southern tribes of Judah, which together form the chosen nation of Israel. **he chose:** The language of divine election (Deut 7:6-7).

33:26 I will reject ... Jacob: Another thing God will never do (1 Sam 12:22; Ps 94:14; Rom 11:1). **one of his descendants:** The royal messianic Branch of 33:15.

34:1-22 Jeremiah predicts the fiery destruction of Jerusalem (34:2), assures King Zedekiah that he will escape death by the sword (34:4-5), and insists that the Lord will hold the city's slave owners accountable for violating their covenant to let slaves go free (34:15-22).

34:1 Nebuchadrezzar: An alternate spelling for Nebuchadnezzar, ruler of the Neo-Babylonian empire from 605 to 562 B.C. **all the kingdoms:** Military support is supplied to Nebuchadnezzar by nations already conquered and made vassals of the Babylonian empire. **fighting against Jerusalem:** During the months leading up to the fall of the city in 586 B.C.

34:2 Zedekiah: The last king of Judah, who reigned from 597 to 586 B.C.

34:3 You ... shall surely be captured: Zedekiah attempts to flee Jerusalem by night, but the Babylonians overtake him

near Jericho (2 Kings 25:4-5). **eye to eye:** Zedekiah will be brought before Nebuchadnezzar, who will slay his sons and gouge out his eyes before sending him into exile (2 Kings 25:6-7).

34:5 You shall die in peace: A promise that Zedekiah will be spared execution, not that he will be spared suffering. He is imprisoned in Babylon until the day of his death (52:11). **spices:** The exiled community will give Zedekiah some semblance of a royal funeral (2 Chron 16:14).

34:7 Lachish and Azekah: Fortified towns of Judah southwest of Jerusalem.

34:8 liberty: Similar to a proclamation of "release" (Heb., *derôr*) at the start of a Jubilee year (Lev 25:10). Here a covenant is made for the immediate emancipation of Judahite slaves who had been kept in a state of servitude beyond the six years allowed by the Mosaic Law (34:14). The reason for this decision is probably twofold: **(1)** Zedekiah wants to seek the Lord's favor in a time of national emergency by calling Judah to a more complete obedience of the Torah; **(2)** he wants to increase the manpower devoted to the city's defense. In any case, the manumission of enslaved kinsmen is "right" in the Lord's eyes (34:15).

34:11 took back the ... slaves: In violation of the covenant just made. It took place when the Babylonians had withdrawn from Jerusalem (34:21), lifting the siege temporarily in order to confront Egyptian forces that had marched into southern Canaan (37:5). Many must have thought the threat was over, when in fact the Babylonians would return quickly to overthrow the city.

of the land of Egypt, out of the house of bondage, saying, [14]"At the end of six[1] years each of you must set free the fellow Hebrew who has been sold to you and has served you six years; you must set him free from your service.' But your fathers did not listen to me or incline their ears to me. [15]You recently repented and did what was right in my eyes by proclaiming liberty, each to his neighbor, and you made a covenant before me in the house which is called by my name; [16]but then you turned around and profaned my name when each of you took back his male and female slaves, whom you had set free according to their desire, and you brought them into subjection to be your slaves. [17]Therefore, thus says the LORD: You have not obeyed me by proclaiming liberty, every one to his brother and to his neighbor; behold, I proclaim to you liberty to the sword, to pestilence, and to famine, says the LORD. I will make you a horror to all the kingdoms of the earth. [18]And the men who transgressed my covenant and did not keep the terms of the covenant which they made before me, I will make like[m] the calf which they cut in two and passed between its parts—[19]the princes of Judah, the princes of Jerusalem, the eunuchs, the priests, and all the people of the land who passed between the parts of the calf; [20]and I will give them into the hand of their enemies and into the hand of those who seek their lives. Their dead bodies shall be food for the birds of the air and the beasts of the earth. [21]And Zedeki'ah king of Judah, and his princes I will give into the hand of their enemies and into the hand of those who seek their lives, into the hand of the army of the king of Babylon which has withdrawn from you. [22]Behold, I will command, says the LORD, and will bring them back to this city; and they will fight against it, and take it, and burn it with fire. I will make the cities of Judah a desolation without inhabitant."

The Rechabites Commended

35 *The word which came to Jeremi'ah from the LORD in the days of Jehoi'akim the son of Josi'ah, king of Judah: [2]"Go to the house of the Re'chabites, and speak with them, and bring them to the house of the LORD, into one of the chambers; then offer them wine to drink." [3]So I took Ja-azani'ah the son of Jeremi'ah, son of Ha"bazzini'ah, and his brothers, and all his sons, and the whole house of the Re'chabites. [4]I brought them to the house of the LORD into the chamber of the sons of Ha'nan the son of Igdali'ah, the man of God, which was near the chamber of the princes, above the chamber of Ma-asei'ah the son of Shallum, keeper of the threshold. [5]Then I set before the Re'chabites pitchers full of wine, and cups; and I said to them, "Drink wine." [6]But they answered, "We will drink no wine, for Jon'adab the son of Re'chab, our father, commanded us, 'You shall not drink wine, neither you nor your sons for ever; [7]you shall not build a house; you shall not sow seed; you shall not plant or have a vineyard;

34:14 At the end of six years: The term limit of a slave's compulsory service according to the laws in Ex 21:2 and Deut 15:12.

34:17 liberty: The subject of a wordplay. Because slave owners reneged on their oath to "release" their slaves permanently, they are now "released" into the fury of the Lord's judgment. **sword ... pestilence ... famine:** Curses of the Mosaic covenant that bring suffering and death to violators of the covenant (Lev 26:25–26).

34:18 the calf which they cut in two: An ancient covenant-making procedure. Partners entering a covenant divided animals in half and walked between the severed parts to ritualize a self-imposed curse. The action was equivalent to saying: "May I become like these animals, slain and dismembered, if I fail to uphold the covenant I am making today." For a biblical example, see Gen 15:7–21, where the Lord passes between divided animals when he swears a covenant oath to give the Promised Land to Abraham's future descendants. The same practice is attested outside the Bible, e.g., in the *Sefire Inscription* of an Aramaic treaty from the eighth century B.C.

34:21 withdrawn: See note on 34:11.

35:1–19 Contrasts the faithfulness of the Rechabites, who heed the instructions of their father (= Jonadab), with the faithlessness of the Judahites, who refuse to listen to their Father (= the Lord). The account stresses how the former "obeyed" (35:8, 10, 14, 18) while the latter has "not obeyed" (35:16).

35:1 Jehoiakim: King of Judah from 609 to 598 B.C.

35:2 the Rechabites: Descendants of a man named Rechab (35:6). The clan stands out from the general population of Judah for its commitment to a nomadic life-style. The Rechabites build no houses, operate no farms or vineyard estates, and decline to drink wine; instead, they dwell in tents (35:6–7). They only seek refuge inside the walls of Jerusalem because the Babylonian army has invaded the land (35:11). Some scholars hypothesize that the Rechabites are ultra-traditionalists who idealize Israel's forty years of encampments in the wilderness before entering the Promised Land (described as a honeymoon period in 2:1–3). The Lord does not endorse their rule of life as such, as though he disapproves of sedentary living or agriculture, but blesses them for honoring their ancestor's commands for multiple generations (35:18–19). **the chambers:** The Temple complex has storage rooms as well as open rooms that can be used for gatherings or even for living quarters (36:10; 2 Kings 23:11; 1 Chron 28:12; Neh 13:4–9).

35:4 the man of God: A title normally used for a prophet (1 Sam 9:6–10; 1 Kings 13:1; 2 Kings 1:9; 4:8–9). **Maaseiah:** Possibly the father of Zephaniah the priest in 21:1; 37:3. **keeper of the threshold:** One of three priests in charge of guarding the Temple precincts (52:24) and seemingly in charge of monies for the upkeep of the sanctuary (2 Kings 12:9).

35:6 drink no wine: In this respect, the Rechabites are similar to persons who take a Nazarite vow to abstain from consuming any produce of the grapevine (Num 6:1–21). **Jonadab:** A shortened from of Jehonadab, who lived during the reign of Jehu, king of Israel, between 841 and 814 B.C. (2 Kings 10:15, 23). **our father:** Here means forefather or ancestor, not biological father.

---

[1]Gk: Heb *seven*.
[m]Cn: Heb lacks *like*.
*35: This chapter is our chief source of information about the little-known sect of Rechabites; cf. 2 Kings 10:15–16, 23. They obeyed what they felt to be a call to serve God in the wilderness and desert places. The ancient nomad life during the Exodus was always looked back to as the time of the greatest fidelity to God.

but you shall live in tents all your days, that you may live many days in the land where you sojourn.' ⁸We have obeyed the voice of Jon'adab the son of Re'chab, our father, in all that he commanded us, to drink no wine all our days, ourselves, our wives, our sons, or our daughters, ⁹and not to build houses to dwell in. We have no vineyard or field or seed; ¹⁰but we have lived in tents, and have obeyed and done all that Jon'adab our father commanded us. ¹¹But when Nebuchadrez'zar king of Babylon came up against the land, we said, 'Come, and let us go to Jerusalem for fear of the army of the Chalde'ans and the army of the Syrians.' So we are living in Jerusalem."

12 Then the word of the LORD came to Jeremi'ah: ¹³"Thus says the LORD of hosts, the God of Israel: Go and say to the men of Judah and the inhabitants of Jerusalem, Will you not receive instruction and listen to my words? says the LORD. ¹⁴The command which Jon'adab the son of Re'chab gave to his sons, to drink no wine, has been kept; and they drink none to this day, for they have obeyed their father's command. I have spoken to you persistently, but you have not listened to me. ¹⁵I have sent to you all my servants the prophets, sending them persistently, saying, 'Turn now every one of you from his evil way, and amend your doings, and do not go after other gods to serve them, and then you shall dwell in the land which I gave to you and your fathers.' But you did not incline your ear or listen to me. ¹⁶The sons of Jon'adab the son of Re'chab have kept the command which their father gave them, but this people has not obeyed me. ¹⁷Therefore, thus says the LORD, the God of hosts, the God of Israel: Behold, I am bringing on Judah and all the inhabitants of Jerusalem all the evil that I have pronounced against them; because I have spoken to them and they have not listened, I have called to them and they have not answered."

18 But to the house of the Re'chabites Jeremi'ah said, "Thus says the LORD of hosts, the God of Israel: Because you have obeyed the command of Jon'adab your father, and kept all his precepts, and done all that he commanded you, ¹⁹therefore thus says the LORD of hosts, the God of Israel: Jon'adab the son of Re'chab shall never lack a man to stand before me."

The Scroll Is Read

36 In the fourth year of Jehoi'akim the son of Josi'ah, king of Judah, this word came to Jeremi'ah from the LORD: ²"Take a scroll and write on it all the words that I have spoken to you against Israel and Judah and all the nations, from the day I spoke to you, from the days of Josi'ah until today. ³It may be that the house of Judah will hear all the evil which I intend to do to them, so that every one may turn from his evil way, and that I may forgive their iniquity and their sin."

4 Then Jeremi'ah called Baruch the son of Neri'ah, and Baruch wrote upon a scroll at the dictation of Jeremi'ah all the words of the LORD which he had spoken to him. ⁵And Jeremi'ah ordered Baruch, saying, "I am debarred from going to the house of the LORD; ⁶so you are to go, and on a fast day in the hearing of all the people in the LORD's house you shall read the words of the LORD from the scroll which you have written at my dictation. You shall read them also in the hearing of all the men of Judah who come out of their cities. ⁷It may be that their supplication will come before the LORD, and that every one will turn from his evil way, for great is the anger and wrath that the LORD has pronounced against this people." ⁸And Baruch the son of Neri'ah

---

35:11 Nebuchadrezzar: An alternate spelling for Nebuchadnezzar, ruler of the Neo-Babylonian empire from 605 to 562 B.C. **Chaldeans … Syrians:** Babylonians and Arameans (2 Kings 24:2).

35:17 all the evil: The curses of the covenant that are triggered by rebellion (Deut 28:15–68).

35:19 never lack a man: A blessing of family preservation. At least one of the sons of Rechab will help to rebuild the walls of Jerusalem in the days of Nehemiah, roughly 150 years after Jeremiah delivers this oracle (Neh 3:14). **to stand before me:** Suggests the Rechabites are granted a form of divine service, but the details are unknown.

36:1–32 Jeremiah dictates his prophecies to Baruch, who writes them down in a scroll (36:4), reads them aloud in the Temple (36:8, 10), and then makes a second, expanded copy of his oracles (36:32) after King Jehoiakim defiantly burns the first scroll (36:21–23).

36:1 the fourth year: 605 B.C. **Jehoiakim:** The king of Judah from 609 to 598 B.C. He is one of Jeremiah's most determined opponents.

36:2 a scroll: A long parchment or papyrus roll (Ezek 2:9). Scribes typically wrote text in columns so that the book could be read section by section as it was unrolled (36:23). **words that I have spoken:** Jeremiah is to dictate, not his own thoughts and ideas, but words given to him by the Lord under the influence of divine inspiration (1:9). **from the days of**

Josiah: Jeremiah was called to be a prophet in 627 B.C. during Josiah's reign as king of Judah (640–609 B.C.). The scroll thus contains an anthology of messages he has received from the Lord over two decades.

36:3 It may be: Judah's doom is not a certainty in 605, as it will be when the Babylonian conquest of 586 B.C. draws closer. At this earlier date, the window of opportunity for Judah's repentance remains open.

36:4 Baruch the son of Neriah: Identified as Jeremiah's *sōpher*, meaning his "secretary" or "scribe" (36:26, 32). His services include writing up deeds of sale (32:12) and recording prophetic oracles that Jeremiah dictates (36:32; 45:1). He also acts as a spokesman for the prophet by reading out Jeremiah's oracles (36:5–6, 10). Baruch's brother, Seraiah, will become quartermaster for King Zedekiah (51:59). Archaeologists digging in Jerusalem unearthed a sixth-century B.C. seal impression or *bulla* that reads: "Belonging to Berekhyahu, son of Neryahu, the scribe"—an artifact that confirms both the historical existence and professional occupation of Jeremiah's collaborator. After the fall of Jerusalem, Baruch went to Egypt with Jeremiah (43:6–7). For his connection to the biblical Book of Baruch, see introduction to Baruch: *Author and Date*.

36:5 I am debarred: No reason is given why Jeremiah is forbidden to enter the Temple, but one suspects it was because of his predictions that the city and sanctuary of Jerusalem are headed for destruction.

did all that Jeremi'ah the prophet ordered him about reading from the scroll the words of the Lord in the Lord's house.

9 In the fifth year of Jehoi'akim the son of Josi'ah, king of Judah, in the ninth month, all the people in Jerusalem and all the people who came from the cities of Judah to Jerusalem proclaimed a fast before the Lord. ¹⁰Then, in the hearing of all the people, Baruch read the words of Jeremi'ah from the scroll, in the house of the Lord, in the chamber of Gemari'ah the son of Sha'phan the secretary, which was in the upper court, at the entry of the New Gate of the Lord's house.

11 When Micai'ah the son of Gemari'ah, son of Sha'phan, heard all the words of the Lord from the scroll, ¹²he went down to the king's house, into the secretary's chamber; and all the princes were sitting there: Elish'ama the secretary, Delai'ah the son of Shemai'ah, Elna'than the son of Achbor, Gemari'ah the son of Sha'phan, Zedeki'ah the son of Hanani'ah, and all the princes. ¹³And Micai'ah told them all the words that he had heard, when Baruch read the scroll in the hearing of the people. ¹⁴Then all the princes sent Jehu'di the son of Nethani'ah, son of Shelemi'ah, son of Cu'shi, to say to Baruch, "Take in your hand the scroll that you read in the hearing of the people, and come." So Baruch the son of Neri'ah took the scroll in his hand and came to them. ¹⁵And they said to him, "Sit down and read it." So Baruch read it to them. ¹⁶When they heard all the words, they turned one to another in fear; and they said to Baruch, "We must report all these words to the king." ¹⁷Then they asked Baruch, "Tell us, how did you write all these words? Was it at his dictation?" ¹⁸Baruch answered them, "He dictated all these words to me, while I wrote them with ink on the scroll." ¹⁹Then the princes said to Baruch, "Go and hide, you and Jeremi'ah, and let no one know where you are."

King Jehoiakim Burns the Scroll

20 So they went into the court to the king, having put the scroll in the chamber of Elish'ama the secretary; and they reported all the words to the king. ²¹Then the king sent Jehu'di to get the scroll, and he took it from the chamber of Elish'ama the secretary; and Jehudi read it to the king and all the princes who stood beside the king. ²²It was the ninth month, and the king was sitting in the winter house and there was a fire burning in the brazier before him. ²³As Jehu'di read three or four columns, the king would cut them off with a penknife and throw them into the fire in the brazier, until the entire scroll was consumed in the fire that was in the brazier. ²⁴Yet neither the king, nor any of his servants who heard all these words, was afraid, nor did they tear their garments. ²⁵Even when Elna'than and Delai'ah and Gemari'ah urged the king not to burn the scroll, he would not listen to them. ²⁶And the king commanded Jerah'meel the king's son and Serai'ah the son of Az'ri-el and Shelemi'ah the son of Abde'el to seize Baruch the secretary and Jeremi'ah the prophet, but the Lord hid them.

Jeremiah Dictates Another Scroll

27 Now, after the king had burned the scroll with the words which Baruch wrote at Jeremi'ah's dictation, the word of the Lord came to Jeremiah: ²⁸"Take another scroll and write on it all the former words that were in the first scroll, which Jehoi'akim the king of Judah has burned. ²⁹And concerning Jehoi'akim king of Judah you shall say, 'Thus says the Lord, You have burned this scroll, saying, "Why have you written in it that the king of Babylon will certainly come and destroy this land, and will cut off from it man and beast?" ³⁰Therefore thus says the Lord concerning Jehoi'akim king of Judah, He shall have none to sit upon the throne of David, and his dead body shall be cast out to the heat by day

---

36:9-26 The scroll of Jeremiah's prophecies is read to three audiences in three different locations: **(1)** Baruch reads the scroll to the people in the Temple (36:10); Baruch reads the scroll to the princes in the secretary's chamber (36:11-19); and **(2)** Jehudi reads the scroll to Jehoiakim and the princes in the king's winter residence (36:20-26).

36:9 the fifth year: 604 B.C. **ninth month:** Kislev, equivalent to November-December. **proclaimed a fast:** Days of community fasting are called for in times of danger and distress so that earnest petition can be made for God's favor and deliverance. Judah may have called a fast after the Babylonians sacked the Philistine city of Ashkelon in 604. See note on Joel 1:14.

36:10 the chamber: See note on 35:2. **Gemariah:** A member of the royal family in Judah. His father had been the secretary of state under King Josiah (2 Kings 22:3). **in the upper court:** Suggests the scroll was read from a second-story window overlooking the Temple court. **the New Gate:** Location uncertain.

36:12 the secretary's chamber: One of the royal offices in Jerusalem.

36:14 Jehudi: Otherwise unknown but tracing his family line back three generations suggests he is a distinguished figure.

36:19 Go and hide: Wise advice, since Jehoiakim has already slain the prophet Uriah for preaching a similar message (26:20-23).

36:22 the brazier: An earthenware pot or metallic kettle used for burning small fires indoors.

36:23 penknife: Used by scribes to cut sheets of papyri and to sharpen reeds into writing pens.

36:24 nor ... tear their garments: A sign of defiant resistance to the word of the Lord and its appeals for repentance. It places the evil Jehoiakim in contrast to righteous kings such as his father, Josiah, who tore his garments when "the book of the law" found in the Temple (= a scroll of all or part of Deuteronomy) was read aloud to him (2 Kings 22:11).

36:30 none to sit upon the throne: Jehoiakim is denied a dynasty. His successor, Jehoiachin, reigns for only three months in 598-597 B.C. before he is exiled to Babylon, where he eventually dies (52:31-34). No other of his descendants exercise kingship. See also note on 22:30. **cast out:** As an unburied corpse. This appears to be a figurative description of the king's dishonorable end, as also in 22:19. The statement "Jehoiakim slept with his fathers" in 2 Kings 24:6 may imply that he was buried in the royal tombs in Jerusalem.

and the frost by night. [31]And I will punish him and his offspring and his servants for their iniquity; I will bring upon them, and upon the inhabitants of Jerusalem, and upon the men of Judah, all the evil that I have pronounced against them, but they would not hear.'"

32 Then Jeremi'ah took another scroll and gave it to Baruch the scribe, the son of Neri'ah, who wrote on it at the dictation of Jeremiah all the words of the scroll which Jehoi'akim king of Judah had burned in the fire; and many similar words were added to them.

Zedekiah Asks Jeremiah's Prayers

37 Zedeki'ah the son of Josi'ah, whom Nebuchadrez'zar king of Babylon made king in the land of Judah, reigned instead of Coni'ah the son of Jehoi'akim. [2]But neither he nor his servants nor the people of the land listened to the words of the LORD which he spoke through Jeremi'ah the prophet.

3 King Zedeki'ah sent Jehu'cal the son of Shelemi'ah, and Zephani'ah the priest, the son of Maasei'ah, to Jeremi'ah the prophet, saying, "Pray for us to the LORD our God." [4]Now Jeremi'ah was still going in and out among the people, for he had not yet been put in prison. [5]The army of Pharaoh had come out of Egypt; and when the Chalde'ans who were besieging Jerusalem heard news of them, they withdrew from Jerusalem.

6 Then the word of the LORD came to Jeremi'ah the prophet: [7]"Thus says the LORD, God of Israel: Thus shall you say to the king of Judah who sent you to me to inquire of me, 'Behold, Pharaoh's army which came to help you is about to return to Egypt, to its own land. [8]And the Chalde'ans shall come back and fight against this city; they shall take it and burn it with fire. [9]Thus says the LORD, Do not deceive yourselves, saying, "The Chalde'ans will surely stay away from us," for they will not stay away. [10]For even if you should defeat the whole army of Chalde'ans who are fighting against you, and there remained of them only wounded men, every man in his tent, they would rise up and burn this city with fire.'"

Jeremiah Is Imprisoned

11 Now when the Chalde'an army had withdrawn from Jerusalem at the approach of Pharaoh's army, [12]Jeremi'ah set out from Jerusalem to go to the land of Benjamin to receive his portion[n] there among the people. [13]When he was at the Benjamin Gate, a sentry there named Iri'jah the son of Shelemi'ah, son of Hanani'ah, seized Jeremi'ah the prophet, saying, "You are deserting to the Chalde'ans." [14]And Jeremi'ah said, "It is false; I am not deserting to the Chalde'ans." But Iri'jah would not listen to him, and seized Jeremiah and brought him to the princes. [15]And the princes were enraged at Jeremi'ah, and they beat him and imprisoned him in the house of Jonathan the secretary, for it had been made a prison.

16 When Jeremi'ah had come to the dungeon cells, and remained there many days, [17]King Zedeki'ah sent for him, and received him. The king questioned him secretly in his house, and said, "Is there any word from the LORD?" Jeremi'ah said, "There is." Then he said, "You shall be delivered into the hand of the king of Babylon." [18]Jeremi'ah also said to King Zedeki'ah, "What wrong have I done to you or your servants or this people, that you have put me in prison? [19]Where are your prophets who prophesied to you, saying, 'The king of Babylon will not come against you and against this land'? [20]Now hear, I beg you, O my lord the king: let my humble plea come before you, and do not send me back to the house of Jonathan the secretary, lest I die

---

37:1–21 Suspected of deserting to the enemy, Jeremiah is arrested (37:13), beaten (37:15), and locked in a dungeon (37:16). In reality, he intended only to conduct some business in his hometown of Anathoth. Zedekiah sympathizes with his plea enough to upgrade his incarceration from a dungeon to "the court of the guard" and supplies him with a daily ration of bread (37:21). Historically, the events in this chapter took place ca. 587 B.C., when the Babylonians briefly suspended the final siege of Jerusalem to fend off reinforcement troops from Egypt coming to the city's aid (37:5, 7).

37:1 Zedekiah: The last king of Judah, who reigns from 597 to 586 B.C. He is placed on the throne by the Babylonians (2 Kings 24:17). **Nebuchadrezzar:** An alternate spelling for Nebuchadnezzar, ruler of the Neo-Babylonian empire from 605 to 562 B.C. **Coniah:** A shortened form of the name Jeconiah (24:1), also known as Jehoiachin, who reigns as king of Judah for three months in 598–597 B.C. before he is taken into exile.

37:3 Pray for us: The king's desperate but vain attempt to win God's favor and escape the consequences of his folly.

Zedekiah refuses to surrender to the Babylonians, contrary to the counsel of Jeremiah (21:1–10).

37:5 Pharaoh: Hophra, king of Egypt from 589 to 570 B.C. (44:30). **out of Egypt:** The army is coming up from the south to help defend Jerusalem, but they will be turned away (37:7). **Chaldeans:** Babylonians.

37:9 will surely stay away: Some delude themselves into thinking the Babylonian threat is over. In fact, Nebuchadnezzar's forces will quickly resume the assault on Jerusalem until the city is fully destroyed (37:8; 52:12–13).

37:12 to receive his portion: Perhaps the prophet is headed for his hometown of Anathoth to inspect or take charge of the land he has bought from his cousin Hanamel (32:6–15).

37:13 Benjamin Gate: Exact location uncertain, but somewhere in the north or northeast wall of Jerusalem opening toward Benjaminite territory. **You are deserting:** According to 38:19, several Jews at this time seek refuge with the besieging army.

37:15 beat him: Not the first time Jeremiah is physically abused (20:2). **the secretary:** Thought to be a secretary of state.

37:19 your prophets: False prophets who claim the Babylonians will never invade Judah (28:2). Jeremiah wonders why he is under arrest for making accurate predictions and not these deceivers who have been proven wrong.

---

[n]Heb obscure.

there." ²¹So King Zedeki'ah gave orders, and they committed Jeremi'ah to the court of the guard; and a loaf of bread was given him daily from the bakers' street, until all the bread of the city was gone. So Jeremiah remained in the court of the guard.

Jeremiah in the Cistern

38 Now Shephati'ah the son of Mattan, Geda-li'ah the son of Pashhur, Ju'cal the son of She-lemi'ah, and Pashhur the son of Malchi'ah heard the words that Jeremi'ah was saying to all the people, ²"Thus says the LORD, He who stays in this city shall die by the sword, by famine, and by pestilence; but he who goes out to the Chalde'ans shall live; he shall have his life as a prize of war, and live. ³Thus says the LORD, This city shall surely be given into the hand of the army of the king of Babylon and be taken." ⁴Then the princes said to the king, "Let this man be put to death, for he is weakening the hands of the soldiers who are left in this city, and the hands of all the people, by speaking such words to them. For this man is not seeking the welfare of this people, but their harm." ⁵King Zedeki'ah said, "Behold, he is in your hands; for the king can do nothing against you." ⁶So they took Jeremi'ah and cast him into the cistern of Malchi'ah, the king's son, which was in the court of the guard, letting Jeremiah down by ropes. And there was no water in the cistern, but only mire, and Jeremiah sank in the mire.

Ebed-melech rescues Jeremiah

7 When E'bed-mel'ech the Ethiopian, a eunuch, who was in the king's house, heard that they had put Jeremi'ah into the cistern—the king was sitting in the Benjamin Gate—⁸E'bed-mel'ech went from the king's house and said to the king, ⁹"My lord the king, these men have done evil in all that they did to Jeremi'ah the prophet by casting him into the cistern; and he will die there of hunger, for there is no bread left in the city." ¹⁰Then the king commanded E'bed-mel'ech, the Ethiopian, "Take three men with you from here, and lift Jeremi'ah the prophet out of the cistern before he dies." ¹¹So E'bed-mel'ech took the men with him and went to the house of the king, to a wardrobe of° the storehouse, and took from there old rags and worn-out clothes, which he let down to Jeremi'ah in the cistern by ropes. ¹²Then E'bed-mel'ech the Ethiopian said to Jeremi'ah, "Put the rags and clothes between your armpits and the ropes." Jeremiah did so. ¹³Then they drew Jeremi'ah up with ropes and lifted him out of the cistern. And Jeremiah remained in the court of the guard.

14 King Zedeki'ah sent for Jeremi'ah the prophet and received him at the third entrance of the temple of the LORD. The king said to Jeremi'ah, "I will ask you a question; hide nothing from me." ¹⁵Jeremi'ah said to Zedeki'ah, "If I tell you, will you not be sure to put me to death? And if I give you counsel, you will not listen to me." ¹⁶Then King Zedeki'ah swore secretly to Jeremi'ah, "As the LORD lives, who made our souls, I will not put you to death or deliver you into the hand of these men who seek your life."

17 Then Jeremi'ah said to Zedeki'ah, "Thus says the LORD, the God of hosts, the God of Israel, If you will surrender to the princes of the king of Babylon,

---

37:21 gave orders: An act of clemency. **court of the guard:** The royal palace-yard in Jerusalem that allows detainees limited interaction with others (32:2). It is more like confinement under "house arrest" than the dungeon cell where Jeremiah has been previously (37:16). The prophet will remain here until the fall of the city (38:28).

38:1–13 Jeremiah is accused of aiding the enemy by deflating the morale of Jerusalem's defenders and seeking the harm of its people (38:4). A charge of treason merited the death penalty (38:4). However, the prophet is not betraying his people; he is advising them to surrender to Nebuchadnezzar to ensure their survival (38:2). Four accusers (38:1), often identified as pro-Egyptian politicians, seize Jeremiah and cast him into a cistern, where he is likely to die of starvation (38:6), while a sympathizer named Ebed-melech orchestrates his rescue (38:7–13).

38:1 Shephatiah: Otherwise unknown. **Gedaliah:** Son of the priest who beats Jeremiah in 20:2. **Jucal:** Probably the Jehucal who is sent to Jeremiah in 37:3. **Pashhur the son of Malchiah:** Sent to Jeremiah in 21:1–2.

38:2 sword ... famine ... pestilence: Curses of the covenant that bring suffering and death to violators of the covenant (Lev 26:25–26; Ezek 7:15). **Chaldeans:** Babylonians.

38:4 put to death: Stands in contrast to the earlier judgment in 26:16.

38:5 he is in your hands: Giving the prophet over to his enemies should have guaranteed Jeremiah's demise, except that the Lord has promised to be his Defender (1:18–19).

38:6 cistern: A stone reservoir used for storing rainwater for the dry summer months. This one is nearly dry, except for some sediment at the bottom, suggesting the event takes place not long before the final conquest of the city in August 586 B.C.

38:7 Ebed-melech: Translates "servant of the king". His life will be spared during the conquest of Jerusalem because he trusts in the Lord, and perhaps also because of his kindness to the Lord's prophet (39:15–18). **eunuch:** A royal officer who may have been castrated. **Benjamin Gate:** See note on 37:13.

38:9 no bread left: The final siege of Jerusalem lasts more than a year so that eventually food supplies in the city run out (37:21).

38:10 Take three men: Jeremiah will be rescued from the cistern by four men, just as he was hurled into the cistern by four men (38:1).

38:11 rags ... clothes: To be used as padding for the ropes that hoist Jeremiah out of the mud (38:12).

38:13 court of the guard: See note on 37:21.

38:14–28 Zedekiah questions Jeremiah about the word of the Lord. The prophet answers (38:17–23) but hesitates to speak because (1) he fears for his safety, and (2) the king has ignored all of his warnings thus far (38:15). He presents the king with two options only: surrender to Nebuchadnezzar, which will spare the city and many lives, or fight against Nebuchadnezzar, which will guarantee the city's demise and the captivity of the royal household.

38:14 the third entrance: Location unknown.

38:16 As the LORD lives: An oath formula invoking the divine name (44:26; 1 Sam 14:45; 1 Kings 1:29).

°Cn: Heb *to under.*

then your life shall be spared, and this city shall not be burned with fire, and you and your house shall live. [18]But if you do not surrender to the princes of the king of Babylon, then this city shall be given into the hand of the Chalde'ans, and they shall burn it with fire, and you shall not escape from their hand." [19]King Zedeki'ah said to Jeremi'ah, "I am afraid of the Jews who have deserted to the Chalde'ans, lest I be handed over to them and they abuse me." [20]Jeremi'ah said, "You shall not be given to them. Obey now the voice of the LORD in what I say to you, and it shall be well with you, and your life shall be spared. [21]But if you refuse to surrender, this is the vision which the LORD has shown to me: [22]Behold, all the women left in the house of the king of Judah were being led out to the princes of the king of Babylon and were saying,

'Your trusted friends have deceived you
    and prevailed against you;
now that your feet are sunk in the mire,
    they turn away from you.'

[23]All your wives and your sons shall be led out to the Chalde'ans, and you yourself shall not escape from their hand, but shall be seized by the king of Babylon; and this city shall be burned with fire."

24 Then Zedeki'ah said to Jeremi'ah, "Let no one know of these words and you shall not die. [25]If the princes hear that I have spoken with you and come to you and say to you, 'Tell us what you said to the king and what the king said to you; hide nothing from us and we will not put you to death,' [26]then you shall say to them, 'I made a humble plea to the king that he would not send me back to the house of Jonathan to die there.'" [27]Then all the princes came to Jeremi'ah and asked him, and he answered them as the king had instructed him. So they left off speaking with him, for the conversation had not been overheard. [28]And Jeremi'ah remained in the court of the guard until the day that Jerusalem was taken.

The Fall of Jerusalem

39 In the ninth year of Zedeki'ah king of Judah, in the tenth month, Nebuchadrez'zar king of Babylon and all his army came against Jerusalem and besieged it; [2]in the eleventh year of Zedeki'ah, in the fourth month, on the ninth day of the month, a breach was made in the city. [3]When Jerusalem was taken,[p] all the princes of the king of Babylon came and sat in the middle gate: Ner'gal-share'zer, Sam'gar-ne'bo, Sar'sechim the Rab'saris, Nergal-sharezer the Rabmag, with all the rest of the officers of the king of Babylon. [4]When Zedeki'ah king of Judah and all the soldiers saw them, they fled, going out of the city at night by way of the king's garden through the gate between the two walls; and they went toward the Ar'abah. [5]But the army of the Chalde'ans pursued them, and overtook Zedeki'ah in the plains of Jericho; and when they had taken him, they brought him up to Nebuchadrez'zar king of Babylon, at Riblah, in the land of Ha'math; and he passed sentence upon him. [6]The king of Babylon slew the sons of Zedeki'ah at Riblah before his eyes; and the king of Babylon slew all the nobles of Judah. [7]He put out the eyes of Zedeki'ah, and bound him in chains to take him to Babylon. [8]The Chalde'ans burned the king's house and the house of the people, and broke down the walls of Jerusalem. [9]Then

---

38:19 the Jews: The people of Judah who have already surrendered to Babylonian forces (39:9).

38:22 feet ... in the mire: Describes a dire predicament that is literally true in Jeremiah's case (38:6).

38:26 I made a humble plea: True, as far as it goes (37:20). **the house of Jonathan:** Location of the dungeon cell where the prophet is imprisoned for a time (37:15–16).

39:1–10 The Babylonian conquest of Jerusalem, which follows a year-and-a-half siege. It takes place one month after a breach is made in the city wall in the midsummer of 586 B.C. Another account is given in 52:4–16, although here we learn the names of the Babylonian officers who take charge of the city.

39:1 ninth year: 587 B.C. The king's tenth year begins in March-April; hence, the long siege of Jerusalem, which begins in January 587 and ends with the burning of the city in August 586, covers an 18-month period that begins late in his ninth year, extends through his tenth year, and ends a few months into his eleventh year (39:2). **Zedekiah:** The last king of Judah, who reigns from 597 to 586 B.C. **tenth month:** Tebet, which corresponds to December-January. **Nebuchadrezzar:** An alternate spelling for Nebuchadnezzar, ruler of the Neo-Babylonian empire from 605 to 562 B.C.

39:2 eleventh year: 586 B.C. **fourth month:** Tammuz, which corresponds to June-July. **a breach was made:** Nebuchadnezzar's forces break through Jerusalem's defensive wall, perhaps on the north side of the city, which is the most vulnerable because it lacks the natural protection of a ravine. The city and Temple are burned one month later (52:12–13; 2 Kings 25:8–9).

39:3 the princes ... sat: Fulfilling the Lord's words that rulers of foreign kingdoms will set their thrones "at the entrance of the gates of Jerusalem" (1:15). **the middle gate:** Location unknown, but likely on the north side to the city. **Nergal-sharezer:** Probably the future king of Babylon, Neriglissar, who reigns from 560 to 556 B.C. **Rabsaris:** Means something like "chief attendant". **Rabmag:** A title of uncertain meaning.

39:4–7 Zedekiah attempts a nighttime escape from the city, only to be apprehended and taken to Babylon. His life is spared, as Jeremiah predicted, but not without bitter suffering: he witnesses the slaying of his sons, and then his eyes are gouged out (39:7; 52:11).

39:4 the king's garden: Near the southeast corner of the city (Neh 3:15). **the Arabah:** The arid lands east of Jerusalem and surrounding the Dead Sea.

39:5 Chaldeans: Babylonians. **plains of Jericho:** Northwest of the Dead Sea. **Riblah:** On the Orontes River in Syria, north of Damascus. It serves as Nebuchadnezzar's base of operations.

39:7 chains: Bronze shackles banded around a captive's wrists and ankles.

39:9 Nebuzaradan: One of Nebuchadnezzar's chief military officers. He oversees both the burning of Jerusalem and its Temple one month after the city is breached (52:12–13)

---

[p] This clause has been transposed from the end of Chapter 38.

Nebu'zarad'an, the captain of the guard, carried into exile to Babylon the rest of the people who were left in the city, those who had deserted to him, and the people who remained. ¹⁰Nebu'zarad'an, the captain of the guard, left in the land of Judah some of the poor people who owned nothing, and gave them vineyards and fields at the same time.

Jeremiah Is Sent to Ebed-melech

11 Nebuchadrez'zar king of Babylon gave command concerning Jeremi'ah through Nebu'zarad'an, the captain of the guard, saying, ¹²"Take him, look after him well and do him no harm, but deal with him as he tells you." ¹³So Nebu'zarad'an the captain of the guard, Nebushaz'ban the Rab'saris, Ner'gal-share'zer the Rabmag, and all the chief officers of the king of Babylon ¹⁴sent and took Jeremi'ah from the court of the guard. They entrusted him to Gedali'ah the son of Ahi'kam, son of Sha'phan, that he should take him home. So he dwelt among the people.

15 The word of the LORD came to Jeremi'ah while he was shut up in the court of the guard: ¹⁶"Go, and say to E'bed-mel'ech the Ethiopian, 'Thus says the LORD of hosts, the God of Israel: Behold, I will fulfil my words against this city for evil and not for good, and they shall be accomplished before you on that day. ¹⁷But I will deliver you on that day, says the LORD, and you shall not be given into the hand of the men of whom you are afraid. ¹⁸For I will surely save you, and you shall not fall by the sword; but you shall have your life as a prize of war, because you have put your trust in me, says the LORD.'"

Jeremiah with Gedaliah the Governor

40 The word that came to Jeremi'ah from the LORD after Nebu'zarad'an the captain of the guard had let him go from Ra'mah, when he took him bound in chains along with all the captives of Jerusalem and Judah who were being exiled to Babylon. ²The captain of the guard took Jeremi'ah and said to him, "The LORD your God pronounced this evil against this place; ³the LORD has brought it about, and has done as he said. Because you sinned against the LORD, and did not obey his voice, this thing has come upon you. ⁴Now, behold, I release you today from the chains on your hands. If it seems good to you to come with me to Babylon, come, and I will look after you well; but if it seems wrong to you to come with me to Babylon, do not come. See, the whole land is before you; go wherever you think it good and right to go. ⁵If you remain, ^q then return to Gedali'ah the son of Ahi'kam, son of Sha'phan, whom the king of Babylon appointed governor of the cities of Judah, and dwell with him among the people; or go wherever you think it right to go." So the captain of the guard gave him an allowance of food and a present, and let him go. ⁶Then Jeremi'ah went to Gedali'ah the son of Ahi'kam, at Mizpah, and dwelt with him among the people who were left in the land.

7 When all the captains of the forces in the open country and their men heard that the king of Babylon had appointed Gedali'ah the son of Ahi'kam governor in the land, and had committed to him men, women, and children, those of the poorest of the land who had not been taken into exile to

---

and the destruction of the city walls (52:14). He is also tasked with organizing the roundup and deportation of Judah's exiles in the aftermath of the conquest (52:15). **carried into exile:** For an inventory of those taken to Babylon, see 52:28–30.

39:10 the poor: A population unlikely to instigate further rebellion.

39:12 do him no harm: Jeremiah is treated well by Nebuchadnezzar, presumably because he has been preaching "surrender" to the besieging army rather than resistance (27:12, 17; 38:2).

39:14 court of the guard: See note on 37:21. **Gedaliah:** Made governor of the non-exiled population left behind in Judah. He is appointed by Nebuchadnezzar after Judah is made a Babylonian province and the Davidic monarchy has come to an end (40:5). His father, Ahikam, protected Jeremiah (26:24), and his grandfather, Shaphan, was Judah's secretary of state under King Josiah (2 Kings 22:8–10). He is not to be confused with the Gedaliah who conspires against Jeremiah in 38:1.

39:15–18 An oracle that predates (rather than postdates) the fall of Jerusalem. Some suspect it originally stood at the end of chap. 38.

39:16 Ebed-melech: The official who facilitated Jeremiah's rescue from the cistern (38:7–13).

39:17 I will deliver you: The same promise was made to Jeremiah in 1:19.

40:1–6 Jeremiah is released from a group of captives headed for Babylon. He had already been given his freedom by Nebuchadnezzar (39:11–12), but apparently he was rounded up by mistake and detained with other Judahites bound for exile (40:1). Upon release, he is given a choice to come to Babylon as a guest or to stay among his people in Judah (40:4). He chooses to stay in the homeland (40:6).

40:1 Nebuzaradan: See note on 39:9. **Ramah:** A town of Benjamin, five miles north of Jerusalem, that serves as a staging area where captives from Judah are assembled in preparation for the long journey to Mesopotamia.

40:3 the LORD has brought it about: A remarkable confession on the lips of a Gentile soldier, who echoes the preaching of Jeremiah that the conquest of Judah was an act of Israel's God. **you sinned:** The pronoun "you" is plural, referring to the sins of the people of Judah, not to the sins of Jeremiah.

40:5 Gedaliah: Appointed governor of Judah (40:7). See note on 39:14. **food and a present:** Jeremiah is given provisions because Nebuchadnezzar has instructed his officers to treat the prophet "well" (39:12).

40:6 Mizpah: A town of Benjamin, seven miles north of Jerusalem, that serves as the administrative center of Judah after the destruction of Jerusalem. The name translates "watchtower". **dwelt with him:** Jeremiah dwells in Mizpah, perhaps in the governor's residence (39:14).

40:7–9 Paralleled by 2 Kings 25:22–24.

40:7 captains of the forces: Commanders of Judah's army who elude capture by the Babylonians by hiding in the countryside.

---

^qSyr: Heb obscure.

Babylon, [8]they went to Gedali'ah at Mizpah—Ish'mael the son of Nethani'ah, Joha'nan the son of Kare'ah, Serai'ah the son of Tan'humeth, the sons of E'phai the Netoph'athite, Jezani'ah the son of the Ma-ac'athite, they and their men. [9]Gedali'ah the son of Ahi'kam, son of Sha'phan, swore to them and their men, saying, "Do not be afraid to serve the Chalde'ans. Dwell in the land, and serve the king of Babylon, and it shall be well with you. [10]As for me, I will dwell at Mizpah, to stand for you before the Chalde'ans who will come to us; but as for you, gather wine and summer fruits and oil, and store them in your vessels, and dwell in your cities that you have taken." [11]Likewise, when all the Jews who were in Moab and among the Am'monites and in E'dom and in other lands heard that the king of Babylon had left a remnant in Judah and had appointed Gedali'ah the son of Ahi'kam, son of Sha'phan, as governor over them, [12]then all the Jews returned from all the places to which they had been driven and came to the land of Judah, to Gedali'ah at Mizpah; and they gathered wine and summer fruits in great abundance.

13 Now Joha'nan the son of Kare'ah and all the leaders of the forces in the open country came to Gedali'ah at Mizpah [14]and said to him, "Do you know that Ba'alis the king of the Am'monites has sent Ish'mael the son of Nethani'ah to take your life?" But Gedali'ah the son of Ahi'kam would not believe them. [15]Then Joha'nan the son of Kare'ah spoke secretly to Gedali'ah at Mizpah, "Let me go and slay Ish'mael the son of Nethani'ah, and no one will know it. Why should he take your life, so that all the Jews who are gathered about you would be scattered, and the remnant of Judah would perish?" [16]But Gedali'ah the son of Ahi'kam said to Joha'nan the son of Kare'ah, "You shall not do this thing, for you are speaking falsely of Ish'mael."

Insurrection against Gedaliah

41 In the seventh month, Ish'mael the son of Nethani'ah, son of Elish'ama, of the royal family, one of the chief officers of the king, came with ten men to Gedali'ah the son of Ahi'kam, at Mizpah. As they ate bread together there at Mizpah, [2]Ish'mael the son of Nethani'ah and the ten men with him rose up and struck down Gedali'ah the son of Ahi'kam, son of Sha'phan, with the sword, and killed him, whom the king of Babylon had appointed governor in the land. [3]Ish'mael also slew all the Jews who were with Gedali'ah at Mizpah, and the Chalde'an soldiers who happened to be there.

4 On the day after the murder of Gedali'ah, before any one knew of it, [5]eighty men arrived from She'chem and Shiloh and Samar'ia, with their beards shaved and their clothes torn, and their bodies gashed, bringing cereal offerings and incense to present at the temple of the LORD. [6]And Ish'mael the son of Nethani'ah came out from Mizpah to meet them, weeping as he came. As he met them, he said to them, "Come in to Gedali'ah the son of Ahi'kam."

40:8 Ishmael: A member of "the royal family" of David (41:1). He was hired to murder Gedaliah by Baalis, king of neighboring Ammon, east of the Jordan (40:14). One suspects the Ammonites are looking for ways both to increase their power and to decrease Babylonian influence in the region. Gedaliah made himself a target by encouraging submission to Babylon (40:9). **Johanan:** The Judahite captain who informs Gedaliah of the assassination plot against his life (40:13-14). He offers to eliminate the threat preemptively (40:15), but his offer is refused, and his warning goes unheeded (40:16). **Maacathite:** Refers to someone from Maacah, north of the Sea of Galilee.

40:9 swore: An oath to protect the captains of Judah from the Babylonians, so long as they accept Babylonian rule peacefully. Submission to Babylon is a theme in Jeremiah's preaching as well (27:12, 17; 29:1-9; 38:2). **Chaldeans:** Babylonians.

40:10 gather wine ... fruits ... oil: Crops harvested in the later summer and early fall (grapes, olives, pomegranates, etc.) need to be gathered to ensure Judah's survival through the coming winter.

40:12 all the Jews returned: Refugees from Judah who fled to lands east of the Jordan (Moab, Ammon) and south of the Dead Sea (Edom) when Babylonians invaded the land in the winter of 588/587 B.C.

40:14 Baalis: His name appears outside the Bible on two seal impressions from the sixth century B.C., one that reads, "Belonging to Baalis, king of the Ammonites", and another that says, "Belonging to Milcomur, servant of Baalis".

41:1-18 Ishmael, a commander of Jewish forces, assassinates Gedaliah at Mizpah (41:2), slaughters mourners heading for Jerusalem (41:7), takes hostages from Mizpah (41:10), and flees toward Ammon, east of the Jordan (41:12). He is overtaken by Johanan, another army commander, who frees the hostages and prepares to flee with the group to Egypt (41:11-14, 16-17). Ishmael, however, escapes and seeks refuge in Ammon with a few of his men (41:15).

41:1 seventh month: Tishri, which corresponds to September-October. The following episode is dated two months after the burning of Jerusalem (52:12-13). **Ishmael:** See note on 40:8. **the royal family:** The descendants of King David. Ridding Judah of its provincial ruler may have been part of a larger plan to reestablish the Davidic monarchy. **Gedaliah:** The governor of Judah. See note on 39:14. **Mizpah:** Seven miles north of Jerusalem. It is the administrative center of Judah under Babylonian rule.

41:2 struck down: Gedaliah was warned of Ishmael's plot to assassinate him, but he dismissed it as a false rumor (40:16).

41:3 all the Jews: Ishmael carries out a bloody massacre, lest one of Gedaliah's pro-Babylonian officials should come forward and succeed him as governor. **Chaldean soldiers:** Babylonian troops.

41:5 Shechem ... Shiloh ... Samaria: Towns in the central hill country of Israel, north of Judah. The mourners belong to the remnant of the northern tribes of Israel who remained in the land after the Assyrian deportations of the eighth century B.C. (cf. 2 Chron 30:1, 10-11). **beards shaved ... clothes torn ... bodies gashed:** Ritual expressions of grief (16:6; 47:5; 48:37). **cereal offerings:** See note on Lev 2:1-16. **incense:** Burned on the altar with a portion of the cereal offering (Lev 2:1-2). **the temple of the LORD:** Destroyed by fire two months prior to this (52:12-13). Bringing sacrificial gifts after this disaster seems to imply that some form of worship, however rudimentary, continues at the Temple site (see Bar 1:10-11). The mourners are probably pilgrims attending the Feast of Booths/Tabernacles, which was celebrated annually in the "seventh month" (41:1; Lev 23:33).

[7]When they came into the city, Ish'mael the son of Nethani'ah and the men with him slew them, and cast them into a cistern. [8]But there were ten men among them who said to Ish'mael, "Do not kill us, for we have stores of wheat, barley, oil, and honey hidden in the fields." So he refrained and did not kill them with their companions.

9 Now the cistern into which Ish'mael cast all the bodies of the men whom he had slain was the large cistern[r] which King Asa had made for defense against Ba'asha king of Israel; Ishmael the son of Nethani'ah filled it with the slain. [10]Then Ish'mael took captive all the rest of the people who were in Mizpah, the king's daughters and all the people who were left at Mizpah whom Nebu'zarad'an, the captain of the guard, had committed to Gedali'ah the son of Ahi'kam. Ishmael the son of Nethani'ah took them captive and set out to cross over to the Am'monites.

Johanan and Ishmael

11 But when Joha'nan the son of Kare'ah and all the leaders of the forces with him heard of all the evil which Ish'mael the son of Nethani'ah had done, [12]they took all their men and went to fight against Ish'mael the son of Nethani'ah. They came upon him at the great pool which is in Gib'eon. [13]And when all the people who were with Ish'mael saw Joha'nan the son of Kare'ah and all the leaders of the forces with him, they rejoiced. [14]So all the people whom Ish'mael had carried away captive from Mizpah turned about and came back, and went to Joha'nan the son of Kare'ah. [15]But Ish'mael the son of Nethani'ah escaped from Joha'nan with eight men, and went to the Am'monites. [16]Then Joha'nan the son of Kare'ah and all the leaders of the forces with him took all the rest of the people whom Ish'mael the son of Nethani'ah had carried away captive[s] from Mizpah after he had slain Gedali'ah the son of Ahi'kam—soldiers, women, children, and eunuchs, whom Johanan brought back from Gib'eon. [17]And they went and stayed at Ge'ruth Chimham near Bethlehem, intending to go to Egypt [18]because of the Chalde'ans; for they were afraid of them, because Ish'mael the son of Nethani'ah had slain Gedali'ah the son of Ahi'kam, whom the king of Babylon had made governor over the land.

Jeremiah Advises Survivors
Not to Go to Egypt

42 Then all the commanders of the forces, and Joha'nan the son of Kare'ah and Azari'ah[t] the son of Hoshai'ah, and all the people from the least to the greatest, came near [2]and said to Jeremi'ah the prophet, "Let our supplication come before you, and pray to the Lord your God for us, for all this remnant (for we are left but a few of many, as your eyes see us), [3]that the Lord your God may show us the way we should go, and the thing that we should do." [4]Jeremi'ah the prophet said to them, "I have heard you; behold, I will pray to the Lord your God according to your request, and whatever the Lord answers you I will tell you; I will keep nothing back from you." [5]Then they said to Jeremi'ah, "May the

---

41:7 slew them: The motive behind Ishmael's deception and slaughter of these innocent travelers is unclear. **cistern:** A stone reservoir used for storing rainwater for the dry summer months. This particular one is "large" since it was built for the entire town of Mizpah to withstand a siege (41:9).

41:8 we have stores: Offered as provisions for Ishmael and his henchmen. It is effectively a bribe to save their lives.

41:9 Asa ... against Baasha: The conflict in 1 Kings 15:16–22.

41:10 took captive all the rest: Jeremiah seems to have been one of the hostages since he is dwelling in Mizpah at this time (40:6). **the king's daughters:** The daughters of Zedekiah, who are "princesses" (43:6). Most of the royal women of his house went into exile (38:22–23).

41:12 the great pool: A giant limestone reservoir with descending stairs along the inner wall. It measures more than 80 feet deep and 35 feet in diameter. It is known as "the pool of Gibeon" (2 Sam 2:13). **Gibeon:** Roughly three miles southwest of Mizpah (modern El-Jib).

41:15 the Ammonites: Ammon is a kingdom east of the Jordan River where Ishmael and his fellow conspirators seek protection. It was the king of Ammon who sponsored Ishmael's plot to eliminate Gedaliah in the first place (40:14).

41:17 Bethlehem: Five miles south of Jerusalem. **Egypt:** A traditional place of refuge for people fleeing disaster or danger in the land of Israel (26:21; Gen 12:10; 46:4; 1 Kings 11:40; Mt 2:13).

41:18 because of the Chaldeans: Johanan fears that Judah will face swift retaliation for the murder of Gedaliah, who was appointed its governor by Nebuchadnezzar himself (40:5; 42:11). His killing would be viewed as a rebellion against Babylonian sovereignty.

42:1–43:7 The remnant in Judah rebels against the word of the Lord. Their leaders claim to seek God's direction (42:2–3), and they express their readiness to obey him (42:6), but when Jeremiah delivers the Lord's answer (42:9–18), they reject it and accuse the prophet of lying (43:2). As it turns out, the people have already made up their minds to flee to Egypt; seeking Jeremiah's intercession is a vain attempt to secure the Lord's approval for a decision already made.

42:1 the commanders: The military leaders of Judah who evaded capture by the Babylonians when Jerusalem was conquered (40:7). **Johanan:** The captain who informed Gedaliah of the assassination plot against him (40:13–14) and rescued the hostages taken by Ishmael after Gedaliah's murder (41:11–14). **Azariah:** One of the "insolent men" of Judah who will accuse Jeremiah of lying (43:2).

42:2 pray to the Lord: Prophets were known for being powerful intercessors (Gen 20:7). See note on 15:1–4. **all this remnant:** The small number of survivors left behind in Judah after the population was greatly reduced by casualties of war and thousands of exiles taken to Babylon (52:28–30).

42:5 May the Lord ... witness: An oath of unconditional obedience. When broken, it will bring the Lord's fearsome wrath upon the remnant (42:21–22). Oaths that invoke the Lord as a witness call upon him to be the Enforcer of its sanctions, i.e., the One who administers blessings and curses for keeping or breaking one's pledge.

---

[r] Gk: Heb *he had slain by the hand of Gedaliah.*

[s] Cn: Heb *whom he recovered from Ishmael.*

[t] Gk: Heb *Jezaniah.*

LORD be a true and faithful witness against us if we do not act according to all the word with which the LORD your God sends you to us. ⁶Whether it is good or evil, we will obey the voice of the LORD our God to whom we are sending you, that it may be well with us when we obey the voice of the LORD our God."

7 At the end of ten days the word of the LORD came to Jeremi′ah. ⁸Then he summoned Joha′nan the son of Kare′ah and all the commanders of the forces who were with him, and all the people from the least to the greatest, ⁹and said to them, "Thus says the LORD, the God of Israel, to whom you sent me to present your supplication before him: ¹⁰If you will remain in this land, then I will build you up and not pull you down; I will plant you, and not pluck you up; for I repent of the evil which I did to you. ¹¹Do not fear the king of Babylon, of whom you are afraid; do not fear him, says the LORD, for I am with you, to save you and to deliver you from his hand. ¹²I will grant you mercy, that he may have mercy on you and let you remain in your own land. ¹³But if you say, 'We will not remain in this land,' disobeying the voice of the LORD your God ¹⁴and saying, 'No, we will go to the land of Egypt, where we shall not see war, or hear the sound of the trumpet, or be hungry for bread, and we will dwell there,' ¹⁵then hear the word of the LORD, O remnant of Judah. Thus says the LORD of hosts, the God of Israel: If you set your faces to enter Egypt and go to live there, ¹⁶then the sword which you fear shall overtake you there in the land of Egypt; and the famine of which you are afraid shall follow hard after you to Egypt; and there you shall die. ¹⁷All the men who set their faces to go to Egypt to live there shall die by the sword, by famine, and by pestilence; they shall have no remnant or survivor from the evil which I will bring upon them.

18 "For thus says the LORD of hosts, the God of Israel: As my anger and my wrath were poured out on the inhabitants of Jerusalem, so my wrath will be poured out on you when you go to Egypt. You shall become an execration, a horror, a curse, and a taunt. You shall see this place no more. ¹⁹The LORD has said to you, O remnant of Judah, 'Do not go to Egypt.' Know for a certainty that I have warned you this day ²⁰that you have gone astray at the cost of your lives. For you sent me to the LORD your God, saying, 'Pray for us to the LORD our God, and whatever the LORD our God says declare to us and we will do it.' ²¹And I have this day declared it to you, but you have not obeyed the voice of the LORD your God in anything that he sent me to tell you. ²²Now therefore know for a certainty that you shall die by the sword, by famine, and by pestilence in the place where you desire to go to live."

Jeremiah Warns of Judgment

43 When Jeremi′ah finished speaking to all the people all these words of the LORD their God, with which the LORD their God had sent him to them, ²Azari′ah the son of Hoshai′ah and Joha′nan the son of Kare′ah and all the insolent men said to Jeremi′ah, "You are telling a lie. The LORD our God did not send you to say, 'Do not go to Egypt to live there'; ³but Baruch the son of Neri′ah has set you against us, to deliver us into the hand of the Chalde′ans, that they may kill us or take us into exile in Babylon." ⁴So Joha′nan the son of Kare′ah and all the commanders of the forces and all the people did not obey the voice of the LORD, to remain in the land of Judah. ⁵But Joha′nan the son of Kare′ah and all the commanders of the forces took all the remnant of Judah who had returned to live in the land of Judah from all the nations to which they had been driven—⁶the men,

---

42:9–18 The remnant is presented with two options: stay in Judah and be blessed with God's protection or seek refuge in Egypt and face the bitter consequences of rebellion against God's will. The prophet's summary of the Lord's message is blunt: "Do not go to Egypt" (42:19). If they do, God will treat them with the same severity he showed to apostate Jerusalem (42:18; 44:13).

42:10 I will build you ... plant you: The Lord promises to establish the remnant safely and securely in the Promised Land. **I repent:** A metaphorical way of saying the Lord will withdraw his punishments from Judah and show the people his favor once again. See note on Jon 3:5.

42:11 Do not fear the king: The concern is that Nebuchadnez-zar, who appointed Gedaliah the governor (40:5), will respond to his assassination with a punitive campaign in Judah (41:2). Because the king of Babylon is the Lord's "servant"–i.e., the instrument of his divine will for shaping the course of history–he can be influenced to show "mercy" toward Judah (42:12) and not simply merciless judgment (25:9). **I am with you ... to deliver you:** The same promise of divine protection that was made to Jeremiah (1:19). The point is that God, being the sovereign Lord of history, is in total control of Judah's well-being, if only his people would trust him with their future (29:11).

42:14 land of Egypt: See note on 41:17. **the trumpet:** The alarm of war. See word study: *Trumpet* at Judg 6:34.

42:15 set your faces: An idiom for resolute determination.

42:17 sword ... famine ... pestilence: Curses of the covenant that bring suffering and death upon violators of the covenant (Lev 26:25–26; Ezek 7:15).

43:1–7 Jeremiah is accused of false prophecy and of scheming with Baruch to hand the survivors of Judah over to the Babylonians (43:2–3). Both the prophet and his scribe are taken to Egypt with the refugees, presumably against their will (43:7). The flight to Egypt is one more act of disobedience on the part of God's people (43:4). See note on 43:6.

43:2 Azariah: One of Judah's military leaders who eluded capture by the Babylonians (42:1). **Johanan:** The captain who informed Gedaliah of the assassination plot against him (40:13–14) and who rescued the hostages taken by Ishmael after Gedaliah's murder (41:11–14).

43:3 Baruch: Jeremiah's companion and scribe. See note on 36:4.

43:5 who had returned: Judeans who found refuge among neighboring peoples when the Babylonians invaded the land. They returned to Judah after the war ended and order was restored (40:11–12).

43:6 also Jeremiah ... Baruch: The text gives no indication whether they joined the group fleeing to Egypt willingly or unwillingly. Coercion seems more likely than not, however, since Jeremiah was adamant that God wanted his people to

the women, the children, the princesses, and every person whom Nebu'zarad'an the captain of the guard had left with Gedali'ah the son of Ahi'kam, son of Sha'phan; also Jeremi'ah the prophet and Baruch the son of Neri'ah. ⁷And they came into the land of Egypt, for they did not obey the voice of the LORD. And they arrived at Tah'panhes.

8 Then the word of the LORD came to Jeremi'ah in Tah'panhes: ⁹"Take in your hands large stones, and hide them in the mortar in the pavement which is at the entrance to Pharaoh's palace in Tah'panhes, in the sight of the men of Judah, ¹⁰and say to them, 'Thus says the LORD of hosts, the God of Israel: Behold, I will send and take Nebuchadrez'zar the king of Babylon, my servant, and heᵘ will set his throne above these stones which I have hid, and he will spread his royal canopy over them. ¹¹He shall come and strike the land of Egypt, giving to the pestilence those who are doomed to the pestilence, to captivity those who are doomed to captivity, and to the sword those who are doomed to the sword. ¹²Heᵛ shall kindle a fire in the temples of the gods of Egypt; and he shall burn them and carry them away captive; and he shall clean the land of Egypt, as a shepherd cleans his cloak of vermin; and he shall go away from there in peace. ¹³He shall break the obelisks of He"liop'olis which is in the land of Egypt; and the temples of the gods of Egypt he shall burn with fire.'"

Denunciation of Idolatry in Egypt

44 The word that came to Jeremi'ah concerning all the Jews that dwelt in the land of Egypt, at Migdol, at Tah'panhes, at Memphis, and in the land of Path'ros, ²"Thus says the LORD of hosts, the God of Israel: You have seen all the evil that I brought upon Jerusalem and upon all the cities of Judah. Behold, this day they are a desolation, and no one dwells in them, ³because of the wickedness which they committed, provoking me to anger, in that they went to burn incense and serve other gods that they knew not, neither they, nor you, nor your fathers. ⁴Yet I persistently sent to you all my servants the prophets, saying, 'Oh, do not do this abominable thing that I hate!' ⁵But they did not listen or incline their ear, to turn from their wickedness and burn no incense to other gods. ⁶Therefore my wrath and my anger were poured forth and kindled in the cities of Judah and in the streets of Jerusalem; and they became a waste and a desolation, as at this day. ⁷And now thus says the LORD God of hosts, the God of Israel: Why do you commit this great evil against yourselves, to cut off from you man and woman, infant and child, from the midst of Judah, leaving you no remnant? ⁸Why do you provoke me to anger with the works of your hands, burning incense to other gods in the land of Egypt where you have come to live, that you may be cut off and become a curse and a taunt among all the nations of the earth? ⁹Have you forgotten the wickedness of your fathers, the wickedness of the kings of Judah, the wickedness of theirʷ wives, your own wickedness, and the wickedness of your wives, which they committed in the land of Judah and in the streets of Jerusalem? ¹⁰They have not humbled themselves even to this day, nor have they feared,

---

"remain" in Judah (42:10) and resist the temptation to "go to Egypt" (42:19).

43:7 Tahpanhes: On the eastern edge of the Nile Delta, south of Lake Manzaleh, over 200 miles from Mizpah in Judah.

43:8–13 Jeremiah announces judgment on Egypt by performing a symbolic action: he buries stones in the forecourt of the Pharaoh's visitation palace in Tahpanhes to mark the spot where Nebuchadnezzar will sit enthroned as Egypt's conqueror. The same catastrophes visited upon disobedient Judah will follow the disobedient remnant of Judah to their new home (e.g., sword, pestilence, temples set on fire, captives taken into exile). For Jeremiah's other symbolic actions, see 13:1–11; 16:1–4; 19:1–13; 27:1–15; 32:1–44.

43:10 Nebuchadrezzar: An alternate spelling for Nebuchadnezzar, ruler of the Neo-Babylonian empire from 605 to 562 B.C. **my servant:** See note on 25:9.

43:11 He shall come and strike: The Babylonian army will invade Egypt in 568 B.C. **captivity:** According to the Jewish historian Josephus, when Nebuchadnezzar's forces conquer Egypt and take many into exile in Babylon (see 46:19), he also takes Jews who are living there (*Antiquities* 10, 180–82). This could explain how Baruch, who comes to Egypt with Jeremiah, ends up in Babylon (Bar 1:1–4).

43:13 the obelisks of Heliopolis: The pillars that adorn the temple of the sun god, Atum-Re, directly northeast of modern Cairo. Because the God of Israel decrees this judgment, the so-called gods of Egypt will prove powerless to protect their nation.

44:1–30 Jeremiah delivers final oracles of judgment against the Judean population that fled to Egypt. This community of survivors, instead of learning from the mistakes of the past (44:9) and making a humble return to the Lord (44:10), reverts to the worship of idols (44:8) and refuses the word of God (44:16). Their defiance guarantees a disastrous outcome: the Lord will bring judgment and woe on them once again, this time reducing his people to a tiny fraction of the surviving remnant, with none left alive to see the homeland of Judah again "except some fugitives" (44:14) who are "few in number" (44:28). Theologically, the apostate Jews in Egypt repudiate the blessings of the Exodus by spurning the Lord, rejecting the teaching of Moses, forfeiting the Promised Land, and returning to Egypt in their hearts (cf. Acts 7:39).

44:1 Migdol: In the eastern Nile Delta. **Tahpanhes:** See note on 43:7. **Memphis:** A major city along the Nile, south of the Delta. The site is located about 13 miles north of modern Cairo. **Pathros:** The name is derived from an Egyptian term meaning "Southern Land". It refers to the land of Upper Egypt, south of the Delta region. Archaeology knows of Jewish settlements as far south as the first Nile cataract (e.g., the colony of Elephantine).

44:2 they are a desolation: As foretold by the Lord through Jeremiah (4:27; 6:8; 9:11; 10:22; 12:11, etc.).

44:7 evil against yourselves: Judah's sin has been the cause of its extreme suffering.

44:8 works of your hands: Idol images, which are nothing more than products of human craftsmanship (Deut 4:28; Ps

---

ᵘGk Syr: Heb *I.*
ᵛGk Syr Vg: Heb *I.*
ʷHeb *his.*

nor walked in my law and my statutes which I set before you and before your fathers.

11 "Therefore thus says the Lord of hosts, the God of Israel: Behold, I will set my face against you for evil, to cut off all Judah. ¹²I will take the remnant of Judah who have set their faces to come to the land of Egypt to live, and they shall all be consumed; in the land of Egypt they shall fall; by the sword and by famine they shall be consumed; from the least to the greatest, they shall die by the sword and by famine; and they shall become an execration, a horror, a curse, and a taunt. ¹³I will punish those who dwell in the land of Egypt, as I have punished Jerusalem, with the sword, with famine, and with pestilence, ¹⁴so that none of the remnant of Judah who have come to live in the land of Egypt shall escape or survive or return to the land of Judah, to which they desire to return to dwell there; for they shall not return, except some fugitives."

15 Then all the men who knew that their wives had offered incense to other gods, and all the women who stood by, a great assembly, all the people who dwelt in Path'ros in the land of Egypt, answered Jeremi'ah: ¹⁶"As for the word which you have spoken to us in the name of the Lord, we will not listen to you. ¹⁷But we will do everything that we have vowed, burn incense to the queen of heaven and pour out libations to her, as we did, both we and our fathers, our kings and our princes, in the cities of Judah and in the streets of Jerusalem; for then we had plenty of food, and prospered, and saw no evil. ¹⁸But since we left off burning incense to the queen of heaven and pouring out libations to her, we have lacked everything and have been consumed by the sword and by famine." ¹⁹And the women said,ˣ "When we burned incense to the queen of heaven and poured out libations to her, was it without our husbands' approval that we made cakes for her bearing her image and poured out libations to her?"

20 Then Jeremi'ah said to all the people, men and women, all the people who had given him this answer: ²¹"As for the incense that you burned in the cities of Judah and in the streets of Jerusalem, you and your fathers, your kings and your princes, and the people of the land, did not the Lord remember it?ʸ Did it not come into his mind? ²²The Lord could no longer bear your evil doings and the abominations which you committed; therefore your land has become a desolation and a waste and a curse, without inhabitant, as it is this day. ²³It is because you burned incense, and because you sinned against the Lord and did not obey the voice of the Lord or walk in his law and in his statutes and in his testimonies, that this evil has befallen you, as at this day."

24 Jeremi'ah said to all the people and all the women, "Hear the word of the Lord, all you of Judah who are in the land of Egypt, ²⁵Thus says the Lord of hosts, the God of Israel: You and your wives have declared with your mouths, and have fulfilled it with your hands, saying, 'We will surely perform our vows that we have made, to burn incense to the queen of heaven and to pour out libations to her.' Then confirm your vows and perform your vows! ²⁶Therefore hear the word of the Lord, all you of Judah who dwell in the land of Egypt: Behold, I have sworn by my great name, says the Lord, that my name shall no more be invoked by the mouth of any man of Judah in all the land of Egypt, saying, 'As the Lord God lives.' ²⁷Behold, I am watching over them for evil and not for good; all the men of Judah who are in the land of Egypt shall be consumed by the sword and by famine, until there is an end of them. ²⁸And those who escape the sword shall return from the land of Egypt to the land of Judah, few in number; and all the remnant of Judah, who came to the land of Egypt to live, shall know whose word will stand, mine or theirs. ²⁹This shall be the sign to you, says the Lord, that I will punish you in this

---

115:4). **incense to other gods:** Sacrifice offered to any god except the Lord invites destruction (Ex 22:20).

44:11–14 The coming judgment will nearly destroy the remnant of Judah in Egypt (44:28).

44:13 sword ... famine ... pestilence: Curses of the covenant that bring suffering and death to violators of the covenant (Lev 26:25–26).

44:14 they desire to return: Implies most of the refugees from Judah are planning only a temporary stay in Egypt until it is safe to return to the homeland.

44:17 the queen of heaven: Ishtar, a Mesopotamian astral goddess of love and war who was associated with the planet Venus (cf. 1 Kings 11:5). She was served by incense offerings, wine libations, cakes baked over a fire, and had many devotees among women and families. Mesopotamian myths identify Ishtar as the wife of the fertility god Tammuz (cf. Ezek 8:14).

She was known in Greek as Astarte. **libations:** Drink offerings of wine. **we had plenty of food:** The men suppose that Ishtar was responsible for Judah's former prosperity and that neglect of the goddess is the reason disaster struck Judah and Jerusalem (a neglect probably connected with King Josiah's religious reform, which had some short-term success in uprooting idolatry from Judah, 2 Kings 23:4–14). It is evidence of their spiritual blindness that they misinterpret the causes of recent history. In realty, they see the situation backward: it was precisely Judah's idolatry that triggered God's wrath against his people (44:22–23).

44:25 perform your vows!: Sarcasm, as in 7:21.

44:26–30 A divine oath of disinheritance, in which God swears by his own life that all but a few of the Jews in Egypt will fall dead, never to see their homeland again. • This recalls the divine oath in Num 14:28–35, in which he swore to the Exodus generation that came out of Egypt that all but a few would fall in the wilderness, never to set foot in the Promised Land (Num 14:28–35).

44:28 mine or theirs: A contest of claims to be settled by the coming events of history.

ˣCompare Syr: Heb lacks *And the women said.*
ʸSyr: Heb *them.*

place, in order that you may know that my words will surely stand against you for evil: ³⁰Thus says the LORD, Behold, I will give Pharaoh Hoph′ra king of Egypt into the hand of his enemies and into the hand of those who seek his life, as I gave Zedeki′ah king of Judah into the hand of Nebuchadrez′zar king of Babylon, who was his enemy and sought his life."

A Word of Comfort to Baruch

45 The word that Jeremi′ah the prophet spoke to Baruch the son of Neri′ah, when he wrote these words in a book at the dictation of Jeremiah, in the fourth year of Jehoi′akim the son of Josi′ah, king of Judah: ²"Thus says the LORD, the God of Israel, to you, O Baruch: ³You said, 'Woe is me! for the LORD has added sorrow to my pain; I am weary with my groaning, and I find no rest.' ⁴Thus shall you say to him, Thus says the LORD: Behold, what I have built I am breaking down, and what I have planted I am plucking up—that is, the whole land. ⁵And do you seek great things for yourself? Seek them not; for behold, I am bringing evil upon all flesh, says the LORD; but I will give you your life as a prize of war in all places to which you may go."

Judgment against Egypt

46 The word of the LORD which came to Jeremi′ah the prophet concerning the nations.

2 About Egypt. Concerning the army of Pharaoh Neco, king of Egypt, which was by the river Euphra′-tes at Car′chemish and which Nebuchadrez′zar king of Babylon defeated in the fourth year of Jehoi′akim the son of Josi′ah, king of Judah:

³"Prepare buckler and shield,
    and advance for battle!
⁴Harness the horses;
    mount, O horsemen!
 Take your stations with your helmets,
    polish your spears,
    put on your coats of mail!
⁵Why have I seen it?
 They are dismayed
    and have turned backward.
 Their warriors are beaten down,
    and have fled in haste;
 they look not back—
    terror on every side!

                    says the LORD.
⁶The swift cannot flee away,
    nor the warrior escape;
 in the north by the river Euphra′tes
    they have stumbled and fallen.

⁷"Who is this, rising like the Nile,
    like rivers whose waters surge?
⁸Egypt rises like the Nile,
    like rivers whose waters surge.
 He said, I will rise, I will cover the earth,
    I will destroy cities and their inhabitants.

46: Is 19; Ezek 29–32; Zech 14:18–19.   **46:5:** Jer 6:25; 20:3, 10; 49:29; Ps 31:13.

44:30 Hophra: Ruler of Egypt from 589 to 570 B.C., at which time he was removed from power by one of his generals. This event is to be a "sign" to the Jews in Egypt that the Lord is about to fulfill his dreadful oath (44:26–29). The Greek historian Herodotus refers to Pharaoh Hophra as "Apries".

45:1 Baruch: The scribe who records Jeremiah's prophecies. See note on 36:4. **fourth year:** 605 B.C., two decades before the events in chaps. 37–44. **Jehoiakim:** The king of Judah from 609 to 598 B.C.

45:3 Woe is me!... I find no rest: The only words of Baruch preserved in the book. He laments his hardships and seems to wonder why the Lord would allow him to suffer so much despite his service to Jeremiah. In fact, it is his close collaboration with the prophet that makes him a target of persecution (see 36:26). The reward for his loyalty: his life will be spared (45:5).

45:4 I am breaking down ... plucking up: The Lord will destroy his work when he brings the Babylonians to conquer Judah and Jerusalem, to burn the Temple where he dwelt, and to terminate the Davidic monarchy in 586 B.C.

45:5 your life as a prize: The same promise was made to Ebed-melech, another one of Jeremiah's friends and helpers (39:18).

46:1—51:58 Jeremiah's oracles against the nations. These chapters form a unit that probably stood originally after 25:13, as in the Greek LXX, although in a different order. Each of the nations listed is about to drink the "cup" of the Lord's wrath for its wickedness (25:15). The nations targeted for divine judgment: Egypt (chap. 46), Philistia (chap. 47), Moab (chap. 48), Amon, Edom, Damascus, Kedar, Elam (chap. 49), and Babylon (chaps. 50–51). These oracles, which foretell the humiliation of prideful peoples and governments, are related to Jeremiah's call to be "a prophet to the nations" (1:5). They also reinforce the prophet's message that the Lord is sovereign over all nations, not just over Israel.

46:2 Pharaoh Neco: Neco II, king of Egypt from 610 to 595 B.C. In 609, he marched north through the land of Israel to join forces with Assyria in opposing the rising power of Babylonia. **Carchemish:** A city on the upper Euphrates River, near the modern border between Syria and Turkey. In 605, at the Battle of Carchemish, the Egyptians were routed by Nebuchadnezzar, who rose to kingship over Babylon shortly thereafter. Egypt's humiliating defeat, followed by its immediate withdrawal from Palestine, gave the Babylonians undisputed control over Judah and its neighbors. **fourth year:** 605 B.C. **Jehoiakim:** The king of Judah from 609 to 598 B.C. He was placed on the throne by Pharaoh Neco (2 Kings 23:34).

46:3–12 A prophetic taunt foretelling Egypt's defeat at the Battle of Carchemish. Part of its purpose is to show Judah that reliance on Egypt as a political and military ally against Babylonia is a foolish mistake.

46:4 mount, O horsemen!: Words of mockery. Evidence suggests that the Egyptian army, unlike the Babylonian army, had neither cavalry nor chariotry at this time in history.

46:5 terror on every side: One of Jeremiah's signature expressions (6:25; 20:3, 10; 49:29; Lam 2:22).

46:8 Egypt rises like the Nile: The yearly inundation of the Nile, in which the river overflows its banks and floods the adjacent plains, is here a poetical image of Egypt pouring out of its lands to conquer the world. It is assumed, however, that the Nile not only rises but quickly recedes (Amos 8:8).

⁹Advance, O horses,
   and rage, O chariots!
Let the warriors go forth:
   men of Ethiopia and Put who handle the
      shield,
   men of Lud, skilled in handling the bow.
¹⁰That day is the day of the Lord GOD of hosts,
   a day of vengeance,
   to avenge himself on his foes.
The sword shall devour and be sated,
   and drink its fill of their blood.
For the Lord GOD of hosts holds a sacrifice
   in the north country by the river Euphra′tes.
¹¹Go up to Gilead, and take balm,
   O virgin daughter of Egypt!
In vain you have used many medicines;
   there is no healing for you.
¹²The nations have heard of your shame,
   and the earth is full of your cry;
   for warrior has stumbled against warrior;
   they have both fallen together."

13 The word which the LORD spoke to Jeremi′ah
the prophet about the coming of Nebuchadrez′zar
king of Babylon to strike the land of Egypt:
¹⁴"Declare in Egypt, and proclaim in Migdol;
   proclaim in Memphis and Tah′panhes;
Say, 'Stand ready and be prepared,
   for the sword shall devour round about you.'
¹⁵Why has A′pis fled?ᶻ
   Why did not your bull stand?
   Because the LORD thrust him down.
¹⁶Your multitude stumbledᵃ and fell,
   and they said one to another,

'Arise, and let us go back to our own people
   and to the land of our birth,
   because of the sword of the oppressor.'
¹⁷Call the name of Pharaoh, king of Egypt,
   'Noisy one who lets the hour go by.'

¹⁸"As I live, says the King,
   whose name is the LORD of hosts,
like Ta′bor among the mountains,
   and like Carmel by the sea, shall one come.
¹⁹Prepare yourselves baggage for exile,
   O inhabitants of Egypt!
For Memphis shall become a waste,
   a ruin, without inhabitant.

²⁰"A beautiful heifer is Egypt,
   but a gadfly from the north has come upon
      her.
²¹Even her hired soldiers in her midst
   are like fatted calves;
yes, they have turned and fled together,
   they did not stand;
for the day of their calamity has come upon them,
   the time of their punishment.

²²"She makes a sound like a serpent gliding away;
   for her enemies march in force,
and come against her with axes,
   like those who fell trees.
²³They shall cut down her forest,

                                    says the LORD,

   though it is impenetrable,
because they are more numerous than locusts;
   they are without number.

46:9 Ethiopia: The land of Cush (= the southern part of modern Sudan). **Put:** A biblical name for Libya in North Africa. **Lud:** Lydia in Asia Minor, which supplies mercenary troops to Egypt (cf. the "hired soldiers" in 46:21).

46:10 a day of vengeance: Egypt's defeat at Carchemish in 605 was a divine act of judgment, here described in the language of the Song of Moses (Deut 32:41-42). **sacrifice:** A metaphorical description of the slaughter that decimated the Egyptian army (cf. Is 34:6; Zeph 1:7-8).

46:11 Gilead: The highlands east of the Jordan River. Gilead exports balsam, extracted from trees and plants, that is used for medicinal purposes (8:22; Gen 37:25). **virgin daughter of Egypt:** In several places the Bible personifies cities and nations in feminine terms (God's people, 14:17; Zion, Lam 2:13; Sidon, Is 23:12; Babylon, Is 47:1).

46:13 Nebuchadrezzar: An alternate spelling for Nebuchadnezzar, ruler of the Neo-Babylonian empire from 605 to 562 B.C. **to strike the land of Egypt:** A reference to Nebuchadnezzar's invasion of Egypt in 568 B.C. This is the second time he has humiliated Egypt, only this time he lays waste to cities such as Memphis and takes captives into exile (46:19).

46:14-24 A prophetic taunt spoken against Egypt before the Babylonian invasion of 568 B.C. It expands on the message that Jeremiah gave to the Jews who resettled in Egypt in 43:11.

46:14 Migdol ... Memphis ... Tahpanhes: The location of Jewish settlements in Egypt. See note on 44:1.

46:15 Apis: This name appears in the Greek LXX. The Hebrew has *'abbîrîm*, meaning "mighty ones" (often animals are in view such as "stallions" in 47:3 and "strong bulls" in Ps 22:12). Apis is an Egyptian god represented as a bull and worshiped at Memphis. It is believed to embody the creator god Ptah. Despite its appearance of strength, it flees in fear before the Lord's judgment.

46:17 Pharaoh: Hophra, whose throne was usurped in 570 B.C. See note on 44:30. **Noisy one ... hour go by:** Often considered a pun that pokes fun at Pharaoh Hophra, although the details of how the wordplay works are debated.

46:18 As I live, says ... the LORD: A divine oath, giving assurance that God will send Nebuchadnezzar as his "servant" (43:10) to execute judgment on Egypt and its idols (43:11-13). For a divine oath against the Jews who flee to Egypt, see 44:26-30. **like Tabor ... like Carmel:** Egypt's conqueror, Nebuchadnezzar of Babylon, will stand tall over his enemy like these prominent peaks of northern Israel, which tower over the Plain of Megiddo.

46:20 a gadfly from the north: The Babylonians. See note on 1:14.

46:23 cut down her forest: Felling trees signifies laying low the pride of mighty nations (e.g., Assyria in Is 10:33-34). **locusts:** Ravenous insects that swarm in large numbers and devastate fields, orchards, and countrysides, making them comparable to armies laying waste to everything in their path (Judg 6:5; Joel 1:4; Nahum 3:15).

ᶻGk: Heb *Why was it swept away.*
ᵃGk: Heb *He made many stumble.*

²⁴The daughter of Egypt shall be put to shame,
  she shall be delivered into the hand of a people
    from the north."

25 The LORD of hosts, the God of Israel, said: "Behold, I am bringing punishment upon A′mon of Thebes, and Pharaoh, and Egypt and her gods and her kings, upon Pharaoh and those who trust in him. ²⁶I will deliver them into the hand of those who seek their life, into the hand of Nebuchadrez′zar king of Babylon and his officers. Afterward Egypt shall be inhabited as in the days of old, says the LORD.

²⁷"But fear not, O Jacob my servant,
  nor be dismayed, O Israel;
for behold, I will save you from afar,
  and your offspring from the land of their
    captivity.
Jacob shall return and have quiet and ease,
  and none shall make him afraid.
²⁸Fear not, O Jacob my servant,
                        says the LORD,
  for I am with you.
I will make a full end of all the nations
  to which I have driven you,
but of you I will not make a full end.
I will chasten you in just measure,
  and I will by no means leave you unpunished."

Judgment against the Philistines

47 The word of the LORD that came to Jeremi′ah the prophet concerning the Philis′tines, before Pharaoh struck Gaza.
²"Thus says the LORD:
Behold, waters are rising out of the north,
  and shall become an overflowing torrent;

they shall overflow the land and all that fills it,
  the city and those who dwell in it.
Men shall cry out,
  and every inhabitant of the land shall wail.
³At the noise of the stamping of the hoofs of his
    stallions,
  at the rushing of his chariots, at the rumbling
    of their wheels,
the fathers look not back to their children,
  so feeble are their hands,
⁴because of the day that is coming to destroy
  all the Philis′tines,
to cut off from Tyre and Si′don
  every helper that remains.
For the LORD is destroying the Philistines,
  the remnant of the coastland of Caphtor.
⁵Baldness has come upon Gaza,
  Ash′kelon has perished.
O remnant of the An′akim,ᵇ
  how long will you gash yourselves?
⁶Ah, sword of the LORD!
  How long till you are quiet?
Put yourself into your scabbard,
  rest and be still!
⁷How can itᶜ be quiet,
  when the LORD has given it a charge?
Against Ash′kelon and against the seashore
  he has appointed it."

Judgment against Moab

48 Concerning Moab.
Thus says the LORD of hosts, the God of Israel:
"Woe to Nebo, for it is laid waste!
  Kir″iatha′im is put to shame, it is taken;
the fortress is put to shame and broken
    down;

47: Is 14:29–31; Ezek 25:15–17; Amos 1:6–8; Zeph 2:4–7; Zech 9:5–7.

46:25 Amon: The Egyptian sun god, Amon-Re, worshiped in the temple of Karnak at Thebes on the upper Nile.

46:27–28 Words of hope for exiled Israelites, whom the Lord promises to save from captivity. Nearly identical words appear in 30:10–11.

47:1 Philistines: One of the so-called "Sea Peoples" who invaded the eastern Mediterranean from Crete and other Greek islands. They established themselves in southwest Canaan in the late second millennium B.C., occupying a coalition of five prominent cites (Ashkelon, Ashdod, Ekron, Gaza, Gath). The Philistines were longtime enemies of Israel. **Pharaoh struck Gaza:** Herodotus, the Greek historian, notes that Neco II conquered the city of Cadytis (thought to be Gaza) after winning a battle at Magdolus (thought to be Megiddo) in the late seventh century, between ca. 609 and 605 (*Histories*, 2, 159).

47:2–7 A prophetic taunt foretelling the humiliation of the Philistines in 604 B.C., when Nebuchadnezzar of Babylon conquered Ashkelon and deported Philistine captives into exile.

47:2 waters are rising: The Babylonian invasion of Philistine territory is pictured as the Euphrates River flooding its banks and pouring down into Canaan. Similar prophetic

warnings are made of Egypt (46:7-8) and Assyria (Is 8:6-8). **the north:** See note on 1:14.

47:4 Tyre and Sidon: Seaport cities of Phoenicia, north of Israel (modern Lebanon). They are allies of the Philistines in opposing Babylonian sovereignty in Syria-Palestine; however, they are powerless to stop Nebuchadnezzar's relentless advance. **Caphtor:** Biblical name for the island of Crete, homeland of the Philistines (Amos 9:7).

47:5 Baldness: Shaving the head and self-laceration of the body were pagan mourning rituals. See note on 16:6. **Gaza ... Ashkelon:** Philistine cities. See note on 47:1. **the Anakim:** A people of imposing stature that dwelt in Canaan before Israel's conquest of the land (Num 13:28; Josh 11:21-22).

47:6 sword of the LORD: Unsheathed to administer divine vengeance (Deut 32:41).

48:1–47 An oracle of judgment against the small state of Moab, which fell to Nebuchadnezzar of Babylon in 582 B.C.

48:1 Moab: The territory directly east of the Dead Sea (modern Jordan). The prophet faults the Moabites for pride (48:29) and foretells the destruction of their cities, the captivity of their people, and even the exile of their chief deity, Chemosh (48:1, 7, 18-19, 21-24). Genesis traces the origin of the Moabites to Abraham's nephew Lot, making them cousins of the Israelites (Gen 19:30-37), although they were longtime adversaries of Israel (Num 22:3-6; Judg 3:12-14;

ᵇ Gk: Heb *their valley.*
ᶜ Gk Vg: Heb *you.*

2   the renown of Moab is no more.
   In Heshbon they planned evil against her:
        'Come, let us cut her off from being a nation!'
   You also, O Madmen, shall be brought to silence;
        the sword shall pursue you.

3"Listen! a cry from Horona'im,
        'Desolation and great destruction!'
4Moab is destroyed;
        a cry is heard as far as Zoar.ᵈ
5For at the ascent of Lu'hith
        they go up weeping;ᵉ
   for at the descent of Horona'im
        they have heard the cryᶠ of destruction.
6Flee! Save yourselves!
        Be like a wild donkeyᵍ in the desert!
7For, because you trusted in your strongholdsʰ
        and your treasures,
        you also shall be taken;
   and Che'mosh shall go forth into exile,
        with his priests and his princes.
8The destroyer shall come upon every city,
        and no city shall escape;
   the valley shall perish,
        and the plain shall be destroyed,
        as the LORD has spoken.

9"Give wings to Moab,
        for she would fly away;
   her cities shall become a desolation,
        with no inhabitant in them.

10   "Cursed is he who does the work of the LORD with slackness; and cursed is he who keeps back his sword from bloodshed.

11"Moab has been at ease from his youth
        and has settled on his dregs;

he has not been emptied from vessel to vessel,
        nor has he gone into exile;
   so his taste remains in him,
        and his scent is not changed.
12   "Therefore, behold, the days are coming, says the LORD, when I shall send to him tilters who will tilt him, and empty his vessels, and break hisⁱ jars in pieces. 13Then Moab shall be ashamed of Che'mosh, as the house of Israel was ashamed of Bethel, their confidence.

14"How do you say, 'We are heroes
        and mighty men of war'?
15The destroyer of Moab and his cities has come
              up,
        and the choicest of his young men have gone
              down to slaughter,
        says the King, whose name is the LORD of
              hosts.
16The calamity of Moab is near at hand
        and his affliction hastens apace.
17Bemoan him, all you who are round about
              him,
        and all who know his name;
   say, 'How the mighty scepter is broken,
        the glorious staff.'

18"Come down from your glory,
        and sit on the parched ground,
        O inhabitant of Di'bon!
   For the destroyer of Moab has come up against
              you;
        he has destroyed your strongholds.
19Stand by the way and watch,
        O inhabitant of Aro'er!
   Ask him who flees and her who escapes;
        say, 'What has happened?'

48: Is 15–16; 25:10–12; Ezek 25:8–11; Amos 2:1–3; Zeph 2:8–11.

---

2 Kings 3:1–27). Several cites mentioned in the chapter have not been securely located. The prophecy is similar to Isaiah's oracle against Moab (Is 15–16). **Woe:** A cry of anguish heard at funerals. See word study: *Woe* at Is 28:1. **Nebo ... Kiriathaim:** Israelite towns east of the Jordan River that were seized by the Moabite king Mesha in the ninth century B.C. (according to the inscription on the *Moabite Stone*). They are also mentioned among the cities of Moab in 48:22–23.

48:2 Heshbon: Capital of Ammon, north of Moab (Num 21:26). **Madmen:** Otherwise unknown. It appears to involve a wordplay on the Hebrew term for "dung-pit" in Is 25:10.

48:3 Horonaim: Location uncertain.

48:7 you also shall be taken: I.e., into exile. **Chemosh:** National god of the Moabites, possibly an astral deity, whose

temples will be plundered of their idol images (Num 21:29; 1 Kings 11:7).

48:8 The destroyer: The Babylonians (48:15, 18, 32). **the valley:** The eastern side of the lower Jordan Valley. **the plain:** The plateau northeast of the Dead Sea, known as "the plains of Moab" (Num 22:1).

48:11 at ease from his youth: Moab's peaceful alliance with the Assyrians makes them complacent and unprepared for the threat of the Babylonians.

48:12 empty his vessels ... break his jars: The Moabites, known for their winemaking, are headed for conquest and exile. Jeremiah pictures this as fermented wine that is poured through a strainer (removing the lees) into another vessel, either a skin or jug, after which the old vessel is smashed. The disappearance of wine also signals the disappearance of joy (49:33).

48:13 ashamed of Bethel: The northern tribes of Israel, taken into exile by the Assyrians, are finally ashamed of the calf idol they worshiped in Bethel (1 Kings 12:28–31; Hos 10:5–6).

48:18 Dibon: A prominent Moabite city roughly 15 miles east of the Dead Sea, just north of the Arnon River (modern Dhiban).

48:19 Aroer: A city a few miles southeast of Dibon.

ᵈGk: Heb *her little ones.*
ᵉCn: Heb *weeping goes up with weeping.*
ᶠGk Compare Is 15:5: Heb *the distress of the cry.*
ᵍGk Aquila: Heb *like Aroer.*
ʰGk: Heb *works.*
ⁱGk Aquila: Heb *their.*

²⁰Moab is put to shame, for it is broken;
  wail and cry!
 Tell it by the Arnon,
  that Moab is laid waste.

21 "Judgment has come upon the tableland, upon Ho'lon, and Jah'zah, and Meph'a-ath, ²²and Di'bon, and Nebo, and Beth"-diblatha'im, ²³and Kir"iatha'im, and Beth-ga'mul, and Beth-me'on, ²⁴and Ker'ioth, and Bozrah, and all the cities of the land of Moab, far and near. ²⁵The horn of Moab is cut off, and his arm is broken, says the LORD.

26 "Make him drunk, because he magnified himself against the LORD; so that Moab shall wallow in his vomit, and he too shall be held in derision. ²⁷Was not Israel a derision to you? Was he found among thieves, that whenever you spoke of him you wagged your head?

²⁸"Leave the cities, and dwell in the rock,
  O inhabitants of Moab!
 Be like the dove that nests
  in the sides of the mouth of a gorge.
²⁹We have heard of the pride of Moab—
  he is very proud—
 of his loftiness, his pride, and his arrogance,
  and the haughtiness of his heart.
³⁰I know his insolence, says the LORD;
  his boasts are false,
  his deeds are false.
³¹Therefore I wail for Moab;
  I cry out for all Moab;
  for the men of Kir-he'res I mourn.
³²More than for Ja'zer I weep for you,
  O vine of Sibmah!
 Your branches passed over the sea,
  reached as far as Jazer,ʲ
 upon your summer fruits and your vintage
  the destroyer has fallen.
³³Gladness and joy have been taken away
  from the fruitful land of Moab;
 I have made the wine cease from the wine
  presses;

no one treads them with shouts of joy;
  the shouting is not the shout of joy.

34 "Heshbon and Ele-a'leh cry out;ᵏ as far as Ja'haz they utter their voice, from Zoar to Horona'im and Eg'lath-shelish'iyah. For the waters of Nimrim also have become desolate. ³⁵And I will bring to an end in Moab, says the LORD, him who offers sacrifice in the high place and burns incense to his god. ³⁶Therefore my heart moans for Moab like a flute, and my heart moans like a flute for the men of Kir-he'res; therefore the riches they gained have perished.

37 "For every head is shaved and every beard cut off; upon all the hands are gashes, and on the loins is sackcloth. ³⁸On all the housetops of Moab and in the squares there is nothing but lamentation; for I have broken Moab like a vessel for which no one cares, says the LORD. ³⁹How it is broken! How they wail! How Moab has turned his back in shame! So Moab has become a derision and a horror to all that are round about him."
⁴⁰For thus says the LORD:
 "Behold, one shall fly swiftly like an eagle,
  and spread his wings against Moab;
⁴¹the cities shall be taken
  and the strongholds seized.
 The heart of the warriors of Moab shall be in that
    day
  like the heart of a woman with her labor pains;
⁴²Moab shall be destroyed and be no longer a
    people,
  because he magnified himself against the LORD.
⁴³Terror, pit, and snare
  are before you, O inhabitant of Moab!
                                   says the LORD.
⁴⁴He who flees from the terror
  shall fall into the pit,
 and he who climbs out of the pit
  shall be caught in the snare.
 For I will bring these thingsˡ upon Moab
  in the year of their punishment,
                                   says the LORD.

48:20 the Arnon: Flows westward through Moabite territory and empties into the midpoint of the Dead Sea.

48:25 horn: A symbol of strength (Ps 18:2; 89:17).

48:26 Make him drunk: I.e., with the wine of the Lord's wrath, which will cause Moab to stagger and vomit (Lam 4:21). See note on 25:15. **magnified himself:** Moab's besetting sin is prideful self-confidence in its own strength (48:29–30). Historically, the Moabites taunted the people of Judah and coveted their lands at the time of the Babylonian conquest (Zeph 2:8).

48:29 the pride of Moab: Noted by other prophets as well (Is 16:6; Zeph 2:8).

48:31 Kir-heres: Ancient capital of Moab, also spelled Kir-hareseth (2 Kings 3:25).

48:32–33 Jeremiah reuses key expressions from Isaiah's oracle against Moab, specifically from Is 16:8–9. Isaiah foretold Moab's punishment in the eighth century; Jeremiah speaks of another chastisement in the sixth century.

48:32 Sibmah: A city of northern Moab.

48:33 shouts of joy: The celebratory shout of farmers who tread the grapes after a bountiful harvest (25:30).

48:35 the high place: An idol shrine of the Moabite national god, Chemosh (48:7).

48:37 shaved ... gashes ... sackcloth: Mourning rituals. See notes on 4:8 and 16:6.

48:40 like an eagle: Nebuchadnezzar of Babylon, who will bring swift judgment on Moab (cf. Deut 28:49).

48:44 flees ... fall ... caught: Indicates that God's judgment will be inescapable.

ʲCn: Heb *the sea of Jazer.*
ᵏCn: Heb *From the cry of Heshbon to Elealeh.*
ˡGk Syr: Heb *to her.*

⁴⁵"In the shadow of Heshbon
    fugitives stop without strength;
for a fire has gone forth from Heshbon,
    a flame from the house of Si'hon;
it has destroyed the forehead of Moab,
    the crown of the sons of tumult.
⁴⁶Woe to you, O Moab!
    The people of Che'mosh is undone;
for your sons have been taken captive,
    and your daughters into captivity.
⁴⁷Yet I will restore the fortunes of Moab
    in the latter days, says the LORD."
Thus far is the judgment on Moab.

Judgment against the Ammonites

49 Concerning the Am'monites.
    Thus says the LORD:
"Has Israel no sons?
    Has he no heir?
Why then has Milcom dispossessed Gad,
    and his people settled in its cities?
²Therefore, behold, the days are coming,
    says the LORD,
when I will cause the battle cry to be
        heard
    against Rabbah of the Am'monites;
it shall become a desolate mound,
    and its villages shall be burned with
        fire;

then Israel shall dispossess those who
        dispossessed him,
    says the LORD.

³"Wail, O Heshbon, for Ai is laid waste!
    Cry, O daughters of Rabbah!
Clothe yourselves with sackcloth,
    lament, and run to and fro among the hedges!
For Milcom shall go into exile,
    with his priests and his princes.
⁴Why do you boast of your valleys,ᵐ
    O faithless daughter,
who trusted in her treasures, saying,
    'Who will come against me?'
⁵Behold, I will bring terror upon you,
    says the Lord GOD of hosts,
    from all who are round about you,
and you shall be driven out, every man straight
        before him,
    with none to gather the fugitives.
6 But afterward I will restore the fortunes of the
Am'monites, says the LORD."

Judgment against Edom

7 Concerning E'dom.
Thus says the LORD of hosts:
"Is wisdom no more in Te'man?
    Has counsel perished from the prudent?
    Has their wisdom vanished?

49:1-6: Ezek 21:28–32; 25:1–7; Amos 1:13–15; Zeph 2:8–11.
49:7-22: Is 34; 63:1–6; Ezek 25:12–14; 35; Amos 1:11–12; Obad; Mal 1:2–5.

48:45-46 A reworking of the Song of Heshbon in Num 21:27-29. It originally recalled how the Amorites seized territory from the Moabites before Israel's conquest of the Transjordan under Moses. Here its lyrics are applied to Moab's seizure at the hand of the Babylonians in the sixth century B.C.

48:45 Sihon: Former king of Ammon (Num 21:21). **forehead of Moab:** An expression from Num 24:17.

48:47 restore the fortunes: A promise of salvation for this Gentile people after judgment. **the latter days:** See word study: *The Latter Days* at Is 2:2.

49:1-6 An oracle of judgment against the small state of Ammon, defeated by Nebuchadnezzar of Babylon when he campaigned in the region in 582 B.C.

49:1 Ammonites: The people of Ammon occupied lands north of Moab and east of the Transjordan strip that belonged to the Israelite tribe of Gad (Josh 13:25-27). Genesis traces the origin of the Ammonites to Abraham's nephew Lot, making them cousins of the Israelites (Gen 19:30-37). Jeremiah faults them for seizing lands belonging to Gad (49:1) and for trusting in their treasures (49:4). Their punishment from the Lord will be conquest (49:2), flight (49:5), and exile (49:3). It is not mentioned here, but the Ammonites also conspired with Judah and other states to resist Babylonian rule (27:3), and the king of Ammon sponsored the assassination plot that killed Gedaliah, the Babylonian-appointed governor of Judah after the fall of Jerusalem (40:13-14). **Milcom:** The Hebrew reads "their king", although the same consonants can be vocalized as the name Milcom, as in the Greek LXX and Latin Vulgate. Milcom is the name of the Ammonite national deity (1 Kings

11:5). **dispossessed Gad:** After the fall of the Northern Kingdom of Israel in the eighth century B.C., when the Assyrians took the tribe of Gad into exile (1 Chron 5:26).

49:2 Rabbah: Capital of Ammon, over 20 miles east of the Jordan River (modern Amman).

49:3 Heshbon: Northeast of Mt. Nebo in the Transjordan (Num 21:26). **Ai:** Otherwise unknown. It is not the town of this name attacked by the Israelites in Josh 7:1-9. The name simply means "ruin". **sackcloth:** A coarse fabric spun from goat hair and worn in times of mourning (Gen 37:34). **go into exile:** The idol image will be taken as spoil by the conquerors (as in 43:12; 48:7; Hos 10:5-6).

49:6 restore the fortunes: A promise of salvation for this Gentile people after judgment.

49:7-22 An oracle of judgment against the small state of Edom. Jeremiah's tirade against Edom is related to Obad 1-16. The exact nature of the relationship between these two oracles remains unclear. It could be that **(1)** Obadiah drew upon Jeremiah, **(2)** Jeremiah drew upon Obadiah, or **(3)** both prophets drew upon a single ancient source that is no longer known to us. Compare, e.g., 49:7 with Obad 8, 49:9-10 with Obad 5-6, 49:12 with Obad 16, and 49:14-16 with Obad 1-4.

49:7 Edom: The rugged highlands south of the Dead Sea. The Edomites were longstanding enemies of Israel and were known in the biblical world as one of the "people of the east" who cultivated wisdom (1 Kings 4:30-31; Obad 8). Genesis traces the origin of the Edomites to Jacob's twin brother, Esau (Gen 25:19-26). Edom faces severe judgment for its prideful heart (49:16), but also because the Edomites took perverse delight in the destruction of Jerusalem in 586 B.C. (Ps 137:7), even handing fleeing Judahites over to the sword (Ezek 35:1-15). No promise of future salvation is given to Edom, unlike

---

ᵐ Heb *valleys, your valley flows.*

90

[8]Flee, turn back, dwell in the depths,
  O inhabitants of De′dan!
For I will bring the calamity of Esau upon him,
  the time when I punish him.
[9]If grape-gatherers came to you,
  would they not leave gleanings?
If thieves came by night,
  would they not destroy only enough for
    themselves?
[10]But I have stripped Esau bare,
  I have uncovered his hiding places,
  and he is not able to conceal himself.
His children are destroyed, and his brothers,
  and his neighbors; and he is no more.
[11]Leave your fatherless children, I will keep them
    alive;
  and let your widows trust in me."

12 For thus says the LORD: "If those who did not deserve to drink the cup must drink it, will you go unpunished? You shall not go unpunished, but you must drink. [13]For I have sworn by myself, says the LORD, that Bozrah shall become a horror, a taunt, a waste, and a curse; and all her cities shall be perpetual wastes."

[14]I have heard tidings from the LORD,
  and a messenger has been sent among the
    nations:
"Gather yourselves together and come against
    her,
  and rise up for battle!"
[15]For behold, I will make you small among the
    nations,
  despised among men.
[16]The horror you inspire has deceived you,
  and the pride of your heart,
you who live in the clefts of the rock,[n]
  who hold the height of the hill.

Though you make your nest as high as the
    eagle's,
  I will bring you down from there,
                                    says the LORD.

17 "E′dom shall become a horror; every one who passes by it will be horrified and will hiss because of all its disasters. [18]As when Sodom and Gomor′rah and their neighbor cities were overthrown, says the LORD, no man shall dwell there, no man shall sojourn in her. [19]Behold, like a lion coming up from the jungle of the Jordan against a strong sheepfold, I will suddenly make them[o] run away from her; and I will appoint over her whomever I choose. For who is like me? Who will summon me? What shepherd can stand before me? [20]Therefore hear the plan which the LORD has made against E′dom and the purposes which he has formed against the inhabitants of Te′man: Even the little ones of the flock shall be dragged away; surely their fold shall be appalled at their fate. [21]At the sound of their fall the earth shall tremble; the sound of their cry shall be heard at the Red Sea. [22]Behold, one shall mount up and fly swiftly like an eagle, and spread his wings against Bozrah, and the heart of the warriors of E′dom shall be in that day like the heart of a woman with her labor pains."

Judgment against Damascus

23 Concerning Damascus.
"Ha′math and Arpad are confounded,
  for they have heard evil tidings;
they melt in fear, they are troubled like the sea[p]
  which cannot be quiet.
[24]Damascus has become feeble, she turned to flee,
  and panic seized her;
anguish and sorrows have taken hold of her,
  as of a woman with labor pains.

49:23–27: Is 17:1–3; Amos 1:3–5; Zech 9:1.

Moab (48:47), Ammon (49:6), and Elam (49:39). For the enmity between Edom and Israel, see Introduction to Obadiah: *Historical Background*. **Teman:** A region in north Edom that produced wise men (Job 2:11).

49:8 Dedan: A trade hub in northwest Arabia. **Esau:** Patriarchal ancestor of the Edomites (Gen 36:1–43).

49:9 grape-gatherers ... thieves: Neither one can take everything without leaving something behind. By contrast, when the Lord brings plundering armies against Edom, they will leave nothing remaining.

49:10 I have stripped ... uncovered: The judgment of Edom is so certain that Jeremiah speaks as if these events had already occurred (= the so-called "prophetic perfect" tense).

49:11 I will keep them alive: God will mercifully preserve a remnant in the midst of judgment.

49:12 drink the cup: The cup of the Lord's wrath (Lam 4:21). See note on 25:15.

49:13 Bozrah: An elevated fortress city about 25 miles southeast of the Dead Sea. Despite its lofty height and natural defenses, the Lord will destroy its sense of security and bring it low (49:16).

49:18 Sodom and Gomorrah: Wicked cities near the Dead Sea that God utterly destroyed in patriarchal times (50:40; Gen 19:24–25).

49:19 a lion: An image of the Lord coming against a sinful nation (25:38; 50:44; Hos 5:14).

49:21 the Red Sea: The Hebrew *yam-sûph* here refers to the Gulf of Aqabah, an inlet of the Red Sea that reaches up to the edge of Edomite territory (cf. 1 Kings 9:26).

49:22 like an eagle: See note on 48:40.

49:23–27 An oracle of judgment against the small Aramean (= Syrian) state of Damascus. Due to the limitations of historical information about sixth-century Syria, scholars have thus far been unable to correlate Jeremiah's prophecy with a specific event that represents its fulfillment.

49:23 Damascus: Capital of one of the Aramean kingdoms of Syria, about 60 miles northeast of the Sea of Galilee. It was conquered by the Assyrians in 732 B.C. and came under the yoke of Babylonian rule after the Battle of Carchemish in 605 B.C. **Hamath and Arpad:** Two other Aramean states, both in the path of armies advancing toward Damascus from the north. See note on 1:14.

---

[n] Or *Sela*.
[o] Gk Syr: Heb *him*.
[p] Cn: Heb *there is trouble in the sea*.

²⁵How the famous city is forsaken,[q]
    the joyful city![r]
²⁶Therefore her young men shall fall in her
        squares,
    and all her soldiers shall be destroyed in that
        day,

              says the LORD of hosts.
²⁷And I will kindle a fire in the wall of Damascus,
    and it shall devour the strongholds of
        Benha′dad."

Judgment against Kedar and Hazor

28 Concerning Ke′dar and the kingdoms of Ha′-zor which Nebuchadrez′zar king of Babylon struck.
    Thus says the LORD:
    "Rise up, advance against Kedar!
    Destroy the people of the east!
²⁹Their tents and their flocks shall be taken,
    their curtains and all their goods;
    their camels shall be borne away from them,
    and men shall cry to them: 'Terror on every
        side!'
³⁰Flee, wander far away, dwell in the depths,
    O inhabitants of Ha′zor!

              says the LORD.

For Nebuchadrez′zar king of Babylon
    has made a plan against you,
    and formed a purpose against you.

³¹"Rise up, advance against a nation at ease,
    that dwells securely,

           says the LORD,

that has no gates or bars,
    that dwells alone.

³²Their camels shall become booty,
    their herds of cattle a spoil.
I will scatter to every wind
    those who cut the corners of their hair,
    and I will bring their calamity
    from every side of them,

              says the LORD.
³³Ha′zor shall become a haunt of jackals,
    an everlasting waste;
no man shall dwell there,
    no man shall sojourn in her."

Judgment against Elam

34 The word of the LORD that came to Jeremi′ah the prophet concerning E′lam, in the beginning of the reign of Zedeki′ah king of Judah.

35 Thus says the LORD of hosts: "Behold, I will break the bow of E′lam, the mainstay of their might; ³⁶and I will bring upon E′lam the four winds from the four quarters of heaven; and I will scatter them to all those winds, and there shall be no nation to which those driven out of Elam shall not come. ³⁷I will terrify E′lam before their enemies, and before those who seek their life; I will bring evil upon them, my fierce anger, says the LORD. I will send the sword after them, until I have consumed them; ³⁸and I will set my throne in E′lam, and destroy their king and princes, says the LORD.

39 "But in the latter days I will restore the fortunes of E′lam, says the LORD."

Judgment against Babylon

50 The word which the LORD spoke concerning Babylon, concerning the land of the Chalde′-ans, by Jeremi′ah the prophet:

49:29: Jer 6:25; 20:3, 10; 46:5; Ps 31:13.   **50–51:** Is 13:1–14:23; 47; Hab 1–2.

49:27 devour the strongholds: Recalls Amos' words against Damascus in Amos 1:5. **Benhadad:** A dynastic throne name borne by several Aramean kings in OT times. See note on 1 Kings 15:18.

49:28–33 An oracle of judgment against the north Arabian peoples of Kedar and Hazor, dwelling in the Syrian desert. According to the *Babylonian Chronicle*, Nebuchadnezzar conducted raids and seized plunder from desert Arabs in 599 B.C.

49:28 Kedar: The Kedarites are tent dwellers (Ps 120:5) and traders in flock animals (Ezek 27:21), which they breed in large numbers (Is 60:7). When the Lord's judgment falls, they will be put to flight (49:30) and robbed of their belongings (49:29, 32). **kingdoms of Hazor:** Perhaps a coalition of tribes centered around a single settlement, the exact location of which is unknown.

49:29 Terror on every side: One of Jeremiah's signature expressions (6:25; 20:3, 10; 46:5; Lam 2:22).

49:30 Nebuchadrezzar: An alternate spelling for Nebuchadnezzar, ruler of the Neo-Babylonian empire from 605 to 562 B.C.

49:31 no gates or bars: Unlike walled cities, desert encampments have little protection from attack.

49:32 cut the corners of their hair: Shaving hair from the temples is a religious rite among ancient Arabian tribes (Herodotus, *Histories* 3, 8).

49:34–39 An oracle of judgment against Elam, a distant nation east of Babylon. Nebuchadnezzar of Babylon may have fought with the Elamites in 596 or 595 B.C. The prophecy is spoken by the Lord in the first person ("I, me, my") and shows that his reign extends to the ends of the earth.

49:34 Elam: In lower Mesopotamia, south of the Zagros mountains (southwest Iran). The Lord will scatter the Elamites to "the four winds" (49:36) and bring the "sword" against them (49:37). **Zedekiah:** King of Judah from 597 to 586 B.C.

49:35 break the bow: An idiom for conquering a nation's military might (Hos 1:5). The image is fitting for the Elamites, who are remembered for being skilled archers (Is 22:6).

49:38 my throne: A sign of the Lord's kingship over Elam (e.g., Nebuchadnezzar asserts his dominion over Egypt by placing his throne in Tahpanhes, 43:10).

49:39 the latter days: See word study: *The Latter Days* at Is 2:2. **restore the fortunes:** A promise of salvation for this Gentile people after judgment. Elamites are among those who attend the Feast of Pentecost in Jerusalem when the Holy Spirit descends upon the Church (Acts 2:9).

50:1–51:58 Chapters 50–51 form a collection of judgment oracles against Babylon, the center of a mighty empire that has political dominance over the entire Near East in Jeremiah's day. Together these chapters mark the climax of the prophet's oracles against the nations. The story following in 51:59–64 tells how Jeremiah recruits Baruch's brother Seraiah to recite these prophecies publicly in Babylon. They announce

---

[q] vg: Heb *not forsaken.*
[r] Syr Vg Tg: Heb *city of my joy.*

2"Declare among the nations and proclaim,
　set up a banner and proclaim,
　conceal it not, and say:
'Babylon is taken,
　Bel is put to shame,
　Mer′odach is dismayed.
Her images are put to shame,
　her idols are dismayed.'

3 "For out of the north a nation has come up against her, which shall make her land a desolation, and none shall dwell in it; both man and beast shall flee away.

4 "In those days and in that time, says the LORD, the people of Israel and the people of Judah shall come together, weeping as they come; and they shall seek the LORD their God. 5They shall ask the way to Zion, with faces turned toward it, saying, 'Come, let us join ourselves to the LORD in an everlasting covenant which will never be forgotten.'

6 "My people have been lost sheep; their shepherds have led them astray, turning them away on the mountains; from mountain to hill they have gone, they have forgotten their fold. 7All who found them have devoured them, and their enemies have said, 'We are not guilty, for they have sinned against the LORD, their true habitation, the LORD, the hope of their fathers.'

8"Flee from the midst of Babylon, and go out of the land of the Chalde′ans, and be as he-goats before the flock. 9For behold, I am stirring up and bringing against Babylon a company of great nations, from the north country; and they shall array themselves against her; from there she shall be taken. Their arrows are like a skilled warrior who does not return empty-handed. 10Chalde′a shall be plundered; all who plunder her shall be sated, says the LORD.

11"Though you rejoice, though you exult,
　O plunderers of my heritage,
though you are wanton as a heifer at grass,
　and neigh like stallions,
12your mother shall be utterly shamed,
　and she who bore you shall be disgraced.
Behold, she shall be the last of the nations,
　a wilderness dry and desert.
13Because of the wrath of the LORD she shall not be
　　inhabited,
　but shall be an utter desolation;
every one who passes by Babylon shall be
　　appalled,
　and hiss because of all her wounds.
14Set yourselves in array against Babylon round
　　about,
　all you that bend the bow;
shoot at her, spare no arrows,
　for she has sinned against the LORD.
15Raise a shout against her round about,
　she has surrendered;
her bulwarks have fallen,
　her walls are thrown down.
For this is the vengeance of the LORD:
　take vengeance on her,
　do to her as she has done.
16Cut off from Babylon the sower,
　and the one who handles the sickle in time of
　　harvest;
because of the sword of the oppressor,
　every one shall turn to his own people,
　and every one shall flee to his own land.

17 "Israel is a hunted sheep driven away by lions. First the king of Assyria devoured him, and now at last Nebuchadrez′zar king of Babylon has gnawed his bones. 18Therefore, thus says the LORD of hosts, the God of Israel: Behold, I am bringing

---

50:8: Jer 51:6, 9, 45; 2 Cor 6:17; Rev 18:4.

Babylon's fall to Medo-Persia in 539 B.C. Similar prophecies appear in Is 13–14. See note on 46:1–51:58.
　50:1 Babylon: Built along the Euphrates River in lower Mesopotamia (southern Iraq). The Lord executes his plan for Judah and its neighbors by wielding the Babylonians as "the hammer of the whole earth" (50:23), a destructive instrument for bringing judgment on rebellious peoples and kingdoms (51:20). Now the time has come for Babylon itself to face "the wrath of the LORD" for its cruelty (50:13). Because it has "sinned" (50:14) and "defied the Lord" (50:29), it will soon be treated just as it has treated others (50:15, 29). God will avenge himself on Babylon for sacrilege as well, i.e., for destroying the Temple in Jerusalem (50:28; 51:11). **Chaldeans:** The Babylonians, whose leading tribe was the Kaldu tribe.
　50:2 Bel: Another name for Marduk, here spelled **Merodach**, chief god of the city of Babylon (Is 46:1).
　50:3 out of the north: Babylon falls to the Persians, who dwell east of Mesopotamia, but the Persian army advances into Babylonian territory from the north. See notes on Is 41:2 and 41:25. **none shall dwell in it:** The language of complete desolation indicates that the Babylonian empire will disappear from history forever (50:13; cf. Is 13:19–22; 14:22–23).

　50:4 Israel ... Judah: For the reunion of Israel's twelve tribes, see note on 3:18.
　50:5 Zion: The mountain height of Jerusalem (31:6). **everlasting covenant:** The "new" and "everlasting" covenant that Jeremiah prophesies in 31:31–34 and 32:40.
　50:6 lost sheep: The exiles of Israel and Judah scattered in distant lands (50:17). **shepherds:** The royal and religious leaders who have led God's people away from obedience to the covenant (10:21; 12:10; 23:1–4).
　50:8 Flee: The exiles of Judah in Babylon are called to return home, as in Is 48:20. The Exile officially ends in 538 B.C., one year after the fall of the city, by an edict of Cyrus II of Persia (Ezra 1:1–4).
　50:13 hiss: See note on 18:16.
　50:15 her walls are thrown down: Stereotypical language for the conquest of a city, not always to be taken literally. The Medo-Persian army of Cyrus II engages the Babylonians in battle at other locations, but in 539 B.C. they seize control of the city of Babylon without a fight.
　50:17 lions: The Assyrians, who destroy the Northern Kingdom of Israel in stages between 734 and 722 B.C. (2 Kings 15:29; 17:5–6; 1 Chron 5:26), and the Babylonians, who

punishment on the king of Babylon and his land, as I punished the king of Assyria. ¹⁹I will restore Israel to his pasture, and he shall feed on Car'mel and in Ba'shan, and his desire shall be satisfied on the hills of E'phraim and in Gilead. ²⁰In those days and in that time, says the LORD, iniquity shall be sought in Israel, and there shall be none; and sin in Judah, and none shall be found; for I will pardon those whom I leave as a remnant.

²¹"Go up against the land of Meratha'im,ˢ
  and against the inhabitants of Pe'kod.ᵗ
Slay, and utterly destroy after them, says the
  LORD,
  and do all that I have commanded
  you.
²²The noise of battle is in the land,
  and great destruction!
²³How the hammer of the whole earth
  is cut down and broken!
How Babylon has become
  a horror among the nations!
²⁴I set a snare for you and you were taken, O
  Babylon,
  and you did not know it;
you were found and caught,
  because you strove against the LORD.
²⁵The LORD has opened his armory,
  and brought out the weapons of his
  wrath,
for the Lord GOD of hosts has a work to do
  in the land of the Chalde'ans.
²⁶Come against her from every quarter;
  open her granaries;
pile her up like heaps of grain, and destroy her
  utterly;
  let nothing be left of her.
²⁷Slay all her bulls,
  let them go down to the slaughter.

Woe to them, for their day has come,
  the time of their punishment.

28 "Listen! they flee and escape from the land of Babylon, to declare in Zion the vengeance of the LORD our God, vengeance for his temple.

29 "Summon archers against Babylon, all those who bend the bow. Encamp round about her; let no one escape. Repay her according to her deeds, do to her according to all that she has done; for she has proudly defied the LORD, the Holy One of Israel. ³⁰Therefore her young men shall fall in her squares, and all her soldiers shall be destroyed on that day, says the LORD.

³¹"Behold, I am against you, O proud one,
  says the Lord GOD of hosts;
for your day has come,
  the time when I will punish you.
³²The proud one shall stumble and fall,
  with none to raise him up,
and I will kindle a fire in his cities,
  and it will devour all that is round about him.

33 "Thus says the LORD of hosts: The people of Israel are oppressed, and the people of Judah with them; all who took them captive have held them fast, they refuse to let them go. ³⁴Their Redeemer is strong; the LORD of hosts is his name. He will surely plead their cause, that he may give rest to the earth, but unrest to the inhabitants of Babylon.

³⁵"A sword upon the Chalde'ans, says the LORD,
  and upon the inhabitants of Babylon,
  and upon her princes and her wise men!
³⁶A sword upon the diviners,
  that they may become fools!
A sword upon her warriors,
  that they may be destroyed!

---

subjugate the Southern Kingdom of Judah in 605 and destroy it by 586 B.C. (2 Kings 24:1–2, 10–17; 25:8–11; Dan 1:1–4). Both conquerors take captives from the land of Israel into exile.

50:19 his pasture: The Promised Land of Canaan. **Carmel:** Rises near the coast of northwest Israel, near modern Haifa. **Bashan:** Fertile lands northeast of the Sea of Galilee. **Ephraim:** The central hill country of Israel. **Gilead:** Highlands east of the Jordan River.

50:20 none shall be found: The Lord's forgiveness, by which he removes the guilt of sin from his people, is a sign of the new covenant he will ratify with his people (31:31–34; cf. Mt 26:27–28).

50:21 Merathaim ... Pekod: Symbolic names for the southern and eastern regions of Babylonia, which have similar sounding names (see textual notes s and t).

50:23 hammer of the whole earth: Babylon is an imperial superpower that pounds smaller states into submission, eventually ruling over the entire Near East (27:5–7).

50:27 Woe: A cry of anguish heard at funerals. See word study: *Woe* at Is 28:1.

50:28 vengeance for his temple: Of all the offences Babylon commits at the height of its power, the desecration and destruction of the Lord's sanctuary in Jerusalem are the most egregious (52:12–13). The Babylonians will thus be repaid for "all the evil that they have done in Zion" (51:24).

50:29 the Holy One of Israel: See note on Is 1:4.

50:34 Redeemer: The Lord is like one who reclaims his kinsmen from slavery by purchasing their freedom. The kinship between God and Israel is that between a Father and his first-born son (Ex 4:22; Deut 8:5; Is 63:16). See word study: *Redeem* at Lev 25:25.

50:35 A sword: An image of the Lord's avenging judgment (Deut 32:40–42). **wise men:** Specialists in dream interpretation and astrology.

50:36 diviners: Claimed to gain knowledge of the future by various superstitious arts (27:9).

ˢ Or *Double Rebellion.*
ᵗ Or *Punishment.*

³⁷A sword upon her horses and upon her chariots,
  and upon all the foreign troops in her midst,
    that they may become women!
A sword upon all her treasures,
    that they may be plundered!
³⁸A drought upon her waters,
    that they may be dried up!
For it is a land of images,
    and they are mad over idols.

39 "Therefore wild beasts shall dwell with hyenas in Babylon, and ostriches shall dwell in her; she shall be peopled no more for ever, nor inhabited for all generations. ⁴⁰As when God overthrew Sodom and Gomor′rah and their neighbor cities, says the Lord, so no man shall dwell there, and no son of man shall sojourn in her.

⁴¹"Behold, a people comes from the north;
    a mighty nation and many kings
  are stirring from the farthest parts of the earth.
⁴²They lay hold of bow and spear;
    they are cruel, and have no mercy.
The sound of them is like the roaring of the sea;
    they ride upon horses,
  clothed as a man for battle
    against you, O daughter of Babylon!

⁴³"The king of Babylon heard the report of them,
    and his hands fell helpless;
  anguish seized him,
    pain as of a woman in labor.

44 "Behold, like a lion coming up from the jungle of the Jordan against a strong sheepfold, I will suddenly make them run away from her; and I will appoint over her whomever I choose. For who is like me? Who will summon me? What shepherd can stand before me? ⁴⁵Therefore hear the plan which the Lord has made against Babylon, and the purposes which he has formed against the land of the Chalde′ans: Surely the little ones of their flock shall be dragged away; surely their fold shall be appalled at their fate. ⁴⁶At the sound of the capture of Babylon the earth shall tremble, and her cry shall be heard among the nations."

51 Thus says the Lord:
Behold, I will stir up the spirit of a destroyer
    against Babylon,
  against the inhabitants of Chalde′a;ᵘ
²and I will send to Babylon winnowers,
    and they shall winnow her,
  and they shall empty her land,
    when they come against her from every
      side
  on the day of trouble.
³Let not the archer bend his bow,
    and let him not stand up in his coat of mail.
Spare not her young men;
    utterly destroy all her host.
⁴They shall fall down slain in the land of the
      Chalde′ans,
    and wounded in her streets.
⁵For Israel and Judah have not been forsaken
    by their God, the Lord of hosts;
  but the land of the Chalde′ansᵛ is full of guilt
    against the Holy One of Israel.

⁶"Flee from the midst of Babylon,
    let every man save his life!
Be not cut off in her punishment,
    for this is the time of the Lord's vengeance,
    the repayment he is rendering her.
⁷Babylon was a golden cup in the Lord's hand,
    making all the earth drunken;
  the nations drank of her wine,
    therefore the nations went mad.
⁸Suddenly Babylon has fallen and been broken;
    wail for her!

51:6, 9, 45: Jer 50:8; 2 Cor 6:17; Rev 18:4. **51:7-8:** Jer 25:15; Rev 14:8, 10; 16:19; 17:4; 18:3.

50:37 foreign troops: Mercenaries.
  50:40 Sodom and Gomorrah: Wicked cities near the Dead Sea that God utterly destroyed in patriarchal times (49:18; Gen 19:24-25). **no man shall dwell there:** See note on 50:3.
  50:41 a people: The Persians, who absorbed the Medes ca. 550 B.C.
  50:44 a lion: An image of the Lord coming against a sinful nation (25:38; 49:19; Hos 5:14).
  51:1 spirit of a destroyer: Or "a destroying wind". A dry, scorching wind that blows in from the desert is sometimes an image of judgment (4:11; 18:17; Is 27:8; Jon 4:8).
  51:2 they shall winnow: Winnowing was part of a process (after threshing) that ancient farmers used to separate wheat and barley grains from their husks, called chaff. It is sometimes an image of judgment in Scripture (15:7; Ps 1:4; Mt 3:12).
  51:5 Israel and Judah: Jeremiah is adamant that the exiled tribes of Israel have not been abandoned to languish in exile forever, but a remnant of both the northern and southern tribes will be gathered and reunited as one family in the bonds of a new covenant (3:18; 31:31). **the Holy One of Israel:** See note on Is 1:4.
  51:6 Flee from ... Babylon: An announcement of Babylon's fall and Judah's release from exile (Is 48:20).
  51:7 golden cup: A sign of royal dignity and wealth. It is the Lord's will that Babylon should bring all the nations of the Near East under the yoke of its empire (27:5-7). In this way, Babylon serves as a divine instrument of judgment on other nations, especially Judah (25:8-11).
  51:8 Babylon has fallen: The fall of Babylon to foreign conquerors in 539 B.C. is so certain that Jeremiah can speak as if it has already happened. Scholars sometimes call this the "prophetic perfect" tense (Is 21:9; Rev 14:8).

ᵘHeb *Leb-qamai*, a cipher for Chaldea.
ᵛHeb *their land*.

Take balm for her pain;
    perhaps she may be healed.
⁹We would have healed Babylon,
    but she was not healed.
Forsake her, and let us go
    each to his own country;
for her judgment has reached up to heaven
    and has been lifted up even to the skies.
¹⁰The Lord has brought forth our vindication;
    come, let us declare in Zion
    the work of the Lord our God.

¹¹"Sharpen the arrows!
    Take up the shields!
The Lord has stirred up the spirit of the kings of the Medes, because his purpose concerning Babylon is to destroy it, for that is the vengeance of the Lord, the vengeance for his temple.
¹²Set up a standard against the walls of Babylon;
    make the watch strong;
set up watchmen;
    prepare the ambushes;
for the Lord has both planned and done
    what he spoke concerning the inhabitants of
    Babylon.
¹³O you who dwell by many waters,
    rich in treasures,
your end has come,
    the thread of your life is cut.
¹⁴The Lord of hosts has sworn by himself:
Surely I will fill you with men, as many as
    locusts,
    and they shall raise the shout of victory over
    you.

¹⁵"It is he who made the earth by his power,
    who established the world by his wisdom,
and by his understanding
    stretched out the heavens.
¹⁶When he utters his voice there is a tumult of
    waters in the heavens,
    and he makes the mist rise from the ends of
    the earth.

He makes lightning for the rain,
    and he brings forth the wind from his
    storehouses.
¹⁷Every man is stupid and without knowledge;
    every goldsmith is put to shame by his idols;
for his images are false,
    and there is no breath in them.
¹⁸They are worthless, a work of delusion;
    at the time of their punishment they shall
    perish.
¹⁹Not like these is he who is the portion of Jacob,
    for he is the one who formed all things,
and Israel is the tribe of his inheritance;
    the Lord of hosts is his name.

²⁰"You are my hammer and weapon of war:
    with you I break nations in pieces;
    with you I destroy kingdoms;
²¹with you I break in pieces the horse and his
    rider;
    with you I break in pieces the chariot and
    the charioteer;
²²with you I break in pieces man and woman;
    with you I break in pieces the old man and
    the youth;
with you I break in pieces the young man and
    the maiden;
²³   with you I break in pieces the shepherd and
    his flock;
with you I break in pieces the farmer and his
    team;
    with you I break in pieces governors and
    commanders.

The Doom of Babylon

24 "I will repay Babylon and all the inhabitants of Chalde′a before your very eyes for all the evil that they have done in Zion, says the Lord.

²⁵"Behold, I am against you, O destroying
    mountain,
                says the Lord,
    which destroys the whole earth;

51:13: Rev 17:1.

51:10 our vindication: The voice of the exiles who suffer at the hands of the Babylonians. **in Zion:** Anticipates a return of exiles to Jerusalem as the focal point of Judah's postexilic restoration (50:28).

51:11 the Medes: A people of ancient Iran, southwest of the Caspian Sea. The Medes were incorporated into the growing Persian Empire by ca. 550 B.C. Babylon surrenders to the combined Medo-Persian forces in 539 B.C. (Is 13:17; Dan 5:30–31). **vengeance for his temple:** See note on 50:28.

51:14 locusts: Represent swarms of enemy soldiers. See note on 46:23.

51:15–19 The God of Israel is the almighty Creator whose power over the elements is witnessed in the thunderstorm. The idols of the nations are no match for him, which means that Babylon's gods will be unable to protect the city from the Lord's impending judgment.

51:15 by his wisdom: See note on Prov 8:22–23. **stretched out the heavens:** The work of creation, with the sky suspended over the earth, is compared to pitching a tent, as often in Isaiah (Is 40:22; 42:5; 44:24; 45:12). This reflects ancient Israel's belief that the world is a cosmic sanctuary, just as Israel's sanctuaries, the wilderness Tabernacle and the Jerusalem Temple, are viewed as replicas of the cosmos. See essay: *The Theology of the Temple* at 2 Chron 5.

51:20 my hammer: Babylon is an imperial superpower that pounds smaller states into submission, eventually ruling over the entire Near East (27:5–7).

51:25 O destroying mountain: The image depicts the height of Babylon's pride (50:31; Is 14:3–14).

I will stretch out my hand against you,
    and roll you down from the crags,
    and make you a burnt mountain.
²⁶No stone shall be taken from you for a corner
    and no stone for a foundation,
but you shall be a perpetual waste,
    says the Lord.

²⁷"Set up a standard on the earth,
    blow the trumpet among the nations;
prepare the nations for war against her,
    summon against her the kingdoms,
    Ar'arat, Minni, and Ash'kenaz;
appoint a marshal against her,
    bring up horses like bristling locusts.
²⁸Prepare the nations for war against her,
    the kings of the Medes, with their governors
      and deputies,
    and every land under their dominion.
²⁹The land trembles and writhes in pain,
    for the Lord's purposes against Babylon stand,
to make the land of Babylon a desolation,
    without inhabitant.
³⁰The warriors of Babylon have ceased fighting,
    they remain in their strongholds;
their strength has failed,
    they have become women;
her dwellings are on fire,
    her bars are broken.
³¹One runner runs to meet another,
    and one messenger to meet another,
to tell the king of Babylon
    that his city is taken on every side;
³²the fords have been seized,
    the bulwarks are burned with fire,
    and the soldiers are in panic.
³³For thus says the Lord of hosts, the God of Israel:
The daughter of Babylon is like a threshing floor
    at the time when it is trodden;
yet a little while
    and the time of her harvest will come."

³⁴"Nebuchadrez'zar the king of Babylon has
    devoured me,
    he has crushed me;
he has made me an empty vessel,
    he has swallowed me like a monster;
he has filled his belly with my delicacies,
    he has rinsed me out.
³⁵The violence done to me and to my kinsmen be
    upon Babylon,"
    let the inhabitant of Zion say.
"My blood be upon the inhabitants of Chalde'a,"
    let Jerusalem say.
³⁶Therefore thus says the Lord:
"Behold, I will plead your cause
    and take vengeance for you.
I will dry up her sea
    and make her fountain dry;
³⁷and Babylon shall become a heap of ruins,
    the haunt of jackals,
a horror and a hissing,
    without inhabitant.

³⁸"They shall roar together like lions;
    they shall growl like lions' whelps.
³⁹While they are inflamed I will prepare them a
    feast
    and make them drunk, till they swoon away^w
and sleep a perpetual sleep
    and not wake, says the Lord.
⁴⁰I will bring them down like lambs to the
    slaughter,
    like rams and he-goats.

⁴¹"How Babylon^x is taken,
    the praise of the whole earth seized!
How Babylon has become
    a horror among the nations!
⁴²The sea has come up on Babylon;
    she is covered with its tumultuous waves.
⁴³Her cities have become a horror,
    a land of drought and a desert,

51:26 a perpetual waste: The language of complete desolation indicates that the Babylonian empire will disappear from history forever (50:13; cf. Is 13:19–22; 14:22–23).

51:27 standard: A military banner used to give directions to soldiers in battle (Is 13:2). **Ararat, Minni, and Ashkenaz:** Peoples and places surrounding upper Mesopotamia that are ruled by the Medes until their absorption into the expanding Persian Empire ca. 550 B.C.

51:28 the Medes: See note on 51:11.

51:29 desolation: See note on 50:3.

51:30 become women: Fear of enemy attackers will turn Babylon's brave soldiers into the equivalent of frightened female civilians (cf. Is 19:16; Nahum 3:13). **bars:** Used to secure city gates.

51:33 daughter of Babylon: A personification of the city. See word study: *The Daughter of Zion* at Lam 1:6. **harvest:** Designates a time of judgment when the Lord intervenes to punish evildoing after it has fully ripened.

51:34 Nebuchadrezzar: An alternate spelling for Nebuchadnezzar, ruler of the Neo-Babylonian empire from 605 to 562 B.C. **like a monster:** The Lord called the king of Babylon to be his "servant" in punishing Judah (25:9), but the king transgressed his mandate by desecrating the Temple (50:28; 51:11) and showing merciless cruelty (50:29; Is 47:5–7; Zech 1:15). **me:** The speaker is Jerusalem/Zion personified (51:35).

51:35 My blood be upon: An imputation of guilt for murderous bloodshed (26:15; Acts 5:28).

51:37 haunt of jackals: Picturing once-populated cities as a home to wild animals is a traditional image of desolation after conquest (cf. 50:39; Is 13:21–23).

51:39 make them drunk: With the wine of divine judgment (25:15–27).

51:41 Babylon is taken: See note on 51:8.

---

^wGk Vg: Heb *rejoice*.
^xHeb *Sheshach*, a cipher for Babylon.

a land in which no one dwells,
    and through which no son of man passes.
⁴⁴And I will punish Bel in Babylon,
    and take out of his mouth what he has
        swallowed.
The nations shall no longer flow to him;
    the wall of Babylon has fallen.

⁴⁵"Go out of the midst of her, my people!
Let every man save his life
    from the fierce anger of the LORD!
⁴⁶Let not your heart faint, and be not fearful
    at the report heard in the land,
when a report comes in one year
    and afterward a report in another year,
and violence is in the land,
    and ruler is against ruler.

⁴⁷"Therefore, behold, the days are coming
    when I will punish the images of Babylon;
her whole land shall be put to shame,
    and all her slain shall fall in the midst of her.
⁴⁸Then the heavens and the earth,
    and all that is in them,
shall sing for joy over Babylon;
    for the destroyers shall come against them out
        of the north,
                    says the LORD.
⁴⁹Babylon must fall for the slain of Israel,
    as for Babylon have fallen the slain of all the
        earth.

⁵⁰"You that have escaped from the sword,
    go, stand not still!
Remember the LORD from afar,
    and let Jerusalem come into your mind:
⁵¹'We are put to shame, for we have heard
    reproach;
    dishonor has covered our face,
for aliens have come
    into the holy places of the LORD's house.'

⁵²"Therefore, behold, the days are coming, says the
    LORD,
    when I will execute judgment upon her
        images,

and through all her land
    the wounded shall groan.
⁵³Though Babylon should mount up to heaven,
    and though she should fortify her strong
        height,
yet destroyers would come from me upon her,
    says the LORD.

⁵⁴"Listen! a cry from Babylon!
    The noise of great destruction from the land of
        the Chalde'ans!
⁵⁵For the LORD is laying Babylon waste,
    and stilling her mighty voice.
Their waves roar like many waters,
    the noise of their voice is raised;
⁵⁶for a destroyer has come upon her,
    upon Babylon;
her warriors are taken,
    their bows are broken in pieces;
for the LORD is a God of recompense,
    he will surely repay.
⁵⁷I will make drunk her princes and her wise men,
    her governors, her commanders, and her
        warriors;
they shall sleep a perpetual sleep and not wake,
    says the King, whose name is the LORD of
        hosts.

⁵⁸"Thus says the LORD of hosts:
The broad wall of Babylon
    shall be leveled to the ground
and her high gates
    shall be burned with fire.
The peoples labor for nothing,
    and the nations weary themselves only for
        fire."

Jeremiah's Command to Seraiah

59 The word which Jeremi'ah the prophet commanded Serai'ah the son of Neri'ah, son of Mahsei'ah, when he went with Zedeki'ah king of Judah to Babylon, in the fourth year of his reign. Seraiah was the quartermaster. ⁶⁰Jeremi'ah wrote in a book all the evil that should come upon Babylon, all these words that are written concerning Babylon. ⁶¹And Jeremi'ah said to Serai'ah: "When you come to Babylon, see that you read all these words, ⁶²and

---

51:48: Is 44:23; Rev 12:12; 18:20.

51:44 Bel: Another name for Marduk, chief god of the city of Babylon (Is 46:1).

    51:45 Go out ... my people!: See note on 51:6.

    51:47 the images: Idols (50:2).

    51:48 destroyers: The Persians and Medes (Dan 5:28). **out of the north:** See note on 1:14.

    51:50 You ... go: Another appeal for the Jewish exiles to flee from Babylon (50:8; 51:6, 45).

    51:51 the LORD's house: The Temple in Jerusalem, defiled and burned by Babylonian conquerors in 586 B.C. (52:13).

    51:57 make drunk: See note on 51:39. **perpetual sleep:** The permanent disappearance of the Babylonian empire is meant.

    51:59–64 A postscript forming the conclusion to Jeremiah's prophecies.

    51:59 Seraiah: The brother of Jeremiah's secretary, Baruch (36:32). **Zedekiah:** The last king of Judah, who reigned from 597 to 586 B.C. **the fourth year:** 594 B.C.

    51:61 all these words: Refers to Jeremiah's prophecy of Babylon's downfall in chaps. 50–51.

say, 'O LORD, you have said concerning this place that you will cut it off, so that nothing shall dwell in it, neither man nor beast, and it shall be desolate for ever.' ⁶³When you finish reading this book, bind a stone to it, and cast it into the midst of the Euphra′tes, ⁶⁴and say, 'Thus shall Babylon sink, to rise no more, because of the evil that I am bringing upon her.' "ʸ

Thus far are the words of Jeremi′ah.

Zedekiah Is Captured

52 *Zedeki′ah was twenty-one years old when he became king; and he reigned eleven years in Jerusalem. His mother's name was Hamu′tal the daughter of Jeremi′ah of Libnah. ²And he did what was evil in the sight of the LORD, according to all that Jehoi′akim had done. ³Surely because of the anger of the LORD things came to such a pass in Jerusalem and Judah that he cast them out from his presence.

And Zedeki′ah rebelled against the king of Babylon. ⁴And in the ninth year of his reign, in the tenth month, on the tenth day of the month, Nebuchadrez′zar king of Babylon came with all his army against Jerusalem, and they laid siege to it and built siegeworks against it round about. ⁵So the city was besieged till the eleventh year of King Zedeki′ah. ⁶On the ninth day of the fourth month the famine was so severe in the city, that there was no food for the people of the land. ⁷Then a breach was made in the city; and all the men of war fled and went out from the city by night by the way of a gate between the two walls, by the king's garden, while the Chalde′ans were round about the city. And they went in the direction of the Ar′abah. ⁸But the army of the Chalde′ans pursued the king, and overtook Zedeki′ah in the plains of Jericho; and all his army was scattered from him. ⁹Then they captured the king, and brought him up to the king of Babylon at Riblah in the land of Ha′math, and he passed sentence upon him. ¹⁰The king of Babylon slew the sons of Zedeki′ah before his eyes, and also slew all the princes of Judah at Riblah. ¹¹He put out the eyes of Zedeki′ah, and bound him in chains, and the king of Babylon took him to Babylon, and put him in prison till the day of his death.

Jerusalem Is Plundered and Burned

12 In the fifth month, on the tenth day of the month—which was the nineteenth year of King Nebuchadrez′zar, king of Babylon—Nebu′zarad′an the captain of the bodyguard who served the king of Babylon, entered Jerusalem. ¹³And he burned the house of the LORD, and the king's house and all the houses of Jerusalem; every great house he burned down. ¹⁴And all the army of the Chalde′ans, who were with the captain of the guard, broke down all the

---

51:63–64: Rev 18:21.   **52:** 2 Kings 24:18—25:30; 2 Chron 36:11–13.

51:63 the Euphrates: Babylon was built along its banks in lower Mesopotamia. The symbolic act of binding the words of the prophecy to a rock that is hurled into the river, never to be seen again, reinforces what is written: the Lord's sentence of judgment will cause Babylon to fall and never rise again (51:64).

52:1-27 The final days of the Southern Kingdom of Judah. Jeremiah's account closely parallels 2 Kings 24:18—25:21.

52:1 Zedekiah: The last king of Judah, who reigns from 597 to 586 B.C. It is his rebellion against King Nebuchadnezzar, Judah's political overlord, that provokes the Babylonian invasion that destroys the Southern Kingdom of Judah once and for all in 586 B.C. (52:12-13). Zedekiah survives the conquest of Jerusalem but is blinded and taken into exile, where he eventually dies (52:7-11). **Hamutal:** Queen of Judah by virtue of being Zedekiah's mother. See essay: *The Queen Mother* at 1 Kings 2. **Jeremiah of Libnah:** Otherwise unknown.

52:2 Jehoiakim: Older brother of Zedekiah and his predecessor on the throne from 609 to 598 B.C.

52:3 rebelled: Probably means that Judah, a vassal state under Babylonian rule, defiantly withheld the payment of tribute demanded by Nebuchadnezzar.

52:4 ninth year: 587 B.C. The king's tenth year began in March–April; hence, the long siege of Jerusalem, which began in January 587 and ended with the burning of the city in August 586, covers an 18-month period that began late in his ninth year, extended through his tenth year, and ended a few months into his eleventh year (39:2). **tenth month:** Tebet, which corresponds to December–January. **Nebuchadrezzar:** An alternate spelling for Nebuchadnezzar, ruler of the Neo-Babylonian empire from 605 to 562 B.C.

52:6 fourth month: Tammuz, which corresponds to June–July. **famine:** Starving survivors resort to cannibalism (Lam 4:10).

52:7-11 Zedekiah attempts a nighttime escape from the city, only to be apprehended and taken to Babylon as a prisoner. His life is spared, as Jeremiah predicted, but not without bitter suffering: he witnesses the slaying of his sons, and then his eyes are gouged out (39:6-7).

52:7 a breach was made: In the summer of 586 B.C., Nebuchadnezzar's forces break through Jerusalem's defensive wall, perhaps on the north side of the city, which is the most vulnerable because it lacks the natural protection of a ravine. The city and Temple are burned one month later (52:12-13; 2 Kings 25:8-9). **the king's garden:** Near the southeast corner of the city (Neh 3:15). **Chaldeans:** Babylonians. **the Arabah:** The arid lands east of Jerusalem and surrounding the Dead Sea.

52:8 plains of Jericho: Northwest of the Dead Sea.

52:9 Riblah: On the Orontes River in Syria, north of Damascus. It serves as Nebuchadnezzar's base of operations (52:26-27).

52:11 chains: Bronze shackles banded around a captive's wrists and ankles.

52:12 fifth month: Av, which corresponds to July–August. Jews in the exilic and early postexilic periods mourned the Temple's destruction by fasting in the fifth month (Zech 7:3). **tenth day:** The seventh day according to 2 Kings 25:8. **Nebuzaradan:** One of Nebuchadnezzar's chief military officers. He oversees the burning of Jerusalem and its Temple one month after the city is breached (52:12-13) along with the destruction of the city walls (52:14). He also organizes the roundup and deportation of Judah's exiles in the aftermath of the conquest.

ʸ Gk: Heb *upon her. And they shall weary themselves.*
*52: Historical supplement which recapitulates and enlarges on 2 Kings 24:18—25:30. Cf. Is 36–39, which was added in the same way.

walls round about Jerusalem. [15]And Nebu'zarad'an the captain of the guard carried away captive some of the poorest of the people and the rest of the people who were left in the city and the deserters who had deserted to the king of Babylon, together with the rest of the artisans. [16]But Nebu'zarad'an the captain of the guard left some of the poorest of the land to be vinedressers and plowmen.

17 And the pillars of bronze that were in the house of the LORD, and the stands and the bronze sea that were in the house of the LORD, the Chalde'ans broke in pieces, and carried all the bronze to Babylon. [18]And they took away the pots, and the shovels, and the snuffers, and the basins, and the dishes for incense, and all the vessels of bronze used in the temple service; [19]also the small bowls, and the firepans, and the basins, and the pots, and the lampstands, and the dishes for incense, and the bowls for libation. What was of gold the captain of the guard took away as gold, and what was of silver, as silver. [20]As for the two pillars, the one sea, the twelve bronze bulls which were under the sea,[z] and the stands, which Solomon the king had made for the house of the LORD, the bronze of all these things was beyond weight. [21]As for the pillars, the height of the one pillar was eighteen cubits, its circumference was twelve cubits, and its thickness was four fingers, and it was hollow. [22]Upon it was a capital of bronze; the height of the one capital was five cubits; a network and pomegranates, all of bronze, were upon the capital round about. And the second pillar had the like, with pomegranates. [23]There were ninety-six pomegranates on the sides; all the pomegranates were a hundred upon the network round about.

24 And the captain of the guard took Serai'ah the chief priest, and Zephani'ah the second priest, and the three keepers of the threshold; [25]and from the city he took an officer who had been in command of the men of war, and seven men of the king's council, who were found in the city; and the secretary of the commander of the army who mustered the people of the land; and sixty men of the people of the land, who were found in the midst of the city. [26]And Nebu'zarad'an the captain of the guard took them, and brought them to the king of Babylon at Riblah. [27]And the king of Babylon struck them, and put them to death at Riblah in the land of Ha'math. So Judah was carried captive out of its land.

The Captives Taken to Babylon

28 This is the number of the people whom Nebuchadrez'zar carried away captive: in the seventh year, three thousand and twenty-three Jews; [29]in the eighteenth year of Nebuchadrez'zar he carried away captive from Jerusalem eight hundred and thirty-two persons; [30]in the twenty-third year of Nebuchadrez'zar, Nebu'zarad'an the captain of the guard carried away captive of the Jews seven hundred and forty-five persons; all the persons were four thousand and six hundred.

Jehoiachin Favored in Captivity

31 And in the thirty-seventh year of the captivity of Jehoi'achin king of Judah, in the twelfth month, on the twenty-fifth day of the month, E'vil-mer'odach king of Babylon, in the year that he became king, lifted up the head of Jehoiachin king of Judah and brought him out of prison; [32]and he spoke kindly to him, and gave him a seat above the seats of the kings who were with him in Babylon. [33]So Jehoi'achin put off his prison garments. And every day of his life he dined regularly at the king's table; [34]as for his allowance, a regular allowance was given him by the king according to his daily need, until the day of his death as long as he lived.

52:15 carried away captive: For an inventory of those taken to Babylon, see 52:28–30.

52:16 poorest of the land: A population unlikely to instigate further rebellion.

52:17–23 The Temple is plundered of its precious metals and sacred implements (cf. 1 Kings 7:15–50). However, no mention is made of the Ark of the Covenant or of the golden altar of incense because Jeremiah reportedly hid them away in a cave before the onset of the Babylonian siege (2 Mac 2:4–5).

52:24 Seraiah: The grandson of Hilkiah, high priest in the days of Josiah (2 Kings 22:3–4). **second priest:** A deputy high priest whose specific responsibilities are unknown. **keepers of the threshold:** Three priests who stand guard as sentries to prevent unlawful encroachment into the sanctuary (2 Kings 12:9).

52:28–30 A headcount of 4600 captives from Judah taken into exile. This figure may refer only to the royal and religious leaders deported to Babylon, since 2 Kings 24:14 numbers 10,000 captives of Judah at the deportation of 597 B.C. alone. Jeremiah does not mention the initial exile of Judahites in 605 B.C. (Dan 1:1–4) but mentions three others: one in 597 (**seventh year**), one in 586 (**eighteenth year**), and a final one in 582 B.C. (**twenty-third year**). Nothing further is known about this last deportation, although it may have been a punitive response to the assassination of Gedaliah (41:1–2).

52:31 thirty-seventh year: About 560 B.C. **Jehoiachin:** The king of Judah taken to Babylon in 597 B.C. (2 Kings 24:12, 15). His survival represents the endurance of the Davidic royal line through the period of the Babylonian Exile, keeping alive the hope in God's promise to send a future messianic king—the righteous "Branch" from David's dynastic line (23:5; 33:15; Mt 1:12–16). **Evil-merodach:** Son and successor of Nebuchadnezzar as king of Babylon (562 to 560 B.C.). The Babylonian form of his name means "Man of (the god) Marduk".

52:34 his allowance: A detail corroborated by the archaeological discovery of clay tablets from ancient Babylon that name Jehoiachin and his sons as recipients of food rations of oil supplied by the royal household.

---

[z] Heb lacks *the sea*.

STUDY QUESTIONS
Jeremiah

Chapter 1

For understanding

1. **1:5.** When did God choose Jeremiah to be a prophet? What image does the Hebrew verb *yāṣar* suggest? What does Catholic tradition infer from this passage? According to St. Cyril of Jerusalem, why is God not unashamed to take human flesh, since he is its Creator? As the language of divine election, what does "I knew you" mean? What does being consecrated accomplish? Although Jeremiah is sent mainly to the people of Judah, to whom else will he speak oracles of judgment? How does Paul allude to this verse in Gal 1:15, and what does he imply about himself?

2. **1:6.** Of whom is Jeremiah's initial objection to God's call typical? In what other figures can the same reaction be seen? How does the Lord respond to the resistance of those he calls to service? Probably how old was Jeremiah when God called him?

3. **1:9.** For what service does Jeremiah's encounter with God equip him? How were Isaiah and Ezekiel similarly prepared for prophetic ministry? What words is the prophet given, and with what is his message invested? How does the passage use language from Deut 18:18? However, in whom is the coming of a prophet of Moses' stature only fully realized?

4. **1:19.** What reception will Jeremiah face? Beyond needing courage, of what is the prophet made aware? Like Isaiah and Ezekiel, with what is Jeremiah tasked? What is characteristic of prophetic ministry in the OT and is likewise a hallmark of apostolic ministry in the NT? According to St. John Cassian, how is a victory worthy of praise to be gained?

For application

1. **1:5.** How does this verse echo Ps 139? How long before you were born did the Lord know you? For what purpose were you born?

2. **1:6.** Have you ever resisted doing something you felt the Lord wanted you to do? If so, what were some of your excuses? What opportunities for grace do you most regret missing? What opportunities are you most grateful for accepting?

3. **1:10.** In a society like ours, what attitudes, ideologies, or practices primarily among Christians do you think Jeremiah would pluck up and tear down, and what would he build and plant? How might your answers reflect upon your own prophetic role?

4. **1:17.** What most dismays or frightens you about the opposition to the Gospel that Christians face today? How have you prepared yourself to stand up to it? What does the Lord mean by saying that if you are dismayed, he will dismay you (cf. Lk 9:26)?

Chapter 2

For understanding

1. **2:3.** What does it mean for Israel to be holy? What are the first fruits? Who were the only ones allowed to eat the first fruits? Theologically, of what harvest is Israel the first fruits, and what is that equivalent to saying? In Jas 1:18, to whom is the same expression applied? As the family of Abraham, what privilege did Israel enjoy?

2. **2:13.** What are cisterns? What do they represent here? What are living waters? For what does Jesus use this expression? According to St. Athanasius, what image have the sacred writers given us of the divine Son?

3. **2:20.** Of what is the yoke an image? After the Israelites were freed from the yoke of bondage in Egypt, to what did they bind themselves? How is breaking the yoke equivalent to breaking the covenant? To what does the expression "high hill and green tree" refer? To what is idolatry compared? What fact does the use of sexual metaphors for idolatry mirror?

4. **2:27.** To what do a tree and a stone refer here? Why does Jeremiah, speaking with sarcasm, reverse the sexual roles of these objects? What does addressing these objects as "You are my father" imply?

For application

1. **2:8.** How does it happen that a theologian who studies Scripture professionally disbelieves its message, or that one who teaches the faith has no personal relationship with God? What can be done to build or restore faith in such a one?

2. **2:13.** What are some of the "broken cisterns" that modern people hew for themselves? Why do these things hold no water?

3. **2:19.** How can one's wickedness chasten him? For example, how might the consequences of a sexually depraved life actually benefit the sinner?

4. **2:20.** The saying "I will not serve" is often attributed to Satan. What was the origin of his refusal to serve his Maker? How do those who refuse to acknowledge sin in their own lives imitate him?

Chapter 3

For understanding

1. **Word Study: Return (3:1).** How often does the Hebrew verb *shûv* appear in the OT? Because it expresses various meanings, including "turn", "turn around", and "turn back", what can the term indicate? As a theological term, how does it speak to Israel's relationship with the Lord? Although Jeremiah makes several appeals for his people to "return" to the Lord in this way, what are Judah and Jerusalem in danger of doing? If they resist the prophet's call, what will God's anger not do?

2. **3:6-11.** To what does the prophet compare the former rebellion of the Northern Kingdom of Israel? Although both kingdoms embraced a culture of sin and so placed themselves under God's judgment, why does Judah bear the greater guilt? Where else in Scripture is the metaphor used of Israel (with its capital, Samaria) and Judah (with its capital, Jerusalem) as wayward sisters?

3. **3:8.** What is a decree of divorce? When would a husband hand this certificate to his wife? Because the tribes of the Northern Kingdom of Israel were sent into exile and never returned home, from whom does it appear that a large part of the covenant people were "divorced"? Why is this not so, however?
4. **3:16.** What was the Ark of the Covenant, and where was it kept? How was the ark lidded, and with what was it topped? According to 2 Mac 2:5-6, what did Jeremiah do with it?

For application
1. **3:7-8.** In what sense does Israel's conduct and refusal to repent constitute scandal toward its sister, Judah? How does the *Catechism* understand the sin of scandal and its gravity (CCC 2284-87)? Has this sin by others ever influenced your behavior? What action or attitude of yours might have been an occasion of scandal to others?
2. **3:10.** Read the note for this verse. In the Sacrament of Reconciliation, how often do you confess the same sins over and over again? Even if the sins confessed seem trivial to you, how seriously do you take the resolution to sin no more that you spoke in the Act of Contrition?
3. **3:13.** When you do something you know is wrong toward a loved one, how often do you rationalize or minimize your behavior? Why is it so hard simply to admit the truth without excusing it, acknowledge the wrong, and ask forgiveness?

Chapter 4

For understanding
1. **4:10.** When is the word "GOD" spelled with capital letters? In a moment of distress and grief, of what does the prophet audaciously accuse the Lord? What do many wrongly suppose about Jerusalem and the Temple? What does the Lord also make clear, however?
2. **4:14.** Why does Jeremiah urge Jerusalem to "wash your heart"? Since prophecies of destruction are initially conditional, on what does their fulfillment depend?
3. **4:23.** How is the same Hebrew expression ("waste and void") translated in Gen 1:2? What does this suggest about the land of Judah?
4. **4:27.** Despite mass devastation, from what will God stop short? Why will he preserve a remnant of his people?

For application
1. **4:1.** Why do Christians reevaluating their faith and seeking a fuller experience of God often turn to other religions first? Why is turning to the one true God often the last thing they want to do? What makes yielding at last to him so difficult, and yet so easy?
2. **4:3.** According to Jesus' parable of the Sower, what happens to the seed that is sown among thorns (cf. Lk 8:14)? Why do anxieties and the pleasures of life interfere with the production of spiritual fruit?
3. **4:4.** Because most males are born with a foreskin, what are some of the reasons, both medical and religious, it is removed? As a metaphor, what does its removal mean for the human heart?
4. **4:14.** Read the note for this verse. How aggressively have modern peoples responded to calls for repentance as given, for example, by our Lady at Fatima? Why do we not feel the need to respond? What are the possible consequences for us?

Chapter 5

For understanding
1. **5:1-3.** What does the Lord challenge Jeremiah to find in Jerusalem, and why? Tragically, what shows that its divine punishment is justly deserved? To what dialogue is this passage similar?
2. **5:12.** To what does the saying that the Lord "will do nothing" amount? Utterly deceived, on what do they insist? What do they proclaim in the midst of violence, and what do they wrongly believe?
3. **5:15.** What is the "nation from afar"? What is the language that Jerusalem does not know? What covenant curses of Deut 28:49-68 is Jeremiah invoking? When did an earlier fulfillment of this curse take place?
4. **5:24.** What is lacking in Judah? During what months do the autumn rains occur? What do they accomplish? During what months do the spring rains occur? What are the weeks appointed for the harvest?

For application
1. **5:3.** Some children do not respond positively to corporal punishment but seem to make "their faces harder than rock". How does one discipline a child who refuses to change behavior after corporal punishment? How might methods of discipline change as a child grows older?
2. **5:4-5.** Why do we expect virtue and integrity from the educated classes rather than the poor? Why is it not the case that the educated elites are any more virtuous than the uneducated poor and, in fact, may be less virtuous? Of the two classes, which is more often the one that persecutes religious people and institutions?
3. **5:7-8.** When a parent gives a child everything he wants, what is likely to happen as he matures? How is indulging a child any better discipline than inflicting severe corporal punishment on one who seems to dare the parent to force a change?
4. **5:12.** According to the rules of Ignatian discernment, how does the evil spirit operate in the soul of one who is going from bad to worse? When lightning does not strike upon an evil act, what is the sinner most likely to conclude about God's judgment?

Chapter 6

For understanding
1. **6:9.** What are the Babylonians given permission to do? In biblical law, what were farmers instructed to leave after harvesting? How does that restriction apply to Judah?

2. **6:14.** What does the Hebrew word *shālôm* imply? What do the false prophets delude the masses into thinking? What does the quotation appear to have been?
3. **6:16.** What do the ancient paths marked out by the Torah show to God's people? When does Jesus borrow Jeremiah's language of "rest for your souls"? With what is his teaching implicitly contrasted?
4. **6:20.** Of what is frankincense a key ingredient? As an ancient trading empire in the southern Arabian Peninsula, what did Sheba export? Of what is sweet cane a key ingredient? Why is God's rejection of Judah's sacrifices not a condemnation of sacrifice per se? Rather, when do Israel's prophets insist that worship becomes displeasing to God? According to the *Apostolic Constitutions*, why did the Lord, before the coming of Christ, reject the sacrifices of the people?

For application
1. **6:1.** According to the note for this verse, where are these cities relative to Jerusalem? As refugees, to where are they to flee? What are some modern refugee centers in the Middle East? From where do these refugees come? For most of them, what is the near-term likelihood of return to their homes?
2. **6:4–5.** Who are the speakers in these verses? What point is the prophet making regarding the welfare of Jerusalem?
3. **6:10.** What pleasure do you derive from the word of the Lord? How open is your ear to hearing it (cf. Ps 40:7–8)? What causes you the most difficulty in taking pleasure or profit from it?
4. **6:15.** When one does wrong, whether deliberately or not, what is the value of shame? How is it possible for one to silence the voice of conscience once and for all?

Chapter 7

For understanding
1. **7:4.** What does Jeremiah call "the temple of the LORD"? If Jerusalem's protection does not lie in the presence of the Lord's house within its walls, where does it lie? On what is the belief that Zion is "inviolable" probably based? What do the people, and the false prophets who deceived them, forget? What is their only secure object of trust?
2. **7:11.** To what is the Temple compared? What will the Lord's house, by contrast, not afford? When does Jesus cite these words, and of what does he accuse the merchants?
3. **7:18.** Who was the queen of heaven? How was she served? How do Mesopotamian myths identify her? How was she known in Greek?
4. **7:22.** At the time of the Exodus, according to the Pentateuch, what did God's original covenant with Israel at Mt. Sinai not include? Of what did it initially consist? Laws mandating sacrifice were not given until *after* Israel did what? For Jeremiah, what does a careful reading of this story show? According to St. Jerome, what did the prophet mean that God first gave his people and, after the passage about the calf, later demanded? How does St. Thomas Aquinas explain why God instituted burnt offerings and sacrifices?

For application
1. **7:4.** What confidence for the survival of Christianity do you place in the centuries-long endurance of certain important Christian sites? How would your faith change if the Vatican and all of its buildings were destroyed? Where should trust rather be placed?
2. **7:8–11.** What are some of the ways that people and organizations hide racketeering activities behind Catholic devotion? What are some of the ordinary ways the "average Catholic" hides sinful behavior beneath a veneer of holiness? How is God's attitude toward these activities different now from what it was in Jeremiah's time?
3. **7:16.** When is intercessory prayer most likely to be successful? When is it least likely to be successful? If the Lord were to tell you that praying for a particular person is pointless, what would you do?
4. **7:22–23.** Look up Mic 6:6–8. What is the goal of the Christian life? What is the value of personal sacrifices made as part of living according to that goal? What is the value of personal sacrifices if one does not live according to that goal?

Chapter 8

For understanding
1. **8:1.** What kind of act is exhuming and exposing the remains of idolaters? Whose bones do the royal tombs of Jerusalem hold? How extensive is religious corruption in Judean society?
2. **8:2.** What does the host of heaven include? What about them is forbidden in Israel, and how is the prohibition regarded?
3. **8:7.** What do the birds of the air know when to begin, thanks to the instinct given them by God? Of what is Judah, by contrast, less perceptive than non-rational animals?
4. **8:17.** To what are the Babylonian hordes compared? What will Judah be unable to avert? How was snake charming practiced in the ancient Near East?

For application
1. **8:1–2.** Why is grave robbery considered a crime by most societies? Why is mutilating a corpse considered an act of desecration? In Catholic burials, why is it important to place the deceased in blessed ground?
2. **8:4.** How might you cite this verse to encourage someone who has sinned and feels hopeless? What virtue does it encourage?
3. **8:11.** What is the typical penance you are given after making your confession? What is the most severe penance you have ever received? Which was more effective at helping you change your behavior? Why does Jesus mention the prospect of hell as often as he does (e.g., Mt 5:22; Mk 9:43–47; Lk 12:5)?
4. **8:22.** Of what is the balm of Gilead an emblem? How can it soothe the sin-sick soul? Of course, once the balm is applied, what is the responsibility of that soul?

Chapter 9

For understanding
1. **9:3.** How is the tongue like a warrior's bow and arrows? To what does a profusion of slander, deception, and lies in Judah point?
2. **9:17.** In what rituals do women and girls play a leading role? How do they fulfill that role? Why is Jerusalem urged to summon these women?
3. **9:25.** For what purpose was circumcision of the male foreskin widely practiced in the Near East? In OT times, how do the Philistines become one of the few peoples that stand out from their neighbors in that regard? When does male circumcision take place in Israel, and for what purpose?
4. **9:26.** In biblical times, when do Arabs circumcise boys? What kind of rite is shaving hair from the temples among Arabian tribes? How does Judah become no different from neighboring peoples outside the covenant? What premise is unstated? What does cutting away the foreskin of the flesh symbolize? But while efforts at circumcising the heart are needed, what will become clear to Jeremiah? What did Moses foresee that the Lord, by an interior act of grace, would someday do? According to Paul, when does this promised circumcision of the heart take place?

For application
1. **9:4–6.** What is the normal function of language? What is its role in building social cohesion? What happens in society when everyone must be wary of his neighbor and no one trusts the truth of what anyone says?
2. **9:17–18.** What is the purpose of a funeral? What public displays of mourning does our culture employ, and what social functions do they serve? In cases of national mourning, such as at the death of a president, what events may be scheduled to include the largest number of people?
3. **9:23–24.** What is the true mark of success in life, according to Jeremiah? In what does the Lord most delight, even now?
4. **9:25.** What practical difference should reception of the Sacrament of Baptism make in a person's daily life? What is the true mark of failure in the life of a baptized person who rejects or ignores his baptismal commitment?

Chapter 10

For understanding
1. **10:1–5.** Why does the Lord declare that idols and astrological signs pose no threat to his people? To what are images of gods and goddesses compared? What are they unable to do?
2. **10:6.** What does it mean that the God of Israel is incomparable? As addressed to God, what is "your name"? What mystery does this name, which was revealed to Moses at the burning bush, bear, and how must it be treated?
3. **10:17.** Why should the Judeans gather up their bundle? When do deportations from Judah to Babylon take place?
4. **10:23–25.** With what do these verses deal? For what does the petitioner, either Jeremiah or the personified city of Jerusalem, ask? Toward whom is God asked to divert some of his wrath?

For application
1. **10:2.** Why, in a supposedly advanced culture like ours, is astrology still so popular? What influence does one's astrological sign actually bear on one's personality, character, or fate? What, or who, actually directs these things?
2. **10:6.** The note for this verse refers to the *Catechism of the Catholic Church*, paragraphs 206–9, which explain the significance of God's name, "at once a name revealed and something like the refusal of a name". What does your name reveal about you, and what does it conceal? If your name is something you want treated with respect, how often do you fail to treat the divine name with at least the same reverence?
3. **10:23–24.** What does Jeremiah think of the ability of a person to forge his own destiny? Although human beings have free will, what are its limits? When it comes to a relationship with God, why is it advisable to pray that he provide correction?

Chapter 11

For understanding
1. **11:2.** Whom does the Mosaic covenant bind together? In what stages were the terms of this covenant gradually revealed?
2. **11:14.** Although prophets typically intercede for others (Gen 20:7), for what is Jeremiah forbidden to pray? Whose prayers will the Lord refuse to answer? Of what is the futility of intercession an ominous sign?
3. **11:16.** Of what is the olive tree an image? How does Paul employ the same image of Israel as an olive tree?
4. **11:19.** Of what is Jeremiah both innocent and unaware? How does the imagery resemble Isaiah's Song of the Suffering Servant? How is Jeremiah thus a messiah-like figure? According to St. Justin Martyr, what can be seen from these words?
5. **11:23.** Who will survive when the Babylonians overrun Anathoth? On whose family will this be another act of divine judgment?

For application
1. **11:1–17.** Read the note for these verses. Why during a period of religious revival such as happened during the height of Josiah's reforms would a prophet invoke the curses of the covenant? Why remind people of the sins of the past when things seem to be improving?
2. **11:14–15.** As Jeremiah hints in these verses, what is the prayer that Judah is offering but to which the Lord will refuse to listen? What, rather, is the prayer to which the Lord will always listen, even at the eleventh hour?
3. **11:20.** For the Christian who suffers as a victim, to whom does vengeance rightfully belong (cf. Deut 32:35)? For a God who does not desire the death of the sinner, what vengeance is to him the sweetest?

Chapter 12

For understanding
1. **12:1.** How does the Lord show that he is righteous? Why is the prophet puzzled and irked? Why does the Lord say that the situation is temporary?
2. **12:7.** Whom has the Lord abandoned? When does Jesus allude to this verse? In both cases, to what is the abandonment of God's dwelling a prelude? How is the covenant people described?
3. **12:14–17.** What function do these verses serve? What will happen to the small nations of Moab, Ammon, and Syria? Nevertheless, how will the Lord show them compassion? With what does the language of the passage ("pluck up, build, destroy") have links?

For application
1. **12:1.** How appropriate is it for you to lodge a complaint to the Lord regarding his handling of reality? What examples can you find in Scripture of people making similar complaints? What is the difference between a serious complaint and mere whining? In prayer, how does one resolve a complaint?
2. **12:5.** Read the note for this verse. What are some more contemporary ways of saying the same thing to a person who is ready to give up when things get difficult?
3. **12:6.** What strains or ruptures exist within your family? To what extent are you or your Christian commitment the focus of these difficulties? What steps have you taken to reconcile the family, and with what effect?
4. **12:16–17.** Compare these verses with the commissioning of the apostles in Mk 16:15–16. What either/or choice do both texts hold out? Why is there no middle ground?

Chapter 13

For understanding
1. **13:1–11.** When Jeremiah buys a new waistcloth, what does he do with it? What did God command these actions to signify? By serving gods other than the Lord, what had the "evil people" of Judah and Jerusalem become?
2. **13:11.** What does the Hebrew verb *dabaq* mean, and what does it signal? To what is it comparable? According to St. Jerome, whom does the loincloth represent?
3. **13:12–14.** In another symbolic action, what does Jeremiah, standing before a collection of empty wine jugs, declare that God is about to do? What does the large number of vessels to be filled with wine signify? Where might the prophet be standing?
4. **13:18.** Which king is Jeremiah addressing? Who is the queen mother? What royal headpiece did both the king and queen wear?

For application
1. **13:1–7.** How is this symbolic action by Jeremiah like a parable? What is the purpose of parables, such as those that Jesus told? For whose benefit is this parable being enacted?
2. **13:8–11.** Here, the Lord explains the meaning of the parable. What is its main point? How would you rewrite Jeremiah's parable using a more modern image that would apply the same point to today's apostate culture?
3. **13:15–16.** Compare these verses with Is 55:6. When is the most opportune time to seek the Lord? How might the Lord allow the "window of opportunity" for seeking him to close? According to Jeremiah, what attitude causes that window to shut?
4. **13:23.** How do we use the proverb in this verse today? To what situations do we apply it? How similar is the meaning we give this proverb to the way Jeremiah uses it?

Chapter 14

For understanding
1. **14:1–6.** Under what does the whole land of Judah, people and animals, groan? Why are water supplies depleted and the landscape denuded of growth? When did these extreme conditions seem to have come? What is the implied background?
2. **14:7–10.** How does Jeremiah intercede for Judah? What does the use of the first-person plural ("we, us, our") show about his role? What does he not excuse or deny, and what does he affirm? If nothing else, for what motive does the prophet desire God to show mercy?
3. **14:11.** How many times has Jeremiah been forbidden to pray for Judah? Of what is the futility of intercession, as well as the people's fasting and sacrifice, an ominous sign? Now what is the only thing the prophet can do?
4. **14:13–16.** How does Jeremiah, unwilling to give up on intercessory prayer, respond? What is his plea? What is the divine reply?

For application
1. **14:2–3.** On what do we rely for our fresh water supply? In our urban environment, how is our water delivered to us? How would those who live in cities obtain water if their electrical systems failed?
2. **14:4.** Similarly, farmers often rely on irrigation to water their crops. How would our food supply be affected if the rains were to cease and the groundwater aquifers were to become dry?
3. **14:13–16.** Jeremiah blames the prophets for misleading the people into accepting false assurances. When both Church leaders and the faithful accept practices like out of wedlock sexual behavior as normal, who must bear the consequences? What kinds of consequences are likely to result?
4. **14:17.** Read the note for this verse. When Jesus blesses those who mourn (Mt 5:4), to what kind of mourning does he refer? How personally affected should you be by the sins of Christians who accommodate their lives to the prevailing culture rather than to the Lord?

Chapter 15

For understanding
1. **15:2.** What function do pestilence, sword, and famine serve? What is the climactic curse of the Mosaic covenant? Of those who escape the curse of death, how will many of them fare? How badly is captivity feared?
2. **15:13-14.** In his response to Jeremiah, whom does the Lord also address? What is about to happen to Judah's wealth, and what will happen to those who survive sword, famine, and pestilence?
3. **15:16.** What does Jeremiah remember? What idea did God's placement of divine "words" into his "mouth" suggest? To what discovery do some relate this passage? What does the word of the Lord become to those who accept it?
4. **15:19.** What does God's statement ("If you return") imply that Jeremiah, at the end of his rope, has decided? What will the Lord do if Jeremiah accepts again his prophetic task to speak God's word? How will he stand before the Lord?

For application
1. **15:1-4.** In today's Church, popular devotion places much emphasis on the Lord's mercy. Why the stark refusal of mercy in these verses? Given the history of the last hundred years, in which millions of innocent people have been slaughtered, what claim on divine mercy do we have that the Judahites did not?
2. **15:10-11.** If you have ever regretted the day you were born, what brought you to that point? Jeremiah faced real hatred from others for doing what God commissioned him to do; did the opposition you faced come from without or from within, from others or from a psychological issue? Has prayer helped you deal with that regret? If so, in what way?
3. **15:15-18.** If, like Jeremiah, you believe you have done everything properly and still feel abandoned by the Lord, what comfort can you take from the lives of saints who experienced similar abandonment? If, like Jeremiah, you question God's favor (v. 18), how do you restore trust in him?
4. **15:19-21.** In God's promise to restore Jeremiah's vocation, what reassurance does the Lord *not* make? Though his repentance will not necessarily improve his circumstances, what is the implied reward? What should be one's inner motivation for undertaking any ministry despite its continuing hardships?

Chapter 16

For understanding
1. **16:1-9.** What things is Jeremiah forbidden to do? In what way are they prophetic signs of judgment for the people and signs of mercy for the prophet? What will not be possible in the dreadful days ahead?
2. **16:6.** Who will survive or remain in the land to grieve over the dead? Why are gashing or lacerating the skin and shaving one's hair forbidden in Israel? However, what expression of grief is known in Israel?
3. **16:15.** What new formula for swearing oaths will replace the old formula in 16:14? What new and greater exodus does the prophet foresee? After the coming judgment, what does he expect to see? What is the north country?
4. **16:19-21.** With what are these verses concerned? How does the prophet foresee Gentiles coming to faith in the God of Israel?

For application
1. **16:1-4.** Sociologists are alarmed at the falling birthrates in the Western world, in some cases well below replacement level. What circumstances in this environment convince many married couples to avoid having children or choosing at most to bear "one and be done"? Why does the Catholic Church require married couples to remain open to the procreation of human life (CCC 2366-71)?
2. **16:5.** Note the irony in this verse. For whom has the Lord's "steadfast love and mercy" become nothing more than a meaningless expression? For whom should it become a reality?
3. **16:10.** When the present generation deliberately hides any recollection of evils perpetrated by previous generations, what guilt for these evils does it share? How do the sins of the fathers explain the sins of their children?

Chapter 17

For understanding
1. **17:5-8.** What contrast do these verses present? What constitutes the difference between them? Upon what does the passage encourage the remnant of devout Jews to rely?
2. **17:9.** Where are inclinations to sin lodged, and what do they affect? How are they a spiritual pathology? Although we still possess free will (Sir 15:11-20), what does Jeremiah recognize about our hearts? What things does Jesus likewise teach come from our hearts? Since sinful man is a mystery to himself, who can know the depths of his heart?
3. **17:15.** Who is it that asks where is the word of the Lord? Why is Jeremiah beginning to look foolish? What is it that scoffers fail to realize?
4. **17:21.** What is the "sabbath day"? Being one of the Ten Commandments, how serious is its obligation, and of what is it a perpetual sign? Here and elsewhere, how is the Sabbath broken?

For application
1. **17:5.** Why does the man who trusts in man merit a curse? Since trust is necessary for social survival, what is the spiritual problem that Jeremiah sees here?
2. **17:7-8.** How does one exhibit trust in the Lord? According to this analogy, what emotional or spiritual problems does trust in the Lord eliminate? What fruit does trust in the Lord enable one to produce?
3. **17:9.** What does the *Catechism* say about the corruption human beings inherit from Original Sin, and how is it different from both Pelagianism and the teaching of the first Protestant reformers (CCC 404-6)? What effect does Baptism have on the human heart?

4. **17:24–26.** According to Jeremiah, what are the social blessings that follow from keeping the Sabbath day holy? In a culture like ours, what natural blessings would follow from observing a seventh-day rest (CCC 2172)? How does the Christian observance of Sunday fulfill the Jewish Sabbath (CCC 2175–76)?

Chapter 18

For understanding
1. **18:1–12.** In this lesson of the potter at his wheel, what does Jeremiah learn? To whom else does the potter and clay as an image of the Lord's authority to form his people go back and by whom is it later used? From which picture does it stem?
2. **18:8.** Since the prophecy is conditional, on what does the outcome depend? How does God deal differently with those who repent and those who refuse to cease their wicked ways? If the notion of God "repenting" is not intended literally, on what analogy is it based? What is it a way of saying? Which kind of evil does God intend?
3. **18:18.** Who are the priests, the wise, and the prophets being discussed here? What were each of them supposed to do? What does their expression "strike him with the tongue" suggest they will do, although what else may be part of the plot?
4. **18:23.** If this is not a prayer for the damnation of one's enemies, for what is Jeremiah praying? Specifically, what does he, who has prayed that fellow Judahites would be spared divine wrath, now pray?

For application
1. **18:1–4.** Some Christian hymns compare God to the potter and the human soul to the clay he shapes. Into what does God wish to shape the human heart? What say does the clay have regarding the shape into which it is being molded?
2. **18:12.** Why do people who leave the faith claim that the Christian way of life is unworkable? What aspects of Christian life do they find most objectionable? Without God, where do their own plans and decisions lead?
3. **18:18.** What kinds of reception do reformers get who challenge the received wisdom or the reigning ideology? When these reformers receive death threats, who takes the threats seriously? Even if the threats are not serious, what is their purpose?
4. **18:23.** If your life were threatened as Jeremiah's was, what would your prayer with respect to your persecutors be like? What kind of action would you pray God to take in their regard?

Chapter 19

For understanding
1. **19:1–13.** When Jeremiah buys a clay vessel, what does he do with it? Why does God command these prophetic actions? How does Judah, in other words, become no longer the malleable clay it was in 18:4?
2. **19:2.** Where is the valley of the son of Hinnom? Of what is it an image in the NT? Where is the Potsherd Gate, and how is it perhaps otherwise known? For what is it probably used?
3. **19:6.** For what is the cult site called Topheth used? What is the meaning of the name? Why is it called the valley of Slaughter?
4. **19:7–9.** What are the calamities in store for Judah and Jerusalem? What do they include?

For application
1. **19:2.** What does the expression "Location, location, location" mean? To what is it usually applied? If you wanted to televise a warning about, say, political corruption, where would you choose to film it? What does the selection of a location like the valley of Hinnom or Topheth suggest for the type of announcement Jeremiah will make?
2. **19:3–6.** The mention of certain place-names can conjure up images of things associated with them. For example, what images or ideas does the name Auschwitz bring to mind? For what purpose did Jesus use the name Gehenna?
3. **19:12.** If a modern prophet were to warn that a major city like New York City would become like Hiroshima and Nagasaki, what fate for the city would he be suggesting? What would be the reaction of his hearers?
4. **19:14.** In what way is Jeremiah's selection of the Temple more significant for his next announcement than was the valley of Hinnom? If Hinnom signified death and decay, what does the Temple signify? How would that significance lend all the more force to Jeremiah's words?

Chapter 20

For understanding
1. **20:7–13.** What is the subject of these verses? What distinguishes them from previous confessions? What personal cost of his preaching is Jeremiah coming to realize? How does his prayer, which begins in great distress, end?
2. **20:7.** In this daring accusation, what causes Jeremiah in his anguish to feel misled? What is he discovering? What accusation does "you are stronger than I" imply that God has done?
3. **20:9.** Why does Jeremiah attempt to keep silent, and why is his attempt unsuccessful? What is his dilemma? At times, what irresistible urge from within did prophets have? What does this image suggest that his message concerns?
4. **20:14–18.** What is the subject of these verses? Like Job in the midst of his agony, what does Jeremiah curse? Why is cursing one's birthday different from cursing one's parents?

For application
1. **20:7.** To what vocation do you believe the Lord has called you? When you considered the vocation but before you made a decision, what did you know about what it would demand of you? After making your decision, have you entertained any second thoughts about it? How content are you with the decision you made?
2. **20:9.** What temptations to abandon your vocation have you faced? What has kept you faithful to it; or, alternatively, how has your desire to continue in it grown stronger or weaker? Since God does not compel obedience, from where does the compulsion to continue with him come?

3. **20:12.** Why does the Lord try the righteous? What would he learn from such a trial that he does not already know? Why might you, like the Psalmist, wish to invite the Lord to probe your heart and try your thoughts (Ps 139:23–24)?
4. **20:14–18.** What has been the lowest point of your life to date? How close to utter despair did you come? What pulled you through it? If you prayed for relief, how did the Lord provide it?

Chapter 21

For understanding
1. **21:1–10.** What assurance does the king of Judah seek from Jeremiah? What does he actually learn? What are the only options left for the city?
2. **21:5.** By what is the fall of Jerusalem assured? Using expressions familiar from the Exodus story, against whom is the dreadful power of God now turned? When did Moses use the same language as in this verse?
3. **21:8.** How is this verse a parody of the "two ways" of the covenant described by Moses? In Jeremiah's day, since the curse of national conquest is certain, what is the only way to save one's life?
4. **21:14.** To what is "her forest" an allusion?

For application
1. **21:2.** What answer do the emissaries hope to receive from Jeremiah? What would be the conditions under which the answer they want might be granted? What virtually guarantees that the miracle they want will be refused?
2. **21:8–9.** To a dedicated military commander, which of the options Jeremiah presents would be preferable? Even when the situation is hopeless, why would a commander refuse to surrender, assuming his soldiers would be spared if he did? On the other hand, what could the commander expect from his superiors if he chose to surrender?
3. **21:13.** Read the note for this verse. While an accident of geography has so far protected the North American continent from foreign attack, what signs exist that suggest this protection is no longer so sure? Rather than facing attacks from without, what are the possibilities of attack from within? As ancient prophets would argue, on what must we base our national security?

Chapter 22

For understanding
1. **22:6.** What and where are Gilead and Lebanon? What does the felling and burning of their trees in 22:7 signify? What will the Southern Kingdom of Judah, which endured for more than three centuries, become?
2. **22:13.** What does Jehoiakim, the seventeenth king of Judah, who reigned from 609 to 598 B.C., care little about? Instead, with what is he preoccupied? Of what is his corrupt regime guilty? Which son of Josiah is Jehoiakim? What does the accusation of making his laborers serve him for nothing suggest that Jehoiakim does? According to Catholic tradition, what is one of the sins that cries out to heaven?
3. **22:19.** What happens with the burial of a donkey? What does this poetic imagery signify? Historically, how is Jehoiakim buried?
4. **22:30.** How is Jeconiah/Jehoiachin to be considered childless? Since he already has several sons, what does the prophecy declare? When will another heir from David's royal line assume David's throne? How does Peter see its fulfillment? Where are Jeconiah/Jehoiachin and his sons mentioned outside the Bible? In harmony with 52:34 and 2 Kings 25:30, of what do they speak?

For application
1. **22:4–5.** According to 2 Sam 7:14–15, what does the Lord promise through the prophet Nathan to David's successor? If, according to Jeremiah, the house of David will become a desolation for not heeding the Lord's words, how will Nathan's prophetic promise to it remain in effect?
2. **22:6.** Have you ever had to destroy a possession or abandon a relationship you cherished? If so, what reasoning led you to your decision? What would lead God to destroy what he cherishes?
3. **22:13.** The note for this verse refers to Catholic tradition regarding the withholding of wages. According to the *Catechism*, what is a just wage (CCC 2434)? How do employers and employees arrive at what constitutes a just wage?

Chapter 23

For understanding
1. **23:5.** What days are prophesied as coming? As a wise and upright king from David's line, when will the future Messiah rule over the reunited family of Israel and Judah? According to St. Leo the Great, what was the one remedy that could help prevent the ruin of the human race, and how did the Lord provide it? What two virtues are required by the kings of Israel and Judah as earthly representatives of God and his rule?
2. **Word Study: Branch (23:5).** What various types of vegetative growth does the Hebrew noun *ṣemaḥ* indicate? Less frequently but more significantly, what sign does the image of a branch represent? In one passage, who is the Lord's branch? In several others, what function does the word serve? Initially, to whom does this "branch" refer? Ultimately, however, for whom is it a title? To what passage in Isaiah is this image of the Messiah as a sprouting "branch" likely indebted?
3. **23:9–40.** Though the prophets of Jeremiah's day present themselves as divine messengers, why are they exposed as false? While they allege having prophetic dreams, from where do their visions come? Worst of all, how do they embolden people to continue in evil?
4. **23:18.** What is the council of the Lord? To what are true prophets like Jeremiah given privileged access? What makes the claims of false prophets to speak for God or his plans for the future fraudulent?

For application

1. **23:3.** Given the ongoing abandonment of Christian faith in today's society, what do people mean who refer to the "remnant"? From where will this "remnant" come? What is the "new evangelization", and what prospects for a return to faith does it hold?
2. **23:6.** Various prayers and litanies approved by the Church contain expressions that affirm God's relationship with us, such as "The Lord our strength", "The Lord our destiny", and so on. How many of them can you think of? As a devotional practice, how useful might it be for you to repeat these during your prayer times?
3. **23:14.** How does religious teaching that is openly false or even subtly misleading strengthen the hands of evildoers? Which strengthens evildoing more: false doctrine or false moral teaching? Which is easier to correct, and why?
4. **23:28-29.** The charism of prophecy is still active in the Church. According to Heb 4:12: What is the word of the Lord like? What effect should it have on its audience? How does one recognize genuine prophecy in the thoughts or insights of the prophet?

Chapter 24

For understanding

1. **24:1-10.** In this vision of the good and bad figs, who are the good figs, and what will eventually happen to them? Who are the bad figs, and for what are they headed? What misunderstanding among the bad figs does the vision correct? What is the vision's key theological premise?
2. **24:1.** For whom is Nebuchadrezzar an alternative spelling? Who is Jeconiah, and how does his name appear in 22:24? What is this vision? When do figs become ripe?
3. **24:7.** What is one of the great hopes of biblical prophecy? How does Moses describe this? How do Jeremiah and Ezekiel describe it? With whom will the covenant between the Lord and Israel (Lev 26:12) be reaffirmed?

For application

1. **24:1-3.** Certain fruits and the trees from which they come may have cultural or religious significance. For example, what was the cultural significance of a fig tree in ancient Israel? What for us might be the religious significance of an apple?
2. **24:4-7.** How can tragedy or great suffering such as a devastating loss or disease work to purify the human heart over time? What beneficial effect has suffering had on your spiritual life?
3. **24:8-10.** If tragedy or great suffering has never been part of your life, how might its absence be a curse instead of a blessing? While you may not wish to pray for the experience of suffering, how can you prepare yourself for it when it comes?

Chapter 25

For understanding

1. **25:9.** What does it mean to say that Nebuchadrezzar is the Lord's servant? What is the Lord, who steers the course of world history, able to direct? How will God similarly raise up Cyrus II of Persia as his anointed servant?
2. **25:11.** To what does the period of seventy years refer, and what will happen at its end? When did this period begin, and how long did it actually last? What does seventy years also represent, and so what is part of the message?
3. **25:15.** Of what is the cup of the wine of wrath an image? Which nations are included among those set to imbibe God's wrath?
4. **25:26.** For what nation is the Hebrew word *shēshakh* a cipher? How is it created?

For application

1. **25:3.** How frustrating would it be to engage in a work to which you were convinced God called you, only to sense that your efforts had been fruitless? What considerations would influence your decision to continue or not?
2. **25:4.** What does it mean to "incline your ear" to hear? How does one incline his ear to hear the Lord? Since Judah has not inclined its ear to hear the Lord, what in effect is that society doing?
3. **25:11.** Read the note for this verse. What is the similarity between the fate of those who will return to Judah at the end of the seventy years and that of the Israelite generation who will first enter the Promised Land under Joshua? Why would it have been necessary in both cases for the earlier generation to die out?
4. **25:29.** Why is it appropriate that the judgment of the world should begin with the household of God (1 Pet 4:17)?

Chapter 26

For understanding

1. **26:1-24.** When is Jeremiah's Temple sermon delivered? Although a fuller account of this sermon appears in 7:1—8:3, on what is attention focused here? In this instance, for what do the religious leaders of Judah clamor, and what do the royal leaders of Judah do? What is Jeremiah's alleged blasphemy? What other prophets utter the same warning?
2. **26:8.** How are Jeremiah's words perceived, and with what is that linked?
3. **26:16.** In whom is the first criterion of a true prophet met? Although false prophets of the day sometimes speak in the name of the Lord, in what other god's name do they speak?
4. **26:18.** When and where does Micah of Moresheth, as one of the Minor Prophets whose oracles are preserved in the Bible, prophesy? What do the court elders argue about sparing Jeremiah's life and heeding his call to repentance? When does Hezekiah reign? What does the citation from Mic 3:12 foretell?

For application

1. **26:12-15.** When Jesus faced a hostile audience, how did he typically comport himself? For example, how did he respond when besieged with questions designed to entrap him (e.g., Mt 22:15ff.; Jn 8:3-11)? When threatened by crowds ready to stone him, what did he do (Jn 10:31-39)? When is the only time he allowed himself to be arrested?

2. **26:16.** When a person exercising a genuine charism of prophecy gives a message in the name of the Lord, what responsibility is he taking upon himself? If he feels the urge to prophesy but is not sure of the message, what should he do? If the prophet deliberately invokes the name of the Lord while knowing that the message is his own invention, what commandment is he violating?

3. **26:20–23.** What did Jesus warn his disciples would happen to those who preach his name (Mt 10:17–23)? What did he say the persecuted should do? What will be the reward of those who endure to the end?

Chapter 27

For understanding

1. **27:1–22.** What message does Jeremiah deliver that Judah and its neighbors must do or face what consequence? Because God gave Nebuchadnezzar the authority to rule these small states for a time, to what does any attempt at rebellion against Babylon amount? What sharp contrast does the episode also draw?

2. **27:2.** What are thongs and yoke-bars? Why does Jeremiah carry such a yoke, and what does it represent?

3. **27:16.** To which vessels does this verse refer? What do false prophets claim about these spoils? How does the opposite prove true? When will they be returned to the Temple?

4. **27:19.** What were these pillars, and where did they stand? What was the sea, and where was it located? What were the stands?

For application

1. **27:8–11.** The note for v. 3 says that these words were addressed to foreign nations through their delegates in Jerusalem. What attention do you think they would pay to a message from the Israelite God? Aside from that, how politically realistic would Jeremiah's message have seemed to them? What would a modern politician say of such a message?

2. **27:12–15.** Recall that Zedekiah was installed as king by Nebuchadnezzar after he deported Jechoiachin and three thousand Judahites to Babylon. Whose subject, therefore, is Zedekiah? On what basis should Zedekiah know that Jeremiah's allegation regarding the court prophets is true? In effect, whom is Jeremiah demanding that the king should trust without corroborating evidence?

3. **27:18.** Read the note for this verse. How would the populace know that the prophets' intercession had succeeded? What, however, does Jeremiah expect will actually happen?

Chapter 28

For understanding

1. **28:1.** What is "that same year"? Who is Hananiah? With what promise is he deceiving the people? How does Jeremiah view all of this? Where is Gibeon?

2. **28:6.** What does the Hebrew acclamation "Amen!" mean? Why is Jeremiah speaking sarcastically?

3. **28:9.** What is the keynote theme of the false prophets in Jeremiah's day? What is one of the tests of a true prophet set forth in Deuteronomy? How is this test applied to the two prophets who square off in this episode?

4. **28:10.** What does Hananiah attempt to do by breaking the yoke-bars that Jeremiah has been carrying? How does the gesture make the outcome more bleak?

For application

1. **28:1–4.** What is Jeremiah wearing that prompts Hananiah's response (27:2)? Against whom is the response publicly directed? What is Hananiah's motive?

2. **28:7–8.** To what authorities does Jeremiah appeal in his reply to Hananiah, and what is the content of their prophecies? What are some modern examples of prophets who made specific predictions that have not come to pass?

3. **28:15–17.** According to Deut 18:20, what is the penalty for a prophet who prophesies falsely? Why was the penalty for false prophecy so drastic? In today's world, what would spiritual leaders think a penalty for false prophecy should be?

Chapter 29

For understanding

1. **29:1–32.** To whom is Jeremiah's letter addressed? What reassurance does he give them? For the time being, what should they be prepared to do? But after the "seventy years" of subjection to Babylon are complete, what will God do? Thus, what are his plans for them? What is the only thing the community still living in Judah can expect?

2. **29:8.** Who are "your prophets"? Who are the diviners? What did these deceivers create? How does Jeremiah counter this?

3. **29:21.** Who are the Ahab and Zedekiah mentioned here? Why does the Lord pronounce judgment on them?

4. **29:22.** What is wished upon others as a curse? Most likely, what was the outcome of Ahab's and Zedekiah's message that Judah's exile was about to end?

For application

1. **29:4–6.** How might Middle Eastern Christian refugees who were forced by war or persecution to flee to other countries apply these verses to themselves? What are the implications for the future in these verses?

2. **29:7.** In what ways should the Christian people concern themselves about the welfare of the nation in which they abide? As a Catholic, what concerns do you have for political developments in our country, and what can you do about them? Do you pray for the welfare of the nation (cf. CCC 1900)?

3. **29:11.** In the original context, what were the Lord's plans for the exiles? As applied to the current situation of the Church in the world, what future might the Lord have in mind? How would you apply this verse to yourself personally?

4. **29:13–14.** What is the key to finding the Lord whom you seek? Why is a half-hearted effort ineffective?

Chapter 30

For understanding

1. **30:3.** How does Jeremiah's vision expand, and whom does it include? For whom is the Lord's promise of restoration thus intended?
2. **30:11.** What made expulsion from the Promised Land and dispersion among the nations necessary? What does the limit to God's judgment mean?
3. **30:19.** What does the Hebrew word *tôdōh* indicate here? How was thanksgiving for salvation also ritualized?
4. **30:22.** What does the promise "you shall be my people, and I will be your God" reaffirm? How do scholars designate such statements of mutual belonging? How many times is it found in Jeremiah's "Book of Consolation"?

For application

1. **30:2.** Why do people write books? Why might the Lord wish his words to be written down? If the Holy Spirit were to grant you a prophecy or a vision, what would you do with it?
2. **30:8.** Compare this verse with Jeremiah's condemnation of Hananiah's prophecy (28:2–4, 10–11). Against whose yoke did Hananiah prophesy? Whose yoke is Jeremiah saying the Lord will break? Why is Jeremiah not contradicting himself?
3. **30:11.** When a parent forgives a child for some wrong, why must punishment still follow? What is the punishment intended to accomplish?
4. **30:21.** How does this verse apply to Jesus? How has he drawn near to the Lord? On whose initiative do you draw near to the Lord?

Chapter 31

For understanding

1. **31:3.** What is God's "everlasting love"? Though this love may be expressed at times as discipline, what does it ensure? Of what has divine love been the foundation? To what does the Hebrew word *ḥesed* refer?
2. **31:15.** What cries echo in Ramah? According to one tradition, whose burial site was in this town? In Jeremiah's time, for what is Ramah a staging point? For what is Rachel said to mourn, but what does the Lord assure her will happen in the future? According to Mt 2:18, when does this passage also find fulfillment? In this instance, how are Rachel's children (= baby Israelites) taken from the land of Israel?
3. **31:31–34.** What are four distinctive features of the "new covenant" Jeremiah prophesies that are unlike the Mosaic covenant? When does Jesus ratify Jeremiah's new covenant? How does Paul see himself as a minister of this new covenant? According to the Book of Hebrews, what does the sacrifice of Jesus accomplish? According to St. Justin Martyr, what is the effect of the New Covenant on the Old, and how long will the New last? According to St. Augustine, what is promised in the New Covenant?
4. **31:34.** To what does "knowing the Lord" refer, and on what is it based in part? According to St. Bede, when—and why—will we no longer need the Scriptures or people to interpret them? To what is "remembering sin" a reference?

For application

1. **31:3.** This verse is intended for the consolation of Israel as a people. How has it consoled you as an individual? How might you use it to help someone who feels abandoned by God?
2. **31:9.** In this verse, how does the Lord show his fatherhood for the returning exiles? In the parable of the Prodigal Son, how does the father demonstrate paternal love for each of the two sons (Lk 15:11–32)?
3. **31:18–19.** According to Prov 13:24, how does the father regard his child when he refuses to discipline him? What is the relationship between parental love and parental discipline? What are some behavioral indications that a child actually wants discipline?
4. **31:33.** At what point in one's life does the Law of God pass from being a law written on stone to a law written in the heart? How does one's life change when that transition occurs?

Chapter 32

For understanding

1. **32:7.** Who is Shallum? What is Anathoth? In ancient Israel, why were efforts made to keep family lands within family lines? In times of financial hardship, when land had to be sold, to whom was it first offered? When would land purchased by someone outside the kinship group revert to the original family owners?
2. **32:10.** How was the original deed of sale processed? Where were duplicate copies of the deed stored? What was the function of witnesses?
3. **32:25.** About what does the prophet have second thoughts? What reassurance does he seek from the Lord?
4. **32:34.** To what abominations does Jeremiah refer? In the late monarchical period, how was the Lord's sanctuary defiled?

For application

1. **32:9–15.** If you have ever closed on the purchase of a house or other property, what closing procedures are involved that are similar to those narrated here? For example, why are the services of a notary public required? What happens to the documents? How does Jeremiah signal that this purchase is a prophetic action?
2. **32:25.** What question, in effect, is Jeremiah asking? Have you ever felt led, either by the Lord or by your own judgment, to do something that was counterintuitive and possibly pointless? What was your reasoning? What was the outcome?
3. **32:36–44.** What was the Lord's answer? In recent times, although Middle Eastern Christians have been driven from their homes by religious extremists and not by any infidelity on their part, what are the prospects for their return?
4. **32:39.** How is fear of the Lord good for the people and for their children? What does it mean for the people to have one heart?

Chapter 33

For understanding
1. **33:3.** The personal pronoun ("you") is singular in both cases, indicating that God is addressing whom? What are the "hidden things"?
2. **33:11.** When will the joyous sounds of wedding celebrations be heard again in Judah? What thank offerings will be offered in the Temple? According to later rabbinic tradition, all sacrifices will cease in the age to come except which one?
3. **33:17–18.** What covenants does God pledge to uphold? In the Davidic covenant, what did the Lord swear to do? In the Levitical covenant, to what did he admit Aaron and his descendants? In view of what are these pledges renewed?
4. **33:20.** What is the Lord's covenant with the day and the night? If people cannot break this covenant, what does that say for God's covenants with David and the Levitical priests?

For application
1. **33:3.** When you call to the Lord as he is inviting you to do, what do you expect of him in reply? What are some of the hidden things about yourself or your environment that you wish him to tell you?
2. **33:8.** Although God's forgiveness is freely offered here, what do Israel and Judah need to do to obtain it? According to Ps 51, what does the Psalmist desire of the Lord besides forgiveness? What kind of sacrifice is he willing to offer to obtain it?
3. **33:11.** Read the note for this verse. Among Christians with valid liturgies, which type of sacrifice is still being offered? Why are other types of sacrifice no longer required?
4. **33:25–26.** What is the Lord claiming here? Since the Lord cannot forget even the smallest part of his creation, what is the likelihood that he would forget you? When you repent and are forgiven of sin, what does restoration mean for you?

Chapter 34

For understanding
1   **34:8.** To what is Zedekiah's proclamation of liberty similar? What covenant is made here? What is probably the twofold reason for this decision? In any case, what does the manumission of enslaved kinsmen amount to in the Lord's eyes?
2. **34:11.** When did violation of the covenant just made take place? What must many have thought of the threat against Jerusalem?
3. **34:17.** Because slave owners reneged on their oath to "release" their slaves permanently, into what are they now "released"? What do the curses of the Mosaic covenant bring to those who violate it?
4. **34:18.** In an ancient covenant-making procedure, what did partners entering a covenant do with the severed parts of animals? What were these actions equivalent to saying? For a biblical example, in Gen 15:7–21, what is the Lord promising when he passes between divided animals? Where is the same practice attested outside the Bible?

For application
1. **34:5.** The note for this verse mentions that Zedekiah's life will be spared, but not suffering. Why does the Lord not spare you suffering? What purposes can suffering serve if you are willing to accept it? How can suffering be transcended?
2. **34:8–11.** In confession, you promise to renounce the sin you just confessed and promise to avoid that sin in the future. How often have you reneged on promises such as that? What have been some of the spiritual consequences of committing that sin again, and possibly repeatedly? If you have no firm intention of avoiding that sin, what does that say for the validity of your confession? If you deliberately make an invalid confession, what additional sin do you commit?
3. **34:18.** The ceremony alluded to here dramatizes the consequences of the failure to keep the covenant. In a culture like ours, how do we ceremonially dramatize what happens if we fail to keep the vows we make? If we have no such ceremony, on what do we rely for assurance that we will keep our vows?

Chapter 35

For understanding
1. **35:1–19.** How do these verses contrast the Rechabites with other Judahites? What does the account stress?
2. **35:2.** Who are the Rechabites? How does the clan stand out from the general population of Judah? How do they live? What is the only reason they seek refuge within the walls of Jerusalem? What do some scholars hypothesize about them? Although the Lord does not endorse their rule of life as such, for what does he bless them? What are the chambers mentioned here?
3. **35:4.** For whom is the title "man of God" normally used? Who is Maaseiah? What is the keeper of the threshold?
4. **35:19.** What blessing does the Lord give Jonadab? What does at least one of the sons of Rechab do for Jerusalem, and when? What does the promise of standing before the Lord suggest that the Rechabites are granted?

For application
1. **35:4.** Some monasteries have a position called a porter; Bl. Solanus Casey was given this function. Why would a porter be necessary? What would a porter do? In Ps 84:10, why would the Psalmist wish to be a porter in the house of God? How might his wish possibly reflect your own?
2. **35:6–10.** What, if any, religious purpose lies behind the Rechabites' pattern of life? Why would a modern family establish a pattern of life based on kinds of food to be eaten or avoided (such as a vegan diet) or an alternative life-style (such as subsistence farming)? If not chosen for religious reasons, what would be the benefits of such a way of life?
3. **35:14.** How do modern secular principles for living a healthy and productive life compare with the Rechabites' determination to obey their father's command? Why do these same principles often serve as an alternative to Judeo-Christian moral principles? What would Jeremiah say about this alternative?
4. **35:18–19.** Why is it important to keep vows that you make, even when they are not religious? How does the effort to build a good character even in non-religious matters help with spiritual growth?

Chapter 36

For understanding

1. **36:2.** How did scribes normally write text on long parchment or papyrus scrolls? What words is Jeremiah to dictate? In what year was Jeremiah called to be a prophet? What does the scroll thus contain?
2. **36:4.** Who is Baruch, son of Neriah? What do his services include? How does he also act as a spokesman for the prophet? What will Baruch's brother, Seraiah, become? What did archaeologists digging in Jerusalem unearth about Baruch? After the fall of Jerusalem, where does Baruch go?
3. **36:24.** What sign of defiant resistance to the word of the Lord and its appeals for repentance do the king and his servants make? How does it place the evil Jehoiakim in contrast to righteous kings such as his father, Josiah?
4. **36:30.** What is Jehoiakim denied? How long does his successor, Jehoiachin, reign? What does it mean for Jehoiakim to be "cast out'? Why does this appear to be a figurative description of the king's dishonorable end?

For application

1. **36:3.** Isaiah urges his audience to "seek the Lord while he may be found" (Is 55:6). When does a time come when the Lord may not be found? According to the note for this verse, what window of opportunity is about to close? What window of opportunity is open to those who seek the Lord today, and under what conditions might it close?
2. **36:5.** St. Stephen was arrested and tried for preaching against the Temple. Why was such preaching regarded as criminal? What might people of Jeremiah's time have thought would happen to the faith of Israel if the center of its worship were destroyed? Now that the Temple has been destroyed and not rebuilt, how has Judaism adapted? Among Christians, what is the new center of worship?
3. **36:16–19.** Why would the princes regard Jeremiah's message as seditious? In addition to predicting the destruction of Jerusalem, against whom by extension are the prophecies on the scroll directed?
4. **36:23–24.** In an age when copying was slow, laborious, and time-consuming, what might the king have supposed destroying the original of a document would accomplish? In the modern age, how might a document critical of the government be circulated even if the original was destroyed? In the age of the Internet, how likely is it that the written word of God would ever be eradicated?

Chapter 37

For understanding

1. **37:3.** How successful is the king's attempt to win God's favor and escape the consequences of his folly? What does he do that is contrary to the counsel of Jeremiah?
2. **37:9.** What do some delude themselves into thinking about the Babylonian threat? In fact, what will Nebuchadnezzar's forces quickly do?
3. **37:19.** To which prophets is Jeremiah referring? What does Jeremiah wonder?
4. **37:21.** In an act of clemency, where does Zedekiah place Jeremiah? What sort of confinement is it more like? How long will the prophet remain there?

For application

1. **37:3.** If someone asked you to pray for the success of a project you were convinced was not of the Lord, what would you do? How would you explain your refusal to pray for the project? If you agreed to pray, what form would your prayer take?
2. **37:13–15.** In this country, what recourse do citizens have who have been arrested and jailed over a false charge? On whom lies the burden of proof if the case comes to trial? If the charge is proven false or the case is dismissed, what recompense has the citizen for the time spent in jail and the damage to his reputation?
3. **37:17.** If you have ever been the possessor of bad news for an authority who hoped to hear the opposite, what courage did you need to communicate it? What reaction were you most afraid of receiving? How did you communicate the message: by giving the straight, unvarnished version or by sugarcoating it as much as possible?
4. **37:21.** Since Zedekiah apparently has some respect for Jeremiah as a prophet (v. 17), why does the king not release him? What would have been the point of keeping him in prison indefinitely?

Chapter 38

For understanding

1. **38:1–13.** How is Jeremiah accused of aiding the enemy? What penalty does the charge of treason merit? However, since the prophet is not betraying his people, what is he advising them to do? Where do four accusers (38:1), often identified as pro-Egyptian politicians, cast Jeremiah, and what does a sympathizer named Ebed-melech do?
2. **38:6.** What is a cistern? Since this one is nearly dry, except for some sediment at the bottom, what does that suggest about when this incident took place?
3. **38:7.** How does the name Ebed-melech translate? Why will his life be spared during the conquest of Jerusalem? What is a eunuch?
4. **38:14–28.** About what does Zedekiah question Jeremiah? Although he answers, why does he hesitate to speak? With what two options does he present the king?

For application

1. **38:4.** What merit is there in the princes' accusation against Jeremiah? The note for this verse says that the princes have reversed their position regarding him. What do you think may have caused their change of opinion? What would happen nowadays to someone accused of publicly advocating surrender to the enemy?
2. **38:6.** Since the princes have the king's permission, why place Jeremiah in a cistern rather than execute him outright? What do they hope will happen to him?

3. **38:17–19.** Have you ever been confronted with a choice of two options, neither of which promises a good outcome (e.g., to quit your job or be fired from it)? If so, what considerations led you to decide one choice might be better than the other? What fears did you face about making any choice?
4. **38:24–27.** The note for v. 26 says that Jeremiah's reply to the princes is "true, as far as it goes"; however, it is not the whole truth, as the princes demanded. What moral dilemma does Jeremiah face regarding the truth? What does the *Catechism* say about when it is appropriate to reveal the whole truth to someone who asks for it (CCC 2488–89)?

Chapter 39

For understanding
1. **39:1.** What year is the king's ninth year? Since his tenth year begins in March-April, how many months does the long siege of Jerusalem, which begins in January 587 and ends with the burning of the city in August 586, cover? What is the tenth month?
2. **39:2.** What year is Zedekiah's eleventh year, and what is its fourth month? Which of Jerusalem's defensive walls do Nebuchadnezzar's forces probably break through, and why was it vulnerable? How long afterward are the city and Temple burned?
3. **39:9.** Who is Nebuzaradan? What does he oversee? What is he also tasked with organizing?
4. **39:14.** Of what is Gedaliah made governor? When is he appointed by Nebuchadnezzar? What roles did his father, Ahikam, and grandfather Shaphan have? With whom is he not to be confused?

For application
1. **39:4.** What is the "fight or flight" response to a perceived danger? Under the circumstances, what would have been the "fight" alternative if Zedekiah had chosen not to flee? Have you ever faced situations where such an alternative presented itself? Which did you take? Which, upon reflection, should you have taken?
2. **39:7.** What is spiritual blindness? How might you work to discover areas of sin to which you have been spiritually blind? To what extent may we be culpable for our own areas of spiritual blindness (cf. Jn 9:40–41)?
3. **39:10.** According to the *Catechism*, to whom do the goods of the earth and its resources belong? When is government appropriation of property legitimate (CCC 2402, 2406)? What does the Church teach about the ownership of private property as it relates to the universal destination of goods (CCC 2403)?

Chapter 40

For understanding
1. **40:1–6.** From what group is Jeremiah released? Though he had already been given his freedom by Nebuchadnezzar (39:11–12), apparently what happened? Upon release, what choice is he given, and what choice does he make?
2. **40:3.** Whose preaching did the remarkable confession of the Gentile soldier echo, and what did he say? Because the pronoun "you" is plural, to what does it refer?
3. **40:6.** What function did Mizpah, a town of Benjamin seven miles north of Jerusalem, serve? How does the name translate? Where does Jeremiah dwell?
4. **40:8.** Who is Ishmael? By whom was he hired to murder Gedaliah? What does one suspect the Ammonites are looking for ways to accomplish? How does Gedaliah make himself a target? When Johanan, the Judahite captain, informs Gedaliah of the assassination plot against his life, what happens? To whom does the term 'Maacathite' refer?

For application
1. **40:4–6.** Nebuzaradan gives Jeremiah four options on where to go upon release. Given Jeremiah's prophecies about the blessings the Lord would bring to the exiles in Babylon and curses on those who remained (cf. Jer 24), why would he decide to stay in Judah?
2. **40:6.** Read the note for this verse. For what else is Mizpah known (cf. Judg 11:11; 20–21;1 Sam 7:6, 16; 1 Mac 3:46)?
3. **40:9–12.** The note for v. 8 says that Gedaliah makes himself a target by encouraging submission to Babylon. How is Gedaliah's a no-win situation for himself? After conquering Judah, why would Nebuchadnezzar appoint a Jew rather than a Babylonian official to govern Judah? Despite the abundance of the summer harvest, what would have been the sentiment of those remaining in Judah regarding submission to Babylon?
4. **40:14–16.** How would Johanan have known of the plot against Gedaliah's life (cf. v. 14)? If you were warned that someone was out to kill you, even if you did not believe the threat, how would you change your behavior? In effect, what does Gedaliah do to protect himself?

Chapter 41

For understanding
1. **41:1–18.** What does Ishmael, a commander of Jewish forces, do? When he is overtaken by Johanan, another army commander, what happens? Where does Ishmael, who escapes, seek refuge?
2. **41:5.** Where are Shechem, Shiloh, and Samaria? To what group do the mourners belong? How is incense used in sacrifice? Since the Temple in Jerusalem was destroyed by fire two months prior to this (52:12–13), what does bringing sacrificial gifts after this disaster seem to imply? What feast are the mourners probably attending as pilgrims?
3. **41:12.** What is the great pool? How large is it, and how is it known? Where is Gibeon relative to Mizpah?
4. **41:18.** What does Johanan fear that Judah will face? How would Gedaliah's killing be viewed by Nebuchadnezzar?

For application
1. **41:1–3.** What might be Ishmael's rationale for bringing with him such a small company of armed men? Why conduct the assassination of Gedaliah and his Jewish attendants during a banquet (a common approach in such episodes in Scripture)?

2. **41:11–15.** Read the note for v. 12. What may have been the cause of Ishmael's slow progress in his escape? Why does Ishmael appear not to have put up a fight against Johanan and his force?
3. **41:16–18.** Read the note for v. 18. Why would Johanan with his soldiers take the captives from Mizpah to Egypt—a large retinue for a small military force—rather than returning them to Mizpah?

Chapter 42

For understanding
1. **42:5.** When an oath of unconditional obedience is broken, what will it bring upon the remnant? What do oaths that invoke the Lord as a witness call upon him to be?
2. **42:9–18.** With what two options is the remnant presented? According to the prophet's blunt summary of the Lord's message, if the remnant adopts the second option, what will God do?
3. **42:10.** What does the Lord promise to do for the remnant if they stay in the Promised Land? What is the Lord's "I repent" a metaphorical way of saying?
4. **42:11.** What is the remnant's concern about how Nebuchadnezzar, who appointed Gedaliah the governor (40:5), will respond to his assassination? Because the king of Babylon is the Lord's "servant", what can he be influenced to show Judah? What is the point of giving the same promise of divine protection that was made to Jeremiah?

For application
1. **42:4.** How eager to intercede for the refugees does Jeremiah appear to be? Why does he insist that he will tell them everything the Lord says, with nothing held back?
2. **42:5–6.** According to the *Catechism*, when may one take an oath (CCC 2151)? Why must the reason for swearing an oath be serious? What is the moral problem with swearing a false oath?
3. **42:10–12.** Given the retribution the refugees feared, what is the Lord asking them to do by promising safety if they stay in Judah? Have you ever faced the challenge of trusting the Lord to care for you although the prospects looked bleak? In any form of prayer, why does the Lord expect trust from petitioners?
4. **42:19–22.** What reply is Jeremiah expecting to receive from the leaders of the refugees? How does his experience validate his concern? How confident does he appear to be that his prophecy is truly the Lord's word?

Chapter 43

For understanding
1. **43:1–7.** Of what is Jeremiah accused? Where are both the prophet and his scribe taken? To what does the flight to Egypt amount?
2. **43:6.** To what does the text give no indication regarding Jeremiah and Baruch? Why does coercion seem more likely than not?
3. **43:8–13.** How does Jeremiah announce judgment on Egypt? What will follow the disobedient remnant of Judah to their new home?
4. **43:11.** When does the Babylonian army invade Egypt? According to the Jewish historian Josephus, when Nebuchadnezzar's forces conquer Egypt, what do they do? How does this explain what happens with Baruch?

For application
1. **43:2–3.** When you pray to the Lord for direction, what should be your attitude toward the outcome? If your prayer assumes that God will bless an outcome decided upon in advance, what answer are you likely to receive?
2. **43:4–7.** The *Catechism* says that "we have a responsibility for the sins committed by others when *we cooperate in them*" (CCC 1868; emphasis in original). Although the refugees in these verses go to Egypt with Johanan and the military commanders, what is most likely their level of willingness to cooperate in the migration? What level of guilt can be imputed to those who go unwillingly, such as Jeremiah (cf. CCC 1736–37)?
3. **43:8–10.** Guilt tends to follow one who tries to evade it. What are some common ways that people try to assuage their guilt? What are some indications in people's behavior that the effort is futile? In effect, what is Jeremiah telling his audience?

Chapter 44

For understanding
1. **44:1–30.** What do these verses document? To what does this community of survivors, instead of learning from the mistakes of the past and making a humble return to the Lord, revert? What disastrous outcome does their defiance guarantee? Theologically, how do the apostate Jews in Egypt repudiate the blessings of the Exodus?
2. **44:17.** Who is the queen of heaven? How was she served? How do Mesopotamian myths identify Ishtar, and what was she known as in Greek? For what do men suppose that Ishtar was responsible? As evidence of their spiritual blindness, they misinterpret the causes of recent history; in realty, how do they see the situation?
3. **44:26–30.** In this divine oath of disinheritance, what does God swear by his own life will happen? How does this recall the divine oath in Num 14:28–35?
4. **44:30.** Who was Hophra, and what happened to him? Of what is this event to be a "sign" to the Jews in Egypt? How does the Greek historian Herodotus refer to Pharaoh Hophra?

For application
1. **44:3.** What does the Lord mean by saying that the people of Jerusalem served "other gods that they knew not"? What does it mean to "know" God? From where would this knowledge have come?
2. **44:9.** What is the hardest lesson you have had to learn about yourself? What event or series of events forced this lesson upon you? Since then, has that lesson needed to be repeated, at least in your memory if not in fact?

3. **44:10.** Psalm 119 is a long meditation on the Psalmist's desire for formation in the Law and its statutes. What is it about them that so repels the wicked and so attracts the Psalmist? How do you relate to what the Psalmist sees in the Law?
4. **44:25.** Why has modern culture taken such pride in "doing it my way"? From the Christian point of view, what is the spiritual folly of doing things our own way?

Chapter 45

For understanding
1. **45:3.** What are the only words of Baruch preserved in the book? What does he lament, and what does he seem to wonder about? In fact, what makes him a target of persecution? What is the reward for his loyalty?
2. **45:4.** When and how will the Lord destroy his own work?

For application
1. **45:3.** What is your favorite complaint about the difficulties of your life? How often do you voice it, and how is the complaint received? If it is justified, what are you doing to resolve the issue?
2. **45:5.** When Jesus assures his disciples that not a hair of their heads will be destroyed during persecution, what does he actually promise them (Lk 21:16–19)? What does it mean that their loyalty to Jesus will secure their lives, since most of them are martyred?

Chapter 46

For understanding
1. **46:2.** Why did Pharaoh Neco II, king of Egypt, march north through the land of Israel to join forces with Assyria? Where is Carchemish? What happened at the Battle of Carchemish? What was the result of Egypt's humiliating defeat, followed by its immediate withdrawal from Palestine?
2. **46:8.** How is the yearly inundation of the Nile, in which the river overflows its banks and floods the adjacent plains, here a poetical image of Egypt? What else is assumed, however, about the Nile?
3. **46:15.** Where does the name Apis appear? What word does the Hebrew have? What is Apis and how is it represented? Whom is it believed to embody? Despite its appearance of strength, what does it do?
4. **46:23.** What does felling trees signify? How are ravenous locusts that swarm in large numbers comparable to armies?

For application
1. **46:5–6.** For a military commander, what happens among his troops when a rout occurs? How hard is it to regain control over the troops? When an army in a foreign land suffers a rout in battle, what mercy are its fleeing troops likely to expect?
2. **46:11–12.** What happens to the morale of a superpower after its armies have suffered a major defeat? What opinion will other nations, both friendly and hostile, have of the same superpower afterward?
3. **46:14–17.** Hophra was Pharaoh when the Egyptian army marched to relieve the siege of Jerusalem but retreated before the Babylonian army. According to the note for v. 15, what can the Jews living in these cities expect from weakened Egyptian power? If you were to give a nickname to a braggart who threatened a fight and then shied away from it, what nickname might you propose?
4. **46:28.** When a parent forgives a child for some wrong, why must punishment still follow? What is the punishment intended to accomplish?

Chapter 47

For understanding
1. **47:1.** Who are the Philistines? When did they establish themselves in southwest Canaan, and what coalition of cities did they occupy? According to Herodotus, the Greek historian, what city did Neco II conquer, and when?
2. **47:2–7.** Whose humiliation did this prophetic taunt foretell?
3. **47:2.** How is the Babylonian invasion of Philistine territory pictured? Of whom are similar prophetic warnings made?
4. **47:4.** Where are the seaport cities of Tyre and Sidon? Although they are allies of the Philistines in opposing Babylonian sovereignty in Syria-Palestine, what are they powerless to do? What is Caphtor?

For application
1. **47:3.** Think of a time when you experienced panic over your physical safety. On what did you focus? If you were in a group at the time, how much of your attention was on protecting them? Did the feeling of panic obstruct all thought? After the experience passed, how did you evaluate your conduct during it?
2. **47:6.** Although in Jeremiah the sword of the Lord may be understood somewhat literally as the sword of the Babylonians, in New Testament terms what is the sword of the Lord? According to Heb 4:12, what does it do? How has it operated in your life?

Chapter 48

For understanding
1. **48:1.** Where is Moab? Faulting the Moabites for pride, what does the prophet foretell about them and their chief deity, Chemosh? To whom does Genesis trace the origin of the Moabites? What happened to Nebo and Kiriathaim, Israelite towns east of the Jordan River?

2. **48:12.** For what are Moabites, known for their winemaking, headed? How does Jeremiah picture this? What does the disappearance of wine also signal?
3. **48:26.** What will make Moab drunk? What is Moab's besetting sin? Historically, how did the Moabites treat the people of Judah?
4. **48:45–46.** Of what song are these verses a reworking? What did it originally recall? To what are its lyrics applied here?

For application
1. **48:10.** This verse seems to be an aside. To whom is it directed? How can the first half of this verse be applied to the way one pursues his vocation or his spiritual life?
2. **48:26.** Why are drunkards a staple of comedy? What about their behavior makes us laugh? From the drunkard's viewpoint, why is intoxication not a laughing matter?
3. **48:29.** How does the sin of pride obstruct one's view of reality? This verse mentions pride, arrogance, and haughtiness. Though these three vices are closely related, how are they different from each other? How can you recognize them in your own behavior?

Chapter 49

For understanding
1. **49:1.** What lands do the people of Ammon occupy? How does Genesis trace the origin of the Ammonites? For what does Jeremiah fault them? What will be their punishment from the Lord? Though it is not mentioned here, with whom did the Ammonites conspire to resist Babylonian rule? Whose assassination does the king of Ammon sponsor? Who is the Ammonite national deity? When do the Ammonites dispossess Gad?
2. **49:7–22.** Against whom is this oracle of judgment addressed? Since Jeremiah's tirade against Edom is related to Obad 1–16, what is the nature of the relationship between these two oracles?
3. **49:7.** Where is Edom located? As longstanding enemies of Israel, how are the Edomites known in the biblical world? How does Genesis trace the origin of the Edomites? For what does Edom face severe judgment? What promise of future salvation is given to Edom? Where is Teman, and what did it produce?
4. **49:28.** Who are the Kedarites? What will happen to them when the Lord's judgment falls? What are perhaps the kingdoms of Hazor?

For application
1. **49:1–2.** Regarding possession of this world's lands and goods, how secure are your possessions? How quickly might your most secure possessions vanish without hope of return or reparation? What would you do if such a disaster were to happen?
2. **49:16.** How does God often deal with prideful people? What is the difference between humility and humiliation, and from where does each originate? In your experience, has humiliation served as a remedy for your pride?
3. **49:18.** How does this vision resemble the condition of sites like Chernobyl and Fukushima, both abandoned because of nuclear meltdowns? With what are Sodom and Gomorrah associated? How is their destruction and subsequent abandonment equivalent to the condemnation of a society to hell?

Chapter 50

For understanding
1. **50:1.** Where was Babylon built? How does the Lord execute his plan for Judah and its neighbors through it? What time has now come for Babylon itself? Because it has "sinned" and "defied the Lord", what will happen to it? For what specific sin will the Lord avenge himself on Babylon as well? Why are the Babylonians called Chaldeans?
2. **50:8.** What are the exiles of Judah in Babylon called to do? When does the exile officially end?
3. **50:27.** Of all the offences Babylon commits at the height of its power, what is the most egregious? For what will the Babylonians thus be repaid?
4. **50:34.** How is the Lord a redeemer? What is the nature of the kinship between God and Israel?

For application
1. **50:4.** Seeking the Lord can sometimes be an emotional pursuit. Why do you think the people of Israel and Judah weep as they return to the Promised Land? Have your own overtures toward the Lord ever been a cause of weeping? If so, on what occasions? What kind of tears were they: tears of sorrow or of joy?
2. **50:8.** In a flock of sheep moving from one grazing ground to another, what do the rams at the head do? In a migration of Israelites returning to their homeland, who would be expected to lead them?
3. **50:15.** This verse suggests that the law of retaliation ("eye for eye, tooth for tooth", etc.) be imposed on Babylon. If you retaliate for an injury by doing to the perpetrator what he did to you, how do you right the wrong he has done? Likewise, how do you set the stage for perpetuation of further injury?
4. **50:34.** According to the Ignatian rules for the discernment of spirits, how does the evil spirit act in a soul that is progressing in virtue? Likewise, how does the good spirit act in the soul that is going from bad to worse? Why would the Lord either cause or allow a sinful soul to experience unrest?

Chapter 51

For understanding
1. **51:5.** About what is Jeremiah adamant? However, what will happen to both the northern and southern tribes?
2. **51:7.** Of what is a golden cup a sign? What is the Lord's will that Babylon should do? In this way, for whom does Babylon serve as a divine instrument of judgment?

3. **51:15.** To what is the work of creation, with the sky suspended over the earth, compared? What belief of ancient Israel does this reflect?
4. **51:63.** Where was Babylon built? What does the symbolic act of binding the words of the prophecy to a rock that is hurled into the river, never to be seen again, reinforce?

For application
1. **51:1.** According to the note for this verse, the "spirit of a destroyer" is a hot, dry wind from the desert. In your part of the country, from which direction do hot, dry winds (such as California's Santa Ana winds) tend to come? What environmental conditions do they bring about? How can such winds be seen as a sign of divine judgment?
2. **51:8.** Read the note for this verse. How does the "prophetic perfect" tense as applied to the city of Babylon resemble the cry of the angel in Rev 18 about the fall of Babylon the great?
3. **51:15.** According to the note for this verse, ancient Israel viewed the world as a cosmic sanctuary and the Temple as a replica of the cosmos. How do we moderns view the world? If it is not a cosmic sanctuary, what is it for us? If we have lost the ability to see the world as a sacred space, how can we regain that view?

Chapter 52

For understanding
1. **52:4.** What is Zedekiah's ninth year? Since the king's tenth year began in March-April, what time period did the long siege of Jerusalem cover? What is the tenth month?
2. **52:12.** What is the fifth month of the year? What do Jews in the exilic and early postexilic periods do in the fifth month? Who is Nebuzaradan, and what is his role in the siege?
3. **52:17–23.** Of what is the Temple plundered? Why is no mention made of the Ark of the Covenant or of the golden altar of incense?
4. **52:28–30.** What do these verses record? Why may this figure refer only to the royal and religious leaders deported to Babylon? Although Jeremiah does not mention the initial exile of Judahites in 605 B.C., which others does he mention? What is known about this last deportation?

For application
1. **52:1–34.** What is an epilogue? What function does it serve in a narrative? If you had to write the history of your grandparents, what might the epilogue to that history look like?
2. **52:9–11, 31–34.** Compare the fate of Zedekiah with that of his predecessor, Jehoiachin, who, though imprisoned in Babylon, eventually was released and ate at the king of Babylon's table. Why the difference? Why is the punishment of an offender who resists capture often more severe than that of one who submits to it?
3. **52:17–23.** What kinds of material treasures does the Catholic Church possess? How might the Church respond if all the treasures of the Vatican were looted? What might be the minimum that the Church requires to keep alive her liturgical forms of worship?

INTRODUCTION TO LAMENTATIONS

Author No claim to authorship is made in the Book of Lamentations. It stands as an anonymous collection of funeral dirges that mourn the destruction of Jerusalem and the Temple in 586 B.C. The contents of the book indicate that its author was a skilled poet who witnessed firsthand many of the atrocities he describes. He identifies himself as "the man who has seen affliction" (3:1), as a persecuted figure who has been "hunted" by his enemies (3:52), and as one of the survivors left behind in Jerusalem after its inhabitants have "gone away" as captives into exile in Babylon (1:5). Since this internal information aligns closely with the personal history of the prophet Jeremiah, Jewish and Christian readers through the centuries have reasonably inferred that Jeremiah is the author of the book. Jeremiah, after all, lived through the Babylonian siege and conquest of Jerusalem (Jer 39:1–10); he suffered greatly for speaking the word of the Lord (Jer 20:1–6; 38:1–28); and he was left behind in the land of Judah (Jer 40:1–6) after many of his fellow Israelites were taken to Babylon (Jer 52:15, 24–30). The earliest witness to this tradition is a prescript in the Greek Septuagint, which attributes the words of the book to Jeremiah. Internal analysis lends credence to this tradition insofar as the books of Lamentations and Jeremiah share a number of expressions and images in common (compare 1:13 and Jer 20:9; 1:16 and Jer 9:18; 2:11 and Jer 4:11; 3:15 and Jer 9:15; 4:2 and Jer 18:6; 4:21 and Jer 25:15). It is further relevant that Scripture remembers Jeremiah as one who composed a famous lament at the death of King Josiah (2 Chron 35:25). Although this particular lament cannot be identified with the Book of Lamentations, it indicates that Jeremiah was known to have produced this type of work.

Modern scholarship has been less inclined to attribute the Book of Lamentations to the prophet Jeremiah than previous ages, so that many are content to identify the author as an anonymous poet who lived at the same time and place as the famous prophet. The main reason for this departure from tradition is the perceived tension between Lamentations and the Book of Jeremiah. For instance, the author's claim that Jerusalem's "prophets obtain no vision from the LORD" (2:9) is difficult to square with Jeremiah's self-awareness as a prophet who delivers oracles in Jerusalem before, during, and after its conquest by the Babylonians. Similarly, the author recalls the hope of his fellow Israelites that Egypt would protect Judah and Jerusalem from Babylonian destruction when he states: "We watched for a nation which could not save" (4:17). Some find it hard to imagine these words coming from Jeremiah, who opposed Judah's reliance on Egypt as a futile attempt to ward off the judgments of God with the help of a political ally (Jer 2:18; 37:5–10). Passages such as these suggest to many scholars that Jeremiah and Lamentations are two unrelated works produced by two different writers.

The authorship of the Book of Lamentations thus remains a disputed question. There are solid grounds for attributing its poems to the prophet Jeremiah, and there are balancing factors that could suggest they come from an unknown author. Thankfully, interpretation of the book depends little on our ability to identify the human personality behind it. It is enough to know that the book comes from one who witnessed firsthand the devastation of Jerusalem in the sixth century B.C. and, beyond that, to recognize that Lamentations is an inspired text of Scripture that communicates the living word of God.

Date It is certain that Lamentations was written after the Babylonian conquest of Jerusalem in 586 B.C., but it remains uncertain how long after this event the composition of the book should be dated. Every indication within the book suggests it was written soon after the event. Memories of the disaster remain painfully vivid in the mind of the poet, and the trauma of witnessing the desecration of God's city and sanctuary hardly seems to have subsided. Also, since Lamentations sees no sign of hope in the events of recent history, it seems more likely than not that its author composed his laments before word reached him from Babylon of King Jehoiachin's release from prison ca. 560 B.C., since this development was the first sign that a restoration of the Davidic kingdom and its capital remained a future possibility (2 Kings 25:27–30; Jer 52:31–34). In view of these considerations, the Book of Lamentations was probably written early in the exilic period between 585 and 565 B.C.

Title Lamentations is known in Hebrew as 'êkāh, a word that translates "How ...!" and stands at the beginning of three of the five chapters of the book (1:1; 2:1; 4:1). Rabbinic writings also refer to Lamentations as qînôt, or "laments". The Greek Septuagint translation supplies the heading *Thrēnoi*, meaning "dirges" or "songs of lamentation". This title is transliterated in the Latin Vulgate as *Threni*. English translations of the Bible typically follow the Greek and Latin titles.

Place in the Canon Jewish and Christian tradition alike revere the Book of Lamentations as part of canonical Scripture, although it appears in different places in their respective canons. In the Jewish Bible, or Tanakh, Lamentations stands in the third division of books (called the *Ketuvim*, or Writings) among a collection of five scrolls that are read in the synagogue on select Jewish feast days (along with Ruth, Ecclesiastes, Song of Solomon, and Esther). It is read each year in late summer on the ninth of Ab, commemorating the time when the Babylonians (and later the Romans) laid waste to the city and Temple of Jerusalem. In the Christian Old Testament, which generally follows the arrangement of books in the Greek Septuagint, Lamentations is tethered to the Books of Jeremiah and Baruch, so much so that ancient lists of the books of Scripture sometimes count all three works as one work under the title Jeremiah. In the Latin Vulgate, Lamentations is joined directly to the end of Jeremiah and constitutes its final five chapters.

Structure The Book of Lamentations is an artfully designed composition made up of five poems, each corresponding to a chapter of the book. Chapters 1–2 as well as 4–5 each have twenty-two poetic verses. Chapter 3, which is the centerpiece of the book, has sixty-six verses and is often considered the most personal and profound of the poems. Internally, Lamentations follows an acrostic pattern that is based on the twenty-two letters of the Hebrew alphabet. In chapters 1, 2, and 4, successive verses of poetry begin with a sequential Hebrew letter. In chapter 3, the alphabetic pattern is expanded so that every cluster of three verses begins with a sequential Hebrew letter. In chapter 5, the alphabetic device is not followed line by line, and yet a total of twenty-two verses is retained. Many scholars hold that Hebrew authors used the acrostic format, not only as a mnemonic device to assist memorization, but also as a literary device to signify completeness. Lamentations thus presents itself as a total outpouring of anguish over the fall of Jerusalem, one that expresses the full range of mournful emotions from A to Z, so to speak.

Content and Themes The Book of Lamentations may be described as an attempt to speak the unspeakable. It seeks to express the pain and confusion of a national tragedy in the vivid language of Hebrew poetry. The poet and other survivors who lived through Jerusalem's destruction in 586 B.C. lament the horrors of the Babylonian siege that led to the conquest of Jerusalem (chap. 4); they mourn the ruin of the city, the desecration of the Lord's Temple, and the exile of many of its inhabitants (chaps. 1–2); and they bemoan the military occupation of Judah that followed the city's demise (chap. 5). At the center of the book, the poet reflects on his personal afflictions as a man who has endured persecution but who refuses to give up hope in the goodness and mercy of God (chap. 3). On literary grounds, the five poems of Lamentations share several features

in common with funeral dirges, with individual and communal psalms of lament, and with laments for fallen cities and temples attested in the literature of the ancient Near East.

The teaching of Lamentations revolves mainly around the themes of divine justice and divine mercy. **(1)** *Divine Justice.* The book first of all provides a theological interpretation of a historical calamity. Despite all appearances, the fall of Jerusalem was not primarily the result of merely earthly forces at work in the affairs of two nations at cross purposes. In fact, the poet never identifies Babylon as the nation who brought destruction upon the city and People of God. It is primarily the Lord himself who is behind this disaster; and it is Israel's covenant with the Lord that explains why it happened (1:5, 15, 17; 2:1–8, 22; 4:11, 16). Judah's humiliation was the outworking of a covenant curse triggered by covenant violation, namely, the people's wanton transgressions and stubborn refusal to repent. Far from being a sign that the Lord has forsaken his beloved city and people, or that he is unable to defend them from their earthly enemies, the events surrounding 586 B.C. show that Israel's God is the sovereign Lord of history and the righteous Lord of the covenant who cannot tolerate sin indefinitely without a just response. **(2)** *Divine Mercy.* The fall of Jerusalem must have felt like an exclamation point at the end of Israel's tumultuous history. But the poet expresses confidence that all is not lost. It is precisely because the Lord is the cause of the calamity that he can also be the solution. His wrath burns hot against brazen disobedience, but grounds for hope remain because "his mercies never come to an end; they are new every morning" (3:22–23). In fact, the book reminds readers that God "does not willingly afflict or grieve the sons of men" (3:33). The Lord takes no delight in bringing his people to judgment. The curses of the covenant, experienced as excruciating suffering and loss, are punishments for the sins of the past (3:39). At the same time, they are much more than this. Their ultimate aim is to bring God's people to repentance and to restore them to obedience in the future. God brings "grief" upon his rebellious people for the greater purpose of showing "compassion" when disaster moves them to mend their ways (3:32). For the survivors in Judah, this means that suffering is neither meaningless nor useless. It is an invitation to confess their sins, to return to the covenant, and to live with a renewed faith in the Lord (3:40–42).

The central poem of Lamentations turns the spotlight on the author as an individual who has endured great suffering. He describes himself as a man who has known "affliction" (3:1) and "bitterness" (3:19) at the hands of "enemies" (3:52) and "assailants" (3:62). These details may suggest the poet is a prophet (such as Jeremiah) whose task of proclaiming the word of the Lord is vigorously and sometimes violently opposed, but this is not stated openly in the text. Whatever his occupation, the author believes that God wills his suffering for the sake of some good. He is persuaded that the Lord is "against" him (3:3), that he has burdened him with "heavy chains" (3:7), and that he "shuts out" his pleas for help, at least for a time (3:8). Perhaps these sufferings are punishments for his own sins, or perhaps not (3:39). Whatever the case may be, the poet is an example for the People of God in their day of distress. He shows that suffering allowed by the Lord is not a cause for despair so long as one calls to mind what is known by faith: "The steadfast love of the LORD never ceases" (3:22) and "the Lord will not cast off for ever" (3:31). The proper response to divine indignation, then, is self-reflection, repentance, and prayer: "Let us test and examine our ways, and return to the LORD! Let us lift up our hearts and hands to God in heaven" (3:40–41).

Christian Perspective The Book of Lamentations is never quoted in the New Testament, but at least one allusion to its wording has been detected. The image in 2:15, with people passing by the ruined site of Jerusalem and its Temple, wagging their heads in mockery, is evoked by the evangelist Matthew when he describes the scene of Jesus' Crucifixion: "And those who passed by derided him, wagging their heads and saying, 'You who would destroy the temple and build it in three days, save yourself!'" (Mt 27:39–40). Use of this language implies a comparison between the devastated Jerusalem and the dying Messiah—both are tragic events that result from sin, yet both are the focal point of a new outpouring of God's mercy. This connection with the Passion narrative may have contributed to the longstanding Christian tradition of reading Lamentations on Good Friday and Holy Saturday. Following the New Testament period, Christian readers discovered additional connections between Christ and Lamentations. Attention was most often focused on 4:20, where the taking away of "the LORD's anointed", originally a reference to the exile of King Zedekiah, was related to the saving death of Jesus Christ.

OUTLINE OF LAMENTATIONS

1. The Desolation of Jerusalem (1:1–22)
    A. The Lonely and Humiliated City (1:1–11a)
    B. The City Mourns Its Sins and Losses (1:11b–22)

2. The Divine Judgment of Jerusalem (2:1–22)
    A. The Lord's Anger Brings Ruin (2:1–17)
    B. Zion Called to Prayer (2:18–19)
    C. An Appeal to the Lord (2:20–22)

3. Lament of the Man Afflicted (3:1–66)
    A. Suffering under God's Hand (3:1–20)
    B. Hope for Divine Mercy (3:21–39)
    C. Exhortation and Expectation of Justice (3:40–66)

4. The Conditions inside Jerusalem (4:1–22)
    A. Scenes of the Siege (4:1–12)
    B. People Scattered for Their Sins (4:13–20)
    C. A Warning to Edom (4:21–22)

5. The Community's Prayer for Jerusalem (5:1–22)
    A. A Prayer for Divine Remembrance (5:1–18)
    B. A Prayer for Divine Restoration (5:19–22)

THE LAMENTATIONS
OF JEREMIAH

The Deserted City

1 How lonely sits the city
　　that was full of people!
How like a widow has she become,
　　she that was great among the nations!
She that was a princess among the cities
　　has become a vassal.

²She weeps bitterly in the night,
　　tears on her cheeks;
among all her lovers
　　she has none to comfort her;
all her friends have dealt treacherously with
　　her,
　　they have become her enemies.

³Judah has gone into exile because of affliction
　　and hard servitude;
she dwells now among the nations,
　　but finds no resting place;
her pursuers have all overtaken her
　　in the midst of her distress.

⁴The roads to Zion mourn,
　　for none come to the appointed feasts;

all her gates are desolate,
　　her priests groan;
her maidens have been dragged away,ᵃ
　　and she herself suffers bitterly.

⁵Her foes have become the head,
　　her enemies prosper,
because the LORD has made her suffer
　　for the multitude of her transgressions;
her children have gone away,
　　captives before the foe.

⁶From the daughter of Zion has departed
　　all her majesty.
Her princes have become like deer
　　that find no pasture;
they fled without strength
　　before the pursuer.

⁷Jerusalem remembers
　　in the days of her affliction and bitternessᵇ
all the precious things
　　that were hers from days of old.
When her people fell into the hand of the foe,
　　and there was none to help her,

1:1–22 A lament over the desolation and disgrace of Jerusalem. The chapter falls into two parts: in 1:1–11b, the poet speaks as an observer who describes the abysmal conditions of the city in the third person ("she, her, hers"); and in 1:11c–22, the poet personifies the city and allows it to speak for itself in the first person ("I, me, my"). Both confess that Jerusalem, far from being an innocent victim of attack, drew this suffering upon itself by its sins against the Lord (1:5, 8, 14, 18, 20).

1:1 How: A distraught cry of emotion that elsewhere appears in funeral laments for the fallen (2 Sam 1:19; Is 14:12; Jer 48:17; Ezek 26:17). It introduces the poems in 2:1 and 4:1 as well. In the Greek LXX, this opening word is preceded by a short prescript, not present in the Hebrew text, that reads: "Now it happened after Israel was taken captive and Jerusalem was left desolate that Jeremiah sat weeping, and he composed this lament over Jerusalem and said...." **lonely:** Death by sword and famine, along with the deportation of captives to Babylon, have greatly reduced Jerusalem's population (1:3–5, 18–19). **like a widow:** The city is likened to a bereaved bride who is overwhelmed with grief. **a vassal:** Judah is now a conquered territory, subject to Babylonian rule and forced to pay tribute to its overlords.

1:2 her lovers: Regional states that were once Jerusalem's political allies by covenant (1:19; Jer 30:14). Not only were

these neighbors powerless to defend the city, but some even betrayed and fought against it alongside the Babylonians (2 Kings 24:2). **none to comfort her:** A theme of the first poem (1:9, 16–17, 21).

1:3 into exile: Thousands of captives from Judah were taken away to Babylon (2 Kings 25:11–12), where they would live as exiles for the next several decades until the return from exile began ca. 538 B.C. (Ezra 2:1–70). See note on 2 Kings 24:14–16. **no resting place:** The manifestation of a covenant curse, as stated in Deut 28:65.

1:4 Zion: Another name for Jerusalem, which became the capital of Israel when David wrested the stronghold of Zion from the control of the Jebusites ca. 1004 B.C. (2 Sam 5:6–10). **appointed feasts:** The religious festivals celebrated at the Temple. Droves of pilgrims traveled to Jerusalem to attend these annual liturgies before the destruction of the sanctuary in 586 B.C. See chart: *The Seven Feasts of Israel* at Lev 23. **her gates:** Normally places of bustling activity in a walled city.

1:5 the head: Babylon has become the master and overlord of the covenant people, who have in turn become "the tail" (Deut 28:44). **the LORD has made her suffer:** A prophetic insight into the fall of Jerusalem, which was not an accident of history but an act of divine judgment on Judah's stubborn persistence in sin. It is stated multiple times in the book that God himself was behind this catastrophe (1:14–15, 17, 21; 2:1–8, 17, 21–22; etc.). **her children:** Jerusalem is pictured as a mother grieving the loss of her exiled children. See note on 1:3.

1:7 precious things: Including the vessels of the Temple, which the Babylonians confiscated as spoils of war (2 Kings 25:13–17; Jer 27:19–22).

This book is traditionally ascribed to Jeremiah but is probably not all by him. It seems rather to have been composed by more than one author, though at about the same period of the siege and exile. The poems, written in the rhythm known as *qinah*, were probably composed for the liturgical services that continued to be held on the site of the temple.
ᵃ Gk Old Latin: Heb *afflicted*.
ᵇ Cn: Heb *wandering*.

the foe gloated over her,
    mocking at her downfall.

⁸Jerusalem sinned grievously,
    therefore she became filthy;
all who honored her despise her,
    for they have seen her nakedness;
yes, she herself groans,
    and turns her face away.

⁹Her uncleanness was in her skirts;
    she took no thought of her doom;
therefore her fall is terrible,
    she has no comforter.
"O LORD, behold my affliction,
    for the enemy has triumphed!"

¹⁰The enemy has stretched out his hands
    over all her precious things;
yes, she has seen the nations
    invade her sanctuary,
those whom you forbade
    to enter your congregation.

¹¹All her people groan
    as they search for bread;

they trade their treasures for food
    to revive their strength.
"Look, O LORD, and behold,
    for I am despised."

¹²"Is it nothing to you,ᶜ all you who pass by?
    Look and see
if there is any sorrow like my sorrow
    which was brought upon me,
which the LORD inflicted
    on the day of his fierce anger.

¹³"From on high he sent fire;
    into my bonesᵈ he made it descend;
he spread a net for my feet;
    he turned me back;
he has left me stunned,
    faint all the day long.

¹⁴"My transgressions were boundᵉ into a yoke;
    by his hand they were fastened
        together;
they were set upon my neck;
    he caused my strength to fail;
the Lord gave me into the hands
    of those whom I cannot withstand.

1:8 nakedness: A cause for shame (Gen 3:7; Is 47:3; Ezek 16:35–37).

1:9 no comforter: See note on 1:2. **O LORD, behold my affliction:** Either a spontaneous prayer of the poet or the voice of personified Jerusalem, anticipating 1:11c–22.

1:10 invade her sanctuary: The desecration of the Jerusalem Temple by the Babylonians, who burned it to the ground (2 Kings 25:8–9). **forbade to enter:** Possibly a reference to Deut 23:3, which forbids foreigners from joining the worshiping assembly of Israel.

1:11 search for bread: Famine gripped the city in the aftermath of its conquest (1:19; 4:4, 9).

1:12–22 Passages that are traditionally read during Holy Week in connection with the Lord's Passion.

1:12 the day: A reference to "the day of the Lord". The prophets announced this as a day of dreadful judgment, when God will manifest his power over nations and bring just recompense for their evildoing (Is 13:6–9; Zeph 1:14–18). Sometimes it is hailed as a day of reckoning for Gentile peoples (Ezek 30:1–5; Jer 50:25–27; Obad 15–16); other times it is a day when the Lord settles accounts with sinful Israel (Ex 32:34; Amos 5:18–20). Theologically, every "day of the Lord" throughout history offers a glimpse of the final and universal Day of Judgment to come at the end of history (Mt 25:31–46; Rev 20:11–15). See essay: *The Day of the Lord* at Joel 1:15.

1:13 fire ... into my bones: The prophet Jeremiah says this about himself in Jer 20:9.

1:14 My transgressions ... a yoke: The guilt of sin is viewed as a burden that weighs heavy upon Jerusalem. Deuteronomy also warns that Israel's subjugation to foreign conquerors will feel like a "yoke of iron" (Deut 28:48).

ᶜ Heb uncertain.
ᵈ Gk: Heb *bones and.*
ᵉ Cn: Heb uncertain.

Word Study

The Daughter of Zion (1:6)

Bat ṣiyyôn (Heb.): a personification of the city of Jerusalem and its people. The expression, which can also be translated "Daughter Zion", appears more than two dozen times in OT poetry. Cities are oftentimes viewed in the Bible as female figures, partly because the Hebrew term for "city" is grammatically feminine and partly because cities are conceived as nurturing communities. Other urban centers of the biblical world described as daughters include Babylon (Ps 137:8) and Tyre (Is 23:10). The significance of the epithet Daughter Zion seems to vary according to the context: sometimes the city is described as a virgin (Lam 1:15) and sometimes as a mother with children (Lam 1:5–6). Either way, Jerusalem is the object of the Lord's affection and care. She is called to rejoice in the presence of the God who lives in her midst (Zeph 3:14; Zech 2:10) and who comes to rescue her from captivity (Is 52:2; 62:11). On the other hand, there are also times when she is brought to judgment and chastised by the Lord for her unfaithfulness (Jer 6:23; Mic 4:10). It is in this latter situation that Lamentations addresses Daughter Zion and bemoans her humiliation as a city laid waste by divine wrath (Lam 2:1, 4, 8, 10, 13; 4:22).

¹⁵"The LORD flouted all my mighty men
  in the midst of me;
he summoned an assembly against me
  to crush my young men;
the Lord has trodden as in a wine press
  the virgin daughter of Judah.

¹⁶"For these things I weep;
  my eyes flow with tears;
for a comforter is far from me,
  one to revive my courage;
my children are desolate,
  for the enemy has prevailed."

¹⁷Zion stretches out her hands,
  but there is none to comfort her;
the LORD has commanded against Jacob
  that his neighbors should be his foes;
Jerusalem has become
  a filthy thing among them.

¹⁸"The LORD is in the right,
  for I have rebelled against his word;
but hear, all you peoples,
  and behold my suffering;
my maidens and my young men
  have gone into captivity.

¹⁹"I called to my lovers
  but they deceived me;
my priests and elders
  perished in the city,
while they sought food
  to revive their strength.

²⁰"Behold, O LORD, for I am in distress,
  my soul is in tumult,

my heart is wrung within me,
  because I have been very rebellious.
In the street the sword bereaves;
  in the house it is like death.

²¹"Hear ᶠ how I groan;
  there is none to comfort me.
All my enemies have heard of my trouble;
  they are glad that you have done it.
Bring ᵍ the day you have announced,
  and let them be as I am.

²²"Let all their evil-doing come before you;
  and deal with them
as you have dealt with me
  because of all my transgressions;
for my groans are many
  and my heart is faint."

God's Warnings Are Fulfilled

2 How the Lord in his anger
  has set the daughter of Zion under a cloud!
He has cast down from heaven to earth
  the splendor of Israel;
he has not remembered his footstool
  in the day of his anger.

²The Lord has destroyed without mercy
  all the habitations of Jacob;
in his wrath he has broken down
  the strongholds of the daughter of Judah;
he has brought down to the ground in dishonor
  the kingdom and its rulers.

³He has cut down in fierce anger
  all the might of Israel;
he has withdrawn from them his right hand
  in the face of the enemy;

1:15 my mighty men: The soldiers of Judah, who were unable to protect Jerusalem or prevent its demise.
1:18 The LORD is in the right: Or "The Lord, he is righteous." Jerusalem acknowledges God's justice in enforcing the covenant he has made with his people, even when this means imposing its curses on the disobedient, as Moses forewarned (Deut 28:15–68). See word study: *Righteous* at Neh 9:8. **I have rebelled:** A confession of sin on behalf of the sinful city (cf. Ezra 9:5–15; Dan 9:3–19).
1:19 my lovers: See note on 1:2.
1:21–22 A prayer for God's judgment to fall on wicked nations who gloat with satisfaction over Jerusalem's humiliation.
2:1–22 A second lament over conquered Jerusalem. Like the first, it sets third-person (2:1–19) and first-person points of view (2:20–22) side by side. Its theme: The Lord himself played the part of the enemy (2:4–5), withdrawing his protection from the city (2:3) so that its Temple was thrown down (2:1, 7) and its defenses were reduced to rubble (2:2, 8). The poet, who is appalled by the city's ruin, pleads with Jerusalem to seek the Lord in prayer (2:18–19).
2:1 How: See note on 1:1. **anger:** The chapter also speaks of the Lord's "wrath" (2:2), "fury" (2:4), and

"fierce indignation" (2:6). Historically, divine anger is manifest in acts of judgment on sin, acts that result in suffering and distress in the world. Theologically, however, God is eternal and unchanging, meaning that he is not moved or swayed by emotions as human beings are. As a result, the language of "wrath" is not to be understood literally but is a way of making God's just response to sin intelligible to human minds. • In God, anger is not a passion of the soul but a just judgment insofar as he wills to punish sin (St. Thomas Aquinas, *Summa Theologiae* I-II, 47, 1). **daughter of Zion:** Or "Daughter Zion". See word study: *The Daughter of Zion* at 1:6. **the splendor of Israel:** The Lord's Temple, once the crown jewel of Jerusalem, is now destroyed (Is 64:11). **his footstool:** The Ark of the Covenant (1 Chron 28:2), or else the Temple where it once resided (Ps 132:7; Ezek 43:7). **the day:** See note on 1:12.
2:2 all the habitations of Jacob: The lands of the northern tribes of Israel were overrun by the Assyrians in the eighth century B.C., and now the lands of the southern tribes of Israel have fallen to the Babylonians in the sixth century B.C. **the kingdom:** The Southern Kingdom of Judah, which came to a permanent end in 586 B.C.
2:3 his right hand: A reference to God's protection. It can also represent God's power to bring judgment, as in 2:4. **the enemy:** The Babylonians.

ᶠ Gk Syr: Heb *they heard.*
ᵍ Syr: Heb *you have brought.*

he has burned like a flaming fire in Jacob,
  consuming all around.

⁴He has bent his bow like an enemy,
  with his right hand set like a foe;
and he has slain all the pride of our eyes
  in the tent of the daughter of Zion;
he has poured out his fury like fire.

⁵The Lord has become like an enemy,
  he has destroyed Israel;
he has destroyed all its palaces,
  laid in ruins its strongholds;
and he has multiplied in the daughter of Judah
  mourning and lamentation.

⁶He has broken down his booth like that of a
    garden,
  laid in ruins the place of his appointed
    feasts;
the Lord has brought to an end in Zion
  appointed feast and sabbath,
and in his fierce indignation has spurned
  king and priest.

⁷The Lord has scorned his altar,
  disowned his sanctuary;
he has delivered into the hand of the enemy
  the walls of her palaces;
a clamor was raised in the house of the Lord
  as on the day of an appointed feast.

⁸The Lord determined to lay in ruins
  the wall of the daughter of Zion;
he marked it off by the line;
  he restrained not his hand from destroying;
he caused rampart and wall to lament,
  they languish together.

⁹Her gates have sunk into the ground;
  he has ruined and broken her bars;
her king and princes are among the nations;
  the law is no more,
and her prophets obtain
  no vision from the Lord.

¹⁰The elders of the daughter of Zion
  sit on the ground in silence;
they have cast dust on their heads
  and put on sackcloth;
the maidens of Jerusalem
  have bowed their heads to the ground.

¹¹My eyes are spent with weeping;
  my soul is in tumult;
my heart is poured out in grief ʰ
  because of the destruction of the daughter of
    my people,
because infants and babies faint
  in the streets of the city.

¹²They cry to their mothers,
  "Where is bread and wine?"
as they faint like wounded men
  in the streets of the city,
as their life is poured out
  on their mothers' bosom.

¹³What can I say for you, to what compare you,
  O daughter of Jerusalem?
What can I liken to you, that I may comfort you,
  O virgin daughter of Zion?
For vast as the sea is your ruin;
  who can restore you?

¹⁴Your prophets have seen for you
  false and deceptive visions;

2:4 his bow: For the Lord as a Divine Archer, see 3:12; Deut 32:23; Ps 7:12–13. **the tent:** Poetic language for Jerusalem, or, more specifically, the Lord's Temple.

2:5 daughter of Judah: Jerusalem. The city is also called "daughter of Zion" (1:6; 2:1, 8, 10, 18), "daughter of Jerusalem" (2:13, 15), and "virgin daughter of Zion" (2:13). See word study: *The Daughter of Zion* at 1:6.

2:6 his booth: A poetic depiction of the Temple. **appointed feasts:** See note on 1:4. **feast and sabbath:** The yearly and weekly holy days of the Israelite calendar (Lev 23:1–44). These feasts are no longer observed in the exilic period, i.e., while Jerusalem's sanctuary lies in ruins. **king and priest:** The city's royal and religious authorities.

2:7 his altar: The bronze altar of sacrifice (Ex 27:1–8) in the outer court of the Temple (1 Kings 8:22). **her palaces:** The royal government buildings in Jerusalem (1 Kings 7:1–12). **a clamor was raised:** Shouts of joy, which characterized Israel's religious feasts, were replaced by the shouts of warriors bringing destruction on the Temple (Ps 74:4–7).

2:8 the wall: The wall around Jerusalem, which the Babylonian army broke down (2 Kings 25:10; Neh 1:3). **the line:** A tool used in the building of a new structure. Here, however, the tool is used to "size up" Jerusalem's defenses for destruction (cf. 2 Kings 21:13; Amos 7:7–9).

2:9 among the nations: I.e., as exiles. **the law is no more:** The Law of Moses can no longer be observed in the absence of the Temple, at least not its precepts for sacrificial worship at the sanctuary. **no vision:** No prophetic guidance or words of divine comfort are given to Jerusalem in the immediate aftermath of its desolation (1:2, 9, 16–17, 21).

2:10 dust on their heads: A mourning ritual (Josh 7:6; Job 2:12; Ezek 27:30). **sackcloth:** A coarse, hair-spun fabric worn next to the skin as an act of sorrow or repentance (2 Kings 6:30; Jer 4:8; Jon 3:6).

2:11 the daughter of my people: Jerusalem. The expression appears only in Lamentations (3:48; 4:3, 6, 10) and Jeremiah (Jer 4:11; 6:26; 8:19, 21–22; 9:1; 14:17). See note on 2:5. **infants and babies:** Forced to suffer the painful consequences of their parents' iniquity (2:12, 19–20).

2:14 Your prophets: The false prophets of Jerusalem. Rather than calling the city to repentance, they gave false

---

ʰ Heb *to the ground.*

they have not exposed your iniquity
    to restore your fortunes,
but have seen for you oracles
    false and misleading.

[15] All who pass along the way
    clap their hands at you;
they hiss and wag their heads
    at the daughter of Jerusalem;
"Is this the city which was called
    the perfection of beauty,
    the joy of all the earth?"

[16] All your enemies
    rail against you;
they hiss, they gnash their teeth,
    they cry: "We have destroyed her!
Ah, this is the day we longed for;
    now we have it; we see it!"

[17] The LORD has done what he planned,
    has carried out his threat;
as he ordained long ago,
    he has demolished without pity;
he has made the enemy rejoice over you,
    and exalted the might of your foes.

[18] Cry aloud [i] to the Lord!
    O [j] daughter of Zion!
Let tears stream down like a torrent
    day and night!
Give yourself no rest,
    your eyes no respite!

[19] Arise, cry out in the night,
    at the beginning of the watches!

Pour out your heart like water
    before the presence of the Lord!
Lift your hands to him
    for the lives of your children,
who faint for hunger
    at the head of every street.

[20] Look, O LORD, and see!
    With whom have you dealt thus?
Should women eat their offspring,
    the children of their tender care?
Should priest and prophet be slain
    in the sanctuary of the Lord?

[21] In the dust of the streets
    lie the young and the old;
my maidens and my young men
    have fallen by the sword;
in the day of your anger you have slain them,
    slaughtering without mercy.

[22] You invited as to the day of an appointed
    feast
    my terrors on every side;
and on the day of the anger of the LORD
    none escaped or survived;
those whom I dandled and reared
    my enemy destroyed.

God's Merciful Love Endures

3 I am the man who has seen affliction
    under the rod of his wrath;
[2] he has driven and brought me
    into darkness without any light;
[3] surely against me he turns his hand
    again and again the whole day long.

---

assurances that it would suffer no harm for its wickedness (Jer 14:13–16; 23:14–22; 29:8–9).

2:15 wag their heads: A gesture of mockery and disdain at the sight of the city's ruin. • An allusion to this passage (as well as Ps 22:7) is made in the Passion narrative when passersby who witnessed the Crucifixion of Jesus "derided him, wagging their heads" (Mt 27:39). **the joy of all the earth:** An epithet for Jerusalem in Ps 48:2.

2:17 his threat: Several times the Lord forewarned Israel that defection from the covenant would bring disaster on the nation (Deut 28:15–68) and its sanctuary (1 Kings 9:6–9). Nevertheless, the suffering imposed on sinful Israel is not a sign that God has rejected his people (Ps 94:14). His plan of salvation includes times of judgment and woe so that the misbehavior of his people can be corrected and obedience restored (3:31–33; Is 40:1–11; 54:7–8).

2:18 Let tears stream down: A call for deep and genuine repentance from sin. The NT calls this "godly grief" (2 Cor 7:10).

2:19 the watches: In ancient Israel, the nighttime hours between sunset and sunrise were divided into three periods of roughly four hours called watches (Judg 7:19). **Pour out your heart like water:** As when the blood of animals, which is forbidden for human consumption, is poured out on the ground

(Deut 12:16, 24). **Lift your hands:** A posture of prayer and petition (1 Kings 8:22, 38; Is 1:15).

2:20 women eat their offspring: A horrifying response to extreme famine (4:10). Cannibalism is envisioned among the curses of the Mosaic covenant (Lev 26:29; Deut 28:53–57).

2:22 terrors on every side: An expression found several times in the Book of Jeremiah (Jer 6:25; 20:3, 10; 46:5; 49:29).

3:1–66 The third and central lament of the book is intensely personal. The fall of Jerusalem still lies in the background, but the focus shifts from the city in distress to the misery of the poet who groans amidst its ruins. He has suffered much at the hands of opponents (3:52–54, 61–63); even more, he senses that God is behind his afflictions (3:1–15). However, just when he reaches the brink of despair (3:16–18), his hope in the Lord's mercy revives (3:22–26, 31–33, 40–41). A short communal lament appears in 3:40–47.

3:1 the rod of his wrath: The poet views his suffering as God's chastisement, perhaps for his own sins as well as for the sins of his people (see 3:39). For more on divine wrath, see note on 2:1.

3:2 darkness: A spiritual darkness in which the Lord's consolation is not experienced (3:6), the burden of suffering weighs heavily (3:7), and prayers for relief seem to fall on deaf ears (3:8, 44). Darkness without light is also a sign that the dreaded "day of the LORD" foretold by the prophets has come upon Judah (Joel 2:1–2; Amos 5:18–20; Zeph 1:14–16). See note on 1:12.

---

[i] Cn: Heb *Their heart cried.*
[j] Cn: Heb *O wall of.*

⁴He has made my flesh and my skin waste away,
  and broken my bones;
⁵he has besieged and enveloped me
  with bitterness and tribulation;
⁶he has made me dwell in darkness
  like the dead of long ago.

⁷He has walled me about so that I cannot escape;
  he has put heavy chains on me;
⁸though I call and cry for help,
  he shuts out my prayer;
⁹he has blocked my ways with hewn stones,
  he has made my paths crooked.

¹⁰He is to me like a bear lying in wait,
  like a lion in hiding;
¹¹he led me off my way and tore me to pieces;
  he has made me desolate;
¹²he bent his bow and set me
  as a mark for his arrow.

¹³He drove into my heart
  the arrows of his quiver;
¹⁴I have become the laughingstock of all peoples,
  the burden of their songs all day long.
¹⁵He has filled me with bitterness,
  he has sated me with wormwood.

¹⁶He has made my teeth grind on gravel,
  and made me cower in ashes;
¹⁷my soul is bereft of peace,
  I have forgotten what happiness is;

¹⁸so I say, "Gone is my glory,
  and my expectation from the LORD."

¹⁹Remember my affliction and my bitterness, ᵏ
  the wormwood and the gall!
²⁰My soul continually thinks of it
  and is bowed down within me.
²¹But this I call to mind,
  and therefore I have hope:

²²The steadfast love of the LORD never ceases, ¹
  his mercies never come to an end;
²³they are new every morning;
  great is your faithfulness.
²⁴"The LORD is my portion," says my soul,
  "therefore I will hope in him."

²⁵The LORD is good to those who wait for him,
  to the soul that seeks him.
²⁶It is good that one should wait quietly
  for the salvation of the LORD.
²⁷It is good for a man that he bear
  the yoke in his youth.

²⁸Let him sit alone in silence
  when he has laid it on him;
²⁹let him put his mouth in the dust—
  there may yet be hope;
³⁰let him give his cheek to the one who strikes him,
  and be filled with insults.

³¹For the Lord will not
  cast off for ever,

3:4 my flesh ... skin ... bones: Not physical injuries directly inflicted by God, but various trials and sufferings that have taken their toll on the poet, making him feel broken and drained of life.

3:6 like the dead: The OT pictures the realm of the dead, called Sheol or the Pit, as a netherworld of shadow and gloom. See word study: *Sheol* at Num 16:30.

3:8 my prayer: Not unheard by the Lord but not answered in the way the poet desires (3:44).

3:9 my paths crooked: The poet feels that afflictions have been placed as obstacles on his path. The passage does not mean that God made the poet a sinner, since God tempts no one to commit sin (Jas 1:13) but provides ways to escape and endure temptations (1 Cor 10:13).

3:10 like a bear ... like a lion: Scripture compares the Lord to a predator when he brings his sinful people to judgment (Hos 13:7–8) and when he allows great suffering into the lives of individuals (Job 10:16).

3:12 his bow: See note on 2:4.

3:15 wormwood: A plant known for its extremely bitter taste (Prov 5:4; Jer 9:15; Rev 8:11).

3:22–26 A burst of new hope surges up from the depths of personal agony. Despite the poet's feeling that the Lord has subjected him to unusually rough treatment, he has not relinquished his belief that the Lord is **good** (3:25) and that he brings **salvation** (3:26) to those who seek him with patient trust.

3:22 steadfast love: The Hebrew term indicates loyalty, commitment, and mercy in a covenant relationship. See word study: *Merciful Love* at Ex 34:7.

3:23 new every morning: God's mercy is abounding and without limit (Ex 34:6; Ps 103:8). This makes forgiveness of sins possible each and every day, as Jesus teaches in the Lord's Prayer (Mt 6:11–12; Lk 11:3–4).

3:24 The LORD is my portion: A sentiment, also expressed in the Psalms, indicating that God is the greatest and most vital part of one's life; everything else fades into insignificance in comparison with him (Ps 16:5; 73:26; 142:5).

3:25 those who wait for him: Those who entrust themselves to the Lord, rely upon his promises, and refuse to give up hope in his goodness and mercy, even in dire circumstances (Ps 37:1–7; Is 30:18). • The motive for loving God is God himself. He loves us first with great tenderness, and we owe him our love in return. He has no gift better than himself. He gives himself as prize and reward. He is refreshment for holy souls, ransom for those in captivity, for "the Lord is good to those who wait for him" (St. Bernard of Clairvaux, *On Loving God* 7). **seeks him:** See word study: *Sought* at 2 Chron 1:5.

3:27 the yoke: A yoke of discipline for sin (1:14).

3:31–33 The poet is reassured that God's judgments in history, though acts of divine discipline, are *not* signs (1) that God has abandoned the covenant people, (2) that his mercy on their behalf has run out, or (3) that correcting his erring children is something in which he delights. Judgments are rather signs of God's love, which aims at purging his people of evil and bringing them to spiritual health and maturity (Prov 3:11–12; Heb 12:5–6, 10).

3:31 not cast off for ever: The duration of Jerusalem's punishment is strictly limited, in contrast to the mercies of God, which "never come to an end" (3:22).

ᵏCn: Heb *wandering*.
¹Syr Tg: Heb *we are not cut off*.

³²but, though he cause grief, he will have
compassion
according to the abundance of his steadfast
love;
³³for he does not willingly afflict
or grieve the sons of men.

³⁴To crush under foot
all the prisoners of the earth,
³⁵to turn aside the right of a man
in the presence of the Most High,
³⁶to subvert a man in his cause,
the Lord does not approve.

³⁷Who has commanded and it came to pass,
unless the Lord has ordained it?
³⁸Is it not from the mouth of the Most High
that good and evil come?
³⁹Why should a living man complain,
a man, about the punishment of his sins?

⁴⁰Let us test and examine our ways,
and return to the LORD!
⁴¹Let us lift up our hearts and hands
to God in heaven:
⁴²"We have transgressed and rebelled,
and you have not forgiven.

⁴³"You have wrapped yourself with anger and
pursued us,
slaying without pity;
⁴⁴you have wrapped yourself with a cloud
so that no prayer can pass through.
⁴⁵You have made us offscouring and refuse
among the peoples.

⁴⁶"All our enemies
rail against us;
⁴⁷panic and pitfall have come upon us,
devastation and destruction;

⁴⁸my eyes flow with rivers of tears
because of the destruction of the daughter
of my people.

⁴⁹"My eyes will flow without ceasing,
without respite,
⁵⁰until the LORD from heaven
looks down and sees;
⁵¹my eyes cause me grief
at the fate of all the maidens of my city.

⁵²"I have been hunted like a bird
by those who were my enemies without
cause;
⁵³they flung me alive into the pit
and cast stones on me;
⁵⁴water closed over my head;
I said, 'I am lost.'

⁵⁵"I called on your name, O LORD,
from the depths of the pit;
⁵⁶you heard my plea, 'Do not close
your ear to my cry for help!'ᵐ
⁵⁷You came near when I called on you;
you said, 'Do not fear!'

⁵⁸"You have taken up my cause, O Lord,
you have redeemed my life.
⁵⁹You have seen the wrong done to me, O
LORD;
do judge my cause.
⁶⁰You have seen all their vengeance,
all their devices against me.

⁶¹"You have heard their taunts, O LORD,
all their devices against me.
⁶²The lips and thoughts of my assailants
are against me all the day long.
⁶³Behold their sitting and their rising;
I am the burden of their songs.

3:35 the Most High: An epithet for the Lord, the maker of heaven and earth (Gen 14:19, 22).

3:36 the Lord does not approve: Either the oppression of peoples or the corruption of rulers who rob them of justice (Ex 23:1–6; Deut 16:19; Ps 94:1–7).

3:38 good and evil: Not a reference to moral actions that are right and wrong, since the power to choose these options is entrusted to man's free will (Sir 15:11–20). The meaning here is closer to "prosperity and adversity" or "good times and bad times".

3:40 return to the LORD: A call to repentance and a renewed commitment to the covenant. See word study: *Return* at Jer 3:1.

3:41 lift up ... hands: A posture of prayer and petition (1 Kings 8:22, 38).

3:42 you have not forgiven: In the sense that God did not hold back the painful judgments that fell on the rebel city.

3:44 with a cloud: Indicates that God has made himself inaccessible to the pleas of his people, at least for a time (3:31–32). The Book of Sirach appears to borrow from the imagery of this passage to reveal an important exception: "The prayer of the humble pierces the clouds" (Sir 35:17).

3:48 rivers of tears: The poet mourns in solidarity with the conquered city (1:2, 16; 2:11, 18; 3:49). **the daughter:** See note on 2:11.

3:51 the maidens of my city: Humiliated and exiled by Babylonian conquerors.

3:52–66 The poet cries out for divine justice. He beseeches the Lord to remember the treachery of his persecutors and to repay them as their evildoing deserves.

3:53 the pit: A traditional image of the grave, suggesting the poet is on the brink of death (Job 33:22; Ps 30:3). The traditional image of drowning in 3:54 conveys the same idea (Ps 69:1–2, 14–15; Jon 2:3). Alternatively, one might see an allusion to the prophet Jeremiah being lowered into a cistern of sludge (Jer 38:1–6).

3:58 redeemed my life: The Lord delivered him from death at the hands of his enemies.

ᵐ Heb uncertain.

[64]"You will repay them, O Lᴏʀᴅ,
  according to the work of their hands.
[65]You will give them dullness of heart;
  your curse will be on them.
[66]You will pursue them in anger and destroy them
  from under your heavens, O Lᴏʀᴅ."[n]

The Punishment and Distress of Zion

4 How the gold has grown dim,
  how the pure gold is changed!
The holy stones lie scattered
  at the head of every street.

[2]The precious sons of Zion,
  worth their weight in fine gold,
how they are reckoned as earthen pots,
  the work of a potter's hands!

[3]Even the jackals give the breast
  and suckle their young,
but the daughter of my people has become cruel,
  like the ostriches in the wilderness.

[4]The tongue of the infant clings
  to the roof of its mouth for thirst;
the children beg for food,
  but no one gives to them.

[5]Those who feasted on dainties
  perish in the streets;
those who were brought up in purple
  lie on ash heaps.

[6]For the chastisement[o] of the daughter of my
    people has been greater
  than the punishment[p] of Sodom,

which was overthrown in a moment,
  no hand being laid on it.[q]

[7]Her princes were purer than snow,
  whiter than milk;
their bodies were more ruddy than coral,
  the beauty of their form[r] was like sapphire.[s]

[8]Now their visage is blacker than soot,
  they are not recognized in the streets;
their skin has shriveled upon their bones,
  it has become as dry as wood.

[9]Happier were the victims of the sword
  than the victims of hunger,
who pined away, stricken
  by want of the fruits of the field.

[10]The hands of compassionate women
  have boiled their own children;
they became their food
  in the destruction of the daughter of my people.

[11]The Lᴏʀᴅ gave full vent to his wrath,
  he poured out his hot anger;
and he kindled a fire in Zion,
  which consumed its foundations.

[12]The kings of the earth did not believe,
  or any of the inhabitants of the world,
that foe or enemy could enter
  the gates of Jerusalem.

[13]This was for the sins of her prophets
  and the iniquities of her priests,

3:65 dullness of heart: Or "anguish of heart".

4:1–22 Chapter 4 returns to the focus of chaps. 1–2 by describing the siege of Jerusalem that ended with the conquest of the city in 586 B.C. Four verses, expressed in the first-person plural ("we, us, our"), give the perspective of the suffering people.

4:1 How: See note on 1:1. **the gold has grown dim:** The splendor of Jerusalem has faded behind the horrors of the Babylonian siege. **The holy stones:** The people of the city, called the "precious sons of Zion" in 4:2, who lie dead in the streets, strewn about like broken potsherds (Is 51:20). Others read this as a reference to the stones of the ruined Temple or to the holy city's dismantled wall (2 Kings 25:10).

4:3 the daughter of my people: Jerusalem. See note on 2:5. **ostriches:** Thought to be heartless animals who leave their eggs unprotected (Job 39:13–16). Jerusalem is no less cruel, for it gives no food or defense to its children.

4:4 beg for food: See note on 1:11.

4:5 purple: Or "scarlet". Clothing dyed this color was very expensive and usually worn by royalty. Not even Judah's wealthy nobility is spared the afflictions of Jerusalem's siege. **ash heaps:** Piles of burned garbage.

4:6 greater: As evidenced by the fact that Jerusalem's suffering is long and drawn out, whereas the wicked city of **Sodom** was overthrown quickly by brimstone and fire (Gen 19:24–25). The prophets compare Jerusalem to Sodom to stress the gravity of its sins (Is 1:10; Jer 23:14; Ezek 16:44–52).

4:7 whiter than milk: The untanned skin of the wealthy, who have no need to labor in the sun for a living. During the siege, however, when hardships come upon all, their appearance is "blacker than soot" (4:8).

4:9 Happier: A quick death by violence is preferred to the slow, agonizing death of starvation.

4:10 boiled their own children: See note on 2:20.

4:11 his wrath: See note on 2:1. **fire in Zion:** The Lord's Temple, the royal buildings, and every great house in the city were destroyed by fire (2:3; 2 Kings 25:9; Is 64:11).

4:12 did not believe: Jerusalem was once thought to be an unconquerable city. Previously it had been besieged and even plundered, but never destroyed (1 Kings 14:25–28; 2 Kings 14:13–14; Is 7:1; 36–37).

4:13 prophets ... priests: Jerusalem's sins are especially grave because they are committed by its religious leaders—persons who should have been models of covenant faithfulness.

---

[n] Syr Compare Gk Vg: Heb *the heavens of the* Lᴏʀᴅ.
[o] Or *iniquity*.
[p] Or *sin*.
[q] Heb uncertain.
[r] Heb uncertain.
[s] Heb *lapis lazuli*.

who shed in the midst of her
  the blood of the righteous.

¹⁴They wandered, blind, through the streets,
  so defiled with blood
that none could touch
  their garments.

¹⁵"Away! Unclean!" men cried at them;
  "Away! Away! Touch not!"
So they became fugitives and wanderers;
  men said among the nations,
  "They shall stay with us no longer."

¹⁶The LORD himself has scattered them,
  he will regard them no more;
no honor was shown to the priests,
  no favor to the elders.

¹⁷Our eyes failed, ever watching
  vainly for help;
in our watching^t we watched
  for a nation which could not save.

¹⁸Men dogged our steps
  so that we could not walk in our
    streets;
our end drew near; our days were numbered;
  for our end had come.

¹⁹Our pursuers were swifter
  than the vultures in the heavens;
they chased us on the mountains,
  they lay in wait for us in the wilderness.

²⁰The breath of our nostrils, the LORD's anointed,
  was taken in their pits,
he of whom we said, "Under his shadow
  we shall live among the nations."

²¹Rejoice and be glad, O daughter of E'dom,
  dweller in the land of Uz;
but to you also the cup shall pass;
  you shall become drunk and strip yourself
    bare.

²²The punishment of your iniquity,
  O daughter of Zion, is accomplished,
  he will keep you in exile no longer;
but your iniquity, O daughter of E'dom, he will
    punish,
  he will uncover your sins.

A Prayer for Mercy

5 Remember, O LORD, what has befallen us;
  behold, and see our disgrace!
²Our inheritance has been turned over to strangers,
  our homes to aliens.
³We have become orphans, fatherless;
  our mothers are like widows.

4:15 Away! Unclean!: Suggests the inhabitants of Jerusalem have become like lepers, who are required to warn others not to approach them in their impure state (Lev 13:45–46).

4:16 the LORD himself ... scattered: The poet asserts that God is ultimately behind Judah's exile to Babylon. See note on 1:5.

4:17 watching vainly for help: Jerusalem waits in vain for the Egyptians to rescue the city from the Babylonian siege. Initially this appears to be a hopeful prospect, but Jeremiah learns from the Lord that Egypt, despite being a powerful ally, will not save the city from destruction (Jer 37:1–10).

4:19 Our pursuers: Babylonian soldiers hunt and seize all who try to flee from the doomed city (2 Kings 25:1–7).

4:20 The breath of our nostrils: I.e., the animating spirit (Heb., *rûaḥ*) of God's people. The Greek LXX translates: "The spirit of our face". • To some extent it is possible to reach an intelligent understanding of the sublime nature and unapproachable power of the Spirit as well as the greatness of his operations by considering the meaning of his title. He is called "Spirit" and "the breath of our nostrils, the anointed of the Lord" (St. Basil of Caesarea, *On the Holy Spirit* 19, 48). **the LORD's anointed:** Zedekiah, the last king of Judah (597–586 B.C.). The people of Judah rely on him as their life-breath and protection, yet even he is taken captive to Babylon, where he eventually dies in prison (Jer 52:11). • Christ is indeed Savior, being both the Son and Word of God; and he is saving because he is Spirit, for he says, "The Spirit of our countenance, the Anointed of the Lord" (St. Irenaeus, *Against Heresies* 3, 10, 2). **his shadow:** Suggests the image of a bird sheltering its young under its wings (e.g., Ps 57:1; 91:4).

4:21 Rejoice: Sarcasm. **daughter of Edom:** The Edomites, who lived in the rugged highlands south of the Dead Sea. Edom is a target of the Lord's judgment for taking full advantage of Judah's conquest in 586 B.C. Instead of coming to Judah's defense, the Edomites took perverse delight in the suffering of God's people and even committed acts of violence, plunder, and treachery against them (Ps 137:7; Joel 3:19; Obad 10–14). **the cup:** Filled with the wine of divine judgment, which will bring confusion and disgrace upon Edom (Jer 49:12; cf. Ps 75:8).

4:22 daughter of Zion: Jerusalem. See word study: *The Daughter of Zion* at 1:6. **accomplished:** The Lord's wrath has been poured out on the city in full; its punishment is complete. As a result, the Lord's mercy and compassion are ready to be revealed, bringing an end to the **exile** of Judah in Babylon (Is 40:1–2). The return from exile would begin after the fall of Babylon in 539 B.C.

5:1–22 The final chapter is a communal lament. Life in the occupied land of Judah is a miserable struggle for survival. Food is scarce, freedom is taken away, and faith in the Lord's concern for his people is stretched to the breaking point. The prayer is that God will see the plight of his people and be moved to pity (5:21).

5:1 Remember: An appeal, not simply to "recall" Judah's humiliation, but to "take action" in its favor (Ps 74:2, 18, 22).

5:2 Our inheritance: The tribal territory of Judah, which is part of the Promised Land that God gave to Israel as an inheritance (Deut 4:21; Josh 11:23). **Strangers ... aliens:** The occupying army of Babylon. The conquest of Canaan, a land once inhabited by Gentiles, has been reversed so that even resources that once belonged to Israel must now be purchased (5:4).

5:3 orphans ... widows: I.e., like persons who are especially vulnerable and tend to suffer most in ancient societies.

---

^t Heb uncertain.

⁴We must pay for the water we drink,
  the wood we get must be bought.
⁵With a yoke ᵘ on our necks we are hard driven;
  we are weary, we are given no rest.
⁶We have given the hand to Egypt,
  and to Assyria, to get bread enough.
⁷Our fathers sinned, and are no more;
  and we bear their iniquities.
⁸Slaves rule over us;
  there is none to deliver us from their hand.
⁹We get our bread at the peril of our lives,
  because of the sword in the wilderness.
¹⁰Our skin is hot as an oven
  with the burning heat of famine.
¹¹Women are ravished in Zion,
  virgins in the towns of Judah.
¹²Princes are hung up by their hands;
  no respect is shown to the elders.
¹³Young men are compelled to grind at the mill;
  and boys stagger under loads of wood.

¹⁴The old men have quit the city gate,
  the young men their music.
¹⁵The joy of our hearts has ceased;
  our dancing has been turned to mourning.
¹⁶The crown has fallen from our head;
  woe to us, for we have sinned!
¹⁷For this our heart has become sick,
  for these things our eyes have grown dim,
¹⁸for Mount Zion which lies desolate;
  jackals prowl over it.

¹⁹But you, O LORD, reign for ever;
  your throne endures to all generations.
²⁰Why do you forget us for ever,
  why do you so long forsake us?
²¹Restore us to yourself, O LORD, that we may be
    restored!
  Renew our days as of old!
²²Or have you utterly rejected us?
  Are you exceedingly angry with us?

5:5 a yoke: See note on 1:14.

5:6 Egypt ... Assyria: Judah once reached out to these nations and formed alliances with them, but doing so only showed a lack of faith in the Lord that contributed to its downfall.

5:7 we bear their iniquities: The victims of the Babylonian conquest stand as the last of several sinful generations that have brought God's judgment on Judah and Jerusalem with such severity. It is a catastrophe multiple decades in the making, thanks to Judah's stubborn persistence in evil (see 2 Kings 21:10–15; 23:26–27; 24:3, 19–20).

5:8 Slaves rule over us: Probably a reference to the Babylonian "officials" who govern the land of Judah after the fall of Jerusalem (2 Kings 25:24). The Hebrew term translated "officials" in the passage can also be translated "servants" or "slaves".

5:12 hung up: Either a means of execution or a public display of corpses appears to be in view.

5:13 grind at the mill: Animals typically performed the task of turning giant millstones.

5:14 old men: Community leaders. **the city gate:** A place of public assembly where elders sat to conduct business and hear legal cases (Deut 22:15; Ruth 4:1–12).

5:16 The crown has fallen: The community laments not only the humiliation of God's people (Job 19:9) but also the fall of the Davidic monarchy in 586 B.C. (Ps 89:39).

5:18 Mount Zion: The height of Jerusalem. See note on 1:4. **jackals:** Haunt the ruins of cities no longer inhabited (Jer 9:11; 10:22).

5:19 you, O LORD, reign for ever: A confession of faith in God's everlasting kingship (Ps 93:1–2; 102:12; 146:10), which endures despite the exile of the Davidic kings of Judah (Jehoachin, 2 Kings 24:15; Zedekiah, 2 Kings 25:7).

5:22 utterly rejected us?: The book ends on a somber note as survivors in Judah wonder whether the Lord has disowned them. Faith knows that his mercy never runs out (3:22); but intense and prolonged suffering can make one feel abandoned (cf. Ps 22:1–5).

ᵘ Symmachus: Heb lacks *with a yoke*.

STUDY QUESTIONS
Lamentations

Chapter 1

For understanding
1. **1:1.** As a distraught cry of emotion that appears elsewhere in funeral laments, what other poems in Lamentations does this initial word "How" introduce? In the Greek LXX, what short prescript, not present in the Hebrew text, precedes this opening word? What conditions have greatly reduced Jerusalem's population? To what is the city likened? As a conquered territory subject to Babylonian rule, what is Judah forced to do?
2. **1:5.** With Babylon as the master and overlord, who is "the tail"? What prophetic insight into the fall of Jerusalem has the poet made? As stated multiple times in the book, who is behind the catastrophe? How is Jerusalem pictured?
3. **Word Study: The Daughter of Zion (1:6).** As a personification of Jerusalem and its people, how often does the expression *bat ṣiyyôn*, which can also be translated "Daughter Zion", appear in OT poetry? Why are cities oftentimes viewed in the Bible as female figures? How does the significance of the epithet Daughter Zion seem to vary according to the context? Either way, as the object of the Lord's affection and care, what is Jerusalem sometimes called to do and sometimes brought to endure? In which of these cases does Lamentations address Daughter Zion?
4. **1:12.** To what is "the day" a reference? How did the prophets announce this day? Theologically, of what does every "day of the Lord" throughout history offer a glimpse?

For application
1. **1:1.** Have you ever visited a true ghost town? How does a city with a booming economy suddenly become so depopulated as to consist of abandoned buildings? On a spiritual level, how might the Church, once resembling a boom town in the culture of our country, come to resemble a ghost town?
2. **1:7.** What is the worst calamity or personal disaster you can imagine happening to you? How would it change your relationships with relatives, friends, and neighbors? What questions would it raise for your faith in God's providential care for you?
3. **1:11.** What are the homeless persons foraging through waste bins and dumpsters looking for? What is your attitude toward them? If you have ever wanted to help them, what have you done about it?
4. **1:12.** How do you think the homeless view you? What would they like you to know about them? How do you think their perception of you might change your view of them?

Chapter 2

For understanding
1. **2:1.** Of what does this chapter speak? Historically, how is divine anger manifested? Theologically, however, what does it mean that God is eternal and unchanging, and so how is the language of wrath to be understood? According to St. Thomas Aquinas, if God's anger is not a passion of the soul, what is it? What was the splendor of Israel, now destroyed? What was God's footstool?
2. **2:9.** What does the poet mean by saying that the law is no more? In the immediate aftermath of Jerusalem's desolation, what is not given to it?
3. **2:17.** Despite the Lord's forewarnings of disaster on the nation and its sanctuary, of what is the suffering imposed on Israel *not* a sign? Why does God's plan of salvation include times of judgment and woe?
4. **2:19.** In ancient Israel, what are the watches? How does one pour out his heart like water? Of what is the lifting up of hands a posture?

For application
1. **2:4–5.** When, in reality, would the Lord behave like an "enemy" to the human soul? Even for one in the state of grace, how can the Lord sometimes come across as indifferent, if not seemingly hostile? What virtues are needed for one experiencing extreme suffering in order to maintain hope?
2. **2:9.** Read the note for this verse. If all the churches in the country were either forbidden to Christians or destroyed, what aspects of worship would be unavailable to them? If all the priests were exiled or killed, what additional means of worship would be denied? Without access to the Eucharist, how would Christian faith survive?
3. **2:13.** This verse is sometimes adapted and applied to Mary at the foot of the Cross. If you had been there with her, how would you have comforted her? Why is it hard to find words to comfort someone in the extremes of grief?
4. **2:18.** The note for this verse refers to "godly grief". What is that? Has the awareness of your own sin ever led to a grief so deep that tears could not be stopped? Why should you thank the Lord for such an experience?

Chapter 3

For understanding
1. **3:2.** What is happening in the kind of darkness the poet is experiencing? Of what is darkness without light also a sign?
2. **3:22–26.** What surges up from the depths of the poet's personal agony? Despite his feeling that the Lord has subjected him to unusually rough treatment, what has he not relinquished?
3. **3:25.** Who are those who wait for the Lord? According to St. Bernard of Clairvaux, what is the motive for loving God?
4. **3:31–33.** Of what three things is the poet reassured regarding God's judgments in history? Rather, as signs of God's love, what is their aim?

For application
1. **3:2.** Have you ever had experiences of spiritual darkness? If so, how intense were these experiences? What occasioned them? What spiritual tools did you use to deal with them?
2. **3:24.** What does it mean for you to have the Lord as your "portion"? How central is the Lord in your life? How might reminding yourself of his centrality help you in times of spiritual darkness?
3. **3:27.** To what yoke does this verse refer? Why is it good for one to bear that yoke in one's youth? How does that help one bear the same yoke when one is older and more experienced with suffering?
4. **3:31–33.** According to St. Ignatius' rules for the discernment of spirits, periods of consolation (the highs) and desolation (the lows) commonly succeed one another. How should one conduct himself during the low periods of desolation? During consolation, how should one prepare for the desolation that will eventually come?

Chapter 4

For understanding
1. **4:1.** What gold has grown dim? What are the holy stones that lie scattered? Of what do others read this as a reference?
2. **4:17.** For what does Jerusalem wait in vain during the Babylonian siege? Although initially this appears to be a hopeful prospect, what does Jeremiah learn from the Lord?
3. **4:20.** What is "the breath of our nostrils"? How does the Greek LXX translate it? According to St. Basil of Caesarea, how is it possible to some extent to reach an intelligent understanding of the sublime nature and unapproachable power of the Spirit? Who is the Lord's anointed? Though the people of Judah rely on him as their life-breath and protection, what happens to him? According to St. Irenaeus, in what way is Christ the Savior, and how is he saving? What does the image of being under the king's shadow suggest?
4. **4:21.** Where do the Edomites live? Why is Edom a target of the Lord's judgment? What cup is referred to here?

For application
1. **4:4.** Whenever you view scenes on news media of children starving, what is your emotional response? What responsibility have you felt for coming to their aid? How have such scenes influenced your prayer life?
2. **4:6.** King David was once given three options as punishment for a particular sin: three years of famine, three months of fleeing from pursuit by enemies, or three days of deadly plague (2 Sam 24:13). What are the advantages and disadvantages of each? If you were in David's position, which would you choose? As a measure of the benefits one receives from punishment, from which would you learn the most about the gravity of your offense?
3. **4:9.** Which kind of death would you prefer, quick but painful or slow but relatively painless? Again, what are the advantages and disadvantages of each? How prepared are you for either?
4. **4:16.** What honor do Catholics usually accord priests and members of the hierarchy? If a priest with whom you are on friendly terms were accused of sexual misconduct, how would your relationship with him change? How does the disgrace of the guilty affect those who are innocent?

Chapter 5

For understanding
1. **5:7.** In what place do the victims of the Babylonian conquest stand? What made the Babylonian conquest a catastrophe multiple decades in the making?
2. **5:8.** By saying that "slaves rule over us", to what does the poet probably refer? How can the Hebrew term translated "officials" in the passage also be translated?
3. **5:16.** In addition to the humiliation of God's people, what does the community lament?
4. **5:22.** How does the Book of Lamentations end? While faith knows that the Lord's mercy never runs out, how can intense and prolonged suffering make one feel?

For application
1. **5:4.** In most modern societies, utility companies provide water, fuel, and electricity for a price. Which of them could most people do without? Who in our society is most likely to suffer because of the cost of these necessities? While paying for them is common for most of us, what makes it so burdensome for the author of Lamentations?
2. **5:7.** Read the note for this verse. For what sins of our forebears do we as a nation bear the consequences? From what social ills do we suffer as a result? How can living a committed Christian life ameliorate or even resolve some of these ills?
3. **5:14.** How does music reflect the state of a society? According to the popular music with which you are familiar, what are some of the concerns, problems, and issues of our society? How does popular music deal with personal relationships, especially between the sexes? What sense of optimism does it either reflect or reject?

INTRODUCTION TO BARUCH

Author and Date The Book of Baruch is a small collection of writings that have been joined together into a single work. Beyond this simple observation, much about the origin and date of the book remains obscure. The first section of the book, 1:1—3:8, is attributed to Baruch, son of Neriah, the personal secretary of the prophet Jeremiah (Jer 36:4, 32; 45:1). The second section, 3:9—4:4, as well as the third, 4:5—5:9, give no explicit information about who wrote them or when they were written. The fourth and final section of the book, 6:1–73, claims to reproduce a letter that Jeremiah sent to the exiles of Judah living in Babylon. The book thus presents itself as the work of (at least) two authors, Baruch and Jeremiah, who engaged in a collaborative ministry before, during, and after the fall of Jerusalem in 586 B.C. The book's internal claims of authorship and date have been generally accepted as historical in Christian tradition.

The prevailing opinion among biblical scholars today is that Baruch, along with the Letter of Jeremiah, which forms its final chapter, are pseudepigrapha, i.e., writings attributed to famous historical persons but not actually written by them. This is based on observations that are said to weigh against a literal interpretation of the book's own claims of authorship and date: **(1)** The introduction in 1:1–14 includes information that is considered historically suspect. For instance, it places Baruch in Babylon in 581 B.C., yet the Book of Jeremiah counts him among those who fled to Egypt after the conquest of Jerusalem in 586 B.C. (Jer 43:4–7). Similarly, the book states that Baruch returned to Jerusalem with the silver vessels of the Temple that had been confiscated by the Babylonians in 597 B.C. (2 Kings 24:10–13), yet this stands in tension with Ezra 1:7–11, which indicates that Mithredath, one of the Jewish exiles released from Babylon, brought the silver and gold vessels of the Temple back to Jerusalem in 538 B.C., several decades after Baruch had allegedly done so. **(2)** A few passages of the book rely on biblical texts that appeared later than Baruch's lifetime. For instance, many claim that the prayer in 1:15—2:10 borrows directly from Daniel's prayer in Dan 9:4–19, yet the latter is explicitly dated to 539 B.C. (Dan 9:1–3), more than forty years after the setting described in Baruch 1:1–4. Likewise, select verses in 4:5—5:9 draw upon the Greek LXX translation of Isaiah (see note on 4:35). This is significant because Isaiah was not rendered from Hebrew into Greek until the third or second century B.C. **(3)** The wisdom poem in 3:9—4:4 portrays its audience as living in exile for many years. They are a people who are "growing old in a foreign country" (3:10). This remark is not easy to reconcile with a document intended for the exiles in Babylon in 581 B.C., only five years after the deportation described in 2 Kings 25:11. Thus, instead of a book written by Baruch and Jeremiah to exiled Jews in Babylon in the sixth century B.C., most scholars hold that the book was written by several unknown authors (and compilers) who wished to address fellow Jews living in the Diaspora, far from the land of Israel, in the centuries after the return of the exiles from Babylon.

While this modern view faces some significant challenges of its own—e.g., the book's references to the Temple in ruins, the city of Jerusalem robbed of its inhabitants, and the imminent return of the exiles fit very uneasily into the Second Temple period (see notes on 2:26; 4:12; 4:25)—it nevertheless seems clear that Baruch is a more complex composition than has been traditionally recognized. Indeed, one can envision the writing, editing, and translating of the various parts of Baruch taking place in stages over a long period of time. Some sections may go back to the sixth century B.C.; other sections, however, appear to have been written (or at least edited) in the Hellenistic period between roughly 300 and 100 B.C. The identity of the scribe(s) responsible for giving the book its final form is simply unknown.

Title The title of the book in the Greek Septuagint is *Barouch*, which is a shortened form of the Hebrew name *Berekhyahu*, meaning "the LORD blesses". The name is taken from 1:1–4, which states that Baruch, the son of Neriah, wrote the words of a book that he read to Jewish exiles in Babylon. The Book of Baruch is sometimes called 1 Baruch to distinguish it from other Jewish writings such as a Syriac Apocalypse called *2 Baruch* and a Greek Apocalypse called *3 Baruch*. Some manuscripts of the Latin Vulgate give the title as *Prophetia Baruch*, "Prophecy of Baruch". It was often the case in ancient times that 6:1–73 circulated as an independent work under the Greek title *Epistolē Ieremiou*, "Letter of Jeremiah".

Place in the Canon Baruch is included in Catholic and Eastern Orthodox canons of Scripture but not in Jewish or Protestant canons. In early copies of the Greek LXX, Baruch 1–5 is placed between Jeremiah and Lamentations, with Baruch 6 appearing as the Letter of Jeremiah after Lamentations. The RSV2CE, which groups all six chapters together after Lamentations, mirrors the structure of the Latin Vulgate (although in this translation the Book of Lamentations is joined directly to the end of Jeremiah, forming its final five chapters). In ancient

Christian times, a few figures such as St. Jerome disputed Baruch's inclusion among the inspired writings of Scripture, but others openly accepted it, including St. Athanasius of Alexandria, St. Cyril of Jerusalem, and St. Epiphanius of Salamis. Baruch and the Letter of Jeremiah both appear in a canon attributed to the Synod of Laodicea (A.D. 364); however, neither is mentioned by name in the list of biblical books drawn up by the Synods of Hippo (A.D. 393) and Carthage (A.D. 397). This might seem to indicate that Baruch was excluded from these lists, except that Lamentations is not mentioned in them, either. Scholars think it more likely that the entire collection of writings associated with the prophet Jeremiah was included under his name alone (i.e., Jeremiah = Jeremiah, Lamentations, Baruch, and the Letter of Jeremiah). This was a customary practice in ancient Christian times, as seen in the writings of the Church Fathers, who routinely cited Baruch under the name Jeremiah.

Structure Baruch divides into four major sections. **(1)** The first begins with a prose introduction (1:1–14) that describes Baruch's visit to the Jewish exiles in Babylon, who commissioned him in turn to bring funds to Jerusalem for sacrifices. Joined to this preface is a communal confession of sin (1:15—2:10) and a communal prayer for restoration (2:11—3:8). **(2)** The second part of the book is a poem on the excellence of wisdom. The poet exhorts readers to learn wisdom (3:9–14) and to recognize that wisdom is found ultimately in God (3:15–37) and historically in the Mosaic Law (4:1–4). **(3)** The third part takes the form of a prophetic exhortation. It explains the exile as God's discipline of his sinful people (4:5–20), announces that he will deliver them from captivity (4:21–29), and encourages Jerusalem with the news that its children are about to return home (4:30—5:9). **(4)** The fourth section purports to be a letter Jeremiah sent to the exiles in Babylon, urging them to preserve their Jewish faith and recognize that pagan idolatry is a sham (6:1–73).

Content and Themes The Book of Baruch is not a work of great originality. Instead of breaking new ground and advancing new ideas, its primary purpose is to restate old ones. It is basically a synthesis of themes and teachings drawn from other Old Testament books. Behind this lies the conviction that the Scriptures of Israel enshrine a wisdom that is truly divine and that never grows old or out of date. Far from being irrelevant, the Bible should animate the prayer of God's people and should serve as a guide for making sense of their history. Baruch's extensive use of scriptural texts illustrates how this works in practice.

Theologically, the book embraces a view of Israel's national history that derives from the Book of Deuteronomy. This vision, especially apparent in Deut 28–32, foresees that the people of Israel will enjoy God's blessings in the land of Canaan for a time, but eventually they will turn against the Lord and bring the curses of his covenant upon themselves. These curses will be manifest most dramatically in the exile of God's people from the Promised Land and their captivity among the nations. This is precisely the situation in which Baruch's original readers find themselves (2:27–30). They have been exiled from Judah and Jerusalem and are "growing old in a foreign country" (3:10). And this is no accident of history. It is because Israel sinned grievously against the Lord that the people have come under the curse of the covenant (1:19–20) and have been scattered far from their homeland (2:4–7; 3:8; 4:6).

Baruch admonishes the exiles of Israel to respond to God's chastisement with repentance. They are urged to "return with tenfold zeal" to seek the Lord amid their exile (4:28). This process begins with the people confessing their sins (1:13; 2:5, 10, 24) and acknowledging that the Lord is righteous, even when he brings his people to judgment (1:15; 2:6, 9), reduces the Temple to ruins (2:26), and makes Jerusalem a grieving mother (4:11, 16) and widow (4:12). The next step is to seek divine mercy, since exile from the land is merely a symptom of the people's spiritual exile from God (2:14–19; 3:2). This includes buying sacrifices to be offered in Jerusalem (1:10–13) while praising the Lord in the lands of captivity (3:6). Lastly, the covenant community must renew its commitment to the wisdom (3:9) that God has made uniquely accessible to Israel in the commandments of the Torah (3:36—4:4). Among the most important of these commitments, the people must take care to worship the Lord alone (6:6) while renouncing the idolatry of the nations as foolishness (6:8–73) and even as service to demons (4:7).

Besides admonishment, Baruch also has words of encouragement for God's children. If the people are truly repentant, they can be confident of restoration in the future. The exiles are to "take courage" (4:5, 21, 27) in the knowledge that God is coming to "deliver" them (4:18, 21) from their captivity and to become their "everlasting Savior" (4:22). Indeed, their enemies, the Babylonians, are about to see "destruction" (4:25; cf. 4:31–35), and the mother city of Jerusalem is told to "take courage" (4:30) because her sons and daughters, which were carried away from her, will soon come streaming home (4:36–37; 5:5). At this point, the exiles will experience "the mercy and righteousness" that come from the Lord (5:9), which is nothing less than the gift of "a heart that obeys" the Law of God (2:31). The climax of this coming restoration is thus the renewal of the covenant. Through the inspired author, God says: "I will make an everlasting covenant with them to be their God and they shall be my people" (2:35). This, according to Baruch, is what Moses meant when he foresaw in Deuteronomy that the Lord would circumcise the hearts of his people, enabling them to walk in his ways (Deut 30:6).

Christian Perspective Baruch is never quoted directly in the New Testament, nor have scholars been able to identify unmistakable allusions to the book. General parallels in thought are evident, however, and these are clearest in the Gospel of John and 1 Corinthians. Baruch's claim that the wisdom of God "appeared upon earth and lived among men" (3:37) in the commandments of the Torah is similar to the evangelist's claim that the Word of God "became flesh and dwelt among us" in the Person of Jesus Christ (Jn 1:14). Thus, what Baruch says of the Mosaic Law, the fourth Gospel says of the Messiah, explicitly comparing them as the lesser and the greater: "For the law was given through Moses; grace and truth came through Jesus Christ" (Jn 1:17). Likewise, Paul makes two significant statements about idols that affirm what Baruch says about idols, even if the apostle is not referring directly to the text of Baruch (compare 1 Cor 8:4 with 6:16, 23, 29 and 1 Cor 10:20 and 4:7). Outside the New Testament, some attention was given to the Book of Baruch in the writings of the Church Fathers and Doctors. The most popular passage was 3:37, which was read as a prophecy of the Incarnation of God in Jesus. Finally, a portion of the wisdom poem (3:9–15, 32—4:4) is featured as one of the Old Testament readings for the Easter Vigil Mass.

OUTLINE OF BARUCH

1. Baruch and the Exiles in Babylon (1:1—3:8)
  A. Baruch's Mission in Babylon (1:1–9)
  B. The Letter and Money Sent to Jerusalem (1:10–14)
  C. The Exiles' Confession of Sin (1:15—2:10)
  D. The Exiles' Prayer for Restoration (2:11—3:8)

2. A Poem on Wisdom (3:9—4:4)
  A. An Appeal for Wisdom (3:9–14)
  B. The Search for Wisdom (3:15–23)
  C. Wisdom and the Law (3:24—4:4)

3. A Prophetic Exhortation (4:5—5:9)
  A. Exile Is Divine Chastisement (4:5–20)
  B. Divine Deliverance Is Coming (4:21–29)
  C. Take Courage, O Jerusalem (4:30—5:9)

4. The Letter of Jeremiah (6:1–73)
  A. Jeremiah's Message from God (6:1–7)
  B. Jeremiah Ridicules Idolatry (6:8–73)

THE BOOK OF

BARUCH

Baruch and the Jews of Babylon

1 These are the words of the book which Baruch the son of Neri′ah, son of Mah′seiah, son of Zedeki′ah, son of Hasadi′ah, son of Hilki′ah, wrote in Babylon, ²in the fifth year, on the seventh day of the month, at the time when the Chalde′ans took Jerusalem and burned it with fire. ³And Baruch read the words of this book in the hearing of Jeconi′ah the son of Jehoi′akim, king of Judah, and in the hearing of all the people who came to hear the book, ⁴and in the hearing of the mighty men and the princes, and in the hearing of the elders, and in the hearing of all the people, small and great, all who dwelt in Babylon by the river Sud.

5 Then they wept, and fasted, and prayed before the Lord; ⁶and they collected money, each giving what he could; ⁷and they sent it to Jerusalem to Jehoi′akim the high priest,ᵃ the son of Hilki′ah, son of Shallum, and to the priests, and to all the people who were present with him in Jerusalem. ⁸At the same time, on the tenth day of Si′van, Baruchᵇ took the vessels of the house of the Lord, which had been carried away from the temple, to return them to the land of Judah—the silver vessels which Zedeki′ah the son of Josi′ah, king of Judah, had made, ⁹after Nebuchadnez′zar king of Babylon had carried away from Jerusalem Jeconi′ah and the princes and the prisoners and the mighty men and the people of the land, and brought them to Babylon.

A Letter to Jerusalem

10 And they said: "Herewith we send you money; so buy with the money burnt offerings and sin offerings and incense, and prepare a cereal offering,

---

1:1 the book: A scroll to be read at liturgical events in Jerusalem (1:14). Its precise contents are uncertain, i.e., whether the scroll encompasses 1:15–5:9 or only 1:15–3:8. **Baruch the son of Neriah:** The scribe who assisted the prophet Jeremiah by writing down his inspired oracles (Jer 36:4, 32; 45:1). His brother Seraiah was a military officer under King Zedekiah (Jer 51:59). Baruch and Jeremiah were among the remnant of survivors in Judah taken to Egypt after the fall of Jerusalem in 586 B.C. (Jer 43:5-7). Archaeologists have uncovered two clays seals, dating from the seventh century, that are stamped with the words in Hebrew: "Berekhyahu, son of Neryahu, the scribe". These finds confirm that Baruch was a historical figure. **son of Zedekiah ... Hasadiah ... Hilkiah:** Three generations beyond what is found in Jer 32:12. **in Babylon:** Baruch's presence in Babylon is not otherwise attested in ancient sources but is affirmed in later rabbinic writings (e.g., *Song of Songs Rabbah* 5, 5). Interestingly, the Jewish historian Josephus states that when the Babylonians conquered Egypt a few years after the fall of Jerusalem, they took Jews who were living there as captives to Babylon (*Antiquities* 10, 180-82).

1:2 the fifth year: 581 B.C., five years after the fall of Jerusalem. **seventh day of the month:** Many scholars suspect this verse was miscopied at an early date. They surmise that a second occurrence of the word "fifth" was accidently omitted, since **(1)** the month of the year is not indicated, and **(2)** the seventh day of the fifth month marks the date when the Babylonians set fire to Jerusalem and its Temple (2 Kings 25:8-9). **Chaldeans:** Babylonians.

1:3 Jeconiah: Another name for Jehoiachin, king of Judah, who was taken captive to Babylon in 597 B.C. (2 Kings 24:12; Jer 27:20) and imprisoned there until ca. 561 B.C. (2 Kings 25:27-30; Jer 52:31-34). This would mean that Baruch read to Jeconiah in his confinement, since the event described here is dated 20 years before his release.

1:4 the mighty men: Persons of influence such as members of the ruling class. **the princes:** Perhaps the sons of Jeconiah/Jehoiachin (1 Chron 3:17-18). **all who dwelt in Babylon:** The community of exiles who were taken in stages from the land of Judah (2 Kings 24:10-16; 25:11; Dan 1:1-4). **the river Sud:** Otherwise unknown but probably a canal in Babylon. The Dead Sea Scrolls mention a river Sur in connection with the Babylonian Exile (4Q389), perhaps referring to the same place, since the letters *d* and *r* are easily confused in Hebrew script.

1:5 wept ... fasted ... prayed: Acts of repentance joined to the confession of sin and the prayer for deliverance in 1:15–3:8. **the Lord:** The Greek is *Kyrios*, a word typically used to translate the sacred name Yʜᴡʜ (= Yahweh) in texts rendered from Hebrew.

1:7 Jehoiakim: Literally, "Joakim", who is otherwise unknown. The line of high priests listed in 1 Chron 6:3-15 ends with the exile of Jehozadak, son of Seraiah. Joakim may have been a senior priest who assumed the office when the high priest was deported to Babylon, though evidence is lacking to confirm this.

1:8 Sivan: The third month of the Jewish year, corresponding to May-June. **silver vessels:** Liturgical items such as shovels, pans, bowls, censors, etc., made to replace the gold and silver articles plundered from the Temple in 597 B.C. (2 Kings 24:10-13). These also were taken to Babylon in 586 B.C. (2 Kings 25:13-17). Baruch's return of the items to Jerusalem anticipates the return of all remaining silver and gold vessels in 538 B.C. (Ezra 1:7-11). This is the only verse in the Bible that speaks of Zedekiah's replacement vessels. **Zedekiah:** The last king of Judah, who reigned from 597 to 586 B.C.

1:10-11 Envisions sacrifices being offered in Jerusalem in 581 B.C. despite the destruction of the Temple in 586 B.C. It is implied in Jer 41:5 that grain and incense offerings continued to be made at the site of the ruined sanctuary.

1:10 we: The exiles in Babylon. **burnt offerings:** See note on Lev 1:3-17. **sin offerings:** See note on Lev 4:1–5:13. **cereal offering:** See note on Lev 2:1-16. **altar of the Lord:** Perhaps an earthen or unhewn stone altar (Ex 20:24-26). The bronze altar of sacrifice was not rebuilt until ca. 538 B.C. (Ezra 3:1-5).

This book, one of the deuterocanonical books, is not extant in Hebrew and is placed here after Lamentations in the Latin Vulgate. It is said to have been composed by Baruch at Babylon during the Exile, but in fact the evidence indicates rather that some of it was composed about the second or even first century B.C. The material may well have been composed at different periods, and the final editing have taken place toward the time of Christ. The particular value of the book is that it gives an insight into Jewish life in the Dispersion.

ᵃ Gk *the priest*.

ᵇ Gk *he*.

and offer them upon the altar of the Lord our God; [11]and pray for the life of Nebuchadnez'zar king of Babylon, and for the life of Belshaz'zar his son, that their days on earth may be like the days of heaven. [12]And the Lord will give us strength, and he will give light to our eyes, and we shall live under the protection[c] of Nebuchadnez'zar king of Babylon, and under the protection[c] of Belshaz'zar his son, and we shall serve them many days and find favor in their sight. [13]And pray for us to the Lord our God, for we have sinned against the Lord our God, and to this day the anger of the Lord and his wrath have not turned away from us. [14]And you shall read this book which we are sending you, to make your confession in the house of the Lord on the days of the feasts and at appointed seasons.

Confession of Sins

15 "And you shall say: 'Righteousness belongs to the Lord our God, but confusion of face, as at this day, to us, to the men of Judah, to the inhabitants of Jerusalem, [16]and to our kings and our princes and our priests and our prophets and our fathers, [17]because we have sinned before the Lord, [18]and have disobeyed him, and have not heeded the voice of the Lord our God, to walk in the statutes of the Lord which he set before us. [19]From the day when the Lord brought our fathers out of the land of Egypt until today, we have been disobedient to the Lord our God, and we have been negligent, in not heeding his voice. [20]So to this day there have clung to us the calamities and the curse which the Lord declared through Moses his servant at the time when he brought our fathers out of the land of Egypt to give to us a land flowing with milk and honey. [21]We did not heed the voice of the Lord our God in all the words of the prophets whom he sent to us, but we each followed the intent of his own wicked heart by serving other gods and doing what is evil in the sight of the Lord our God.

2 "'So the Lord confirmed his word, which he spoke against us, and against our judges who judged Israel, and against our kings and against our princes and against the men of Israel and Judah. [2]Under the whole heaven there has not been done the like of what he has done in Jerusalem, in accordance with what is written in the law of Moses, [3]that we should eat, one the flesh of his son and another the flesh of his daughter. [4]And he gave them into subjection to all the kingdoms around us, to be a reproach and a desolation among all the surrounding peoples, where the Lord has scattered them. [5]They were brought low and not raised up, because we sinned against the Lord our God, in not heeding his voice.

1:11 pray for: Urging prayer for the Babylonian king recalls Jeremiah's plea for the exiles to pray for the city of Babylon (Jer 29:7). Intercession for government rulers was practiced in Israel (Ezra 6:10) as well as the early Church (1 Tim 2:1-2). **Nebuchadnezzar:** Reigned over the Neo-Babylonian empire from 605 to 562 B.C. It is notable that Jewish exiles and residents of Jerusalem should pray for him, since Nebuchadnezzar was the destroyer of Jerusalem (2 Kings 25:8-10). **Belshazzar:** Deputy regent over Babylon while his father, Nabonidus, the king from 556 to 539 B.C., lived abroad in Arabia. See note on Dan 5:1. **his son:** Often labeled an error, since Belshazzar was the son of Nabonidus, not of Nebuchadnezzar. This judgment may be hasty, however, since **(1)** some historical evidence has been read to suggest that his mother was Nebuchadnezzar's daughter, thus making him a grandson, and **(2)** the language of father-and-son may be a way of speaking about a ruler and his (acting) successor. See note on Dan 5:2.

1:13 the anger of the Lord: See note on Lam 2:1.

1:14 days of the feasts: The yearly liturgical festivals observed in Israel (Lev 23:1-44; Deut 16:1-17).

1:15—2:10 A national confession of sin. Those who survived Jerusalem's destruction, whether exiled to Babylon or remaining in Judah, acknowledge the justice of suffering for their sins as well as the justice of God in punishing their sins. • The prayer is remarkably similar to Dan 9:4-19, with language taken from Deuteronomy and Jeremiah as well. It is uncertain whether Baruch relied upon Daniel, Daniel relied upon Baruch, or both drew upon a common tradition.

1:15 Righteousness belongs to the Lord: God has shown himself faithful to the covenant by enforcing its penalties against Israel's disobedience (2:6). See word study: *Righteous*

at Neh 9:8. **confusion of face:** An idiom for shame and disgrace (Dan 9:7; 2 Chron 32:21).

1:17 we have sinned: A confession of the Jewish survivors in Judah (1:15), as distinct from that of the Jewish exiles in Babylon (2:12; 3:2).

1:19 until today: From the Exodus to the Exile, Israel's history has been a long struggle with sin (2 Kings 21:15).

1:20 clung to us: Wording reminiscent of Deut 28:21, 60. **the curse:** Exile from the Promised Land is the culminating curse that Moses warned about in Lev 26:32-39 and Deut 28:63-68. The prophet Daniel, himself exiled to Babylon (Dan 1:1-6), also viewed the Exile in these terms (Dan 9:11). **flowing with milk and honey:** Describes the bountiful land of Canaan (Ex 3:8; Num 13:27; Deut 6:3).

1:21 the prophets: Sent by God to call his people to repentance but repeatedly rejected. Jeremiah speaks in similar terms (Jer 7:25-26; 25:4-7), as does Jesus in the parable of the Wicked Tenants (Mt 23:34; Lk 11:39). **wicked heart:** Similar to Jeremiah's assessment: "The heart is deceitful above all things, and desperately corrupt" (Jer 17:9). For the Lord's solution to this problem, see 2:31-33.

2:1 confirmed his word: The Lord fulfilled his oath to administer the curses of the covenant when his people refused to repent of evildoing (2:24; Lam 2:17). This follows a recurring pattern in the history of Israel, from the days of the **judges** and the rise of the **kings** to the demise of the Northern Kingdom of **Israel** and the Southern Kingdom of **Judah**.

2:3 eat ... flesh: Parents cannibalizing their children during a food shortage was foretold by Moses as a sign of the covenant curse on an evil generation (Deut 28:52-57). Atrocities of this kind occurred when the Babylonians conquered Jerusalem (Lam 4:10; cf. Jer 19:8-9).

2:4 them: The Jewish exiles in Babylon, viewed from the perspective of Jews living in Judah. The latter are the recipients of the book sent from Babylon (1:14).

---

[c]Gk *in the shadow.*

6 "'Righteousness belongs to the Lord our God, but confusion of face to us and our fathers, as at this day. [7]All those calamities with which the Lord threatened us have come upon us. [8]Yet we have not entreated the favor of the Lord by turning away, each of us, from the thoughts of his wicked heart. [9]And the Lord has kept the calamities ready, and the Lord has brought them upon us, for the Lord is righteous in all his works which he has commanded us to do. [10]Yet we have not obeyed his voice, to walk in the statutes of the Lord which he set before us.

Prayer for Deliverance

11 "'And now, O Lord God of Israel, who brought your people out of the land of Egypt with a mighty hand and with signs and wonders and with great power and outstretched arm, and have made you a name, as at this day, [12]we have sinned, we have been ungodly, we have done wrong, O Lord our God, against all your ordinances. [13]Let your anger turn away from us, for we are left, few in number, among the nations where you have scattered us. [14]Hear, O Lord, our prayer and our supplication, and for your own sake deliver us, and grant us favor in the sight of those who have carried us into exile; [15]that all the earth may know that you are the Lord our God, for Israel and his descendants are called by your name. [16]O Lord, look down from your holy habitation, and consider us. Incline your ear, O Lord, and hear; [17]open your eyes, O Lord, and see; for the dead who are in Hades, whose spirit has been taken from their bodies, will not ascribe glory or justice to the Lord, [18]but the person that is greatly distressed,[d] that

goes about bent over and feeble, and the eyes that are failing, and the person that hungers, will ascribe to you glory and righteousness, O Lord. [19]For it is not because of any righteous deeds of our fathers or our kings that we bring before you our prayer for mercy, O Lord our God. [20]For you have sent your anger and your wrath upon us, as you declared by your servants the prophets, saying: [21]"Thus says the Lord: Bend your shoulders and serve the king of Babylon, and you will remain in the land which I gave to your fathers. [22]But if you will not obey the voice of the Lord and will not serve the king of Babylon, [23]I will make to cease from the cities of Judah and from the region about Jerusalem the voice of mirth and the voice of gladness, the voice of the bridegroom and the voice of the bride, and the whole land will be a desolation without inhabitants.'

24 "'But we did not obey your voice, to serve the king of Babylon; and you have confirmed your words, which you spoke by your servants the prophets, that the bones of our kings and the bones of our fathers would be brought out of their graves;[e] [25]and behold, they have been cast out to the heat of day and the frost of night. They perished in great misery, by famine and sword and pestilence. [26]And the house which is called by your name you have made as it is today, because of the wickedness of the house of Israel and the house of Judah.

God's Covenant Recalled

27 "'Yet you have dealt with us, O Lord our God, in all your kindness and in all your great compassion, [28]as you spoke by your servant Moses

---

2:6 Righteousness: See note on 1:15.

2:8 turning: The language of repentance. See word study: *Return* at Jer 3:1.

2:11—3:8 A communal prayer for mercy (2:19; 3:2) and a pledge to praise the Lord in the lands of exile (3:6–8). Memories of the Exodus from Egypt, which demonstrated God's power to save his people, inspire the hope that he will deliver them from captivity among foreign nations once again. • The prayer closely resembles Dan 9:15–19, while select verses summarize messages drawn from Jeremiah (2:21–23) and Deuteronomy (2:29–35).

2:11 signs and wonders: The miracles of the Exodus (Ex 7:3; Deut 4:34; 6:22; Neh 9:10).

2:13 few in number: One of the curses of the covenant (Deut 28:62) and a reversal of the blessing of extraordinary fruitfulness promised to Abraham (Gen 17:2–6).

2:15 Israel: The patriarch Jacob, whom God renamed Israel, meaning "he who strives with God" (Gen 32:28; 35:10).

2:16 your holy habitation: The Lord's Temple in heaven (Deut 26:15; Ps 11:4).

2:17 Hades: The realm of the dead. For the biblical concept, see word study: *Sheol* at Num 16:30. **will not ascribe glory:** Echoes an ancient belief that the spirits of the dead (in OT times) did not praise God in the darkness of the netherworld (Ps 6:5; 30:9; Sir 17:27–28; Is 38:18).

2:19 not ... righteous deeds: God's mercy is sought as an undeserved grace, as in Deut 9:5 and Dan 9:18.

2:20 your anger: See note on Lam 2:1.

2:21–23 A summary of teachings delivered by the prophet Jeremiah, who urged the people of Judah and Jerusalem to submit to Babylonian rule; otherwise, conquest, desolation, and exile would be assured (Jer 7:34; 27:8, 12).

2:24 confirmed your words: See note on 2:1. **bones of our kings:** Jeremiah warned that the remains of deceased kings and others would be dishonored (Jer 8:1–2; 22:19; 36:30).

2:25 famine ... sword ... pestilence: Curses of the Mosaic covenant (Lev 26:25–26) as often repeated by Jeremiah (Jer 14:12; 24:10; 32:36; 38:2).

2:26 the house: The Lord's Temple in Jerusalem (1 Kings 9:1–3). **as it is today:** Still in ruins in 581 B.C., having been burned by the Babylonians (2 Kings 25:8–9). It is unclear how this detail fits the modern hypothesis that Baruch was addressed to the Jewish Diaspora long after the time of the Babylonian Exile, since the Second Temple was operational from 515 B.C. until A.D. 70. Some avoid this problem by dating the Book of Baruch in the late first century A.D. **house of Israel:** The northern tribes of Israel, who forsook the Temple in 930 B.C. (1 Kings 12:25–33). **house of Judah:** The southern tribes of Judah and Benjamin, who defiled the Temple before its destruction in 586 B.C. (2 Kings 23:4–7).

2:28 write your law: Echoes the ancient belief that Moses wrote the laws of Deuteronomy (Deut 31:9) as well as other parts of the Pentateuch (Ex 17:14; 24:4; Num 33:2).

---

[d] The meaning of the Greek is uncertain.

[e] Gk *their place.*

on the day when you commanded him to write your law in the presence of the people of Israel, saying, [29]"If you will not obey my voice, this very great multitude will surely turn into a small number among the nations, where I will scatter them. [30]For I know that they will not obey me, for they are a stiff-necked people. But in the land of their exile they will come to themselves, [31]and they will know that I am the Lord their God. I will give them a heart that obeys and ears that hear; [32]and they will praise me in the land of their exile, and will remember my name, [33]and will turn from their stubbornness and their wicked deeds; for they will remember the ways of their fathers, who sinned before the Lord. [34]I will bring them again into the land which I swore to give to their fathers, to Abraham and to Isaac and to Jacob, and they will rule over it; and I will increase them, and they will not be diminished. [35]I will make an everlasting covenant with them to be their God and they shall be my people; and I will never again remove my people Israel from the land which I have given them."

In Praise of Wisdom

3 "'O Lord Almighty, God of Israel, the soul in anguish and the wearied spirit cry out to you.

[2]Hear, O Lord, and have mercy, for we have sinned before you. [3]For you are enthroned for ever, and we are perishing for ever. [4]O Lord Almighty, God of Israel, hear now the prayer of the dead of Israel and of the sons of those who sinned before you, who did not heed the voice of the Lord their God, so that calamities have clung to us. [5]Remember not the iniquities of our fathers, but in this crisis remember your power and your name. [6]For you are the Lord our God, and you, O Lord, will we praise. [7]For you have put the fear of you in our hearts in order that we should call upon your name; and we will praise you in our exile, for we have put away from our hearts all the iniquity of our fathers who sinned before you. [8]Behold, we are today in our exile where you have scattered us, to be reproached and cursed and punished for all the iniquities of our fathers who forsook the Lord our God.'"

[9]Hear the commandments of life, O Israel;
   give ear, and learn wisdom!
[10]Why is it, O Israel, why is it that you are in the
   land of your enemies,
   that you are growing old in a foreign
   country,
that you are defiled with the dead,

2:29–35 A paraphrase of Deut 30:1–10, where Moses looks into the future and foresees Israel's rebellion, repentance, and restoration.

2:30 come to themselves: They will come to their senses, acknowledge their sins, and seek forgiveness (cf. Lk 15:17–18).

2:31 a heart that obeys: Refers to Moses' prophecy that the Lord will "circumcise" the hearts of his people and give them a new ability to love as he commands (Deut 30:6; cf. Jer 24:7; Ezek 36:26–27). Circumcision of the heart will be the "sign" of the everlasting covenant to come (2:35), just as circumcision of the flesh was the sign of God's covenant with Abraham (Gen 17:11). • Obedience is the gift of God, and yet we urge people to obey. Those who hear the exhortation of truth with obedience have received this gift, while those who do not have not. The Lord himself shows from whom this gift is received when he says: "I will give them a heart to know me, and ears to hear" (St. Augustine, *On the Gift of Perseverance* 37).

2:35 everlasting covenant: A new and permanent covenant. For similar prophecies that relate this expectation to messianic times, see Jer 31:31–34; 32:40; Ezek 37:26–27. **their God ... my people:** A traditional covenant formula, indicating that God's relationship with his people is deeply personal and not merely contractual (see also Ex 6:7; Lev 26:12; Jer 31:1; Ezek 37:27).

3:1 anguish ... wearied: The spiritual and emotional burdens of living in exile (Deut 28:65).

3:2 we have sinned: A confession of the Jewish exiles in Babylon, as distinct from that of the Jewish survivors in Judah (1:15–17).

3:3 enthroned for ever: Despite the collapse of the Davidic monarchy, the Lord's kingship is everlasting (Ps 9:7; 29:10; 102:12; Lam 5:19).

3:4 the dead of Israel: Many scholars surmise that the original Hebrew text of Baruch read *m tê Yiśrā'ēl*, "the men of Israel", which a Greek translator mistakenly read as *mētê Yiśrā'ēl*, "the dead of Israel". This is possible but not certain.

If the Greek text is correct, however, the passage reflects a belief that the souls of the deceased, while not engaged in praising God (as stated in 2:17), could still pray to God for the redemption of Israel. Such a belief is historically plausible insofar as Jewish views of the afterlife developed in new ways after the Babylonian Exile, e.g., the Jews came to believe that the deceased of Israel could benefit from prayers and sacrifices offered by the living (2 Mac 12:38–45).

3:7 the fear of you: A reverence for God (Jer 32:40) that dissuades people from committing sin (Ex 20:20). See note on Prov 1:7.

3:8 cursed: See note on 1:20. **iniquities of our fathers:** Not a deflection of the responsibility for sin, as 3:2 makes clear, but a recognition that generations of rebellion have led to the Exile (Lam 5:7).

3:9–4:4 A poem on wisdom addressed to the exiles of Israel. It opens with a summons to learn wisdom (3:9–14), continues with a reflection on the elusiveness of wisdom outside Israel (3:15–23), and ends by declaring that wisdom is found within Israel in the precepts of the Torah (3:24–4:4). • The poem is indebted to OT passages such as Deut 4:1–6 and Job 28:1–28. The identification of wisdom with the Law of God, explicit in 4:1, is also made in Sir 24:23–26.

3:9 Hear: An appeal to heed instruction (Deut 5:1; Prov 1:8; 4:1; 5:7). **the commandments of life:** Observance of the covenant leads to blessings of life (Deut 4:1; 5:33; 30:15–16).

3:10 growing old in a foreign country: Suggests to many scholars that the second part of Baruch (3:9–4:4) was written later than the first part (1:1–3:8), which is dated only five years after the conquest of Jerusalem (1:2). This conclusion is not demanded, however, since the Babylonians took Judeans into exile as early as 605 B.C. (Dan 1:1–4) and again in 597 B.C. (2 Kings 24:10–17), meaning there were some exiles living in Babylon for a decade or more prior to Jerusalem's demise. **defiled with the dead:** A description of life in exile, where God's people are surrounded by the uncleanness of idolatry and pagan culture (Ezek 20:31).

11 that you are counted among those in Hades?
12You have forsaken the fountain of wisdom.
13If you had walked in the way of God,
 you would be dwelling in peace for ever.
14Learn where there is wisdom,
 where there is strength,
 where there is understanding,
 that you may at the same time discern
 where there is length of days, and life,
 where there is light for the eyes, and peace.

15Who has found her place?
 And who has entered her storehouses?
16Where are the princes of the nations,
 and those who rule over the beasts on the
 earth;
17those who have sport with the birds of the air,
 and who hoard up silver and gold,
 in which men trust,
 and there is no end to their getting;
18those who scheme to get silver, and are anxious,
 whose labors are beyond measure?
19They have vanished and gone down to Hades,
 and others have arisen in their place.

20Young men have seen the light of day,
 and have dwelt upon the earth;
 but they have not learned the way to knowledge,
 nor understood her paths,
 nor laid hold of her.
21Their sons have strayed far from her f way.
22She has not been heard of in Canaan,
 nor seen in Te'man;
23the sons of Hagar, who seek for understanding on
 the earth,

the merchants of Merran and Te'man,
 the story-tellers and the seekers for
 understanding,
have not learned the way to wisdom,
 nor given thought to her paths.

24O Israel, how great is the house of God!
 And how vast the territory that he possesses!
25It is great and has no bounds;
 it is high and immeasurable.
26The giants were born there, who were famous of
 old,
 great in stature, expert in war.
27God did not choose them,
 nor give them the way to knowledge;
28so they perished because they had no wisdom,
 they perished through their folly.
29Who has gone up into heaven, and taken her,
 and brought her down from the clouds?
30Who has gone over the sea, and found her,
 and will buy her for pure gold?
31No one knows the way to her,
 or is concerned about the path to her.
32But he who knows all things knows her,
 he found her by his understanding.
 He who prepared the earth for all time
 filled it with four-footed creatures;
33he who sends forth the light, and it goes,
 called it, and it obeyed him in fear;
34the stars shone in their watches, and were glad;
 he called them, and they said, "Here we are!"
 They shone with gladness for him who made
 them.
35This is our God;
 no other can be compared to him!

3:11 Hades: See note on 2:17.

3:12 forsaken the fountain: Similar to Jeremiah's words in Jer 2:13.

3:14 where ... where ... where: Wisdom's location will be made known in 4:1 as "the law that endures for ever". **strength:** I.e., encouragement to make choices pleasing to God. **length of days ... life ... peace:** The same benefits of wisdom spelled out in Prov 3:13–17.

3:15 Who has found ... ?: Implied answer: only the Lord (3:32), who made it known to Israel in "the book of the commandments" (4:1). **her:** The pronoun is feminine because the nouns translated "wisdom" in the preceding context are both grammatically feminine (*phronēsis*, 3:9, 14; *sophia*, 3:12).

3:16 princes: Exercise great power, possess enormous wealth, and have more leisure for the pursuit of wisdom than most, yet even they fail to lay hold of it (Job 28:12–13).

3:19 Hades: See note on 2:17.

3:22 Canaan: Phoenicia, the northwestern coast of Canaan, was renowned in biblical times for wisdom and wealth (Ezek 28:1–6; Zech 9:2). **Teman:** A city of Edom, south of the Dead Sea, famous for its sages (Job 2:11; Jer 49:7).

3:23 the sons of Hagar: The Ishmaelites of northern Arabia (Gen 25:12–18). **Merran:** The city is otherwise unknown,

but possibly settled by descendants of Abraham's sons Medan or Midian (Gen 25:2).

3:24 the house of God: Not the sanctuary in Jerusalem, but the whole of creation, which is viewed as the Lord's Temple (Is 66:1). See essay: *Theology of the Temple* at 2 Chron 5.

3:26 giants: Men of colossal stature, called the Nephilim, who are said to have walked the earth before the flood (Gen 6:4; Num 13:33). The Bible describes them as arrogant (Wis 14:6) rebels (Sir 16:7) who perished in the floodwaters "because they had no wisdom" (3:28).

3:29–30 Wisdom is described in terms that Moses used to stress the nearness of God's commandments to the people of Israel (Deut 30:11–14). The point here, by contrast, is that wisdom is difficult to find for the nations beyond Israel.

3:30 buy her for pure gold: Recalls the adage that wisdom "cannot be gotten for gold" (Job 28:15).

3:32 he who knows all things: The one true God, who "sees everything under the heavens" (Job 28:24) and is "perfect in knowledge" (Job 37:16).

3:33 called it, and it obeyed: Refers to God speaking creation into being (Gen 1:3; Ps 33:6, 9).

3:34 They shone with gladness: the stars respond with joy when called by their Creator (cf. the stars being called by name, Ps 147:4; Is 40:26).

---

f Other authorities read *their*.

³⁶He found the whole way to knowledge,
  and gave her to Jacob his servant
  and to Israel whom he loved.
³⁷Afterward she appeared upon earth and lived
  among men.

Encouragement for Israel

4 She is the book of the commandments of God,
  and the law that endures for ever.
 All who hold her fast will live,
  and those who forsake her will die.
²Turn, O Jacob, and take her;
  walk toward the shining of her light.
³Do not give your glory to another,
  or your advantages to an alien people.
⁴Happy are we, O Israel,
  for we know what is pleasing to God.

⁵Take courage, my people,
  O memorial of Israel!
⁶It was not for destruction
  that you were sold to the nations,
 but you were handed over to your enemies
  because you angered God.
⁷For you provoked him who made you,
  by sacrificing to demons and not to God.

⁸You forgot the everlasting God, who brought
  you up,
  and you grieved Jerusalem, who reared
  you.
⁹For she saw the wrath that came upon you from
  God,
  and she said:
 "Listen, you neighbors of Zion,
  God has brought great sorrow upon me;
¹⁰for I have seen the captivity of my sons and
  daughters,
  which the Everlasting brought upon them.
¹¹With joy I nurtured them,
  but I sent them away with weeping and
  sorrow.
¹²Let no one rejoice over me, a widow
  and bereaved of many;
 I was left desolate because of the sins of my
  children,
  because they turned away from the law of
  God.
¹³They had no regard for his statutes;
  they did not walk in the ways of God's
  commandments,
  nor tread the paths of discipline in his
  righteousness.

3:36 Jacob his servant: The people of Israel, called to bear witness in the world to the truth about God. The expression echoes Isaiah's references to "Jacob" as the Lord's "servant" (Is 41:8; 44:1–2; 45:4; 48:20).

3:37 she: The gender of the subject is ambiguous in Greek. The RSV2CE translates it to mean "wisdom" has appeared; others have read it to mean "God" has appeared (3:35). See note on 3:15. **Appeared ... lived among men:** Wisdom is personified as one who came down from heaven (Wis 9:10) in order to dwell in Israel, residing in the commandments of the Mosaic Law (4:1). This is one of many passages of the OT that prepare for the Incarnation, in which the Son of God "dwelt among us" as a man (Jn 1:14). • Do you want to know that he who was born of the Father and later became man is God? Hear the words of the prophet that say: "This is our God; no other compares to him! He found all the way of knowledge.... After this he was seen upon earth and lived among men" (St. Cyril of Jerusalem, *Catechesis* 11, 15). Human nature cannot exist apart from sensible matter. Even if it could subsist in this way, it would not be fitting for the Word of God to have assumed it, since it would not be sensible but intelligible. The Son of God assumed human nature in order to be visible to men, according to Baruch (St. Thomas Aquinas, *Summa Theologiae* III, 4, 4).

4:1 the law: The teaching that "wisdom" is embodied in the precepts of the Torah goes back to Deut 4:5–6 and is likewise developed in Sir 24:23–25.

4:2 the shining of her light: For commandments as a light for our path, see Ps 119:105 and Prov 6:23.

4:3 your advantages: Knowing the Law, and thus knowing what pleases God (4:4), was a great advantage for Israel over other nations, for whom wisdom was not easily discovered (3:15–23). • Paul likewise views possessing the "oracles of God" as one of the advantages of the Jews not shared by Gentiles (Rom 3:1–2).

4:5—5:9 A prophetic exhortation, encouraging Jewish exiles in Babylon with the news that God is coming to deliver them (4:18, 21–29). Two voices can be heard: the prophet speaks to the exiles (4:5–9a), Jerusalem speaks to Israel's neighbors and then to the exiles (4:9b–29), and the prophet addresses Jerusalem (4:30–5:9). This third section of the book draws extensively from older books of the OT, especially from Deuteronomy and Is 40–66.

4:5 Take courage: A refrain, also in 4:21, 27, 30. **my people:** Israel's covenant relationship with the Lord is reaffirmed. See note on 2:35. **memorial of Israel:** The remnant of Israel in exile bears the name of Jacob-Israel, their founding father, and thus remains the heir of God's promises to his descendants.

4:6 sold to the nations: I.e., sent into the slavery of exile (Is 50:1; 52:3).

4:7 sacrificing to demons: The worship of idols is service to evil spirits according to Deut 32:17; Ps 106:37–38. • The apostle Paul concurs with this assessment in 1 Cor 10:20.

4:8 brought you up: Literally, "nursed you" or "nourished you" (cf. Hos 11:4). **Jerusalem:** The city is personified as a mother in mourning. She is saddened by the sins of her children, which have driven them into captivity (4:10). For Jerusalem's motherhood, see also Is 54:1–3; Tob 13:9.

4:9 wrath: See note on Lam 2:1. **Listen:** From here until 4:29, Jerusalem speaks for itself in the first person ("I, me, my"). **neighbors of Zion:** Peoples surrounding Israel who learned of Jerusalem's conquest (4:24).

4:10 the Everlasting: Or "the Eternal One". This title, which recalls Isaiah's claim that "the Lᴏʀᴅ is the everlasting God" (Is 40:28), is used throughout the prophetic exhortation in 4:14, 20, 22, 24, 35; 5:2.

4:12 widow: Jerusalem after its destruction in 586 B.C. (Lam 1:1; Is 54:4). It is unclear how this picture of the desolated city squares with the modern view that Baruch was written to Diaspora Jews long after the Babylonian Exile, since Jerusalem's repopulation began as early as 538 B.C. and the city was not robbed of its inhabitants again until the Roman conquest of A.D. 70.

4:13 righteousness: Observance of the Mosaic Law leads to righteousness according to Deut 6:25. However, the moral weakness of Israel (and all nations) is such that righteousness can only be a gift that comes "from God" (5:2, 9; Phil 3:9).

¹⁴Let the neighbors of Zion come;
 remember the capture of my sons and daughters,
  which the Everlasting brought upon them.
¹⁵For he brought against them a nation from afar,
 a shameless nation, of a strange language,
who had no respect for an old man,
 and had no pity for a child.
¹⁶They led away the widow's beloved sons,
 and bereaved the lonely woman of her daughters.

¹⁷"But I, how can I help you?
¹⁸For he who brought these calamities upon you
 will deliver you from the hand of your
  enemies.
¹⁹Go, my children, go;
 for I have been left desolate.
²⁰I have taken off the robe of peace
 and put on the sackcloth of my supplication;
 I will cry to the Everlasting all my days.

²¹"Take courage, my children, cry to God,
 and he will deliver you from the power and
  hand of the enemy.
²²For I have put my hope in the Everlasting to save
  you,
 and joy has come to me from the Holy One,
because of the mercy which soon will come to
  you
 from your everlasting Savior.ᵍ
²³For I sent you out with sorrow and weeping,
 but God will give you back to me with joy and
  gladness for ever.
²⁴For as the neighbors of Zion have now seen your
  capture,
 so they soon will see your salvation by God,
which will come to you with great glory
 and with the splendor of the Everlasting.
²⁵My children, endure with patience the wrath that
  has come upon you from God.

Your enemy has overtaken you,
 but you will soon see their destruction
  and will tread upon their necks.
²⁶My tender sons have traveled rough roads;
 they were taken away like a flock carried off
  by the enemy.

²⁷"Take courage, my children, and cry to God,
 for you will be remembered by him who
  brought this upon you.
²⁸For just as you planned to go astray from God,
 return with tenfold zeal to seek him.
²⁹For he who brought these calamities upon you
 will bring you everlasting joy with your
  salvation."

³⁰Take courage, O Jerusalem,
 for he who named you will comfort you.
³¹Wretched will be those who afflicted you
 and rejoiced at your fall.
³²Wretched will be the cities which your children
  served as slaves;
 wretched will be the city which received your
  sons.
³³For just as she rejoiced at your fall
 and was glad for your ruin,
 so she will be grieved at her own desolation.
³⁴And I will take away her pride in her great
  population,
 and her insolence will be turned to grief.
³⁵For fire will come upon her from the Everlasting
  for many days,
 and for a long time she will be inhabited by
  demons.

³⁶Look toward the east, O Jerusalem,
 and see the joy that is coming to you from God!
³⁷Behold, your sons are coming, whom you sent
  away;
 they are coming, gathered from east and west,

4:15 nation from afar: The Babylonians, described in the language of Deut 28:49–51.

4:17 how can I help you?: Implies that Jerusalem is powerless to recover its children from exile. It therefore cries out to God in prayer (4:20) and pleads with its children to do the same (4:21), confident that the Lord will be their "Savior" (4:22).

4:20 sackcloth: A coarse, hair-spun fabric worn next to the skin in times of mourning.

4:22 the Holy One: A title for the God of Israel, who is holy in the highest degree (Is 6:3). See note on Is 1:4.

4:25 their destruction: Foretells the fall of Babylon in 539 B.C. Further description is given in 4:31–35. It is unclear how these prophecies of Gentile demise fit the modern hypothesis, which holds that Baruch was written to Diaspora Jews long after the fall of Babylon. **tread upon their necks:** Signifies triumph over an enemy. The expression is elsewhere found in the LXX version of Deut 33:29.

4:27 you will be remembered: Not that God has forgotten his exiled people, but that he will take action on their behalf.

4:28 return: An appeal for repentance, which Moses prophesied was the precondition for Israel's restoration from exile (Deut 30:1–3). **seek him:** A spiritual movement of the heart. For the idea in Hebrew, see word study: *Sought* at 2 Chron 1:5.

4:30 he who named you: The Lord, who chose the city and sanctuary of Jerusalem as the place where his name should dwell on earth (1 Kings 8:15–21; 2 Chron 6:6). **comfort:** Summarizes Isaiah's message to Jerusalem on the eve of Babylon's downfall (see Is 40:1–2; 51:12).

4:31 those who afflicted you: The Babylonians.

4:34 her pride: Babylon was infamous for its arrogance (Is 13:3, 11; 14:13–14).

4:35 inhabited by demons: Drawn from the prophecy of Babylon's desolation in the LXX version of Is 34:14, where the Greek translations render as "demons" what appears in the Hebrew MT as "wild animals".

4:37 gathered from east and west: A poetic description of God's promise to restore his scattered people (cf. Is 43:5–7; Ps 107:3; Zeph 3:20).

ᵍ Or *from the Everlasting, your Savior.*

at the word of the Holy One,
  rejoicing in the glory of God.

Encouragement for Jerusalem

5 Take off the garment of your sorrow and affliction, O Jerusalem,
  and put on for ever the beauty of the glory
    from God.
²Put on the robe of the righteousness from God;
  put on your head the diadem of the glory of
    the Everlasting.
³For God will show your splendor everywhere
  under heaven.
⁴For your name will for ever be called by God,
  "Peace of righteousness and glory of
    godliness."

⁵Arise, O Jerusalem, stand upon the height
  and look toward the east,
and see your children gathered from west and
  east,
    at the word of the Holy One,
    rejoicing that God has remembered
    them.
⁶For they went forth from you on foot,
  led away by their enemies;
but God will bring them back to you,
  carried in glory, as on a royal throne.
⁷For God has ordered that every high mountain
  and the everlasting hills be made low

and the valleys filled up, to make level ground,
  so that Israel may walk safely in the glory of
    God.
⁸The woods and every fragrant tree
  have shaded Israel at God's command.
⁹For God will lead Israel with joy,
  in the light of his glory,
    with the mercy and righteousness that come
    from him.

A Letter of Jeremiah to the Captives

6 [h] A copy of a letter which Jeremi'ah sent to those
who were to be taken to Babylon as captives
by the king of the Babylonians, to give them the
message which God had commanded him.

2 Because of the sins which you have committed
before God, you will be taken to Babylon as captives by Nebuchadnez'zar, king of the Babylonians.
³Therefore when you have come to Babylon you
will remain there for many years, for a long time, up
to seven generations; after that I will bring you
away from there in peace. ⁴Now in Babylon you will
see gods made of silver and gold and wood, which
are carried on men's shoulders and inspire fear
in the heathen. ⁵So take care not to become at all like
the foreigners or to let fear for these gods[i] possess
you, when you see the multitude before and behind
them worshiping them. ⁶But say in your heart, "It
is you, O Lord, whom we must worship." ⁷For my
angel is with you, and he is watching your lives.

5:1–9 The high point of the prophetic exhortation is a collage of borrowings from Isaiah. Like the prophet, Baruch invites Jerusalem to **put on** beautiful attire (Is 52:1), a **robe** of **righteousness** (Is 61:10) and a **diadem** of **glory** (Is 28:5), and to **arise** (Is 51:17) and **stand** upon the heights (Is 40:9) in order to watch its children **carried** home (Is 49:22) from **west and east** (Is 43:5). At that time, every **mountain** will be leveled, every **valley** will be filled in (Is 40:4–5), and Israel's path will be shaded by every sweet-smelling **tree** (Is 41:19). The poetry underscores the abundance of God's goodness to the exiles. In the ancient Church, OT prophecies about a glorified Jerusalem are related to the celestial Jerusalem, the eternal city of angels and saints unseen in heaven (Gal 4:26; Heb 12:22; Rev 21:10).

5:4 Peace of righteousness: The peace that comes with pursuing righteousness (Is 32:17).

5:5–9 These verses bear a striking resemblance to part of a nonbiblical Jewish work: *Psalms of Solomon* 11, 1–7. Scholars debate whether Baruch relied upon the *Psalms* or vice versa.

5:9 light of his glory: Divine glory is often depicted as radiant light (e.g., Is 60:1–4, 19–20).

6:1–73 The Letter of Jeremiah, not originally part of the Book of Baruch, but attached to it in the Latin Vulgate and several modern translations. It is a tirade against the veneration of idols. Images of false gods are lifeless, speechless, and powerless to impact people's lives; for this reason, they must not be worshiped or feared (the refrain in 6:16, 23, 29, 40, 44, 52, 56, 65). The most ancient form of the letter survives in Greek, but it may have been written originally in Hebrew. A tiny fragment of the letter, dated about 100 B.C., was found

among the Dead Sea Scrolls (7Q486). Modern scholars (as well as St. Jerome, preface to *Commentary on Jeremiah*) consider it a composition written in Jeremiah's name rather than a letter from the hand of the prophet. See introduction: *Author and Date.* • The letter draws its critique of idolatry from other passages of the OT, especially Jer 10:1–16, but also Ps 115:3–8; 135:15–16; Is 44:9–20; 46:5–7.

6:1 Jeremiah: The prophet from Anathoth whose oracles appear in the Bible (Jer 1:1). He sent a letter to the exiles in Babylon, excerpts of which appear in Jer 29:1–32. This letter, by contrast, is sent to the people of Judah before they are taken into exile, either in 597 (2 Kings 24:14) or 586 B.C. (2 Kings 25:11). Its purpose is to prepare them to resist the allurements of Babylon's idol cults.

6:2 Nebuchadnezzar: See note on 1:11.

6:3 seven generations: Jeremiah said the Babylonian Exile would last 70 years (Jer 29:10). How this calculation relates to that figure is uncertain, since seven generations would extend the Exile to almost 300 B.C., which is problematic on historical grounds (counting 40 years as a generation, Num 13:33). Some think the figure signifies a long time without specificity.

6:4 on men's shoulders: An allusion to the Near Eastern festivals in which priests carried images of the gods in public procession (Is 46:6–7; Jer 10:5).

6:6 It is you, O Lord, whom we must worship: A reminder of the first commandment laid upon Israel: "I am the LORD your God.... You shall have no other gods before me" (Ex 20:2–3; Deut 5:6–7). Idol worship is a twofold offense against the Mosaic Law, which mandates both monotheism (belief in one God, Deut 4:35, 39) and imageless worship (banning artistic representations of God, Deut 4:15–17).

6:7 my angel: A protector and guide of God's people (Ex 23:20). Daniel identifies Israel's patron angel as Michael (Dan 12:1).

---

[h] The King James Version prints *The Epistle of Jeremy* as Chapter 6 of the book of Baruch, and the chapter and verse numbers are here retained.
[i] Gk *for them.*

The Futility of Idols and Idolatry

8 Their tongues are smoothed by the craftsman, and they themselves are overlaid with gold and silver; but they are false and cannot speak. [9]People[j] take gold and make crowns for the heads of their gods, as they would for a girl who loves ornaments; [10]and sometimes the priests secretly take gold and silver from their gods and spend it upon themselves, [11]and even give some of it to the harlots in the brothel. They deck their gods[k] out with garments like men—these gods of silver and gold and wood, [12]which cannot save themselves from rust and corrosion. When they have been dressed in purple robes, [13]their faces are wiped because of the dust from the temple, which is thick upon them. [14]Like a local ruler the god[l] holds a scepter, though unable to destroy any one who offends it. [15]It has a dagger in its right hand, and has an axe; but it cannot save itself from war and robbers. [16]Therefore they evidently are not gods; so do not fear them.

17 For just as one's dish is useless when it is broken, so are the gods of the heathen,[m] when they have been set up in the temples. Their eyes are full of the dust raised by the feet of those who enter. [18]And just as the gates are shut on every side upon a man who has offended a king, as though he were sentenced to death, so the priests make their temples secure with doors and locks and bars, in order that they may not be plundered by robbers. [19]They light lamps, even more than they light for themselves, though their gods[n] can see none of them. [20]They are[o] just like a beam of the temple, but men say their hearts have melted, when worms from the earth devour them and their robes. They do not notice [21]when their faces have been blackened by the smoke of the temple. [22]Bats, swallows, and birds light on their bodies and heads; and so do cats. [23]From this you will know that they are not gods; so do not fear them.

24 As for the gold which they wear for beauty—they will not shine unless some one wipes off the rust; for even when they were being cast, they had no feeling. [25]They are bought at any cost, but there is no breath in them. [26]Having no feet, they are carried on men's shoulders, revealing to mankind their worthlessness. [27]And those who serve them are ashamed because through them these gods[n] are made to stand, lest they fall to the ground. If any one sets one of them upright, it cannot move of itself; and if it is tipped over, it cannot straighten itself; but gifts are placed before them just as before the dead. [28]The priests sell the sacrifices that are offered to these gods[p] and use the money; and likewise their wives preserve some with salt, but give none to the poor or helpless. [29]Sacrifices to them may be touched by women in menstruation or at childbirth. Since you know by these things that they are not gods, do not fear them.

30 For why should they be called gods? Women serve meals for gods of silver and gold and wood; [31]and in their temples the priests sit with their clothes torn, their heads and beards shaved, and their heads uncovered. [32]They howl and shout before their gods as some do at a funeral feast for a man who has died. [33]The priests take some of the clothing of their gods[q] to clothe their wives and children. [34]Whether one does evil to them or good, they will not be able to repay it. They cannot set up a king or depose one. [35]Likewise they are not able

---

6:10 priests secretly take: The Letter of Jeremiah not only ridicules idols but accuses their attendants of selfishness and sin (6:18, 28, 33, 55).

6:11 brothel: The Greek term indicates a roofed hall or chamber, leaving it unclear whether religious or non-religious prostitution is meant. The Torah outlawed religious prostitution as well as giving money gained from prostitution to the Lord's Temple (Deut 23:17–18).

6:12 purple robes: A sign of royal power (Jer 10:9). The author finds it pathetic that idols clad in such regalia cannot even dust themselves off (6:13).

6:16 not gods ... do not fear them: A different perspective on idol worship from that of 4:7, which states that sacrifices to idols are made to demons. The two views are not in conflict, however, since the Letter of Jeremiah focuses on the physical images of the idols.

6:17 dish ... broken: An utterly useless thing (Jer 22:28).

6:18 may not be plundered: Decorating idols with precious metals made them targets for thieves, as explained in 6:57–58.

6:22 Bats: Unclean animals according to the Mosaic Law (Lev 11:19).

6:25 no breath in them: I.e., they are not living beings (Ps 135:17; Jer 10:14).

6:26 carried: See note on 6:4.

6:27 made to stand, lest they fall: Idols have to be secured in place with hardware, lest they topple over and become damaged (Wis 13:16; Jer 10:4). **as before the dead:** The heathen practice of bringing food offerings to gravesites is no different from bringing food to idols, since the intended beneficiaries are not alive and cannot eat them (Sir 30:18–19).

6:28 none to the poor: Pagan disregard for the poor is implicitly contrasted with Scripture, where concern for them is pronounced (Deut 15:11; Ps 41:1; Jas 1:27).

6:29 menstruation ... childbirth: Both render women temporarily unclean and unfit to participate in public worship according to the Mosaic Law (Lev 12:1–8; 15:19–23).

6:31–32 Shaving and crying out are ritual expressions of mourning, perhaps in connection with the Babylonian cult of Tammuz, a vegetation god that was believed to die and descend into the underworld every summer, only to rise again in the spring (Ezek 8:14).

6:34 cannot set up a king: Unlike Israel's God (Dan 2:21).

6:35 not able to give ... wealth: Unlike Israel's God (1 Sam 2:7). **will not require it:** Unlike Israel's God (Deut 23:21).

---

[j] Gk *They.*
[k] Gk *them.*
[l] Gk *he.*
[m] Gk *of them.*
[n] Gk *they.*
[o] Gk *It is.*
[p] Gk *to them.*
[q] Gk *them.*

to give either wealth or money; if one makes a vow to them and does not keep it, they will not require it. [36]They cannot save a man from death or rescue the weak from the strong. [37]They cannot restore sight to a blind man; they cannot rescue a man who is in distress. [38]They cannot take pity on a widow or do good to an orphan. [39]These things that are made of wood and overlaid with gold and silver are like stones from the mountain, and those who serve them will be put to shame. [40]Why then must any one think that they are gods, or call them gods?

Besides, even the Chalde′ans themselves dishonor them; [41]for when they see a mute man, who cannot speak, they bring him and pray Bel[r] that the man may speak, as though Bel[s] were able to understand. [42]Yet they themselves cannot perceive this and abandon them, for they have no sense. [43]And the women, with cords about them, sit along the passageways, burning bran for incense; and when one of them is led off by one of the passers-by and is lain with, she derides the woman next to her, because she was not as attractive as herself and her cord was not broken. [44]Whatever is done for them is false. Why then must any one think that they are gods, or call them gods?

[45] They are made by carpenters and goldsmiths; they can be nothing but what the craftsmen wish them to be. [46]The men that make them will certainly not live very long themselves; how then can the things that are made by them be gods? [47]They have left only lies and reproach for those who come after. [48]For when war or calamity comes upon them, the priests consult together as to where they can hide themselves and their gods.[t] [49]How then can one fail to see that these are not gods, for they cannot save themselves from war or calamity? [50]Since they are made of wood and overlaid with gold and silver, it will afterward be known that they are false. [51]It

will be manifest to all the nations and kings that they are not gods but the work of men's hands, and that there is no work of God in them. [52]Who then can fail to know that they are not gods?[u]

[53] For they cannot set up a king over a country or give rain to men. [54]They cannot judge their own cause or deliver one who is wronged, for they have no power; they are like crows between heaven and earth. [55]When fire breaks out in a temple of wooden gods overlaid with gold or silver, their priests will flee and escape, but the gods[v] will be burned in two like beams. [56]Besides, they can offer no resistance to a king or any enemies. Why then must any one admit or think that they are gods?

[57] Gods made of wood and overlaid with silver and gold are not able to save themselves from thieves and robbers. [58]Strong men will strip them of their gold and silver and of the robes they wear, and go off with this booty, and they will not be able to help themselves. [59]So it is better to be a king who shows his courage, or a household utensil that serves its owner's need, than to be these false gods; better even the door of a house that protects its contents, than these false gods; better also a wooden pillar in a palace, than these false gods.

[60] For sun and moon and stars, shining and sent forth for service, are obedient. [61]So also the lightning, when it flashes, is widely seen; and the wind likewise blows in every land. [62]When God commands the clouds to go over the whole world, they carry out his command. [63]And the fire sent from above to consume mountains and woods does what it is ordered. But these idols[w] are not to be compared with them in appearance or power. [64]Therefore one must not think that they are gods nor call them gods, for they are not able either to decide a case or to do good to men. [65]Since you know then that they are not gods, do not fear them.

6:36 cannot ... rescue the weak: Unlike Israel's God (Ex 20:2).

6:37 cannot restore sight: Unlike Israel's God (Ps 146:8).

6:38 cannot take pity on a widow: Unlike Israel's God (Ps 68:5).

6:40 Chaldeans: Babylonian magicians and wise men. See note on Dan 2:2.

6:41 Bel: Means "lord" in Akkadian. It is another name for Marduk, a god of healing and the chief deity of the Babylonian pantheon (Is 46:1; Jer 50:2; Dan 14:3).

6:43 lain with: Religious prostitution. Ancient sources indicate that Babylonian women had a once-in-a-lifetime obligation to the goddess Ishtar/Aphrodite to have sexual relations with any man who selected them from the temple precinct with a payment of money (Herodotus, *Histories* 1, 199; Strabo, *Geography* 16, 1, 20). **cord was not broken:** I.e., the woman had not been chosen for sex.

6:51 the work of men's hands: A common way of describing idols in the Bible (Deut 4:28; Ps 115:4; Jer 10:9; Hab 2:18).

6:53 cannot set up a king ... or give rain: Unlike Israel's God (1 Sam 12:13; Deut 11:13–14).

6:54 like crows: The original Hebrew may have read "like clouds".

6:55 will be burned: The wooden core of the idol, which was gilded with metal and fitted with clothes.

6:56 offer no resistance: Babylon's temples were plundered by various enemies in ancient times, including the Hittites, Assyrians, and Persians.

6:59 utensil ... door ... pillar: Things more beneficial to people than idols.

6:60–69 The forces and creatures of the natural world, though merely servants of God's will, are more impressive than idols made by human hands.

---

[r] Or *they bring Bel and pray.*
[s] Gk *he.*
[t] Gk *them.*
[u] The Greek text of this verse is uncertain.
[v] Gk *they.*
[w] Gk *these things.*

66 For they can neither curse nor bless kings; [67]they cannot show signs in the heavens and[x] among the nations, or shine like the sun or give light like the moon. [68]The wild beasts are better than they are, for they can flee to cover and help themselves. [69]So we have no evidence whatever that they are gods; therefore do not fear them.

70 Like a scarecrow in a cucumber bed, that guards nothing, so are their gods of wood, overlaid with gold and silver. [71]In the same way, their gods of wood, overlaid with gold and silver, are like a thorn bush in a garden, on which every bird sits; or like a dead body cast out in the darkness. [72]By the purple and linen[y] that rot upon them you will know that they are not gods; and they will finally themselves be consumed, and be a reproach in the land. [73]Better therefore is a just man who has no idols, for he will be far from reproach.

6:66 neither curse nor bless: Unlike Israel's God (Deut 28:1–68).

6:67 signs in the heavens: The heavenly luminaries determine days and months of the year as well as the times of Israel's religious feasts (Gen 1:14).

---

[x] Other ancient authorities omit *and*.
[y] Cn: Gk *marble*, Syr *silk*.

6:70 Like a scarecrow in a cucumber bed: A simile drawn from the Hebrew version of Jer 10:5. In both texts, the author pokes fun at idols as well as those who worship them. Idol images are no more alive than scarecrows; and their devotees are no less deceived than birds who think that a stuffed figure in a garden is something to be feared.

6:71 thorn bush: An annoyance to the gardener. **dead body:** A corpse is not only lifeless but defiling to others according to the Mosaic Law (Num 19:11–22).

STUDY QUESTIONS
Baruch

Chapter 1

For Understanding
1. **1:1.** In what form was the book of Baruch used? What about its contents is uncertain? Who was Baruch, especially in his relation to Jeremiah? What have archaeologists uncovered about him? Although Baruch's presence in Babylon is not otherwise attested in ancient sources, where is it affirmed? Interestingly, what does the Jewish historian Josephus state about the Babylonian conquest of Egypt a few years after the fall of Jerusalem?
2. **1:3.** When was Jeconiah/Jehoiachin, king of Judah, taken captive to Babylon, and how long was he imprisoned? Where would this mean that Baruch read the book to him?
3. **1:8.** What is the month of Sivan? What liturgical items are referred to here? What does Baruch's return of these items to Jerusalem anticipate? Which other verses in the Bible speak of Zedekiah's replacement vessels?
4. **1:11.** What does urging prayer for the Babylonian king recall? Among whom was intercession for government rulers practiced? Why is it notable that Jewish exiles and residents of Jerusalem should pray for Nebuchadnezzar? Who was Belshazzar? Why is the note that Belshazzar was the son Nebuchadnezzar labeled an error, and why might that judgment be hasty?

For application
1. **1:3–5.** How was the reading of Jeremiah's prophecies to Jehoiachim, Jeconiah's father, received before the Exile (Jer 36:22–23)? What accounts for the different reception Baruch receives before Jeconiah?
2. **1:10.** Why is a monetary offering requested for certain religious functions such as weddings, funerals, and Masses for special intentions? Although the amount for the offering is set by Church authorities, what happens if a person is too poor to pay it (cf. CIC 848)?
3. **1:11.** Why does St. Paul recommend to Timothy that prayers be offered for persons in authority (1 Tim 2:1–2)? Which authorities are typically included in the general intercessions of the Mass? Why should we include secular authorities in our private prayers as well?
4. **1:15–21.** Whose sins are the exiles confessing in these verses? Why does Mass usually begin with a penitential rite? In the Confiteor, who is at fault for the sins we confess? Why do we add that our sins are "grievous"?

Chapter 2

For understanding
1. **2:3.** How did Moses speak of parents cannibalizing their children during a food shortage? When did atrocities like this occur?
2. **2:11–3:8.** What do these verses narrate? What do memories of the Exodus from Egypt, which demonstrated God's power to save his people, inspire? While the prayer closely resembles Dan 9:15–19, what messages do select verses summarize?
3. **2:26.** Why is it unclear how the detail of the Temple's ruins in 581 B.C. fits the modern hypothesis that Baruch was addressed to the Jewish Diaspora long after the time of the Babylonian Exile? How do some scholars avoid this problem? When did the "house of Israel" forsake the Temple, and until when did the southern tribes of Judah and Benjamin continue to defile it?
4. **2:31.** To what does God's offer of a "heart that obeys" refer? Of what will "circumcision of the heart" be the sign? According to St. Augustine, how do we know who has received the gift of obedience from God?

For application
1. **2:6.** In their confession, what do the exiles mean by "confusion of face"? How does awareness of having hurt someone cause confusion in one's approach to that person? How does this confusion show itself on the face or in other body language?
2. **2:14–15.** According to the exiles' prayer, why do they want to be granted favor in the sight of those who carried them into exile? As suggested in the note for this verse, what is the divine name by which the exiles are called? As a Christian, by whose name are you called?
3. **2:18.** How does this verse describe the spiritual condition of the exiles themselves? What self-conception is best calculated to win a favorable hearing from the Lord?
4. **2:31.** The note for this verse refers to St. Augustine, who describes obedience as a gift of God. How does obedience build character? What is the difference between servile and virtuous obedience?

Chapter 3

For understanding
1. **3:4.** How do many scholars surmise that the original Hebrew of this text of Baruch reads in contrast to that of a Greek translator? If the Greek text is correct, what belief does the passage reflect, and how is such a belief historically plausible?
2. **3:10.** What does Baruch's note about growing old in a foreign country suggest to many scholars? Why is this conclusion not demanded, however? How does defilement with the dead describe life in exile?
3. **3:29–30.** How is wisdom described in terms that Moses used? By contrast, what is the point here?
4. **3:37.** While the gender of the subject of this verse is ambiguous in Greek, how do the RSV2CE and others translate it? How is Wisdom personified? Like many passages in the OT, for what does this passage prepare? How does St. Cyril of

Jerusalem interpret the passage? According to St. Thomas Aquinas, why, according to Baruch, did the Son of God assume human nature?

For application
1. **3:4.** Read the note for this verse. How does the developing Jewish view of the afterlife resemble the Christian doctrine of Purgatory? How do the souls in Purgatory depend on the prayers of the living (CCC 1032)? For whom can these souls pray?
2. **3:10.** In what ways can our secular, materialist, and often atheist culture be considered a foreign country for committed Christians who live in it? What does it mean to grow old in such a culture? How can Christians be in the culture without becoming contaminated by it?
3. **3:14.** What is wisdom (as distinct, for example, from knowledge or understanding)? According to Scripture, where does one begin to learn it (Prov 9:10; Sir 1:14)? What is the relation of wisdom to the Holy Spirit?
4. **3:22–23.** What is the difference between the practical wisdom gained from business experience, political shrewdness, and good civic behavior and the kind of wisdom that Baruch has in mind? While the former is important for getting along in society, how is the latter superior?

Chapter 4

For understanding
1. **4:3.** What great advantage does Israel have over other nations? How does Paul likewise view this advantage?
2. **4:5—5:9.** With what news does this prophetic exhortation encourage Jewish exiles in Babylon? Which two voices can be heard? From what sources does this third section of the book draw extensively?
3. **4:12.** Who is the widow here? Why is it unclear how this picture of the desolated city squares with the modern view that Baruch was written to Diaspora Jews long after the Babylonian Exile?
4. **4:13.** To what does observance of the Mosaic Law lead, according to Deut 6:25? Because of the moral weakness of Israel (and all nations), from where alone can this gift come?

For application
1. **4:2.** How does the word of God act like a lamp for your feet and a light for your path (Ps 119:105)? According to Ps 119, where in Scripture are you most likely to find passages that illuminate your way? How many synonyms for "your word" does the psalm use?
2. **4:7.** The note for this verse cites Deut 32:17, which alludes to gods that were new to Israelites. What are some of the new gods that our culture worships? How can they be characterized as demonic? How do those who worship them become like them?
3. **4:20.** As a Christian, why would you choose to wear sackcloth? How would it serve as an accessory to prayer? How would Jesus' injunction to pray or fast in secret (Mt 6:6, 17–18) apply to its use?
4. **4:28.** In what periods of a young person's life is he most likely to stray from Christianity? What are some common reasons for this? What attractions do non-Christian religions provide? What ultimate questions do these religions fail to answer that might prompt a return to the Christian faith?

Chapter 5

For understanding
1. **5:1–9.** What is the high point of the prophetic exhortation? Like Isaiah, what does Baruch invite Jerusalem to do? At that time, what will happen? What does the poetry underscore? In the ancient Church, to what are OT prophecies about a glorified Jerusalem related?
2. **5:5–9.** To what nonbiblical Jewish work do these verses bear a striking resemblance? What do scholars debate in regard to that work?
3. **5:9.** How is divine glory often depicted?

For application
1. **5:3.** At the Last Judgment, what about human behavior will be revealed? Before whom will it be revealed (CCC 678, 1039)? How can we prepare for that event?
2. **5:6.** At the end of time, how will this prophecy be fulfilled in the resurrection of the dead? What enemy led people away, and to where? With what glory will they return? According to St. Paul, how will the rest of creation participate in that glory (Rom 8:19–21)?

Chapter 6

For understanding
1. **6:3.** How long did Jeremiah say the Babylonian Exile would last? Why is it uncertain how this text's calculation of seven generations relates to that figure? What do some think this figure signifies?
2. **6:11.** What does the Greek term for a brothel indicate, and what is unclear about it? What did the Torah outlaw regarding prostitution?
3. **6:27.** How do idols have to be secured in place? Why is the heathen practice of bringing food offerings to gravesites no different from bringing food to idols?
4. **6:43.** What once-in-a-lifetime obligation to the goddess Ishtar/Aphrodite do ancient sources indicate that Babylonian women had? What did it mean for a woman that her cord was not broken?

For application

1. **6:4.** Compare the pagan practice of this verse with the Christian practice of carrying statues of the Blessed Virgin and other saints in procession. How come the latter does not merit Jeremiah's condemnation? What sort of fear should the Christian practices inspire in the faithful?

2. **6:7.** What bothers some people about the presence of God's angel (or God himself) watching their lives? Why might they object to divine oversight? Is God's watchfulness a matter of mere surveillance or something more benign, and if the latter, what?

3. **6:9.** Many parishes have the practice of crowning a statue of Mary with flowers during the month of May. Under what title is Mary venerated at such times? What other Marian devotions are practiced during this month? How are these practices compatible with the worship reserved to God alone?

4. **6:19.** Why are candles used in Catholic churches for liturgical worship and other devotions? What is the special significance of the Easter candle, and how is it used outside of the Easter season? What is the purpose of the votive candles placed near statues of Mary, Joseph, and other saints?

BOOKS OF THE BIBLE

THE OLD TESTAMENT (OT)	
Gen	Genesis
Ex	Exodus
Lev	Leviticus
Num	Numbers
Deut	Deuteronomy
Josh	Joshua
Judg	Judges
Ruth	Ruth
1 Sam	1 Samuel
2 Sam	2 Samuel
1 Kings	1 Kings
2 Kings	2 Kings
1 Chron	1 Chronicles
2 Chron	2 Chronicles
Ezra	Ezra
Neh	Nehemiah
Tob	Tobit
Jud	Judith
Esther	Esther
Job	Job
Ps	Psalms
Prov	Proverbs
Eccles	Ecclesiastes
Song	Song of Solomon
Wis	Wisdom
Sir	Sirach (Ecclesiasticus)
Is	Isaiah
Jer	Jeremiah
Lam	Lamentations
Bar	Baruch
Ezek	Ezekiel
Dan	Daniel
Hos	Hosea
Joel	Joel
Amos	Amos
Obad	Obadiah
Jon	Jonah
Mic	Micah
Nahum	Nahum
Hab	Habakkuk
Zeph	Zephaniah
Hag	Haggai
Zech	Zechariah
Mal	Malachi
1 Mac	1 Maccabees
2 Mac	2 Maccabees

THE NEW TESTAMENT (NT)	
Mt	Matthew
Mk	Mark
Lk	Luke
Jn	John
Acts	Acts of the Apostles
Rom	Romans
1 Cor	1 Corinthians
2 Cor	2 Corinthians
Gal	Galatians
Eph	Ephesians
Phil	Philippians
Col	Colossians
1 Thess	1 Thessalonians
2 Thess	2 Thessalonians
1 Tim	1 Timothy
2 Tim	2 Timothy
Tit	Titus
Philem	Philemon
Heb	Hebrews
Jas	James
1 Pet	1 Peter
2 Pet	2 Peter
1 Jn	1 John
2 Jn	2 John
3 Jn	3 John
Jude	Jude
Rev	Revelation (Apocalypse)